Institutions and Economic Development

The Johns Hopkins Studies in Development

Vernon W. Ruttan and T. Paul Schultz, Consulting Editors

Institutions and Economic Development

Growth and Governance in Less-Developed and Post-Socialist Countries

EDITED BY **Christopher Clague**

THE JOHNS HOPKINS UNIVERSITY PRESS

BALTIMORE AND LONDON

© 1997 The Johns Hopkins University Press
All rights reserved. Published 1997
Printed in the United States of America on acid-free paper
06 05 04 03 02 01 00 99 98 97   5 4 3 2 1

The Johns Hopkins University Press
2715 North Charles Street, Balitmore, Maryland 21218-4319
The Johns Hopkins Press Ltd., London

ISBN 0-8018-5492-X
ISBN 0-8018-5493-8 (pbk.)

Library of Congress Cataloging-in-Publication Data will be
found at the end of this book.

A catalog record for this book is available from the British Library.

Contents

VI　*Implications for Development Practice*

Foreword

The Center on Institutional Reform and the Informal Sector at the University of Maryland at College Park (IRIS), established in 1990 by Mancur Olson, with support from the U.S. Agency for International Development, has pursued two goals: (1) to increase understanding of the role of institutions in development, and (2) to work with reformers and scholars in developing and postcommunist countries to test this understanding and bring it to bear on current and important problems.

Leading thinkers in developing countries and in donor organizations are increasingly recognizing that a country's main resource is the quality of its political and economic institutions. IRIS's work with reformers in twenty-eight countries has led to important reforms of both economic and political institutions: a new civil code in Russia, simplified business licensing in Nepal, a broadened and energized consensus in India on the costs of special interest democracy, progress on secured lending across Central Europe, new pressure for an independent judiciary in Madagascar, a range of reforms in Mongolia leading to positive economic growth . . . these and many others are all outcomes of the application of ideas that have guided IRIS's work. In Almaty, Antananarivo, Bishkek, Cairo, Dhaka, Gaza City, Kathmandu, Kiev, Moscow, New Delhi, Phnom Penh, Rabat, Sofia, Skopje, Ulaanbaatar, Vilnius, Warsaw, and Yerevan—and dozens of other places outside these capitals—IRIS economists and lawyers have worked with local scholars, officials, and reformers, using ideas about institutions and incentives.

This growing focus on institutions certainly does not fit any one academic discipline. While economic ideas are at the heart of IRIS's work, contributions from law, sociology, anthropology, and political science all contribute. Although this approach does not have simple answers for many of the world's problems, especially the developing world's, it does provide a framework for thinking about the challenges of development, both in broad policy and in local projects, which can lead to more realistic solutions and more effective strategies for reform.

The importance of improved institutions can be illustrated by focusing on the problem of poverty. In even the poorest countries, there are wealthy people. But who are most injured by these countries' lack of fundamental rights to property and contract enforcement, the lack of safe places to accumulate savings, by bureaucratic arbitrariness or corruption, and by the lack of a voice in decisions about these issues? It is the poor. And both experience and theory suggest that the poor benefit most from the improvement of institutions.

How to bring about this sort of change has been the challenge of reformers and donors for several decades. In the past, difficulty understanding the sources of poor arrangements and the often political nature of reform have led to measures that ignored the fundamental importance of these issues. The lesson of the research and reform efforts of IRIS is that there is not an "engineering" solution to the problem of poor institutions, that reformers looking for recipes will be led to unrealistic and inappropriate models, and that donors providing "technical" assistance would be better off increasing the local capacity to think about sources and solutions. This is not simply a suggestion for more education for the idea leaders of developing countries, but, rather, a call for assistance to be more educational in method across a broader view of the problem. For example, Nepal does not simply need a better contract law—it needs a community of officials and consumers of that law that understands the incentives inherent in various substantive and implementation options. The solution they pursue will then be both tailored to the locality and owned by the community.

This volume builds on work at IRIS and by dozens of others, including the authors of the individual chapters who draw on their own experience and insight. Those at IRIS who have spent long periods overseas in places like Mongolia, Nepal, Russia, Poland, and Chad have all been important colleagues in the development of the ideas in this collection. Colleagues in College Park who serve as essential links in the development and sharing of ideas among field efforts and research activity deserve credit for enhancing and testing this approach. Counterparts in various USAID country missions, World Bank country offices, and in Washington have provided valuable insight and criticism. Reformers and scholars in reforming societies are, of course, the best sources of inspiration, for it is their situations and their thinking that force us to be clear in our own thinking, relevant in our advice, and quick about our work.

All of this accumulated effort and insight does not pour effortlessly into a book of this reach. Christopher Clague has kept the vision of this volume clear over the months of planning for the October 1994 conference that drew these authors and others together and in his thoughtful interactions since then with all of us who have contributions. Christopher Bartlett has been the skillful implementer of much of the intellectual shaping of this volume, editing and suggesting with an eye trained in economics and scissors informed by the need to communicate concisely. Their steady work is an important reason for such success as IRIS has had overall and is certainly responsible for this volume. Mancur Olson, whose ideas drew most of us to IRIS in the first place, has welcomed competing ideas and encouraged extensions and challenges to his own work. This intellectual environment as well as Mancur's energy and keen interest in the work of IRIS's far-flung operations are of great value to each of as at IRIS and also to those whose support keeps us working at these issues.

While IRIS draws financial support from several sources, the work that contributed to this volume was supported by a cooperative agreement with the U.S. Agency for International Development. The contributors to this volume are grateful to USAID for its support as well as for the intellectual interaction that comes with it. Without diminishing the value of the interaction, it is necessary, however, to make the usual disclaimer—the views expressed here are not necessarily those of USAID. On the other hand, we hope that our colleagues at USAID and other readers find these ideas useful and relevant to their own scholarship and development activity.

Charles Cadwell

Acknowledgments

This book, the idea for which emerged from a conference held at the U.S. Agency for International Development by IRIS in October 1994, represents for me the culmination of research and reflection over a number of years. I have been thinking intensively about the interaction between institutions and economic development since shortly before IRIS came into existence. I would like to express my appreciation to my colleagues at IRIS for the stimulating intellectual environment in which these issues could be contemplated.

The Agency for International Development has supported IRIS since its inception. The IRIS Scholars Program funded several of the chapters in this volume and has provided us with valuable interaction with researchers around the world who are thinking along similar lines. The support by USAID of IRIS in general, and of the conference in particular, is gratefully acknowledged.

Christopher Bartlett did a superb job of editing the papers and preparing the manuscript for the Press. I am also very grateful to Karla Hoff and Robert Klitgaard, who carefully read my contributions and made valuable suggestions. The volume has benefited in addition from the insightful comments of two anonymous referees.

Christopher Clague

Institutions and Economic Development

1   Introduction

Christopher Clague

Much has been learned about economic development in recent decades. This is not grounds for congratulations, since our previous ignorance was so wide and deep. While a great deal of what we have learned can be characterized as the dispelling of misconceptions based on theories that have been clearly contradicted by events, a new appreciation has emerged for some of the propositions of standard economics. It has been found time and again that countries disregard at their peril the laws of supply and demand and of macroeconomic balance. In fact, there has developed a broad consensus among economists and others on the kinds of policies that countries ought to follow to achieve economic development.

This new consensus raises two new questions. First, why don't less-developed countries put these policies into place? Presumably, in most poor countries the people yearn for economic betterment and the leaders are aware of this fact and profess their own aspirations for the country's progress, and yet the necessary policies do not materialize. The second question may be a partial answer to the first. Why is it that when the recommended policies are put into place (often under the guidance of—and pressure from—the International Monetary Fund and the World Bank), the hoped-for results do not materialize quickly?

Both of these questions can be illuminated by a serious analysis of institutions. The first question concerns the political institutions of the country and how these influence economic policy formation and its administrative implementation. The second question concerns the economic institutions of property rights and contract enforcement, and the manner of interaction between government agencies and civil society.

The new academic literature on institutional analysis is a response to forces of both demand and supply. The demand arises from the wider recognition that poor countries are held back in their development efforts by their failure to adopt and implement appropriate policies and to nourish the appropriate economic institutions. The supply of such analysis has been greatly facilitated by a reorientation, which has occurred for largely unrelated reasons, in economic theory. The new institutional analysis, which goes by a variety of names, is appearing in other social sciences and is also being used in the field by development practitioners. A major purpose of this book is to explain and illustrate this new type of analysis so that it can be applied more widely.

An important part of this new style of analysis is the New Institutional Economics (henceforth, NIE). As explained in chapter 2, the NIE in its various branches represents an expanded economics, in the sense that it relaxes some of the strong assumptions of traditional economics with respect to the motivations of, and the information available to, individual decision makers, and it widens the scope of economics to include political phenomena and the evolution of institutions. Institutions are the "rules of the game": the humanly devised constraints on social interaction. *The emergence and evolution of these rules is understood in terms of the motivations and decisions of the individual actors in the collectivity.*

To illustrate how a focus on institutions changes the perception of a problem, consider the role of investment in development. From the beginning of economic development as a separate field of study after World War II, investment in physical capital has been considered the driving force of development. The scarcity of domestic savings in poor countries has usually been regarded as a critical obstacle to investment and as a justification for foreign governments to provide capital assistance. A focus on institutional differences among countries suggests, however, that investment, while necessary for development, is an endogenous variable. A country with a low rate of investment is also likely to be one in which the policy and institutional environment does not make investment profitable. Where this environment is favorable, according to the institutionalist argument, the capital for investment will appear from somewhere, from sources either foreign or domestic.

The emphasis on investment as a driving force for growth in the early development economics literature was compatible with a leading government role in making the investments or in directly stimulating them through tax incentives, subsidized credit, protected markets, or other measures. Such a conception neglects the institutional environment in which the investments are made. The same criticism applies when human capital is treated in a manner parallel to physical capital. The communist countries provide a dramatic illustration that a high rate of physical capital accumulation and a well-educated labor force are not sufficient for sustained economic growth in an environment where the economic institutions are unfavorable. Other examples can be provided from the developing world. Argentina, Uruguay, and Chile had comparatively well-educated populations in 1950 and yet grew relatively slowly over succeeding decades, and Argentina and India in the 1960s and 1970s channeled substantial domestic savings into physical capital accumulation and yet achieved unimpressive rates of growth. Chapter 4 discusses econometric evidence supportive of an interpretation in which a key obstacle to growth is an unfavorable policy and institutional environment, rather than an inability to postpone consumption.

When economic policy and institutions are put at the heart of the development problem, attention naturally focuses on the behavior of politicians, political parties, voters, and interest groups. Since economic policies and outcomes affect the opinions of voters and the emergence and strength of organized interest groups, the analyst needs to study the interaction of economic and political processes. The nature of the feedback from economic policies to rewards for policy makers can be very different for different kinds of policies. For example, macroeconomic stabilization can sometimes be carried out fairly quickly by a small team of technocrats who have the backing of the president or the dictator, and success in stabilization often brings its own political rewards to the political leader. On the other hand, reform of the system of tax collection or the judicial apparatus is a much more institution-intensive process, requiring a longer period of investment of political capital and yielding a much less visible economic benefit.

An aspect of economic development that has been relatively neglected by economists is the administrative capacity of government. Development practitioners have long been acutely aware of the enormous gaps between policy pronouncements and implementation on the ground, but this recognition has often been missing from accounts by economists of the determinants of prosperity. The NIE has called attention to the vital role of government administrative capacity in shaping the institutional environment of business. Moreover, the NIE—and in particular the new economics of organization—may help to explain why bureaucracies perform well or badly and how the inefficient and corrupt ones might be reformed.

The NIE offers powerful insights into many phenomena in economic development, insights that are likely to be missed in approaches that neglect either institutions or economics. The theory and intellectual development of the NIE is described in part 1. The NIE is applied to the effects of economic and political institutions on economic development (part 2), to the determinants of success or failure in community organizations (part 3), to the enormous institutional challenges facing formerly communist countries (part 4), and to the improvement of government administrative performance (part 5). The concluding section (part 6) draws some of the implications for development practice.

The rest of this introduction gives a brief description of the chapters. Part 1, "Theoretical Approaches," provides some of the intellectual background. Chapter 2 by Christopher Clague, "The New Institutional Economics and Economic Development," explains the reorientation in economic theory mentioned above and describes five branches of the NIE: transaction cost economics, the economics of imperfect information, the economics of property rights, collective action theory, and the evolution of rules and norms. The chapter then presents some contributions of NIE analysis to our understanding of economic development and economic history.

Chapter 3, by Mancur Olson, "The New Institutional Economics: The Collective Choice Approach to Economic Development," illustrates how collective choice theory can illuminate the behavior of political actors. The chapter draws on his earlier work on the motivations of narrow and encompassing interests and on some very recent work on the incentives of those with political power to use that power in such a way as to create an environment favorable to economic development. Olson shows that a stable democracy can provide a security of property rights and contract enforcement that is beyond the reach of an autocracy, which inevitably faces the problem of succession. On the other hand, he shows that even a selfish autocratic leader may have an incentive to provide a reasonably favorable environment for development, and he contends that a great deal of the economic progress in history has taken place under such a form of government.

Part 2, "The Effects of Economic and Political Institutions on Economic Development," contains chapters that make the case that societal differences in institutions are profound and that these differences have a large impact on rates of economic progress. Chapter 4, by Christopher Clague, Philip Keefer, Stephen Knack, and Mancur Olson, "Institutions and Economic Performance," presents evidence from cross-country statistical analysis that measures of property rights and contract enforcement help to explain differences in income, growth rates, and rates of investment. These measures of property and contract rights are of two types. First, there are assessments of countries' respect for rule of law, quality of bureaucracy, corruption, risk of government repudiation of contracts, and other such variables by rating services that sell these judgments to companies contemplating investment in the countries. In addition, the chapter makes use of a recently constructed indicator of the state of these rights, called contract-intensive money, which is the proportion of liquid assets that people choose to hold in the form of financial assets rather than currency; assets held in this form are vulnerable when property and contract rights are insecure, and hence this proportion provides a window on the state of these rights in a society.

The following two chapters explore the relationships between democracy and economic development. An interesting paradox is that, while all of the richest countries of the world are democracies, the replacement of autocracy by democracy in poor countries is not always, or even usually, accompanied by an increase in the rate of economic growth. A common way of resolving this paradox is to say that democracy is something that people demand when they become rich, so that the causation runs from income level to democracy. These chapters consider another hypothesis, which is that some features of democracy are favorable to growth while other features are not.

Chapter 5, by Clague, Keefer, Knack, and Olson, "Democracy, Autocracy, and the Institutions Supportive of Economic Growth," provides empirical evidence that democracies at a given level of income tend to provide better property and contract rights than autocracies. They also find that both democracies and autocracies that last longer provide better protection of these rights, but the replacement of a dictator by a new democratic regime is typically associated with a deterioration in the state of property rights, while a change in regime in the reverse direction is usually associated with an improvement in these rights. This finding may be partly explained by the tendency for democracies to give way to dictatorships when they are doing badly economically, while dictatorships frequently turn into new democracies when economic conditions are favorable.

Stephan Haggard, in chapter 6, "Democratic Institutions, Economic Policy, and Development," explains how different institutional features of democracy affect economic policy. He argues that well-organized interest groups can facilitate the compromises needed for effective policy reform, and thus they can play a much more positive role in promoting growth than envisaged in Olson's work (Olson 1982, and chapter 3 of this book). He distinguishes the political requirements for dramatic macroeconomic reforms (namely strong executive authority, without the requirement of institutions of consultation) from those for an institutional environment supportive of sustained economic progress. He also discusses the effects of presidential versus parliamentary systems and of different types of party configurations.

Part 3, "Participation and Local Institutions," deals with institutions and institutional reform at the local level, with a main focus on rural water projects. A common observation about irrigation systems in less-developed countries is that the systems are designed and constructed by national government agencies with little input from the farmers who are to operate and maintain them, and the result is that maintenance is neglected and agricultural productivity is much lower than it could be. Many observers have thought that participation by farmers in the design, construction, and operation of irrigation projects could greatly increase the rates of return to such investments.

In chapter 7, "Investing in Capital, Institutions, and Incentives," Elinor Ostrom explains the ways in which social capital is created and maintained. Careful attention to the structure of rules can make a big difference in how community organizations function. She reports both on a highly successful project to enable farmers from well-functioning irrigation associations to help other associations to work better as well as on an interesting but unfortunate example of externally financed irrigation construction projects in Nepal that reduced agricultural productivity by undermining the basis for cooperation among farmers.

Melinda Smale and Vernon Ruttan in chapter 8, "Social Capital and Technical Change," describe how a particular cultural practice among the Mossi tribes in Burkina Faso was adapted for use in agricultural cooperation. The *kombi-naam* were traditionally mutual assistance associations of young men and women of the same age who worked together for one year, assisting members of the community and collecting remuneration, which was used for a festival at the end of the year. Under the guidance of a local sociologist, the associations were expanded to include other age groups and were converted to ongoing organizations engaged in cooperative technical change projects.

Deepa Narayan, in chapter 9, "Focus on People's Participation," reports on a statistical study of projects supported by the World Bank and the United Nations Development Program. While there is a large literature extolling the virtues of participation in development projects, there has been little hard evidence that a high level of participation makes projects more effective. These variables were carefully and independently measured, and in a multiple regression analysis overall beneficiary participation was found to have a positive effect on project effectiveness.

Vernon Ruttan's chapter 10, "Participation and Development," is in part an extended comment on the chapters in parts 2 and 3. He first traces the evolution of thinking on the role of democracy and autocracy in promoting development and then reviews the history of efforts to encourage the empowerment of local institutions in developing countries. The current emphasis on participation follows the community development movement of the 1950s and the integrated rural development and basic needs initiatives of the 1970s. He draws lessons from some of these earlier experiences for the design of rural development programs.

The Center for Institutional Reform and the Informal Sector (IRIS) at the University of Maryland has been engaged in institutional reform activities in formerly communist countries since its inception in the fall of 1990. Mongolia was the first country in which IRIS was involved, followed by Poland in 1991, by Russia in 1993, and by most of the states of the former Soviet Union in 1994. Some of the lessons from IRIS experiences are described in part 4, "Implementing Institutional Reform in Formerly Communist Societies." In chapter 11, "Missed Policy Opportunities during Mongolian Privatization," Peter Murrell, one of the directors of the IRIS project in Mongolia, draws attention to the absence of informational feedback about the consequences of economic policies. Some of the difficulties encountered in the mass privatization of the large state enterprises have been due to failures to collect and utilize information, rather than to political struggles or interest group influence on policy. Murrell suggests that external assistance might play a useful role in building policy analysis institutions.

In chapter 12, "Implementing Legal Reform in Transition Economies," Charles Cadwell, director of IRIS, describes the conditions in Russia that impede the establishment of a rule of law—the contested authority between the federal executive and legislature, between the center and the regions, and within the federal executive itself. In this environment, Cadwell argues, donors can be most helpful if they think of particular policy debates as opportunities to educate many different political actors about how policy should be formulated and implemented rather than as specific laws to be corrected.

Part 5, "Improving Government Performance," is concerned with the quality of government administration and its effects on development. Vito Tanzi and Anthony Pellechio, in chapter 13, "The Reform of Tax Administration," point out that those who have worked extensively on tax administration generally do not write about it, while those who write about it have not been immersed in the details of it. This chapter is an exception to that generalization. Drawing on their extensive experience in the International Monetary Fund with efforts to reform the administration of tax systems in many countries, the authors describe the factors that influence whether a tax reform project is likely to succeed. This chapter, which grew out of field experience, illustrates many of the ideas of the NIE.

Chapter 14, by Robert Klitgaard, "Information and Incentives in Institutional Reform," applies some ideas from the new economics of organization to the problem of reforming public administration in developing countries. Using an incentive intensity principle from Paul Milgrom and John Roberts, he discusses the conditions under which individual employees or groups of employees might usefully be remunerated on the basis of performance measures. He contrasts this economic approach to administrative reform with traditional public administration doctrines, which have generally not produced much administrative reform in developing countries.

In chapter 15, "Rational Compliance with Rationalized Bureaucracy," Margaret Levi and Richard Sherman explain the vital role of an honest and efficient bureaucracy in the functioning of a market economy and a democratic polity. Such a bureaucracy helps to make it rational for citizens and businesses to comply in a quasi-voluntary manner with the rules of society. Quasi-voluntary compliance involves a choice to obey even if the individual costs of compliance outweigh the individual benefits, but it is a choice within a situation of sanctions being applied against those who break the rules. The features of a bureaucracy that enable it to play this role are a combination of Weberian characteristics (such as recruitment based on qualifications, internal promotion based on merit, insulation from special interest political pressures) and a "corporate culture" or "corporate community" that sustains extra effort and initiative.

In brief, part 2 of the book says that countries differ in their institutional environments and that these differences vitally affect their development performance. Part 3 provides evidence that participatory forms of organization tend to increase the efficiency of water use in irrigation associations and suggests that such forms of organization can emerge when careful attention is paid to the structure of rules. The intellectual progress that has been made in understanding the structure of institutions offers hope that the third wave of external donor interest in promoting grassroots participation will have more success than the first two. But that remains to be demonstrated on a large scale. One of the lessons that has emerged from the descriptions of IRIS experiences in part 4 is that an important part of institutional reform is changing people's intellectual frameworks. Perhaps the term *technical assistance* is a misnomer. Often what is needed is not the technical specifications of an appropriate law or regulation but a change in the way government officials and businesses think about their roles in a market economy. Part 5 conveys a message parallel to that in part 3: careful attention needs to be paid to the structure of rules and to flows of information in government agencies and their relationships with civil society. Changes in these structures need to be nonmarginal to escape from current inefficient equilibria.

Part 6, "Implications for Development Practice," continues a theme touched on in many of the preceding chapters, namely, that the new perspective on development provided by the NIE requires a rethinking of the design and implementation of development programs. Whereas any factor of production—capital, skilled labor, raw materials, or technical knowledge—can be purchased on the international market, new institutions are not so easily put in place. What we think we know about institutions suggests that they cannot be transplanted but must evolve from the decisions of the many participants, who start with their inherited mental models and patterns of behavior. An institutional focus directs attention toward the politics of economic policy and the functioning of various types of organizations.

Robert Picciotto, director-general of operations evaluation at the World Bank, in chapter 16, "Putting Institutional Economics to Work," argues that institutional economics can play an important role in guiding the activities of development practitioners. He presents a conceptual framework, derived from the NIE, for thinking about institutional design in terms of hierarchy, market, and participation principles, and he describes some of the ways in which institutional economics has been put to use and could be further utilized in the Bank's activities. In chapter 17, "The New Institutional Economics and Institutional Reform," Christopher Clague contrasts an institutional approach to development programs with two other approaches, which he calls institution-free standard economics and incentive-free social engineering. An institutional approach, which neglects neither incentives nor the institutional environment, attempts to devise strategies for reform that are incentive-compatible. The chapter draws lessons for development practice from the book's analysis of rural development projects, government bureaucracy and corruption, the functioning of democratic and authoritarian regimes, and the possible roles of external donors.

Reference

Olson, Mancur. 1982. The *Rise and Decline of Nations*. New Haven: Yale University Press.

I THEORETICAL APPROACHES

2   The New Institutional Economics and Economic Development

Christopher Clague

1   From Physical Capital to Human Capital to Social Capital

In the early postwar period, when economists turned their attention to economic development, they thought that the key difference between rich and poor countries lay in the amount of physical capital per person. What was needed to launch a country on the path of self-sustained growth was a rise in the ratio of investment to income from 5 percent to 12 percent, or more. Poor countries were unable to do this on their own, since people were so impoverished that their consumption could not be compressed any further. Thus, foreign aid in the form of investable resources was essential to enable poor countries to escape the poverty trap created by their inability to save and their rapid rates of population growth. In the 1960s, after the remarkably successful Marshall Plan assistance in Europe and the disappointing experience of foreign aid in the less-developed countries, the concept of capital was broadened to include human capital, the lack of which was considered another critical obstacle to development in poor countries.

Although both physical and human capital accumulation are essential to economic growth and development, interpretations of the problem of economic development have shifted in recent decades. First, we have observed countries where high rates of physical capital accumulation have been accompanied by only modest economic growth. Second, we have observed some countries in sub-Saharan Africa and South America where education has expanded rapidly but growth has not taken place. Third, and most fundamentally, we have broadened our focus to include the incentive structures that lead to the accumulation of physical and human capital and to technological progress. In this endeavor, attention has turned to the explanation of economic policies and fundamental economic and political institutions. In some formulations, these institutional arrangements have been called "social capital" (Coleman 1990). Whether we try to understand

I thank Karla Hoff and Robert Klitgaard for perceptive comments on drafts of this chapter. The usual disclaimer applies.

social capital or institutions generally, we need to think about types of social interactions that were long not part of standard economics.

Economists and other social scientists studying less-developed countries have been aware that the institutional environment in these countries differed from that in industrialized countries. In the early postwar decades there were intense debates about the degree to which standard neoclassical economics needed to be modified to apply to less-developed countries. The view was frequently expressed that standard neoclassical economics was based on institutions that existed in industrialized countries but that did not necessarily exist in the underdeveloped countries. There emerged after World War II a subdiscipline called development economics, which made alternative assumptions about how the economy worked. In this sense, development economics assumed that the institutions of the economy were different, but there was little attention among economists to the evolution of these institutions or to deep explanations of them.

By the early 1980s standard economics was making a comeback in the field of development; Hirschman (1983, chap. 1) could say that most economists accepted "monoeconomics," or the idea that the same type of economics applied to both developed and less-developed countries. This view represented a rejection of one of the claims of development economics, that a different type of economics was needed to address the problems of less-developed countries. Today it is even more true than when Hirschman wrote that the same tools of economics are used in the study of development as in the rest of economics. However, the increasing acceptance of standard economics in the analysis of the problems of poor countries owes a great deal to a reorientation of the field of economics to make it more amenable to examining the determinants and consequences of institutions.

The following section explains this reorientation in economic theory, and the following one describes the various strands of literature that are called the New Institutional Economics (hereafter, NIE). Section 4 then presents some contributions of the NIE to economic history and economic development.

2   Reorientation in Economic Theory

The core of economics can be defined in terms of its basic assumptions and its subject matter. The basic assumptions are individual utility maximization with exogenous preferences and a well-defined structure of information; the core subject matter is decisions within markets of consumers, producers, investors, and traders. In the last couple of decades, these basic assumptions have been modified, primarily by the incorporation into the heart of theory of the phenomena of costly information and of limitations on the human capacity to process it. The subject matter of economics has been extended to such nonmarket phenomena as the operation of organizations and the behavior of politicians, bureaucrats, and voters.

With a well-defined information structure, exogenous preferences, and unlimited capacity for processing information, models tend to be "clean," that is, they give strong, unambiguous conclusions. Utility maximization under these conditions is a powerful engine, which traditionally has set economics apart from the "softer" social sciences. However, pervasive uncertainty is an undeniable fact of life, as is the fact that in modern economies people spend a great deal of time and effort in acquiring and processing information. These observations have two important implications. One is that people simplify their decision making by employing rules of thumb rather than continuously optimizing in all dimensions. The other is that trust in others becomes important, in part because it greatly reduces uncertainty and the cost of acquiring information.

In recent decades, the subject matter of economics has expanded in many directions (Hirschleifer 1985); of particular interest in the present context is the application of economic reasoning to the rules of the game, in two senses. One sense is the decision of individuals whether to obey the existing rules; the other is the collective action of people to change the inherited set of rules. Neoclassical economics had assumed that the rules of social interaction were given, in the form of the rules of a market economy, and that people obeyed the rules of the game. These assumptions made sense in the neoclassical world of perfect information, for violations of the rules could be easily detected and the perpetrators punished. Once the question was posed, however, its salience could not be denied, and a great deal of research effort has gone into trying to explain how the rules of the game might evolve in theory and how they have evolved in history.

The extension of the subject matter of economics has reinforced the modification of the basic assumptions. The core set of assumptions of utility maximization with exogenous preferences under well-defined information structures is less appealing when applied to politicians, bureaucrats, voters, organization members, criminals, and mothers than when applied to the traditional subject matter of neoclassical economics. In particular, the study of the evolution of cooperation via the theory of repeated games leads to a recognition of the important role of focal points, which can become symbols with affective content. The study of the evolution of norms leads to economic theories of how moral sentiments develop (e.g., Sugden 1986). This is an example of an economic theory in which preferences are endogenous. As is discussed in more detail below, this step represents the crossing of a line that economists have traditionally regarded as a firm boundary of their discipline.

Many economists have felt that a phenomenon has not been properly explained unless it emerges from a model based exclusively on rational self-interest. If the analyst appealed to altruistic motivation, or if she said that choices were constrained by cultural norms, that was regarded as an unsatisfactory explanation. In recent years, economists have been more willing to countenance relaxation of the traditional assumptions. There has been work on the benefits to individuals of having a conscience (Frank 1988) and on the efficiency gains resulting from shared mental models (Denzau and North 1994). This willingness to accommodate a richer conception of human motivation and to countenance greater limitations on rational calculation of individual advantage has emerged, in my opinion, because of the broadened subject matter of economics as well as the reorientation of the basic assumptions of economic theory.

Methodologically, there is no compelling reason to stick to the postulate of rational self-interested calculation with exogenous preferences. Stiglitz (1986) suggests criteria by which we judge theories; these include simplicity (fewer assumptions are better), internal completeness (the assumptions should be as "primitive" as possible), consistency with available data, predictive power (predicting empirical regularities that have not yet been noted), and the ability to make specific predictions in a variety of contexts. If people form groups and internalize group goals in predictable ways, then models incorporating these regularities will perform better by the various criteria than models based on the postulate of individual self-interested motivation.

The New Institutional Economics, described in the next section, represents a kind of "expanded economics." Like standard economics, it focuses on the choices people make in their lives. But it enriches the simple rational choice model by allowing for the pervasiveness of information problems and human limitations on processing information, the evolution of norms, and the willingness of people to form bonds of trust. The NIE seeks to explain not only individuals' choices with a given set of institutions but, more important, the way that individuals' beliefs and choices affect the evolution of the institutions themselves.

One way of illustrating the new orientation of the NIE is to consider the role of culture in economic outcomes. Economists have often made light of cultural explanations, arguing, first, that people in different cultures tend to want the same things and, second, that since cultural variables have not been satisfactorily measured, explanations based on culture have been empirically vacuous. Economists who have downplayed cultural explanations, such as Balassa (1988) in his remarks on the successful economic development in East Asian countries, stress that what matters are policies and incentives. The analyst following the NIE approach can agree with Balassa that this is what matters, but she can point out that *individuals' incentives depend on the behavior patterns and the cultural norms of the rest of society* (see the discussion of corruption in section 4.5 of this chapter, and chaps. 13–15).

In this connection, it is useful to distinguish between *individual culture* and *community culture*. Individual culture is what the individual carries with him as a result of having been brought up in a particular culture. It is what differentiates an immigrant from the natives in a country. There is abundant evidence that migrants tend to adopt the behavior patterns of their new homes, at least in their economic decisions, and in this sense individual culture is usually not a serious obstacle to economic progress. (See Borjas 1987, 1994 on the earnings of immigrants in the United States.) Community culture, on the other hand, is the set of norms, attitudes, and values of an entire community, and it of course affects the incentives of individuals to behave in particular ways. Community culture tends to reinforce and be reinforced by the patterns of behavior in the community, and it is obvious that the behavior patterns (institutions) and the associated cultural norms can be a serious obstacle to economic progress in the community (for example, corruption in government and popular disdain for politicians and bureaucrats).

3   The New Institutional Economics

In the NIE institutions are defined as socially devised constraints on individual action (North 1994). They are sets of rules that are recognized and frequently followed by members of the community and that impose constraints on the actions of individual members. Of course, the fact that people follow the rules may make the community much better off than it would be in the absence of any rules, and in that sense institutions are liberating rather than constraining. Nevertheless, at the individual level they impose constraints on behavior.

Thus, broadly defined, institutions can be many things (Nabli and Nugent 1989). They can be organizations or sets of rules within organizations. They can be markets or particular rules about the way a market operates. They can refer to the set of property rights and rules governing exchanges in a society. (The individual actors that are constrained by the rules may be organizations and, indeed, frequently are.) They may include cultural norms of behavior. The rules can be either formally written down and enforced by government officials or unwritten and informally sanctioned. The rules need not be uniformly obeyed to be considered institutions, but the concept does imply some degree of rule obedience. If the rules are generally ignored, we would not refer to them as institutions. Thus we may speak of the selection and replacement of political leaders in a particular country as not being "institutionalized," as Huntington (1968) does.

It is useful to distinguish different categories of institutions. Following Feeny (1993), who draws on North (1981), Ostrom, Feeny, and Picht (1993), and Oakerson (1993), we identify (1) the constitutional order, (2) the institutional arrangements, and (3) the cultural endowments. The constitutional order is the fundamental set of rules, both written and unwritten, within which the institutional arrangements are devised by the collective and individual actions of the members. Cultural endowments include the normative behavioral codes of society and the mental models that people use to interpret their experience. The cultural endowments of a society change slowly, as does the constitutional order (except during revolutionary periods). Partly for this reason, much (but not all) of the analysis of institutional innovation in this book and elsewhere consists of examinations of changes in institutional arrangements, taking the constitutional order and the cultural endowments as given.

There are several different strands of literature in what is called the New Institutional Economics.[1] For our purposes, these may be distinguished as follows.

3.1 Markets and hierarchies, or transaction-cost economics

This branch is closely associated with the work of Williamson (1975, 1985). His early work addressed a question that had been largely ignored in the economics literature, although it was raised by Coase in 1937:

---

[1]Although the categories are somewhat different, my conception of the NIE is basically consistent with Lin and Nugent (1995), who provide a fuller treatment of many of the topics mentioned here.

Why did certain transactions take place within organizations rather than between separate firms in a market? The topic is central to industrial organization, and it has important implications for the understanding of vertical integration, mergers, and antitrust policy, and in this sense Williamson's work deals with the core subject matter of economics. However, Williamson altered the basic assumptions of economic analysis with his emphasis on the complexity of economic life, pervasive uncertainty, bounds on rationality, and opportunism. He argued that to understand why firms internalize transactions, one must take account not only of the limitations of human beings (that is, bounded rationality and opportunism) but also of their capacity and willingness to develop relationships of trust. Transaction-cost economics has gone on to study the employment relationship, the nature of contracts in the business world, and many of the topics that are also treated under the following heading.

3.2   Economics of imperfect information

This broad category might be called the "economics of costly and asymmetric information." This literature began with two problems in the insurance industry: adverse selection and moral hazard. It has come to include the economics of screening and statistical discrimination, principal-agent models, theories of mechanism design, the economic theory of organizations, bargaining theory, and theories of incentive-compatible contracts. In contrast to transaction-cost economics, this literature typically does not introduce moral considerations or other "soft" assumptions. The information structure is spelled out precisely, and people are usually individualistic utility maximizers. Much of this literature is quite technical.

It is worth noting that some of the pioneering contributions in this literature were inspired by reflection on problems encountered in poor countries: Akerlof's (1970) lemons principle, Stiglitz's (1974) work on screening, and the large literature on sharecropping, which evolved into the literature on optimal contracts and merged with principal-agent theory. This observation helps to explain why mainstream economics is more applicable to less-developed countries than was thought to be the case in the 1950s and 1960s.

3.3   The economics of property rights

The property-rights literature that emerged in the 1960s (classic references include Alchian 1965 and Demsetz 1964) made the point that the structure of property rights is crucial to economic efficiency and economic progress. At a conceptual level, this literature clarified the dimensions of individual rights to use, rent, sell, destroy, modify, donate, and transform property and the ways in which the rights of some parties to treat their property affect the rights of others. One of the themes of this literature is that a variety of property-rights structures can be reasonably efficient, provided that individuals are free to enter into contracts and that these contracts can be enforced. Thus, whether the responsibility for damages caused by a defective product initially lies with the buyer or the seller is not important if the responsibility can be shifted by contractual provision. Similarly, if tenants suddenly acquire property rights in the land they have been renting, in theory there is no barrier to efficiency as long as these rights can be traded.[2] What this literature has condemned as particularly inefficient is a situation in which such contracts are either prohibited by law or for other reasons are not enforceable in practice and, consequently, landlords discharge tenants or refuse to take them on for fear of losing their property rights to the land.

The view that the initial allocation of property rights does not have efficiency implications has been strongly qualified by recent work in the economics of asymmetric information. In that literature, the initial allocation of wealth has implications for the efficiency of resource allocation, even if there is complete freedom of contract that courts will enforce (subject to the information limitations of the judicial process). For example, a potential creditor may be willing to lend to a potential entrepreneur only if the latter has enough wealth to make credible his commitment to the project (for other examples, see Hoff 1994).

Structures of property rights have varied through history, and scholars have attempted to explain both why property rights changed in particular periods and how these structures affected economic efficiency and progress. The delimitation and enforcement of property rights is a costly process; one of the early insights of this literature was that societies generally do not define and enforce property rights to resources that are not scarce, but as particular resources become scarce, through say population growth or technological change, societies tend to establish property rights in these resources (Demsetz 1967; Feeny 1988).

An explanation of property-rights structures requires (1) an understanding of the behavior of the state, which normally plays an important role in defining and enforcing property rights, and (2) consider-

---

[2]I ignore here the question of whether the process by which the property rights are changed alters expectations about their continuation.

ation of custom, social norms, intellectual structures, and ideology (North 1981, 1990). This is a tall order, and economists do not usually claim to have comprehensive theories of these phenomena. Nevertheless, they have attempted to use the tools of economics to gain insight into these matters. Some of these attempts are described under the next heading.

3.4 Collective action

Olson (1965) saw that the concept of a public good, which he defines by the nonexcludability criterion, and the associated free-rider problem, could fruitfully be applied to a great variety of group goals, not just to the construction of pieces of physical infrastructure. Olson was keenly aware of the cost of information, and the rational ignorance of members of a large group plays a central role in his theory.

The theory of collective action is concerned with the conditions under which groups of people with a common interest will perceive that interest and act to achieve it. (For a recent review of this literature, see Sandler 1992.) Groups are more likely to act when the number of individuals concerned is small, when they interact frequently and can communicate easily with one another, and when they share common values and beliefs. Large groups can act collectively but, usually, only when political entrepreneurs create organizations that provide rewards to the entrepreneurs and "selective incentives" to the members—individual punishments or rewards that provide incentives for individuals to contribute to collective goals. Many potential large groups remain latent. Groups are more likely to form when there are a few members with a significant stake in the outcome. In the case of very large groups, in which no members have significant size in relation to the total group, where the technology of supply is that of summation of individual efforts, people will typically not make large sacrifices of personal welfare in order to contribute to the supply of the public good. People will make small sacrifices, such as bothering to vote or making small contributions to charity, even when the personal payoff is less than the cost, and on infrequent occasions some people will make large sacrifices, including even risking their lives, for collective goals. However, most people in the ordinary run of their lives do not make large contributions to public goods unless there are enough private benefits from their actions (i.e., selective incentives) to make it worthwhile. Large groups come into existence mainly through institutional devices that provide these private benefits.

3.5   The evolution of cooperation and norms

Cooperation can emerge spontaneously between two parties, even when both are egoists and potentially in conflict. In the last two decades a large literature in game theory has explored the conditions under which cooperation may emerge. The likelihood of cooperation depends on the nature of the game (whether it is prisoner's dilemma, chicken, assurance, etc.) and on the probability of continued play with the same partner. This literature has merged with the literature on collective action as researchers try to understand cooperation in groups of all sizes and try to design institutional structures that make cooperation the best strategy in two-person encounters.

Noncooperative game theory has been fruitfully applied to the explanation of the institutions that preserve and maintain common property resources (Ostrom 1990; Ostrom, Gardner, and Walker 1994). In order to explain the empirical phenomena of cooperation as observed both in the field and in the experimental laboratory, these researchers have found it useful to modify the assumptions of classical game theory to place less emphasis on the ability or willingness of participants to calculate their best strategies and more emphasis on their ability to find workable heuristics or norms that structure their cooperative efforts. Noncooperative game theory has also been used to explain the phenomenon of social order in stateless societies (see Bates 1983, chap. 1, on the Nuer in Africa; and Eggertsson 1990, 305–10, on the Icelandic Commonwealth, AD 930–1262). But as Johnson (1994) forcefully points out, particularly for the case of the Nuer, this social order relied on shared symbols, or cultural focal points. These symbols structure the way people think about their options.

3.6   The effects on efficiency of institutional innovation

The study of institutions inevitably includes their evaluation from a normative point of view. There are some interesting differences among the five branches in this regard. In the Williamson-inspired transaction-cost literature, in which the constitutional order of property rights and political institutions are taken as given, there is normally a tendency for organizational forms and types of contract to evolve toward efficiency, from the point of view of the participants. The principle of competition applies to organizational forms and types of contracts just as it does to choices of technology. Given a regime of private property, and in the absence of important externalities, the organizations and contracts that private parties arrange would tend to evolve toward social efficiency as well.[3]

Although the early property-rights literature included many examples of the emergence of private property rights in conditions where efficiency called for them, it was soon recognized that changes in institutions require cooperation and collective action, which may not emerge at all, or which may emerge among groups with narrow interests that are sharply in conflict with those of society at large (North 1990). To the extent that the powerful set the rules, there may be a tendency for the rules to benefit the powerful, but that does not necessarily imply a tendency toward social efficiency (Knight 1992). Moreover, the rules may emerge out of the uncoordinated actions of different parties and may not serve the interests of any of them.

The factors facilitating and blocking changes in institutional arrangements have been characterized in a supply-demand framework by Feeny (1993). He explicitly takes the constitutional order and cultural endowments as givens. Demand-side factors include relative product and factor prices, technology, and size of market. Supply-side factors include the costs of institutional design, the existing stock of knowledge, the responsiveness of the political order to the innovative efforts of political entrepreneurs, the prevailing cultural values and norms, and especially the expected benefits for elite decision makers. There are many examples in history where changes in demand-side factors have created a social need for new property-rights regimes, and new institutional arrangements have been forthcoming. In many of these episodes, however, the changes have been brought about by narrow interest groups seeking their own goals, which happened to benefit society; examples are the role of the merchant guild, the expansion of medieval trade (Greif, Milgrom, and Weingast, 1993), and the emergence of property rights in land in nineteenth-century Hawaii (Roumasset and LaCroix 1994).

---

[3]The imperfect-information school, however, shows that information problems generate externalities, so that contracts that are *pairwise* Pareto-efficient can often be socially inefficient, and thus there are many opportunities for an honest and efficient government to remedy market failures (Hoff, Braverman, and Stiglitz, 1993, chap.1). For example, where individuals can spend resources to acquire information to increase their shares of a fixed pie, as often occurs in insurance markets, it may be efficient to have a government regulation that prohibits people from collecting or using that information. Whether actual governments can efficiently remedy these market failures is, of course, another question.

4 Illustrations of an Institutional Approach to Problems in Economic Development

This section is intended to give the reader the flavor of some of the NIE analyses that have been applied to less-developed countries and to the economic history of the now developed countries.[4] A recurrent theme is that, in order to deal with the questions posed, an expanded economics is necessary.

4.1 Induced technological and institutional innovation

Technological change is at the heart of economic progress, and economists have devoted considerable effort to try to understand its determinants. One of the insights emerging in this literature in the middle decades of this century is that invention and technological innovation are affected by factor scarcities. Seekers of new techniques of production tend to concentrate their efforts on ways of economizing on factors that are relatively expensive or are getting more so. In the 1970s, Hayami and Ruttan drew on models of induced technological change to construct a theory of induced institutional change (Hayami and Ruttan 1971; Binswanger and Ruttan 1978). These theories of both technological and institutional change emphasize demand factors. The basic idea was that the emergence of a need for a new institutional arrangement would lead to efforts by political entrepreneurs to create such arrangements.

Hayami and Ruttan and their coauthors provide rich historical descriptions of the emergence of agricultural research and extension institutions in the United States, Japan, and other countries. Implicit in many of these descriptions and analyses is the assumption that the constitutional order and cultural endowments were favorable to these socially productive institutional innovations. In later work (Ruttan and Hayami 1984; Hayami and Ruttan 1985), they developed a broader framework for analyzing economic change. This framework includes the traditional variables in economic analysis, resources and technology, and adds the new variables, institutions and cultural endowments. The interrelationships among all four are considered, although the authors state that the role of cultural endowments is the least understood.

---

[4]Many other examples are provided in the nice survey by Feeny (1993).

4.2   Interpretations of rates of growth and income differences

Why do poor countries remain poor? A long tradition in economics addresses this question with the intellectual framework of the aggregate production function. In a simple version of this approach, poor countries are poor because they lack physical and human capital.[5] In this view, growth rates are interpreted as the results of accumulation of these factors, or in other words as the result of investment rates and growth of education and training. The vast literature on the "sources of growth," following Denison's pioneering work, is based on the idea that countries are on the frontier of some sort of production function, and a large literature in international economics has interpreted income differences and comparative advantage in terms of factor endowments and common production functions.

It is true that poor countries have small amounts of physical capital per head and have labor forces that are not highly educated. But it does not seem to be true that these factors of production are highly remunerated in poor countries, as would be the case if the simple aggregate production function story were true. In fact, highly skilled workers generally earn much more in rich countries than in poor ones, and capital flows from South to North as well as from North to South.

Of course, economists familiar with less-developed countries have long been aware of the perversities of policies and institutions that lower the productivity of capital and labor or, in other words, that make production functions differ across countries. But systematic analyses of *how* the policies and institutions change the relationships between inputs and outputs have been rare.

In recent years, economists have become aware of the importance not only of the economic policies of governments but also of the *credibility* of government promises to carry out announced policies (Brunetti and Weder 1994). Underlying differences in the credibility of policy announcements are differences in the institutions of policy making. In many less-developed countries, policies are changed by executive decree with no prior notice and without reconciliation of new decrees and prior ones. In such an environment, property rights cannot be secure. In addition, government bureaucrats may have a great deal of discretion in the application of business

---

[5]For a recent exposition and defense of this approach, see Mankiw (1995), and for trenchant criticisms see the comments on Mankiw's paper by Phelps and Romer.

regulations, and their decisions are not predictable. The challenge is to come up with evidence that these differences in institutions matter to growth.

Researchers with an institutional focus have made two sorts of contributions in this area. One is to find *systematic* deviations of economic outcomes from those predicted by an aggregate production function approach. Such deviations provide indirect evidence that institutional differences are at work in generating these outcomes. The second is to find direct measures of the institutional environment of countries and to relate these to economic outcomes. Examples of each are given below.

Consider a scatter diagram where, on the vertical axis, we plot the rate of growth of per capita income of countries from 1960 to 1990 and, on the horizontal axis, we plot the level of per capita income at the beginning of the period. A regression line fitted to these data will have approximately a zero slope; that is, there is no strong tendency for poor countries to grow faster or slower than rich countries. However, the dispersion of the rates of growth is much larger for poor than for rich countries. Thus the data resemble a cone, with the large end of the cone at the bottom of the income scale and the small end at the top. This pattern is consistent with the interpretation that poor countries that get their institutions and policies right will grow faster than rich countries, because the poor ones have greater opportunities for "catch-up" growth, while countries that have their institutions and policies badly wrong will not only be poor but will also have low rates of growth.

Now consider adding other variables to the growth rate regression. In addition to initial income level, a standard set of "conditioning" variables includes level of primary and secondary education, some measure of political instability, and some measure of government intervention in the economy (Barro and Sala-I-Martin 1995; Brunetti 1995; Alessina and Perotti 1994). With these variables controlled for, the relationship between initial income and subsequent growth is now strongly negative. This is the phenomenon of "conditional convergence," which says that if a low-income country provides education to its labor force, avoids the wrong sorts of government intervention in the economy,[6] and avoids political instability, it will grow rapidly.

---

[6]It is not clear *which* measures of government policy and political instability explain growth, as the results depend on which other variables are in the regression equation. See Levine and Renelt (1992).

This evidence, which is consistent with an institutional interpretation of growth rates, is quite indirect. Recently, some researchers at IRIS and elsewhere used direct measures of the institutional environment of countries in explanations of economic growth. These include "risk guide" variables, which are assessments by experts of the risk of investing in particular countries, a measure of "contract-intensive money" that reflects property and contract rights, and entrepreneurs' perceptions of the risk that they will be adversely affected by changes in government regulations. When added to standard growth and investment regression, these institutional variables turn out to be statistically and economically significant (see chap. 4, below, and the references cited there).

4.3 Comparative costs and comparative advantage

Why are services cheap in poor countries? Why do poor countries have comparative advantage in primary products? Questions involving comparative advantage and comparative costs have usually been addressed in the economics literature in the framework of the factor proportions model. The comparative advantage of countries in particular products depends, in this model, on the factor endowments of countries and the factor intensities of the commodities. This model has affinity with the aggregate function approach described in the previous section, in that countries' production functions are often assumed to be the same or to differ in a way that is neutral across commodities.

An institutional approach to comparative advantage would recognize that commodities differ in the degree to which they depend on a well-functioning institutional environment that provides secure property rights, effective contract enforcement, and reliable physical infrastructure. In addition to the concepts of capital-, labor-, and skill-intensive goods, we might think of property- and contract-intensive goods and services, such as banking and insurance. Casual observation seems to bear out the prediction that countries with good institutional and physical infrastructure would have comparative advantage in these services.

Clague (1991) presents a model of comparative advantage in which goods are distinguished according to whether their production can benefit from either large organizations or extensive interaction among enterprises. Some commodities and services are quite "self-contained," in that their production does not benefit much from an elaborate division of labor that requires coordination within large organizations or across firms. The hypothesis from the model, then, is that countries with poor property rights, contract enforcement, and physical infrastructure would tend to have comparative advantage in self-contained goods and comparative disadvantage in goods that are the opposite of self-contained. The model helps to explain why some services (those provided by restaurants, hotels, taxicabs, barbers, and repair persons) tend to be cheap in poor countries: these services are relatively self-contained. The model also helps to explain the strong tendency for poor countries to have comparative advantage in primary products, for these tend to be more self-contained than manufactured products. Within manufactures, poor countries tend to have comparative advantage in the goods that, even in the favorable institutional environment of rich countries, are relatively self-contained and are produced in relatively small organizational units.

4.4   Sharecropping

In many countries, sharecroppers are near the bottom of the socioeconomic ladder and are often perceived by observers as victims of exploitation by landlords, who are typically much better off economically and higher ranking in the social and political spheres. The practice was widely considered to be "feudal," or in other words, a remnant of a domination relationship between landlord and tenant, and it was legally prohibited in many countries as part of land reforms. The topic attracted considerable interest among economists during the 1970s, and one of the successes of the emerging theory of asymmetric information was a convincing account of why landlords and tenants would *both* prefer a sharecropping contract to either a fixed-rent contract or a wage contract. A wage contract has the obvious disadvantage of giving the cultivator little incentive to apply effort above that required to avoid being discharged, and it imposes a burden of labor monitoring on the landowning employer. A fixed-rent contract, which makes the cultivator the residual income recipient of the outcome of the crop season, provides a strong incentive for effort, but it forces the cultivator to bear the risk of crop variability, a risk that the poor cultivator is usually thought to be less willing to bear than the richer landowner. Furthermore, an annual rental contract gives the cultivator-renter little incentive to build up the fertility of the soil, since the landowner has the right to replace the current tenant (or threaten to do so) and raise the rent.

Even when risk considerations are left aside, it can be shown that the sharecropping contract provides a more efficient harmonization of the interests of landlord and cultivator than either of the other two alternatives, in conditions where building up the fertility of the soil is a relevant consideration. One intuitive explanation of this result is that each of the other contracts involves one large distortion, or gap between effort and reward, while the share contract involves two smaller distortions. Since the efficiency loss of a distortion is approximately proportional to the square of the size of the distortion, the sharecropping contract is less inefficient than the other two (Barzel 1989).

But this explanation still leaves a puzzle. According to Barzel's theory, the terms of the sharecropping contract, that is, the share of the crop allocated to the cultivator and to the landowner, as well as ancillary conditions such as the production responsibilities of the two parties, should vary with the relative scarcities of land and labor. Yet a striking empirical regularity of the sharecropping literature is that the shares tend to be simple fractions (such as equal halves or one-third/two-thirds) and that the shares in a given community are remarkably stable, even as labor and land scarcities vary over time.

How can this puzzle be explained? The following explanation is based on Murrell (1983). In view of the importance in many agricultural contexts of building up the fertility of the soil, it is highly desirable for the landlord and the cultivator to have a long-term relationship based on mutual trust. The cultivator wants to be confident that the landowner will not replace him as long as he works diligently and invests in the fertility of the land. The landlord wants to find a tenant who will do just that. A disadvantage of the fixed-rent contract is that it presents the parties with a conflict situation when circumstances, such as prices, change. A change in the rent is perceived as a gain for one party at the expense of the other. In a sharecropping contract, this conflict is muted, since the parties' returns move together automatically as prices change. Moreover, a landowner who proposes a share that departs from the standard one in the community is likely to be perceived as unfair and untrustworthy, and he will suffer the consequences of that perception. Consequently, as prices and resource scarcities change, it is the ancillary conditions of the contract rather than the shares that change. The ancillary conditions are less precisely defined and less easy to compare across contracts than the shares and, hence, can be changed somewhat without incurring the charge of unfairness.

4.5   Corruption, bureaucracy, and development

Corruption in less-developed countries, once eschewed as politically incorrect (Myrdal 1968), has recently attracted a great deal of attention from economists. One issue is what determines the prevalence of corruption in a society. Another is the effect of corruption on economic development.

On the first issue, a number of models show how societies starting from similar situations may wind up with different levels of corruption

(Andvig and Moene 1990, Clague 1993, Sah 1988). In other words, in these models there are "good" and "bad" equilibria, with low and high levels of rule obedience. The models depict different situations, but a common theme is that the probability of getting caught and punished for breaking the rules declines as the number of violators increases. Thus in the "good" equilibrium, an individual who contemplates rule violation faces a high probability of getting caught and punished, and so people rationally choose to obey the rules. In the bad equilibrium, on the other hand, the probability of getting caught is low, and so people rationally choose to violate the rules. The modification of attitudes along with behavior tends to reinforce the conclusion that societies evolve along different paths and that, in particular, it is difficult to escape from a "bad" equilibrium where there is pervasive corruption. The difference between individual and community culture (see section 2 above) is again illustrated by the observation that, when individuals leave a society where corruption is rampant and migrate to a society where it is rare, they tend to adapt themselves to the new environment, where there are typically strong incentives not to break the rules.

Another determinant of the prevalence of corruption is the nature of government activity. Where the state limits its role to the protection of property rights and the enforcement of contracts between private parties, the enforcement of the rules is made easier by the fact that, usually, at least one of the private parties is eager to help the state perform its duty. People want to have their property protected and to see that other parties live up to their contracts with them, and they are usually willing to cooperate with the authorities in providing information and otherwise to help the authorities bring violators to justice. When, on the other hand, the state intervenes in the operation of the private market in such a way as to forbid private parties from making a transaction that both parties want, the task of law enforcement is much more difficult. The so-called victimless crimes of gambling and prostitution are examples of law violations that are extremely difficult to prevent. In many countries, governments attempt to control prices, license foreign exchange, and impose burdensome regulations on business, and these rules create strong incentives for bribes of government officials to look the other way. Of course, a government needs to provide physical infrastructure and to collect taxes, so its activity cannot be limited to the "night watchman" role.

The second issue concerns the effects of corruption on economic growth. Shleifer and Vishny (1993) provide an analysis of the industrial organization of corruption when government permits must be obtained to carry out an economic activity. Where the permits are controlled by a bureaucracy that is effectively controlled from the top, there is a monopoly in the supply of permits and the monopolist will set his bribes (and the associated quantity of permits) so as to maximize his revenue. In this case, the briber "gets what he pays for." Where the permits are controlled by independent authorities, the per-unit bribe will be higher, and the level of output lower, than in the monopolist equilibrium. The different authorities impose negative externalities on one another, which they do not take into account in their independent decisions, and the consequence is that the aggregate amount of bribe revenue and the level of output both suffer. The worst case is where there is free entry into bribe collection, for in that case, the per-unit bribe rises without limit and the economic activity that depends on the permits declines toward zero. This analysis is in striking analogy to Olson's roving bandit (see chap. 3, below). The case of monopoly in the issue of permits corresponds to the autocrat who establishes secure property rights, whereas the case of free entry into bribe collection is one where the government is too weak to guarantee the permit holders the right to carry out the activity to which the permit is supposed to entitle them.

It is often remarked that corruption exists in all societies, including rich and rapidly growing ones. It is easy to imagine circumstances in which corruption does little or no harm to economic growth. If the government imposes burdensome regulations on business, the nonenforcement of these regulations, purchased by bribes, may be more efficient than enforcement. To take another example, if the costs of government contracts for infrastructure are inflated by 10 percent by required payoffs to politicians, the deadweight loss from these transfers is likely to be small, if the needed infrastructure is provided[7]. On the other hand, corruption can be extremely costly to growth when it severely impairs the incentives of potential innovators (Murphy, Shleifer, and Vishny 1993; Olson 1982, chap. 3), as it is likely to do when it accompanies heavy government regulation of the private sector. Established businesses will tend to have ongoing cooperative relationships with corrupt officials, and they will have enough financial resources to pay hefty bribes. Potential entrepreneurs armed only with good ideas are not likely to be able to break into the charmed circle.

The study of bureaucracy, like that of corruption, has traditionally lain outside the purview of economists, including those working on economic development. These topics have been left to other social sciences,

---

[7]To be sure, in these cases one must consider the effects of rule violations on the attitudes of the rest of society toward rule obedience.

where there are large literatures on them. However, the economics of organization (Moe 1986; Milgrom and Roberts 1992; Laffont and Tirole 1993), which is a branch of the economics of imperfect and asymmetric information, has in the last two decades offered a different perspective on organizations from that of classical sociology, behavioral political science, and public administration. As would be expected, in the economics of organization the emphasis is on reward systems, monitoring systems, and individual and group incentives (see Klitgaard, chap. 14, below).

The application of these ideas to bureaucracy in less-developed countries is long overdue. It is clear that the performance of government bureaucracies has a major impact on the pace and character of economic development. Major positive contributions to development have been made by bureaucracies in Japan, Korea, Taiwan, and Botswana (Levi and Sherman, chap. 15, below; Clague 1994), while ineffective and corrupt bureaucracies have held back development in many other countries. A deeper understanding of why government bureaucracies perform the way they do would contribute a lot to our understanding of why growth rates differ.

References

Akerlof, George. 1970. "The Market for Lemons: Quality, Uncertainty, and the Market Mechanism." *Quarterly Journal of Economics* 84: 488–500.

Alchian, Armen. 1965. "Some Economics of Property Rights." *Il Politico* 30: 816–829 (Originally published in 1961 by the Rand Corporation; reprinted in Alchian, *Economic Forces at Work*, Indianapolis: Liberty Press, 1977.)

Alessina, Alberto, and Roberto Perotti. 1994. "The Political Economy of Growth: A Critical Survey of Recent Literature." *World Bank Economic Review* 8: 351–71.

Andvig, Jens Chr., and Karl Ove Moene. 1990. "How Corruption May Corrupt." *Journal of Economic Behavior and Organization* 13: 63–76.

Balassa, Bela. 1988. "Lessons of East Asian Development." *Economic Development and Cultural Change* 36 (suppl.): 273–90.

Barro, Robert, and Xavier Sala-I-Martin. 1995. *Economic Growth.* New York: McGraw-Hill.

Barzel, Yoram. 1989. *Economic Analysis of Property Rights.* Cambridge: Cambridge University Press.

Bates, Robert. 1983. *Essays on the Political Economy of Rural Africa.* Cambridge: Cambridge University Press.

Binswanger, Hans P., and Vernon W. Ruttan, eds. 1978. *Induced Innovation: Technology, Institutions, and Development.* Baltimore: Johns Hopkins University Press.

Borjas, George. 1987. "Self-Selection and the Earnings of Immigrants." *American Economic Review* 77: 531–54.

———. 1994. "Ethnicity, Neighborhoods, and Human Capital Externalities." *American Economic Review* 85: 365–90.

Brunetti, Aymo. 1995. "Political Variables in Cross-Country Growth Analysis: A Survey of the Literature." Department of Economics, Harvard University.

Brunetti, Aymo, and Beatrice Weder. 1994. "Political Credibility and Economic Growth in Less-Developed Countries." *Constitutional Political Economy* 5: 23–43.

Clague, Christopher. 1991. "Relative Efficiency, Self-Containment, and Comparative Costs of Less-Developed Countries." *Economic Development and Cultural Change* 39: 507–30.

———. 1993. "Rule Obedience, Organizational Loyalty, and Economic Development." *Journal of Institutional and Theoretical Economics* 149: 393–414.

———. 1994. "Bureaucracy and Economic Development." *Economic Dynamics and Structural Change* 5: 273–97.

Coase, Ronald C. 1937. "The Nature of the Firm." *Economica* 4: 386–405.

Coleman, James. 1990. *Foundations of Social Theory.* Cambridge: Harvard University Press.

Demsetz, Harold. 1964. "The Exchange and Enforcement of Property Rights." *Journal of Law and Economics* 3: 1–44.

———. 1967. "Toward a Theory of Property Rights." *American Economic Review Papers and Proceedings* 57: 347–59.

Denzau, Arthur and Douglass North. 1994. "Shared Mental Models: Ideologies and Institutions." *Kyklos* 47: 3–31.

Eggertsson, Thrain. 1990. *Economic Behavior and Institutions.* Cambridge: Cambridge University Press.

Feeny, David. 1988. "The Development of Property Rights in Land: A Comparative Case Study." In *Toward a Political Economy of Development*, ed. Robert Bates. Berkeley: University of California Press.

————. 1993. "The Demand for and Supply of Institutional Arrangements." In *Rethinking Institutional Analysis and Development,* ed. Ostrom, Feeny, and Picht.

Frank, Robert. 1988. *Passions within Reason.* New York: Norton.

Greif, Avner, Paul Milgrom, and Barry Weingast. 1994. "Coordination, Commitment, and Enforcement: The Case of the Merchant Guild." *Journal of Political Economy* 102: 745–76.

Hayami, Yujiro, and Vernon W. Ruttan. 1971 (1985). *Agricultural Development: An International Perspective.* Baltimore: Johns Hopkins University Press.

Hirschleifer, Jack. 1985. "The Expanding Domain of Economics." *American Economic Review* 75: 53–68.

Hirschman, Albert. 1983. *Essays in Trespassing: Economics to Politics and Beyond.* Cambridge: Cambridge University Press.

Hoff, Karla. 1994. "The Second Theorem of the Second Best." *Journal of Public Economics* 45: 223–42.

Hoff, Karla, Avishay Braverman, and Joseph Stiglitz. 1993. *The Economics of Rural Organization: Theory, Practice, and Policy.* New York: Oxford University Press.

Huntington, Samuel. 1968. *Political Order in Changing Societies.* New Haven: Yale University Press.

Johnson, James. 1994. "Symbolic Dimensions of Social Order." Department of Political Science, University of Rochester.

Knight, Jack. 1992. *Institutions and Social Conflict.* Cambridge: Cambridge University Press.

Laffont, Jean-Jacques, and Jean Tirole. 1993. *A Theory of Incentives in Procurement Regulation.* Cambridge: MIT Press.

Levine, Ross, and David Renelt. 1992. "A Sensitivity Analysis of Cross-Country Growth Regressions." *American Economic Review* 82: 942–63.

Lin, J. Y., and Jeffrey Nugent. 1995. "Institutions and Economic Development." In *Handbook of Development Economics*, ed. Jere Behrman and T. N. Srinivasan, Vol. 3. Amsterdam: North-Holland.

Mankiw, N. Gregory. 1995. "The Growth of Nations." *Brookings Papers on Economic Activity.* 1: 275–326 (with comments by Edward Phelps and David Romer).

Milgrom, Paul, and John Roberts. *Economics, Organization, and Management.* Englewood Cliffs, N.J.: Prentice-Hall.

Moe, Terry M. 1987. "The New Economics of Organization." *Journal of Political Economy* 83: 739–77.

Murphy, Kevin, Andrei Shleifer, and Robert Vishny. 1993. "Why Is Rent-Seeking So Costly to Growth?" *American Economic Review Papers and Proceedings* 83: 409–14.

Murrell, Peter. 1983. "The Economics of Sharing: A Transaction Cost Analysis of Contractual Choice in Farming." *Bell Journal of Economics* 14: 283–93.

Myrdal, Gunnar. 1968. *Asian Drama*. Vol. 2. New York: Twentieth Century Fund.

Nabli, Mustapha, and Jeffrey Nugent. 1989. "The New Institutional Economics and Economic Development." *World Development* 17: 1333–47.

North, Douglass. 1981. *Growth and Structural Change*. New York: Norton.

———. 1990. *Institutions, Institutional Change, and Economic Performance*. Cambridge: Cambridge University Press.

———. 1994. "Economic Performance through Time." *American Economic Review* 84: 359–68.

Oakerson, Ronald J. 1993. "Reciprocity: A Bottom-Up View of Political Development," in Ostrom, Feeny, and Picht, *Rethinking Institutional Analysis.*

Olson, Mancur. 1965. *The Logic of Collective Action*. Cambridge: Harvard University Press.

———. 1982. *The Rise and Decline of Nations*. New Haven: Yale University Press.

Ostrom, Elinor. 1990. *Governing the Commons: The Evolution of Institutions for Collective Action*. Cambridge: Cambridge University Press.

Ostrom, Elinor, Roy Gardner, and James Walker. 1994. *Rules, Games, and Common-Pool Resources*. Ann Arbor: University of Michigan Press.

Ostrom, Vincent, David Feeny, and Hartmut Picht, eds. 1993. *Rethinking Institutional Analysis and Development: Some Issues, Choices, and Alternatives*. San Francisco: Institute for Contemporary Studies Press.

Roumasset, James, and Sumner J. LaCroix. 1993. "The Coevolution of Property Rights and Political Order: An Illustration from Nineteenth-Century Hawaii." In Ostrom, Feeny, and Picht, *Rethinking Institutional Analysis and Development.*

Ruttan, Vernon W., and Yujiro Hayami. 1984. "Toward a Theory of Induced Institutional Innovation." *Journal of Development Studies* 20: 203–23.

Sah, Raaj Kumar. 1988. "Persistence and Pervasiveness of Corruption: New Perspectives." Discussion Paper 560, Economic Growth Center, Yale University.

Sandler, Todd. 1992. *Collective Action: Theory and Applications*. Ann Arbor: University of Michigan Press.

Shleifer, Andrei, and Robert W. Vishny. 1993. "Corruption." *Quarterly Journal of Economics* 108: 599–607.

Stiglitz, Joseph. "Incentives and Risk-Sharing in Sharecropping." *Review of Economic Studies* 41: 219–55.

Stiglitz, Joseph. 1986. "The New Development Economics." *World Development* 14: 257–65.

Sugden, Robert. 1986. *The Economics of Rights, Cooperation, and Welfare*. Cambridge: Blackwell.

Williamson, Oliver. 1975. *Markets and Hierarchies: Analysis and Antitrust Implications*. New York: Free Press.

———. 1985. *The Economic Institutions of Capitalism*. New York: Free Press.

3   The New Institutional Economics: The Collective Choice Approach to Economic Development

Mancur Olson

Neither economics nor any other discipline offers an integrated theory of *both* economic and political development. Everyday economics teaches us many profoundly important lessons. One of these lessons is that, with ideal economic policies and markets, the participants in an economy face incentives to maximize the efficiency and output of the society. But what incentives do political leaders in the Second and Third Worlds have to establish these ideal policies and institutions? And how could the countries and international organizations that provide foreign aid improve the incentives facing decision makers in developing countries? Everyday economics offers no answers to these questions. Though political science, anthropology, sociology, and the law offer a wealth of pertinent ideas and information, they do not subsume the logic of the market nor provide any general theoretical frameworks that can guide research into this question nor mobilize and summarize knowledge for the policy maker. A unified set of ideas (that is, a general theory) is needed not only to focus research but also to assist strategic decision making in developing countries and in aid-giving organizations.

Such a unified set of ideas or general theory has been emerging in recent years and is coming to have significant and increasing influence in economics and in other social sciences as well. This set of ideas is not only able to guide research but also to provide some practical insights for policy makers. But the theory is so rich and far-reaching—and has been developed by such a wide array of scholars in so many different specialties—that there is not yet any agreed-upon name that serves to identify it. Researchers coming from varying intellectual traditions and specialties use different names for what is essentially the same set of ideas or general theory. Perhaps the best analogy is with the streams that form a great river. Those who are rowing down one stream choose a name for it, and those who are

---

This chapter was partly inspired by (and involves extraordinary amounts of borrowing from) colleagues at IRIS and the work of IRIS fellows and scholars. It has also profited greatly from criticisms by IRIS colleagues. The inspiration and borrowing are cited in only a few special cases. The shortcomings are, however, entirely my responsibility.

rowing down another stream choose another. But ultimately the streams flow together, and the exertions of each crew bring them into the same wide river. In the river, they all have the same opportunity to expand their boats and take on bigger loads.

One large stream flowing into the river is the New Institutional Economics, and, as Clague demonstrates in the previous chapter, this stream is itself the confluence of several other substantial tributaries. Yet, just as the Ohio River, the Mississippi, and the Missouri (the longest of the three), come together at about the same place, so other great streams of research come together at about the same point. These junctures tend to make the river both deeper and wider.

One of these other streams is most comprehensively called "collective choice," but it in turn is the confluence of several sources and again has several names, such as "public choice," "social choice," and "neoclassical political economy." The upstream lakes that created this stream include not only the work on collective action described by Clague but also Arrow's important discoveries about intransitive social choices in *Social Choice and Individual Values* (Arrow 1963), Buchanan and Tullock's fundamental work on constitutions in *The Calculus of Consent* (Buchanan and Tullock 1962), Downs' seminal economic approach to political choices in *An Economic Theory of Democracy* (Downs 1957), and the influential work on coalition formation in Riker's *Theory of Political Coalitions* (Riker 1962). Another of these streams is the field of "law and economics" growing out of the pioneering work of Calabresi, Posner, and others. Another is "rational choice" sociology, arising in part of out of the work of Coleman. Still another is the approach to conflict and strategic interaction arising out of the insights of Schelling and many others. Last but not least, there are the works of North and Williamson and the other important sources that Clague summarizes in the preceding chapter.

There can be no doubt that these several streams of intellectual effort have all been coming together. They all use the economist's method of starting with purposive individuals who are assumed to have exogenously given preferences and then deducing social outcomes. They all are, because of this common method, readily integrated with the traditional economic analysis of markets, yet all go beyond the marketplace to analyze governments and other organizations, the legal system, politics, and interaction in social groups—in short, they all focus on institutions. Together, they make possible an integrated and comprehensive view of development. Though the lack of a single, generally accepted name for all the one resulting stream causes some confusion, it also testifies to the wide array of talents and disciplines that are converging on this new integrated approach.

The best way to make clear the character and uses of the emerging theory is with a specific illustration. While a single illustration of an intellectual method that has countless applications cannot be nearly as important as the method itself, it can be much less abstract. The illustration presented below was chosen because it is simple yet has immediate implications for economic development and foreign aid. The remainder of this chapter, accordingly, is devoted to this illustration.

1   The Logic of Power

Let us begin with a question that everyday economics leaves out: What incentives do leaders in the Second and Third Worlds have to choose the economic policies and institutions that bring economic growth and alleviate poverty? Almost everyone agrees that, whatever the form of government, economic progress tends to occur in societies in which there are clear incentives to produce, invest, and engage in mutually advantageous trade. By contrast, societies in which predation is the norm—whether through a Hobbesian war of each against all or through a government that seizes most assets for itself—are unlikely to be productive. But what determines whether those with power in a society have an incentive to use their power constructively, to provide a peaceful order and other public goods, or destructively, to seize the harvest of the subjects' labor and thereby discourage sowing?

Admittedly, what actually happens in a country depends on more than the incentives that face those with power. One major determinant of the choices societies make is their "climate of opinion" about what institutions and policies the society ought to have. If the elites and opinion leaders of a society have sound ideas about what choices that society should make, the society is, of course, more likely to do well than if choices are guided by mistaken ideas. Since aid-giving organizations, through programs such as international exchanges and education and training, can affect the intellectual climate in client countries, this is an important matter for policy in aid-giving organizations, and I return to it later. The character or temperament of the leaders of a country also helps to determine what happens. As everyone knows, cruel leaders sometimes impose gratuitous suffering on their people, and humanitarian leaders sometimes bring substantial improvements in human welfare. But the problem that confronts us will become impossibly complex if we do not take things one at a time. Thus I shall, initially, leave aside the climate of ideas, the personalities of leaders, and such, and focus only on the *incentives*, or the inducements to self-interested action, that face those with power.

Partly to make it obvious that I am now analyzing only self-interested behavior, I use criminal metaphors to guide the analysis. Clearly, one cannot understand theft without focusing on the thief's self-interest, and this will make it possible for us to gain some insights that are obscured when we think about the altruistic element in human nature. Using a criminal metaphor should also remind us that most people are not criminals but, rather, individuals who engage in benevolent as well as self-interested behavior, and that we must ultimately take these benevolent motives into account.

1.1   The incentives of the individual criminal

Consider the incentives facing the individual criminal in a populous society. Other things being equal, a criminal is better off in a rich than in a poor society: there is more to steal. Theft also makes societies less prosperous than they would otherwise be, because the time devoted to theft produces nothing but reduces the rewards from productive work and investment and induces a diversion of resources from production into guards, locks, police, courts, and the like. Therefore, the crime committed by each criminal reduces the wealth of society and, thus, also reduces the amount available to steal. Does the individual criminal curtail his crime because crime reduces the amount that is there to steal?

Everyone already knows that he does not, but it is important to see why. The typical individual thief in a society of, say, a million people, might bear something like one-millionth of the loss to society that occurs because his crime reduces society's output, but he alone bears the loss of whatever opportunities for theft he passes up. Thus the gain to criminals from a wealthy society and the fact that crime reduces society's wealth does *not* keep crime from paying. It is only society's punishment of criminals that, sometimes, keeps crime from paying. The stake of each criminal in the prosperity of society is so minuscule that the criminal ignores it.

1.2   The incentives with organized crime

Now let us shift from the individual criminal to the head of a Mafia "family" or other criminal gang that can monopolize crime in some neighborhood, stealing more or less as it pleases and preventing anyone else from committing crime. Obviously, the Mafia family has an incentive to keep other thieves out of its domain. But will it gain from taking all that it can on its own ground?

Clearly not. If crime makes business in this domain unprofitable or prompts migration away from the neighborhood, then the neighborhood won't generate much income and there won't be much to steal. Indeed, the Mafia family with a true and continuing monopoly on crime in a neighborhood *will not commit any robberies at all.* If it monopolizes crime in the neighborhood, it will gain from promoting business profitability and safe residential life. Thus the secure Mafia family will maximize its take by selling "protection"—both against the crime it would (if not paid) commit itself as well as that which (if it did not provide protection) would be committed by others. Other things being equal, the better the community is as an environment for business and for living, the more the protection racket will bring in. Accordingly, if one family can monopolize crime, there is, paradoxically (apart from the protection racket) little or no crime. The considerable literature on monopolized crime makes it clear that a secure monopolization of crime does lead to protection rackets rather than ordinary crime and that outbreaks of theft and violence in such environments are normally a sign that the controlling gang is losing its monopoly (and, I would argue, therefore also its encompassing interest).[1] A Mafia family that can monopolize local crime has an incentive to take account of the adverse impact of theft on community income, unlike the individual criminal in a populous society. The gang that can securely monopolize crime in a neighborhood has a large stake, or an "encompassing interest," in the income of that neighborhood.[2] Whereas the individual criminal in a society of a million might bear only one-millionth of the social loss from his crime, a gang with a secure monopoly over crime in a neighborhood will be able to obtain a large fraction of the total income of the community from its protection "tax," and it then bears a large share of any social loss that comes from robbery and burglary in its domain.

Even though it has the power to monopolize crime in a neighborhood, a gang may not, however, be stronger than the national army. Thus, though it could obviously charge more for protection if it could keep the central government's tax collectors out, it may not be able to do this. What would happen if it could?

---

[1]See, for example, Gambetta (1993).

[2]For the concepts of encompassing and narrow interests, see Olson (1982).

1.3   From roving to stationary banditry

Part of the answer to this question came to me by chance when I was reading years ago about a Chinese warlord (Sheridan 1966). In the 1920s, China was in large part under the control of various warlords, men who led some armed band with which they conquered territory and who then appointed themselves lords of that territory. They taxed the population heavily and pocketed much of the proceeds. The warlord Feng Yu-hsiang was noted for the exceptional extent to which he used his army for suppressing bandits and for his defeat of the relatively substantial army of the roving bandit White Wolf. Apparently, most people in Feng's domain found him much preferable to the roving bandits. At first, this puzzled me; why should warlords who were stationary bandits continuously stealing from a given group of victims be preferred, by those victims, to roving bandits who soon departed? The warlords had no traditional legitimacy and had not been chosen by the population or by anyone else.

In fact, if a roving bandit settles down and takes his theft in the form of regular taxation, and at the same time maintains a monopoly on theft in his domain, then those from whom he exacts tax theft have an incentive to produce, which they do not have if they will be picked clean by roving robbers. A stationary bandit takes only a part of his subjects' income in taxes, because he can exact more income if he leaves them with an incentive to generate income, which he can tax. Thus the victims of the stationary bandit, like the bandit himself, are better off than with roving banditry. If the stationary bandit successfully monopolizes theft in his domain, then his victims do not need to worry about theft by anyone else. Since all of the settled bandit's victims are for him a source of tax payments, he also has an incentive to protect them. With the monopolization of theft, the victims of the theft can also expect to retain whatever capital they accumulate out of after-tax income. Therefore, they also have an incentive to save and to invest, increasing their own future income and tax receipts for the stationary bandit.

In a world of roving banditry, there is little or no incentive for anyone to produce or accumulate anything, since it may be stolen. Thus, there is little for bandits to steal. Bandit rationality, accordingly, induces the bandit leader to seize a given domain, to make himself the ruler, and to provide a peaceful order and other public goods for its inhabitants, thereby obtaining more in tax theft than he could have obtained from migratory plunder. We have, then, what I have previously described as "the first blessing of the invisible hand": the self-interested roving bandit leader is led, as though by an invisible hand, to settle down, to wear a crown, and to replace anarchy with government (Olson 1993a). The gigantic increase in output that normally arises from the provision of a peaceful order and other public goods gives the stationary bandit a far larger take than he could obtain if he did not provide government. Thus, government for groups larger than tribes normally arises not because of social contracts or voluntary transactions of any kind but rather because of rational self-interest among those who can organize the greatest capacity for violence. These violent entrepreneurs naturally do not call themselves bandits but, on the contrary, give themselves and their descendants exalted titles. They sometimes even claim to rule by divine right. Since history is written by the winners, the origins of ruling dynasties are, of course, conventionally explained in terms of lofty motives rather than self-interest.

Since the stationary bandit takes a part of total production in the form of tax theft, it will also pay him to provide other goods, besides a peaceful order, that the market will not provide. It is now widely understood that the market will not provide such goods as flood control, quarantine against contagious disease, or defense, whose benefits inevitably go to a broad population; the individual who strives to obtain such goods for himself will find that he reaps only a minute part of the benefits. Thus, individuals and firms in the market will not have an incentive to obtain or provide a peaceful order or any other "collective" or "public" goods (Olson 1965). But the rational stationary bandit has such an incentive: any public good that increases the productivity or size of the population he controls increases his tax receipts.

2   Narrow versus Encompassing Interests

We can see the precise and general logic behind the foregoing stories. As we recall, the individual criminal's minuscule interest in the prosperity of the society is not worth his while to take into account, and his interests are best served simply by taking all of the cash in any till he robs. But the Mafia family that can monopolize crime in a given neighborhood, but not keep the government tax collector out, will steer away from socially costly crimes like robbery and strive for a protection racket instead. In this protection racket it will *not* rationally demand everything in the till—it will not take 100 percent of the assets a business or household possesses. This would lead to the failure or out-migration of the very businesses and households that the Mafia family, given the encompassing interest in the neighborhood provided by its criminal monopoly, hopes will thrive, thereby enabling absolutely larger protection tax payments. So the rational protection racket has a *less than 100 percent* protection tax.[3]

The stationary bandit leader with secure autocratic power will not raise the percentage of his tax theft beyond the point where the distortions due to this tax theft reduce the society's total income so much that his *share* of this loss is as great as his gain from obtaining a larger percentage of the total (McGuire and Olson 1996). To see this, suppose there is a simple flat tax and that the tax rate maximizing the tax take for a given autocrat were exactly 50 percent. Then the last dollar collected in taxes would reduce the national income by two dollars, and the autocrat would bear half of this loss, so he would be at a point of indifference (i.e., at the peak of his tax revenue function). More generally, the stationary bandit finds that he cannot gain from increasing the share, S, of the national income that he takes beyond the point where the national income goes down by $1/S$. The stationary bandit's encompassing interest in the society means that he is led, again as though by an invisible hand, to limit the rate of his theft.

This encompassing interest also makes him provide public goods. Specifically, he gains from using his resources to provide public goods up to the point where the national income increases by $1/S$ times the marginal cost of the public goods. If his optimal tax rate is 50 percent, he gains from spending an extra dollar on public goods so long as that dollar adds two dollars or more to the income of his domain. A secure stationary bandit uses his power, in part, constructively.

---

[3]If there is both a Mafia family and a maximizing autocrat extracting resources, the combined protection racket tax plus autocrat's tax will be higher than if only one of them could tax. The Mafia family has no incentive to take reduced governmental taxes into account in deciding on the rate of protection payment it demands. If a Mafia family were, like our bandit gang that settles down, strong enough so that its protection racket charge was the only tax, then the aggregate tax rate imposed on citizens would be lower and the income of the neighborhood would be higher. In other words, *competition* among autocratic rulers for power over the same domain is worse for the subjects than *monopoly* by a single ruler. By contrast, competition in a democracy between two parties to obtain a majority, which gives the winning party a term when it has a monopoly of government, means a significantly lower tax rate than under a single autocrat and a much lower tax rate than results from a stationary bandit plus a Mafia.

2.1   The logic of power for autocrats and majorities

How would government by a rational, self-interested autocrat compare with a democracy? (Or with other nonautocratic and pluralistic governments with some electoral base in the society, which I shall for brevity call democratic, whether or not there is anything resembling universal suffrage.) It would be wrong to give democracy an unfair advantage by assuming better motivation, so it is best to stick with our criminal metaphors. Thus, I impartially assume that the democratic political leaders and democratic voters are just as self-interested as the stationary bandit and will use any expedient to obtain majority control.

Observation of two-party democracies tells us that incumbents like to run on a record of "you never had it so good." An incumbent obviously would not leave himself with such a record if, like the self-interested autocrat, he took for himself the largest possible net surplus from the society. But we are too favorable to democracy if we assume that the incumbent party or president will maximize his chances of reelection simply by making the electorate as a whole as well off as possible. A candidate needs only a majority to win, and he or she might be able to "buy" a majority by transferring income from the population at large to a prospective majority. The taxes needed for this transfer would impair incentives and reduce society's output just as an autocrat's redistribution to himself does. Would this competition to buy votes generate as much distortion of incentives through taxation as a rational autocracy does? That is, would a vote-buying democratic leader, like the rational autocrat, have an incentive to push tax rates to the revenue-maximizing level?

No. Though both a majority and an autocrat have an encompassing interest in the society because they control tax collections, a majority—or any ruling group that earns some income in the marketplace—has a more encompassing interest in the society's productivity. The majority's interest in its market earnings induces it to redistribute less to itself than an autocrat redistributes to himself. Moreover, if a majority or other ruling interest earns a sufficient proportion of market income, it will not redistribute to itself at all and will treat the unrepresented minority as well as it treats itself! Though this result runs against one's initial intuition, it has been proven logically (McGuire and Olson 1996). Thus a sufficiently encompassing ruling interest—a "superencompassing" interest—will act with a surprising synecdoche: the part will, out of rational self-interest, act as though it were the whole.

2.2   The logic of power for special interests

Observation suggests to most of us that the foregoing argument, by itself, is perhaps excessively optimistic about real-world democracies, and this is, in fact, the case. Suppose that the firms or workers in an industry or the individuals employed in some occupation or profession are organized to act collectively, as a lobby or a cartel. The firms or workers in any single industry or occupation are unlikely to be a majority of the electorate and unlikely to earn any substantial percentage of the national income. Because they are not a majority, they cannot obtain complete control of the taxation and spending power of a government. They must instead take advantage of the "rational ignorance" of the electorate about the details of public policy and about their particular industry or occupation. They will then, often through lobbying, obtain such measures such as protection against imports, regulations that limit entry and competition, tax loopholes, or subsidies. They may also be able to cartelize or collude to obtain monopoly prices or wages.

To what extent will the organizations for collective action that represent particular industries or occupations have an incentive to refrain from any redistribution to themselves that will do great damage to economic efficiency? The profits, and even the value added, in a typical industry, or the wages in a typical craft or occupation, are a small fraction of national income. Suppose, for ease of calculation, that a given organized interest obtains exactly 1 percent. Then it will pay this organized interest to press for both governmental and cartelistic redistributions to itself up to the point where the social losses are a hundred times as great as the amount it obtains. Only then will its marginal share of these social losses be as great as its gain at the margin from further redistribution. Thus the typical special interest group has a very narrow, rather than an encompassing, interest. It therefore faces incentives that are much more detrimental to society than those facing the secure stationary bandit, often also worse than those that face the gang with a protection racket, and not much better for society than those facing the individual criminal.

Those in particular industries and occupations are sometimes not organized for collective action, especially in newly established or reestablished societies. Collective action must overcome the free-rider problem.[4] It can emerge only when the gains from organization benefit only a small number of actors (like the few big firms in a concentrated industry) or when

---

[4]Olson 1965.

there are selective incentives (rewards or punishments that, unlike the collective good the organization provides its constituents, can be applied to or withheld from individuals depending on whether or not they contribute to the costs of the collective action). Even when small numbers or potential selective incentives make organization for collective action possible, it normally takes a long time to work it out. Thus, only long-stable societies have dense and powerful networks of organizations for collective action. As we shall soon see, over the passage of time the continuities and discontinuities of history will play an important and profoundly dualistic role in the present argument.

2.3   Why many autocrats confiscate

Now let us take the logic that shows that a roving bandit leader, if he can secure and hold a given domain, has an incentive to become a king providing public goods—and stand the logic on its head. An autocrat by definition has sovereign power and, thus, the power unilaterally to take any asset he wants. A rational autocrat with a long time horizon will not confiscate his subjects' assets, because this will reduce investment and future income and, thus, his own long-run tax receipts.

Now suppose the autocratic ruler is uncertain about whether he will be in charge much longer. He may be uncertain about this because he fears invasion from a yet-more-powerful domain, a coup d'état, a revolution, or an assassination. When uncertainty gives him a short-term view, he has an incentive, no matter how gigantic his empire or how exalted his lineage might be, to seize any asset whose total value exceeds the discounted present value of its tax yield over his short-term horizon. With a sufficiently short planning horizon, it pays any autocrat not only to confiscate all readily seizable assets but also to repudiate his debts and to generate inflation by printing money for his own use, no matter how great the long-run cost. In other words, just as the roving bandit leader who can securely hold a domain has an incentive to make himself a king, so any autocrat with a short time horizon has an incentive to become, in effect, a roving bandit. An encompassing interest in a society is conducive to the productivity of that society only if it is expected to be maintained long enough for the encompassing interest to harvest much of the gain from this productivity.

Any autocracy must sooner or later have a short time horizon. In addition to the external and internal enemies and accidents that can end any autocracy, there is the fundamental problem of succession. If an autocrat were to create a body with the power to guarantee an orderly succession, that body would have to have more power than anyone else in the society. But it could only have this power if it had more power than the autocrat—and thus the capacity to overrule the autocrat—in which case the society by definition would not be an autocracy.[5] Even in traditional monarchies in which it is customary for the succession to be decided by inheritance, there are in practice often uncertainties about succession: crown princes are often the focus of opposition against the kings and are sometimes destroyed by their fathers, or they are infants at the time of succession, or they are manifestly unviable as leaders. Though the expectation that the customary heir will inherit rule is itself a source of power for him, it remains true that there is in an autocracy no body with the power to ensure that the customary rule is followed. Thus disputes and uncertainties about succession characterize the histories even of autocracies with the strongest customary rules about succession; such disputes are almost the norm in autocracies without such rules. Therefore, we must conclude that autocracies of all types sooner or later must suffer autocrats who engage in confiscation, debt repudiation, and the debasement of coin or currency. This deprives societies of the security of property, contracts, and price levels that they need for development.

3   Lasting Democracy and Secure Property Rights

Admittedly, there are also examples of democracies that saw that their days were numbered and that, after trying desperate expedients, collapsed into autocracy or anarchy. Thus, simply setting up a democratic government provides no automatic exemption from succession crises. But what would happen if a more-or-less democratic government—that is, a government based on the rule of law and chosen through electoral competition, whatever the breadth of suffrage—did last?

No government can last as a democracy unless the legal requirement is followed that the defeated government be replaced after losing an election. Neither can it last as a democracy if there is not considerable freedom of speech and protection of the property and persons for those who oppose the current government. If the leader of a government can unilaterally set aside laws or punish citizens, even by seizing their assets or abrogating their rights under the contracts they have made, the society is presumably not democratic and, certainly, not a democracy that will last.

---

[5]As is evident from Olson (1993a), hereditary succession is not as absurd a system of selecting successors in autocracies as most of us would initially assume.

Therefore, though lasting democracies (like other forms of government) may have innumerable unwise policies, they can never have leaders who revert to roving banditry and, thereby, make a mockery of the property and contract rights of their subjects. In all democracies that are expected to last, individuals and companies routinely invest in long-lived capital assets with confidence that these assets will not be seized (at any event without compensation), and they frequently draw up long-term contracts that they are confident will be enforced with some impartiality. The same dispersion of power, rule of law, and independent courts that make a society a continuing or institutionalized democracy ensure that it will have considerable respect for individual rights, including individual rights to property and to contract enforcement. Of course, the same stability of individual rights also implies freedom of organization, so a lasting democracy—like any other tranquil and continuing regime—will also find that, as time goes on, more and more industries and occupations are organized for collective action.

3.1   Growth under autocracy: The historical evidence
How does this theory, inspired by a criminal metaphor, fit the facts? It certainly has no difficulty with the absence of any populous societies that have prospered under anarchy. It is only societies as small as the hunter-gatherer bands in the most rudimentary communities, and mere handfuls of people in other contexts (such as, perhaps, medieval Iceland), that have been able to provide collective goods and to last without organized government. According to the theory, large populations cannot provide themselves with a peaceful order or other collective goods without selective incentives. Is there even one compelling example of a prosperous anarchy, anywhere in the world or at any time in all of human history? It appears, instead, that in any populous society without government, individual power is used destructively, there is a war of each against all, and virtually no production (except that which can be consumed promptly on the spot) pays off. Thus anarchic populous societies are not only not prosperous, they don't even survive. They do not survive because of the great profit to any roving bandit—or anyone who can conquer and hold an anarchic domain—from becoming a stationary bandit. Thus, from not long after settled agriculture generated the growth and density of population that made for populous societies, human history is mostly a record of stationary banditry interrupted by episodes of roving banditry.

But the logic suggests that not only the secure stationary bandit but his subjects, as well, should share in the gains from the *pax banditica* and the other public goods that the secure ruler has an incentive to provide. The subjects of the stationary bandit receive the increase in income that is not taken in taxes. The stationary bandit, we recall, does not have the incentive to use power in the purely destructive way as the individual criminal in a populous society. He has, on the contrary, an encompassing interest in his domain: he receives a significant proportion of any increase in the society's income in tax receipts and his purse shrinks whenever the economy of his domain weakens. Thus from the time of Hammurabi if not of Sargon, and in China, Europe, and Mesoamerica as well as in the Middle East and South Asia, there have been innumerable periods of economic progress under strong autocrats. This progress occurred even though these autocrats characteristically strived to obtain as much tax revenues as they possibly could for their pyramids, palaces, and (especially) for the armies that an autocrat who would keep up with—or get ahead of—the Joneses must have. At the boundaries of competing domains there might not be even brief security of tenure, only the roving plunder of rival armies; yet near the keep of the castle, there were periods where an autocrat—and thus also his subjects and their properties—were relatively secure.

The economically successful autocracies of recent vintage seem to fit the pattern. In his insecure years on the mainland, Chiang Kai-shek was certainly not above roving banditry. But on Taiwan, courtesy of the United States, he had a domain with secure (and not expandable) borders and good prospects of ruling there for the rest of his life (as he did, until he died a natural death and was succeeded by his son). By the late 1950s, with some counsel from an American government on which he was militarily dependent, he began to find economic policies through which he could expand the output of the domain in which he had such an encompassing interest, and thus he enjoyed a great increase in the resources under his immediate control. Both because the Japanese colonial regime had not allowed indigenous organizations and because of his own dictatorial suppression of independent sources of political power, the firms and workers in Taiwan were not generally able to organize for collective action on behalf of their industries or occupations. Such industry-specific interventionism as his regime thought expedient was, in contrast to most other societies, inspired mainly by his regime's perception of its own interests rather than that of the organized interests of the industry in question. The extraordinary economic growth that grew out of this encompassing (and relatively well-advised) interest is well known.

Park and Chun in South Korea had much the same encompassing interest, secure borders, and economic counsel as Taiwan. They also had, for the same reasons, economic policies that were largely unaffected by special interest lobbying and product and labor markets that were largely free of cartels. The South Korean economy also enjoyed rapid economic growth. The situations in Chile and Singapore were not dramatically different.

3.2   Growth under democracy: The historical evidence

This said, we must remember that the vast majority of autocratic governments, whether in recent times in Africa and Latin America or on all continents in earlier times, have not succeeded in bringing economic progress or in alleviating poverty. Even when secure, they have mostly failed to find the policies that would promote rapid economic advance, and they have often engaged in little more than roving banditry. Moreover, many of the most remarkable periods of economic progress over the course of recorded history appear to have occurred in relatively nonautocratic, or somewhat democratic, jurisdictions that have soared ahead of the absolutist regimes around them.

The existing knowledge—or at least my knowledge—of ancient Athens and the Roman Republic is insufficient for any confident conclusions. Yet it does appear that these societies were, by the standards of the time, relatively nonautocratic. The Roman Republic had at least the beginnings of the rule of law. Even in ancient Athens, the system of justice with respect to contract enforcement was apparently sufficient that borrowing and lending occurred not only among kin but also among unrelated individuals and, sometimes, even involved individuals or enterprises that specialized in credit (Millett 1991). In both ancient Athens and the Roman Republic there were certainly citizens and families who had relatively secure property rights to land and tangible goods (and—tragically for the victims —also in slaves). These societies also expanded through war and colonization. It is natural to suppose that this could not have happened had they not had more of the sinews of war—better economic organization and more total output—than most of the societies with which they were in competition.

The evidence on northern Italian city-states during the Renaissance is more extensive. Certainly, Florence, Venice, and Genoa had extended periods of nonautocratic government.[6] Certainly also, these societies were, for a considerable time, leaders in long-distance trade, banking, and many other types of economic activity. It is hard to repress the thought that these property-intensive and contract-intensive activities owed something to the relatively secure rights that at least some of their citizens enjoyed. At the

---

[6]See, for the case of Genoa, Greif (1994).

same time, societies that were stable for so long were also likely to find that diverse industries and occupations would be cartelized and that these cartels would lobby or even partly control the government. It appears that these societies did in fact come to be ridden by guilds and, eventually, lost their economic dynamism.

The Netherlands in its golden age in the seventeenth century fits this pattern. By the standards of contemporary societies—such as Spain, against which it had rebelled—the Netherlands was relatively nonautocratic. Its success in capital-intensive activities like shipbuilding and shipping and the emergence of the first large-scale bourse, or capital market, suggest that property and contract rights were, by the standards of the time, relatively secure. Again, this society, just as it appears to have profited from a long period of stability without banditry, also appears gradually to have lost its dynamism.

The case of the United Kingdom after the Glorious Revolution appears to be relatively clear-cut. Certainly, the settlement of 1688–89 prohibited various infringements of rights (of which the Stuarts were at times guilty), promulgated a bill of rights, stipulated that judges could not be removed without cause, and limited any future monarchical banditry. The following century saw extensive long-term lending and borrowing at interest rates that were relatively modest even by today's standards. In due course, the enforceability and reliability even of contracts with the government were good enough that Britain was, by the Napoleonic Wars, able to borrow so much that its government debt was larger in relation to gross domestic product than the U.S. government debt incurred during World War II. The autocratic regimes of France and Spain could not do anything comparable. And, as almost everyone knows, the consolidation of individual and more or less democratic rights provided during the Glorious Revolution was followed by the Industrial Revolution. The long period of stability and freedom of organization also facilitated the organization of industries, professions, crafts, and the like for collective action. Britain has, with the gradualism and group-by-group profile that the theory suggests, developed the British disease of slow growth (Olson 1982).

Medieval and early modern European experience show the same general pattern. As deLong and Shleifer (1993) show, the growth of cities—where most of the readily confiscable capital could be found—was systematically more rapid in the less autocratic or more democratic environments in Europe from about 1000 through 1800 than in more autocratic and absolutist situations. This is, of course, consistent with the argument that problems of succession and other difficulties ensure that any autocratic system sooner or later reverts to roving banditry and that secure individual rights, especially to property and to contract enforcement, are extremely important for economic progress. The secure individual rights, the predictability of succession, and the relative freedom from banditry that have arisen from the U.S. Constitution and its durability have also apparently had beneficial economic effects, but these are so well known that no more will be said of them here, nor of the sclerotic processes that have hindered twentieth-century U.S. economic performance, especially in the country's longest settled and longest stable regions.

3.3   Economic performance under different political arrangements

What, from the perspective of the theory and history offered here, is the best form of government for economic success? Clearly not roving banditry or any form of anarchy—the incentives in these cases are essentially those of the individual criminal in a populous society. As we have seen, the encompassing interest of a well-advised stationary bandit should lead to better results. The secure autocrat who looks forward to an extended period of rule not only has an incentive to limit the rate of tax theft and to provide public goods, but he also does not have to indulge the narrow special interests of organizations representing particular industries or occupations.

But any autocrat has the power to unilaterally seize any readily confiscable asset and—whenever he has a short time horizon—the incentive to do so. Although an autocracy cannot over the long run provide secure property and contract enforcement rights, a lasting democracy can do this. The very same rule of law and individual rights needed for continued constitutional government protect individual contract and property rights. A democratic system has the further advantage over an autocracy that a majority, because it earns income in the marketplace at the same time that it controls the government, has a more encompassing interest than an autocrat. Some large majorities even have superencompassing interests, which give them an incentive to redistribute nothing whatever to themselves and to treat the minority as well as they treat themselves.

The same institutionalization of succession that facilitates capital accumulation and long-term contracts, however, also facilitates organization for collective action by the firms and workers in particular markets. The difficulties of collective action can usually be overcome only in the fullness of time, so it is only stable societies that have extensive networks of special interest organizations. These organizations normally represent only a narrow interest and will rationally serve that interest by redistributions to it even if social costs are many times larger than the amount redistributed. This suggests that, if a democracy for any reason emerges in a society without much industrial or occupational organization for collective action, it will, if other conditions are right, enjoy good economic performance. Unfortunately, a new democracy, simply because it is new, may not be expected to last. Accordingly, there is usually only limited confidence in the property, contract enforcement, and other individual rights that the new democracy provides, and this works against good economic performance.

There are certain special cases in which there can be a high level of confidence in property and contract rights even in a new democracy. This confidence can arise from special circumstances that generate social consensus or from foreign influence. These special circumstances prevailed in both West Germany and Japan after World War II. The failures of the defeated dictatorships had been so catastrophic that there was a near consensus in these societies that a democratic government was best. In the case of West Germany, the privations of the people in the part of Germany under communist control further strengthened support for a democratic society and a market economy. But there was not only social consensus: West Germany and Japan were also garrisoned by the armies of the victorious powers that were determined to prevent both communist and fascist dictatorships. The defeated societies wanted democracy with a market economy and knew that, in any event, they had no choice. Both citizens and foreign firms, accordingly, could have more confidence in their property and contract rights than is normal in a new democracy.

With these secure individual rights, and with relatively little narrow organization for collective action, the former Axis societies went on, as the theory here suggests, to enjoy economic miracles. Of course, these miracles would not, by the logic of the theory, be expected to last: their successful postwar stability has permitted relatively extensive networks of special interest organizations to develop, and the economic miracles have, naturally, also ceased. The gradual disappearance of these economic miracles, like their totally unexpected emergence, helps tell us what type of government is best for economic growth: a government that provides secure contract and property rights at the same time that it abstains from the special interest legislation and cartelization that narrow organized interests seek.

3.4   The payoff to poor countries from better institutions

Though an economic miracle requires relatively good economic policies and institutions, the lesson of the historical examples discussed is that, in our contemporary world, a country does not need the best government, or ideal institutions and economic policies, to enjoy economic progress. In times past, it took not only good institutions and economic policies but fairly good luck, as well, to obtain sustained growth of per capita income. If we go back more than 250 years, we find that economic advance never proceeded long at a rate that exceeded population growth. Economic advance in historic times meant higher total income for a society as a whole and the growth of cities. In imposing and somewhat democratic societies of early times, such as Athens, the Roman Republic, and the city-states of the north Italian Renaissance, it could also make possible great artistic and cultural achievements. But it never led to any substantial sustained increase in income for the mass of the population.

Even in the absence of any sclerosis or relapse into autocracy or anarchy, the growth of per capita income could not long continue, because it brought about an increase in population that matched any possible growth in total output. Thus, even when the growth of total income and the advance of civilization continued, per capita income growth did not. Some new technologies were discovered and improvements in economic institutions and policies arose from time to time, but they could not make a society's output increase so much that it exceeded the society's rate of population growth. Thus, the mass of the population had rather low incomes even in Europe on the eve of the Industrial Revolution—per capita food supplies, for example, were not sufficient to enable the majority of the population of Europe to grow to full stature. Though Malthus's theory did not predict the future of the developed world, it received instant celebrity because it described historic reality. Then, in the Industrial Revolution that began in Britain in the mid-eighteenth century (as we recall, not very long after the final defeat of absolutism in the Glorious Revolution), there were so many inventions and improvements in economic organization in close succession that economic growth was able to creep ahead—and stay ahead—of population growth: sustainable economic development occurred for the first time, albeit at a glacial pace.

In the nineteenth century, the United States, several countries of continental Europe, and the countries of the British Commonwealth were able to achieve *faster* economic growth than Britain had achieved. That is, they enjoyed catch-up growth; their output could increase especially rapidly because they benefited from the technological and organizational advances that were occurring, and at the same time, they could copy the superior technologies that had emerged in the Industrial Revolution. Thus, those countries that had the institutions and economic policies that enabled them to realize the opportunities of the time grew not only more rapidly than population but *much* more rapidly. The rates of economic growth in these countries in the second half of the nineteenth century were far higher than the rate of economic growth that Britain had experienced in the Industrial Revolution. They were also higher than those of Britain itself, not only because of the beginnings of sclerosis in the British economy but also because these other countries, such as Germany, could enjoy the more rapid catch-up growth that was not available to Britain, the country that was then the technological leader.

By the end of World War II, technology and organization had, of course, progressed vastly beyond the levels of the nineteenth century, not to mention the levels of preindustrial societies, and the United States was the technological leader. In a couple of decades, the democracies of continental Europe, which were nearly destitute at the end of World War II, nearly caught up to the United States. Even Stalin's Soviet Union and its satellites, in spite of notorious inefficiencies, grew rapidly and gained on the United States in the first two decades after World War II. When Taiwan and South Korea changed their economic policies in about 1960 (even though they made some mistakes and suffered from uncertainties about succession and their long-run stability), they grew at rates so rapid that they rivaled the economic miracle societies of Germany and Japan. This economic growth reached all major classes of the population and brought about extraordinary reductions in the extent of poverty. The catch-up opportunities were even more remarkable when Deng changed economic policies in impoverished mainland China beginning in 1978. Thus, in spite of countless shortcomings in its economic institutions and policies, mainland China has also enjoyed extremely rapid rates of economic growth.

In short, in the late twentieth century the available technologies and opportunities are so great that a backward country, if it adopts relatively good institutions and economic policies, can double its income in a decade and continue doing this in successive decades, thereby obtaining an eightfold increase in income in thirty years. This is not a theoretical maximum—it is something that some societies since World War II have actually achieved. It does not even require an ideal government dedicated to the welfare of the people; even a well-advised stationary bandit can be sufficient.

Therefore, when a government liberates the energies and enterprise of its people and provides even passable institutions that enable them to obtain the gains from social cooperation through trade and specialization, this generates extraordinarily rapid economic progress (given the technological and other opportunities of our age). The advances that result from better institutions and economic policies are so large that they dwarf any other influence on economic performance. Admittedly, some critics claim that this is true only for certain countries and that other poor countries are so lacking in natural or human resources that they cannot develop no matter what institutions and policies prevail; this argument was commonly made with respect to East Asia as recently as the 1950s. In fact, other research demonstrates that, however countries and peoples might differ in their potential for development, no such differences can explain the vast differences in per capita incomes across countries. Better institutions and economic policies can bring large increases in standards of living in every part of the world (Olson 1993b).

4 Economic Growth Is Egalitarian

In most cases, the economic growth that results from superior institutions and economic policies also reaches all broad classes of the population and dramatically reduces poverty. The best available evidence indicates that economic growth in the Third World has not only increased absolute incomes of most low-income people but has also (in a large majority of the developing countries on which there are the needed data) maintained or even increased the percentage of the national income received by those with relatively low incomes (Squire 1993). This should not be surprising. Production requires labor, and the firms in a growing economy compete to obtain the labor they need. Scarce and valuable skills can always command a higher wage, but in a rapidly expanding economy there are strong incentives to profit by using (and sometimes even training) the least costly unskilled labor. In the most successful developing societies, this often takes the form of specializing in the export of labor-intensive products. Investment in capital also raises the marginal productivity—and thus the wages—of labor.

At least some of the exceptions to the generalization that economic growth reduces poverty in about the same proportion that it increases average income are mainly explained by the greater capacity for collective action in the established upper and middle reaches of the income distribution than among the poor. The study of collective choice reveals that, contrary to earlier beliefs, the capacity to organize for collective action is disproportionately in the middle and, especially, the upper reaches of society, so that the impairment of economic progress that results from special interests is overwhelmingly inegalitarian (IRIS 1994).

4.1   Fishing with nets rather than with hooks

These results have important implications for development policies
in both the Third World and formerly communist countries—and for foreign
aid. The implication for the countries of the Second and Third Worlds is
that improving their institutions and economic policies is extraordinarily
important—much more important both for development and for poverty
reduction than whatever option is in second place. With even reasonably
good arrangements, any developing country or nation in transition from
communism can grow rapidly and see a quick alleviation of the plight of
even its poorer classes. Without some arrangements that provide incentives
for socially useful production, no country can grow, no matter what else it
does or how much aid it receives.

The implications of these results for aid-giving organizations are no
less clear-cut: They cannot have any decisive and favorable impact on their
client countries without helping to improve the institutions and economic
policies of these countries. The overwhelming importance of this factor in
relation to other factors is starkly illustrated by comparing private cross-
border capital flows with the budgets of aid-giving organizations. The gross
flow of capital across the borders of the United States is a *trillion* dollars on
the average business *day*, but aid budgets are only a few *billion* dollars a
year. The flood of foreign capital that will go to countries like Russia or
India, if they substantially improve their institutions and policies, would
make all of the foreign aid budgets in the world look trivial. And these huge
capital inflows, in turn, would usually be greatly exceeded by the productive
mobilization of domestic capital: whenever poor economies improve their
arrangements sufficiently, their citizens find amazing amounts of capital in
the woodwork, on arms decorated with gold, and even in the dark vaults of
Zurich. When arrangements are good, this abundance of capital is quickly
combined with the best technologies of the age and with the vast reserves of
energy, mother wit, and enterprise that exist in every population, no matter
how often it has been belittled by chauvinists in more fortunate countries.

Thus, aid programs that promote improvements in institutions and
policies can greatly accelerate the pace of development. They can, above all,
alleviate poverty. The salience such programs must have for any aid-giving
organization can be made evident by extending the familiar metaphor about
fishing: you can feed the hungry by giving them fish, but if you make it
possible for them to catch fish, they will have food for a lifetime. The
metaphor can be extended: programs that improve institutions and policies
are akin to fishing with a net, whereas programs that attempt to alleviate
poverty by providing resources—and even resources for production—out of

the slender means of donor agencies are like fishing with a hook. Admittedly, fishing with a hook is satisfying to the fisherman. Most of the fish caught by fishhooks in the United States are surely not caught because of the pleas of cooks, much less by the cries of hungry children, but rather because the fishermen like to fish. In general, when the concern is to put food on the table, fish are caught with nets. In the same way, when we are sincerely concerned with moral outcomes, with the urgent goal of reducing destitution and poverty around the world, we must use nets rather than hooks. We must help weave the institutions and policies that can bring feasts of loaves and fishes to our brethren in the poorer countries of the world. (Of course, there are also circumstances, such as the emergencies generated by natural disasters, where there is no time to weave the necessary net of institutions and policies.)

4.2   When to demand democracy and when not to

It is time to return specifically to democracy and dictatorship and, especially, to the warning at the beginning of this chapter about the need to take account of the richness of human motivation. Human beings rarely act out of unmixed motives. In many specific situations, the idiosyncratic characters of political leaders are decisive in determining outcomes. The assumption of rational self-interest that was brought into bold relief by the criminal metaphor is, of course, far too simple. I hope that the criminal metaphor will remind everyone that, even though drastic simplifications help us obtain new insights, they are not sufficient for making policy in any specific situation. In general, I take it for granted that the many qualifications and caveats that the present argument requires will be evident to the reader. But where the excessive starkness of the criminal metaphor is immediately evident is in the case of the benevolent despot—the Good King Wenceslas and other public-spirited autocrats. It is clear that many of the people, especially in Asia, who believe that dictatorship is best for development are assuming that autocrats will be, at least in some considerable degree, benevolent. There can, of course, be benevolent autocrats, and this makes the argument inspired by the criminal metaphor too simple.

Nonetheless, the bandit model of autocracy is surprisingly robust. The insights and conclusions it provides usually survive the demonstration that it rests on an assumption that is far simpler than reality. An examination of the history of absolutism in early modern Europe, in Asia in historic times, and more recently in Latin America and Africa makes it clear that the conclusions of the model usually hold. Thus, if it is used with appropriate caution and an awareness of the importance of other factors, the foregoing framework can illuminate many strategic choices facing the nations of the Second and Third Worlds and the aid-giving organizations that help them.

Most notably, it tells us something about the appropriateness of democracy as a goal for developing nations and as a criterion for aid-giving organizations. The foregoing argument makes clear that democracy has not only its well-known moral appeal but, often, also important practical virtues that have not previously been understood. A democratic majority has a more encompassing interest in a society than a dictatorship and, thus, even if it is totally selfish, a greater incentive to limit its redistributions to itself. A society can, in addition, obtain the full range of gains from markets only if its individuals and firms have secure individual property and contract rights. As we have seen, it is only in lasting democracies that these rights are secure in successive generations—they are protected by the same juridical mechanisms and the same predictable succession under law that are necessary for the viability of a democratic political system. It is no accident that the only societies that have enjoyed high levels of capital accumulation across successive generations are the durable democracies. Every society with autocratic rulers sooner or later is victimized by roving banditry from the top. Thus, there are compelling and normally neglected practical as well as moral reasons why the United States should make the promotion of democracy a priority.

At the same time, the foregoing argument tells us that a secure and well-advised autocrat, even if his motives are simply those of a stationary bandit, will be far better for his subjects than anarchy. Though an autocrat has a less encompassing interest than a majority, he has a more encompassing interest than the typical special interest group that dominates an industry or occupation. This point generates a separate and more detailed implication of the theory for foreign aid policy related to democracy. The foregoing logic shows that organizations representing the firms or workers in individual industries or occupations or other markets have socially perverse incentives—if they work to make a country more prosperous, they obtain only a minute percentage of the gain yet bear all of the costs of what they do; if they work to redistribute income to themselves through special interest legislation or through combinations to monopolize price or wage setting, they obtain all of the amounts redistributed to themselves yet bear only a minute percentage of the loss to society. Thus, the overwhelming bulk of the evidence, in society after society and in many historic periods, indicates that these organizations are mainly bad for economic performance. Since the poor and the unemployed are almost never organized for collective action, these organizations are also bad for poverty reduction. They also tend to make politics more divisive, since they shift the focus more toward distributional struggles, with winners and losers, rather than toward activities that advance the interests of the society as a whole.

Thus some civil society democracy programs—those that strive to develop lobbying and cartelistic power among particular industries or occupations in Second and Third World societies—actually more often retard than advance the economic and democratic development of recipient countries. The goals behind democracy programs are better served by an emphasis on such things as the rule of law and elections rather than by civil society activities. Unfortunately, in populous societies, democracy emerges only under favorable conditions or with extensive and patient out-side help.[7] In any society with a significant population, the gains from democracy are a collective good for a large group, and the collective action that is needed to obtain this collective good does not emerge spontaneously. By contrast, autocracy emerges all too easily and naturally—the autocrat's job pays uncommonly well. Whoever is strongest has an enormous incentive to give himself the job and, then, to dig in against the calls for democracy, both from his own people and from other governments.

The theory tells us that United States often cannot buy democracy on the cheap. Autocratic control over a country like China is worth incomparably more to the autocrat than most-favored-nation status. Warlordship over even a significant portion of Somalia is worth fighting the United Nations, and even the United States, to retain. If a society does not have either a lucky balance of forces that prevents autocratic takeovers or an elite with an intellectual appreciation of the value of democracy, countries like the United States cannot, inexpensively, give it democracy.

This, in turn, has other implications. One is that, in promoting democracy in difficult circumstances, the United States should not bite off half of the cherry. It should either devote the considerable investment of resources and patience needed to make the effort succeed, or else not intervene at all. The other implication is that the promotion of democracy is in large part an educational problem: it requires giving elites in countries without democracy an appreciation of the extraordinary practical value of the secure contract, property, and other individual rights that lasting democracies provide. These elites often think of rights as luxuries that poor countries cannot afford.

---

[7] These favorable conditions are explained in Olson (1993a).

5   The New Institutional Economics or Collective Choice Approach to Development

The foregoing argument is offered as a single but specific illustration of the nature and the uses of the New Institutional Economics, or
collective choice, method. Whatever the shortcomings of the argument, it
nonetheless illustrates the unity and breadth of the set of ideas or theory at
issue. Everyday economics, the incentives of the market, and the large
contributions that competitive markets can make to economic development
are part of the intellectual framework used. Also, the analysis of autocrats,
like the analysis of majorities and special interest groups in democracies, is
derived in exactly the way economists typically derive their conclusions
about markets: the analysis of both the actors in the market and the actors in
the polity is grounded in purposive individual behavior—in each case, with
the preference orderings or the utility functions of the individuals involved
and the constraints that they face.

As the use of the criminal metaphor reminds us, the method used
definitely does *not* imply that individuals are always or only self-interested:
altruistic acts and actions motivated by principles and moral beliefs are
commonplace. The emphasis in the foregoing argument on the impartial
enforcement of contract and property rights, especially in the lasting
democracies, arises precisely because judges and the members of juries in
most cases do make their decisions on the basis of the principles and moral
beliefs they were brought up to uphold and, thus, to a great degree in terms
of the laws of the society. By social design, some societies—and all of the
lasting democracies—arrange to have disputes arising under the laws of the
society made by disinterested parties: that is, by parties who have no material
or personal stake in how the dispute is resolved and who, therefore, typically
resolve the dispute in terms of the laws and moral principles of the society.

Thus the unified approach at issue does not assume that all behavior
is selfish, or error free, or dispassionate, much less that it is based on perfect
or even extensive information. The approach nonetheless embodies a
unified view of human motivation, because it does not arbitrarily (and
contrary to a good deal of evidence) assume that, say, careers in corporations
operating in the marketplace are motivated by self-interest, whereas careers
in politics, or in lobbying organizations, or in the civil service are motivated
by the public interest. It credits ambition impartially in all walks of life. It
is the same type of people, and sometimes the same individuals, who operate
in the marketplace and in other spheres of life, and thus behavior in all

domains of life can be understood only in terms of the purposes or plans of the individuals involved. This unified approach to motivation means that analyses of the market, of politics, and of institutions can readily be integrated—that we really do have an integrated view of economic and political development. With this approach, we look not only at the rules of the game but also at the incentives of those who make the rules; not only at the constraints on individual behavior but also at how such constraints arise mainly out of the purposive behavior of interacting individuals.

The unified approach depicted in this chapter and chapter 2 have inspired most of the research and fieldwork at IRIS. It is true that there has also been an effort to profit from the criticisms of those with opposing views. But orthogonal approaches—those that neither resonate with nor provide a counterpoint to what IRIS is doing—have been avoided. The hope is that this means that the work is responsive to criticism but, at the same time, coherent.

In economics, as in the other social sciences and in science generally, the truth of today is not usually the error of tomorrow. More often, the truth of today is the special case of the truth of tomorrow. As time goes on, because of the efforts of many people with various specializations and backgrounds—and because of practical experience as well as research —we learn more. If research is honest, serious, and sustained, it is cumulative. The creeks really do flow into the streams and the streams into the rivers. And there are oceans to discover ahead.

References

Arrow, K. J. 1963. *Social Choice and Individual Values.* New York: John Wiley.

Buchanan, J. M., and G. Tullock. 1962. *The Calculus of Consent.* Ann Arbor: University of Michigan Press.

deLong, J. Bradford, and Andrei Shleifer. 1993. "Princes and Merchants." *Journal of Law and Economics* 36: 671–702.

Downs, Anthony. 1957. *An Economic Theory of Democracy.* New York: Harper and Row.

Gambetta, Diego. 1993. *The Sicilian Mafia.* Cambridge: Harvard University Press.

Greif, Avner. 1994. "On the Political Foundation of the Late Medieval Commercial Revolution: Genoa during the Twelfth and Thirteenth Centuries." *Journal of Economic History* 54: 271–87.

IRIS. 1994. Conference Report "The Paradoxes of Poverty." Working Paper 137. IRIS, College Park, Md.

McGuire, Martin, and Mancur Olson. 1996. "The Economics of Autocracy and Majority-Rule: The Hidden Hand and the Use of Force." *Journal of Economic Literature* 34: 72–96.

Millett, Paul. 1991. *Lending and Borrowing in Ancient Athens.* Cambridge: Cambridge University Press.

Olson, Mancur, Jr. 1965. *Logic of Collective Action.* Cambridge: Harvard University Press.

———. 1982. *Rise and Decline of Nations.* New Haven: Yale University Press.

———. 1993a. "Dictatorship, Democracy, and Development." *American Political Science Review* 87: 567–76.

———. 1993b. "Why Are Differences in Per Capita Incomes So Large and Persistent?" In *Economic Growth in the World Economy,* ed. Horst Siebert. Tübingen: Mohr.

Riker, W. H. 1962. *The Theory of Political Coalitions.* New Haven: Yale University Press.

Sheridan, James E. 1966. *Chinese Warlord: The Career of Feng Yu-hsiang* Stanford: Stanford University Press.

Squire, Lyn. 1993. "Fighting Poverty." *American Economic Review* 83: 377–82.

II THE EFFECTS OF ECONOMIC AND POLITICAL INSTITUTIONS ON ECONOMIC DEVELOPMENT

4   Institutions and Economic Performance: Property Rights and Contract Enforcement

Christopher Clague, Philip Keefer, Stephen Knack, and Mancur Olson

Beginning with Adam Smith, economists have extolled the virtues of specialization. Specialization among individuals, organizations, regions, and countries enhances efficiency through economies of scale, comparative advantage, learning by doing, and technical change. Specialization implies exchange, but without the institutions to support them, neither specialization nor exchange is rational for individuals engaging in them.

The institutions that support an elaborate division of labor in a market economy include legal provisions for rights to property, mechanisms to enforce contracts, and government entities that can provide physical security of property and impartial enforcement of contracts. In short, the rights must exist on paper, and government entities (police, the courts) must be capable of enforcing them. Threats to these rights come from both private parties and the government itself. Thus the existence of these rights depends on a set of political arrangements that give government officials incentives to use their power to protect members of the private sector from one another, but not to use their power to expropriate or defraud private parties.[1]

It is our contention that societal differences in property rights and contract enforcement mechanisms are an important part of the explanation of why some countries prosper while others do not. In section 1, we describe how these institutions provide incentives for investment and innovation; section 2 then presents some empirical measures of these institutional characteristics of countries, developed by ourselves and others. These measures reveal very large differences among countries in property and

Research assistance for chapters 4 and 5 was ably provided by Gary Anderson, Suzanne Gleason, Christos Kostopoulos, Jennifer Mellor, and Ricardo Sanhueza. Data were generously provided by Robert Barro and Holger Wolf, Ross Levine, and Ted Haner of BERI. Computer time was provided by the University of Maryland Computer Science Center. Valuable comments were received from Robert Klitgaard.

[1]The next chapter deals with the relationship between political arrangements on the one hand, and property and contract rights on the other.

contract enforcement institutions. Section 3 shows that these empirical measures of institutional characteristics do help to explain international differences in rates of investment and economic growth. Section 4 deals with the relationship between these institutions and the alleviation of poverty. We reject the common supposition that well-defined and protected property rights and reliable contract enforcement mechanisms benefit the rich at the expense of the poor. Section 5 discusses how our focus on these institutions relates to certain keys to development that have recently been put forward by other researchers. The keys we discuss are investment in machinery and equipment, education, and financial sector development. We argue that these keys will not unlock the potential for development unless a basic institutional framework is in place. We conclude in section 6 by considering the implications of our findings for reform efforts.

1   Property Rights, Contract Enforcement, and Economic Progress

In a society with well-functioning institutions, individuals enter into complex, long-term transactions that contemplate, either explicitly or implicitly, multiple possible states of the world and outcomes of exchange. The sale of a house, for example, is a fairly complex transaction, involving as it does the possibility that the purchaser may not get a loan and the possibility that the house contains hidden defects of which the seller is aware. A modern capital market contains much more complex arrangements. The possibility of entering into such arrangements permits individuals to make highly advantageous trades, as the following examples illustrate.

A rich, elderly couple can transfer capital to a poor but capable and energetic young entrepreneur in exchange for a share in her venture, because the couple can rely on institutions to enforce an agreement that the entrepreneur might otherwise find easy to violate. A potential entrepreneur with an idea can go to a venture capital company that offers advice and training as well as capital for the project. An inventor need not be a capable manager to profit from his discovery, as he can patent his invention and sell it to a company with the capability of bringing it to market. An entrepreneur will sensibly contract out routine aspects of an innovative project so that she can devote more time and energy to what is new and difficult in the enterprise. She will buy insurance against well-defined risks in order to limit the chance that she will lose her entire stake. Many other examples could be cited. The point is that an environment in which contracts can be reliably enforced lowers the cost of innumerable types of exchanges that are advantageous to the participants and that encourage innovation and technical progress.

In societies without well-functioning contract enforcement institutions, individuals and companies choose to be more self-sufficient and engage less frequently in complex and non-self-enforcing transactions. In the extreme, peasants produce most of their own food rather than relying on market exchange. In less extreme cases, factories maintain large stocks of inventories and spare parts and extra electricity-generating capacity. Companies produce component parts of products internally rather than purchasing them from subcontractors. Economies of scale are forgone, as diversification is preferred to specialization by entrepreneurs worried that governments may expropriate one or another line of business activity. Entrepreneurship tends to be limited to members of wealthy families, who are not necessarily the most creative or efficient innovators or producers. Potential inventors have little incentive to devote time and money to making technical improvements, for they are unlikely to possess the entire package of ingredients—capital, marketing skills, managerial ability, and so forth—required to make the innovations profitable.

Insecure property rights and contract enforcement are likely to be much more harmful to the incentive to invest than is nonarbitrary taxation. Impartial and predictable taxation leaves business competition on a level playing field and thus does not impair the incentive to produce efficiently, and properly designed taxation, while it may reduce the return to investment, does not endanger the principal. Insecure property rights and contract enforcement, on the other hand, threaten the investor with the loss of assets. The risk of such loss is greater the more one specializes and the more one depends on complex exchanges. Yet it is precisely this kind of transaction that facilitates innovation and technical change, as the examples given above illustrate.

Contract compliance is not only a function of clear laws and courts where contracts can be enforced. Most transactions are carried out without explicit compulsion by outside enforcement entities. Businesses routinely go to considerable lengths to keep disagreements out of the courts, which are relatively cumbersome instruments for resolving complex disputes (Macaulay 1963; Williamson 1985). Businesses develop their own private mechanisms for resolving disputes and for punishing those who violate agreements. But the emergence and continued functioning of these private arrangements for contract compliance depends on the political and judicial institutions of the society. The government must provide a stable order within which such arrangements can evolve and must serve as the ultimate enforcement authority when private arrangements break down.

2   Measuring Institutions

2.1   Contract-intensive money

The same property rights and contract enforcement institutions that support complex and non-self-enforcing transactions also influence the form in which people hold their assets. In societies where an unstable legal and policy environment makes it sensible to conceal one's activities and assets from the government, people will make extensive use of currency to carry out their transactions. Currency is frequently less convenient than checks, credit cards, or other formal means of payment, but the risks of government confiscation or taxation can easily outweigh these considerations. Moreover, if formal contracts are of little advantage because they cannot be reliably enforced in court, or are avoided because they leave written records of transactions that one wishes to conceal from the government, then currency becomes more attractive because it completes the concealment of the transaction. People may also prefer to hold assets in the form of currency rather than financial claims because they lack confidence in the integrity of banks or other issuers of financial claims or because they doubt the government's competence in the prudential regulation of financial institutions.

In societies where property rights are secure and contracts can be reliably enforced, on the other hand, people have little reason either to use currency for large transactions or to maintain extensive currency holdings. They prefer that transactions be formally recorded in case there is a dispute to be resolved, and they are relieved of the inconvenience and danger of dealing in large amounts of currency. Even for small transactions, people often prefer to use checks or credit cards to facilitate their own record keeping or for documentation for the tax authorities.

The foregoing discussion suggests a means of measuring how conducive the institutional environment is for contract-intensive activity. In an earlier paper (Clague et al. 1995), we introduced the contract-intensive money ratio, or CIM, as a measure of the state of contract compliance and security of property rights in a country. This variable is defined as the ratio of noncurrency money to the total money supply, or $(M_2 - C)/M_2$, where M_2 is a broad definition of the money supply and C is currency held outside banks. The numerator of this ratio consists of financial assets such as checking accounts, time deposits, and other claims on financial institutions, while the denominator is the sum of these assets and currency holdings. The line of reasoning presented above suggests that this ratio is a reflection of the state of property rights and contract enforcement in a society. The higher this ratio, the more favorable these institutions are judged to be.[2]

2.2   Political risk indicators

Knack and Keefer (1995) employ institutional indicators obtained from two private international investment risk services: International Country Risk Guide (ICRG) and Business Environmental Risk Intelligence (BERI). While these companies (and others) publish cross-country ratings for investor risk, the virtue of these two sources is the detailed ratings provided for large samples on various dimensions of investment climate that are closely related to those institutions emphasized by North (1990) and other theorists.

The ICRG variables *expropriation risk* and *rule of law* are easily interpretable as proxies for the security of property: A high risk of expropriation and a lack of established peaceful mechanisms for adjudicating disputes will diminish the quantity and efficiency of capital investment (including investment in human capital), as the probability an investor will be able to retain its marginal product—or even the original investment—is reduced. Enforceability of contracts is likely to be problematic in countries scoring low on rule of law.

Repudiation of contracts by government is a second indicator of contract enforcement: governments not respecting their own contracts with private parties will arguably be less likely to respect and enforce contracts between two private parties. Repudiation may also reflect government credibility: regimes with the freedom to modify or repudiate contractual agreements unilaterally will likely be unconstrained in numerous other areas impinging on economic activity. Such governments will evoke suspicion regarding the possibility of confiscatory taxation or outright expropriation.

---

[2]The CIM ratio may be confused with measures of financial development, but it is quite distinct. A country may have a simple financial system, with the bulk of financial assets in the form of savings deposits and without a stock market or other manifestations of a modern financial system, and yet have a high CIM ratio. Finland, Iceland, and Botswana are examples of such countries. In fact, the simple correlation of CIM with M_2/GDP (a common measure of financial development) is only 0.44 in our sample of countries. We discuss the effect of financial development on economic development in section 6 below.

Corruption in government and *quality of the bureaucracy* proxy the general efficiency of provision of government services, as well as the extent and damage of rent-seeking behavior.[3] If the awarding of contracts, the granting of business and trade licenses, police protection, and so on are decided on the basis of criteria other than those of allocative and technical efficiency, the resulting distortions in investment and trade may reduce the quantity and efficiency of capital investment and of the licensing of foreign technology.

Available indicators from BERI include *contract enforceability, infrastructure quality, nationalization potential,* and *bureaucratic delays.* These measures cover much the same ground as the ICRG indicators. For more detailed descriptions, see Knack and Keefer (1995).

The ICRG has published its ratings since 1982, updating them monthly. BERI first provided its scores in 1972, updating them quarterly. We sum the ICRG and BERI measures, respectively, to create the composite variables ICRG index and BERI index.[4] Rather than taking an average of the available institutional scores over the period since 1982 (for the ICRG) or 1972 (for BERI), the earliest available data point for each source is taken, to minimize any problems of reverse causation leading from high or growing incomes to improvements in property and contract rights (Rosenberg and Birdzell 1986; Tornell 1993). Unlike the case with our objective measure CIM—where we use the average value over the entire period to explain investment and growth—it is also possible that subjective measures of institutional quality are biased by the coders' knowledge of a country's recent economic performance, giving us more reason to favor early-in-the-period values for the subjective indicators. In any event, our measures of institutional quality are fairly stable over time, as the correlation between the ICRG index values for 1982 and 1992 is .82, while the correlation between the BERI index for 1972 and 1992 is .87.

On conceptual grounds, we favor CIM and the ICRG and BERI political risk indexes over other available proxies for institutional quality.

---

[3]These two variables, as well as rule of law, may be thought of as empirical counterparts to Clague's concept of "rule obedience" (Clague 1993).

[4]All BERI variables are scored from 0–4, for a maximum possible index score of 16. For ICRG, 3 variables are 6-point scales while 2 are 10-point scales. We multiply the 6-point scales by 10/6 to create 5 10-point scales, for a maximum possible value of 50 on ICRG Index. Alternative weighting schemes produce indexes highly correlated with these indexes.

Nonetheless, we would have reason to question their validity if they failed to predict other measures of rights, stability, and checks on executive power. Reassuringly, we find that each of our three variables is strongly correlated with the frequency of revolutions and coups, with Gastil's (1987) subjective indexes of political and civil liberties, and with Gurr's (1990) index of constraints on the executive.

Others show that economic performance across nations is positively correlated with financial development (King and Levine 1994) and negatively correlated with inflation (Fischer 1993). One might suspect that cross-country variations in CIM—currency's proportion of the money supply—are explained primarily by variations in financial development and inflation rather than by property rights and contract enforceability. We show elsewhere that the variation in CIM is far better explained by other property rights measures than by M_2/GDP (the usual financial development indicator) and by currency depreciation, a measure of inflation. Furthermore, the same property rights variables that account for half of the variation in CIM account for only 28 percent of the variation in M_2/GDP and 12 percent of the variation in currency depreciation (Clague et al. 1995).

3   Institutions, Investment, and Growth

3.1   Why poor nations don't catch up

A comparison of distributions of real per capita incomes for developing (non-OECD) countries for 1960 and 1990 starkly confirms the well-known fact that many formerly poor nations have rapidly advanced into the middle-income ranks, while numerous others remained behind—with a few even showing declines in income. What accounts for this differential success among developing nations, with some displaying remarkable progress toward developed-nation status while others stagnate or even regress?

It is often argued that "a bit of backwardness" is advantageous to rapid growth, as middle-income developing countries have the human capital and infrastructure successfully to borrow foreign technology while extremely poor nations are unable to make productive use of advanced technology. This view is belied, however, by the cases of Korea, Taiwan, Botswana, and Mauritius, which were among the poorest in the world thirty-five years ago. Middle-income status is arguably not only unnecessary to attract foreign capital and technology, it is not sufficient either; witness the Southern Cone countries and Venezuela, all of which surpassed six current OECD members in per capita income in 1960.

We show elsewhere (Keefer and Knack forthcoming; Knack 1996) that differences in our measures of institutional quality go a long way toward accounting for which less-developed nations are successful in taking advantage of the opportunities for catch-up growth. Variations in growth rates over nations are uncorrelated with initial per capita income levels: on average, relative backwardness does not appear to confer any advantage, contrary to the importance theorists place on opportunities for catch-up. However, we consistently find that, for a given level of institutional quality, poorer countries grow faster than richer countries. Thus, poorer countries as a group have grown somewhat less rapidly than rich countries, not because they are inevitably doomed to fall further behind but because the majority of them have failed to establish mechanisms for securing rights to property, for enforcing contracts, and for establishing efficient public bureaucracies.[5] Table 4.1 compares samples of countries notorious for their economic performance—both good and bad—over the last generation or two. The underperforming African and Latin American economies exhibit low scores on our property rights measures relative to the East Asian countries, particularly given relatively high initial income levels in Latin America.[6]

The East Asian countries are not the only ones successfully catching up with the benefit of relatively secure property rights, enforceability of contracts, and efficient public administration. Several OECD members— Greece, Ireland, Japan, Portugal, Spain, and Turkey—actually had lower per capita incomes around the time the organization was founded than those of several nonmembers—Argentina, Chile, Saudi Arabia, Trinidad, Uruguay, and Venezuela. The table suggests that variations in institutional quality help account for this differential success.[7]

---

[5]Barro (1991) has shown that education is also an important determinant of catch-up growth. Holding education constant, however, we still find that better institutional quality enhances the positive growth effects associated with initial backwardness.

[6]Contrasts in property rights scores are even more dramatic when Japan—an underdeveloped country not long ago—is included in the East Asian grouping.

[7]Differences in human capital levels are surely also relevant. We argue below that education is itself in large part a function of institutional quality.

Table 4.1

Country Groupings, by Property Rights, Human Capital, and Economic Performance

	East Asia[a]	Sub-Saharan Africa	Latin America	OECD Six[b]	Ex Ante Rich Six[c]
ICRG index	36.6	22.2	21.7	38.2	26.0
BERI index	9.4	7.7	6.9	10.1	6.7
CIM average, 1969–90	0.83	0.68	0.80	0.86	0.81
Primary education enrollment	0.91	0.43	0.86	1.06	0.85
Secondary education enrollment	0.21	0.03	0.19	0.35	0.23
Average annual per capita income growth, 1969–90	5.7	0.4	0.5	3.0	0.04
Investment/GDP, average for 1969–90	0.27	0.11	0.17	0.29	0.18

[a]East Asian countries include Hong Kong, Indonesia, Korea, Malaysia, Singapore, Taiwan, and Thailand.

[b]OECD six include Greece, Ireland, Japan, Portugal, Spain, and Turkey, all with 1960 GDP per capita <$2900.

[c]Non-OECD ex-ante rich six include Argentina, Chile, Saudi Arabia, Trinidad, Uruguay, and Venezuela, all with 1960 GDP per capita >$2900.

3.2 Multivariate tests

In tables 4.2 and 4.3 we present the results of multivariate analyses in which we control for other relevant factors commonly included in cross-country tests of economic performance (see Barro 1991, for example): initial income levels, human capital levels, and (in investment equations) the relative price of investment goods. We use three alternative institutional measures: CIM, the ICRG index, and the BERI index. For simplicity and comparability, our dependent variables cover the 1969–90 period for all regressions; that is the period for which we have data on CIM for a large sample. In equations including CIM, we include as additional regressors measures of financial development (M_2/GDP, averaged over the 1969–90 period) and inflation (the average annual rate of currency depreciation over the period)[8] to prevent CIM from capturing any effects more properly attributed to those factors.

For tests including all nations with available data, including the OECD nations, each of our institutional variables exhibits positive and statistically significant impacts on investment and growth (see equations 1, 3, and 5 in tables 4.2 and 4.3). In most cases, these impacts are greater than those of human capital, financial development, and inflation variables.[9]

In nearly every case, these strong results for our institutional indicators are replicated for samples including only developing (i.e., non-OECD) nations (see equations 2, 4, and 6 in tables 4.2 and 4.3). Thus, our measures are not simply capturing differences across the two groups of nations, developing and developed. Rather, we find strong evidence that those underdeveloped nations respecting property and contract rights accumulate capital and increase the incomes of their populations at substantially higher rates than other developing countries—even when controlling for the large variations in starting points, in levels of schooling, and in the price of investment goods.

Coefficients for the institutional variables indicate relatively large effects on economic performance. An increase of one percentage point in investment/GDP (e.g., from 18% to 19%) is associated with increases of about .06 in CIM (e.g., from .75 to .81), or about five points in the ICRG index (e.g., from twenty to twenty-five), or about one point in the BERI index (e.g., from eight to nine). Increases in ICRG of eight or nine points and in BERI of a little more than two points are associated with a rise in per capita income growth of about one percentage point—a very large increase, given that African and Latin American countries collectively grew only about one-half of a percentage point annually over the 1969–90 period.

---

[8]Higher inflation should reduce CIM, as it penalizes holders of currency.

[9]These comparisons employ standardized coefficients: the impact on the dependent variable, measured in standard deviation units, of a one standard deviation change in an independent variable.

Table 4.2

Institutional Quality and Average Investment/GDP, 1969–1990

Institutional Measure	CIM		ICRG Index		BERI Index	
	World	LDCs	World	LDCs	World	LDCs
	Eq. 1	Eq. 2	Eq. 3	Eq. 4	Eq. 5	Eq. 6
Constant	-4.79	-1.17	11.38	13.58	14.54	15.95
	(7.34)	(8.41)	(1.75)	(7.56)	(8.29)	(9.94)
Log 1969	0.59	-0.07	-0.23	-0.59	-1.68	-2.09
GDP per capita	(1.16)	(1.33)	(1.03)	(1.15)	(1.29)	(1.43)
Primary	3.99	6.35	8.41**	7.77**	11.38**	8.87
enrollment, 1960	(2.79)	(3.33)	(2.36)	(2.95)	(3.48)	(4.92)
Secondary	4.69	-7.60	8.01*	12.15	-2.50	5.64
enrollment, 1960	(4.36)	(8.36)	(4.11)	(7.17)	(5.14)	(10.55)
Currency depreciation,	-3.95	-0.97				
mean 1969–90	(5.22)	(5.90)				
M_2/GDP, mean	9.64**	14.06**				
1969–90	(2.91)	(4.32)				
Price of investment	-2.96**	-3.03**	-4.89**	-4.36**	-3.53**	-3.19**
goods, 1969	(0.94)	(0.98)	(0.90)	(0.97)	(0.98)	(0.99)
Institutional variable:	18.07**	16.55**	0.21**	0.20**	1.61**	1.83**
CIM, ICRG, or BERI	(5.73)	(5.99)	(0.05)	(0.07)	(0.36)	(0.40)
Adjusted R^2	.68	.54	.69	.56	.70	.70
N	96	74	101	78	48	28
Mean, dependent variable	18.3	15.3	18.6	15.7	22.6	18.8

Note: Standard errors are in parentheses; they are calculated from White's heteroskedastic-consistent variance-covariance matrix.
*Significant at .05 level, two-tailed test; **significant at .01 level.

Christopher Clague et al.

Table 4.3

Institutional Quality and Per Capita Income Growth, 1969–1990

	CIM		ICRG Index		BERI Index	
	World	LDCs	World	LDCs	World	LDCs
Institutional Measure	Eq. 1	Eq. 2	Eq. 3	Eq. 4	Eq. 5	Eq. 6
Constant	6.89**	7.27**	10.17**	8.82**	15.81**	18.6**
	(2.05)	(2.66)	(2.02)	(2.64)	(2.75)	(4.19)
Log 1969	-1.48**	-1.54**	-1.77**	-1.68**	-2.70**	-3.23**
GDP per capita	(0.33)	(0.43)	(0.31)	(0.38)	(0.41)	(0.57)
Primary	2.20**	2.51*	2.30**	1.63	3.97**	4.72*
enrollment, 1960	(0.82)	(1.19)	(0.78)	(1.17)	(1.01)	(1.9)
Secondary	2.74**	1.13	1.39	4.54*	1.86	4.63
enrollment, 1960	(0.86)	(2.54)	(0.90)	(2.27)	(1.13)	(3.59)
Currency depreciation,	-2.65	-2.22				
mean 1969-90	(1.37)	(1.86)				
M_2/GDP,	1.24	2.64				
mean 1969-90	(0.65)	(1.49)				
Institutional variable:	4.53*	3.70	0.11**	0.13**	0.43**	0.42**
CIM, ICRG, or BERI	(2.01)	(2.36)	(0.02)	(0.02)	(0.10)	(0.13)
Adjusted R^2	.31	.23	.43	.41	.53	.61
N	96	74	101	78	48	28
Mean, dependent	1.82	1.17	1.83	1.18	1.93	1.22
variable						

Note: All equations are estimated using weighted least squares, with initial per capita GDP as weights. R^2 in weighted least squares does not have its usual interpretation. Standard errors are in parentheses; they are calculated from White's heteroskedastic-consistent variance-covariance matrix.

*Significant at .05 level, two-tailed test; **significant at .01 level.

Institutions appear to affect growth predominantly through capital accumulation: when investment is included as a regressor in growth regressions, CIM and BERI no longer significantly predict growth. We nevertheless believe that property rights and contract enforceability influence the efficiency with which physical and human capital is employed and also the speed of technological transfer and innovation. Coefficients for all three of our institutional indicators retain their positive signs, with ICRG retaining its statistical significance. Further, technological advances are often embodied in machinery and other capital; many of these efficiency increases may be attributable to institutional quality but will be largely captured statistically by investment measures.

In addition to financial development and inflation, we have elsewhere considered the possibility that our institutional indicators are spuriously correlated with investment and growth due to omitted policy variables. In all of our regressions, adding measures of government size, trade openness, and macroeconomic stability fails to reduce substantially the estimated impact of our property rights and contract enforceability indicators. Most of our findings are robust to the deletion or inclusion of outliers, countries that strongly influence the institutional variable coefficients.[10]

The potential for reverse causation exists in any empirical analysis of institutions and economic performance: as the volume and average size of transactions increase, the payoffs to establishing commercial law and an independent judiciary increase, for example. For several reasons, we conclude that the statistical correlation measured here is not primarily attributable to such feedback mechanisms, however, and that the causal arrow points primarily in the other direction. First, we are able to trace the major portion of institutional effects on growth through investment channels, as our theory predicts. Second, the BERI indicator is measured early (1972) in the 1969–90 period we examine. Third, while CIM is averaged throughout the period, early-period CIM measures produce nearly identical findings

---

[10]In growth regressions, CIM is particularly sensitive to the inclusion of Yemen, which exhibits a high growth rate—due largely to the impact of remittances from Saudi Arabia—but a low CIM, as most remittances never enter the primitive banking system (Burrowes 1987). Yemen is omitted from our regressions due to missing data on financial development and currency depreciation. Malta and Syria—both with high growth and low CIM—are included, however, and each of these two cases reduces CIM's coefficient more than the most extreme positive outlier (Botswana) raises it.

(Clague et al. 1995). Finally, while the ICRG is measured over halfway into the period, we show elsewhere that it successfully predicts performance in periods with later starting point (Knack and Keefer 1995).

4   The Poor and Improved Property Rights

There is a widespread perception that secure property rights and effective contract enforcement benefit primarily the rich. This perception derives from images of rich property owners enforcing property rights or contract provisions against poor tenants, workers, borrowers, and consumers. We contend, however, that secure property rights and effective contract enforcement mechanisms are not in themselves inegalitarian institutions. In fact, they have powerful equality-promoting effects. These institutions enable individuals with little property and no political connections to make investments in themselves and in their small enterprises. Fair and transparent procedures for property, contracts, and government regulation of business facilitate the entry of low- and middle-income people into many areas of economic life. They also promote the accumulation of physical and human capital, which raises wages. Thus, the reforms in policies and institutions that enhance growth are largely the same as those that raise the welfare of the poor.

One can go further and argue that much of the poverty in the Third World results from policies and arrangements chosen by well-placed individuals and well-off groups in their own interests. Burdensome red tape is often the product of corruption, with government bureaucrats seeking to make illegal all sorts of transactions or to require permits and licenses, opening up possibilities for bribes. Urban, well-established, and well-to-do groups obtain monopoly power through favorable regulations and protective decrees and legislation.[11] Agricultural pricing policies of most developing countries subsidize relatively advantaged urban populations at the expense of the mass of peasant farmers (Krueger, Schiff, and Valdes 1993). Inefficiencies associated with insecure property rights, red tape, corruption, inept management of public infrastructure, and market-distorting policies are

---

[11]These monopoly grants reduce the value of physical and human assets belonging to would-be competitors as well as to entrepreneurs dependent on the monopoly's output for use as an input.

particularly damaging to the poor,[12] because the poor are almost never as politically organized as other groups—especially given low levels of literacy and the high costs of transportation and communication in much of the Third World (van Bastelaer, forthcoming).

Where institutions and policies are deficient, providing direct aid to poor people in the form of goods and services can have only temporary and limited benefits. Programs to teach the poor how to cope better in their existing economic environment through literacy programs, microenterprise credit and training, and family planning may have somewhat greater, although still relatively limited, payoffs. Ultimately, improvements in the economic environment through policy and institutional reforms are necessary for creating maximum incentives to invest in human and physical capital, and to maximize the return to a nation's human and natural resources.[13]

5 Institutions and Other Keys to Development

Various researchers have put forward theories coupled with supporting statistical evidence pointing to a crucial role in development for one variable or another. Such keys to economic development include investment in human capital, financial sector development, investment in equipment, trade openness, fiscal policy, and macroeconomic stability. Without denying the importance of any of these factors, we believe that there are important interactions between policy reform in these areas and the quality of institutions: in the absence of secure rights to property, enforceable contracts, and a relatively honest and competent government bureaucracy, the full benefits of such policy reforms cannot be achieved. Here we comment on only the first three purported keys to development mentioned above.

5.1 Human capital

Citing the historical record of currently industrialized and developing nations, Easterlin (1981) blames the inability of poor nations success-

---

[12] Nearly all households in Istanbul use backup water supply systems such as wells, rivers, and street vendors due to the unreliability of publicly supplied water. These backup systems cost only 1% of household income for the richest households but 5% for the poorest (World Bank 1994, 30).

[13] For further discussion of these points, see Olson (1994).

fully to borrow and adapt advanced foreign technology on their low levels of human capital. This evidence is consistent with the model constructed by Nelson and Phelps (1966), in which the rate of technological advance by followers is a positive function of the gap between the leader and followers and of human capital levels.

Viewing levels of human capital as the key to growth ignores troubling anomalies, however. Secondary-school enrollment in Chile was virtually identical to that of Hong Kong in 1960, 1970, and 1985. For slow-growing Argentina and Uruguay, secondary-school enrollment in 1960 matched enrollment in Singapore and Italy and far exceeded that of Spain, Portugal, Korea, Malaysia, Thailand, and Hong Kong. Cross-country comparisons of estimates of average years of education for the labor force (Kyriacou 1991) or population (Barro and Lee 1993) yield similar findings. Schooling rates for most of East Asia did not exceed those of South America until the 1980s. Argentina's labor force was better educated in 1965 than most of East Asia's was twenty years later (Kyriacou 1991).

Expanding education may be necessary but not sufficient for sustained and rapid growth. Where the economic environment is poor, people may be unable to convert their skills into higher standards of living. This seems to be the case in sub-Saharan Africa, where many countries have experienced considerable educational expansion but where per capita incomes have actually declined since the middle 1970s. Education produces less of a social payoff in countries with poor institutions for two reasons: relatively corrupt, incompetent, and unaccountable governments are probably less effective at educating students, but more important, economic environments in those regions typically fail to make efficient use of existing human resources.[14]

High levels of corruption make economic advancement largely the product of cultivating political connections rather than of accumulating socially productive knowledge and skills. A poor economic environment can thus reduce incentives for people to invest in socially productive human capital and, by distorting the allocation of investment in education, can

---

[14]Our argument is not inconsistent with the empirical finding that additional years of education of an individual are associated with much higher levels of earnings, so that conventionally calculated social rates of return in sub-Saharan Africa are quite high (Psacharapoulos 1993).

reduce the social rates of return to whatever investments are made.[15]

While recent investments in human capital by many developing countries show disappointing results, Barro (1991) and others demonstrate that the economies of developing nations with high 1960 literacy rates and school enrollment levels have performed well subsequently. A favorable economic environment in these countries arguably increased perceived rewards for the acquisition of human capital. These investments, in turn, contribute to growth, but they would not have occurred in the absence of appropriate institutions and policies. Thus, regression coefficients for CIM, ICRG, and BERI when education is controlled for may underestimate the true impact of institutional quality on economic outcomes.

High educational enrollments in 1960 may also be a signal of accountability to the population as a whole: governments emphasizing the education of women, the poor, and rural residents are generally not those with narrow constituencies. They are likely to be the same governments that provide human and economic rights to the population as a whole and that balance social benefits and costs when choosing policies rather than the interests of a few key supporters. To the extent that these growth-enhancing policies are not adequately measured in cross-national statistical analyses, differences in 1960 literacy and school enrollment levels may capture some of their effects.

5.2   Financial development

Financial development is closely related to property rights and contract enforcement. A country cannot develop a sophisticated financial system if these basic institutions are absent. For this reason, empirical studies showing substantial growth effects of financial sector development (e.g., King and Levine 1994) are entirely consistent with the emphasis in this chapter on the institutional underpinnings of economic progress.

However, a country may have a good system of property rights and contract enforcement and still have a relatively simple financial system (see the examples cited in footnote 2 above). One reason for this fact is that it takes considerable time for a sophisticated financial system to develop once property rights and contract enforcement institutions are in place. Another

---

[15]On the latter point, see Murphy, Shleifer, and Vishny (1991), who argue that economies that reward rent seeking rather than socially productive activities will have more lawyers. They present cross-national empirical evidence suggesting that a high ratio of lawyers to engineers reduces growth rates.

is that, since there are cost advantages in international specialization in financial services, a country with good institutions may nonetheless make considerable use of financial services provided by a foreign financial center.

Why is financial sector development associated with high levels of income and rapid rates of economic growth? The prior literature on the subject emphasizes the role of the financial sector in allocating capital across sectors and among entrepreneurs of varying quality (McKinnon 1973; King and Levine 1994). While this role is undeniably important, a well-developed financial sector surely reflects an institutional environment that supports a wide variety of complex exchanges, many of which do not involve the market for capital. We contend that the basic institutional environment, as well as the financial sector itself, contributes to countries' economic performance.

Thus our results on CIM provide an alternative interpretation for previous findings of strong effects of financial development on economic growth and investment, which have usually been interpreted to mean that countries with underdeveloped financial sectors require only technical assistance to build them up. Rather than placing emphasis on the mechanics of capital markets and on the human capital required to conduct the types of transactions carried out in highly developed financial markets,[16] the interpretation here stresses the regulatory and legal apparatus that defends contractual and property rights in financial markets. The evidence summarized in section 4 suggests that collateral law and prudential regulation must be enforceable and credible, characteristics that emanate from the larger institutional framework into which these laws and regulations are introduced.

5.3   Equipment investment

DeLong and Summers (1991) present evidence indicating that rapid growth requires high rates of investment in machinery and equipment. They note that their findings are consistent with the emphasis of economic historians on the role of mechanization and are in opposition to the currently widespread view among development and growth economists that the importance of capital accumulation was exaggerated by an earlier generation of development economists (deLong 1992).

Socially productive investment in machinery does not occur in an

---

[16]Note, for example, the emphasis placed on stock markets in the reform programs of some of the postcommunist societies. For an assessment of this emphasis, see Stiglitz (1992).

institutional vacuum: entrepreneurs' decisions to purchase equipment will crucially depend on the quality of a nation's institutions and policies.

We show above that secure property rights and enforceable contracts encourage capital investment. Investment in structures—shown by deLong and Summers to have far lower social rates of return—will clearly be sensitive to institutional quality. Structures are difficult to move or hide and, thus, easily taxed or expropriated. They depreciate relatively slowly, so that prospects for medium- and even long-term policy instability may substantially deter investment. Although machinery, by contrast, depreciates more rapidly and is more mobile, it is arguably more often dedicated to particular uses and is likely to have little resale value in comparison to structures. Thus, machinery investment should also be highly sensitive to property rights security.

Variations in equipment investment as a share of GDP across countries turn out to be strongly related to variations in our measures of institutional quality. The strong and positive connection between institutional quality and machinery investment proves robust to multivariate analyses controlling for differences across nations in income and educational levels (see equations 1, 3, and 5 in table 4.4).[17] Equipment price levels, when added to these models, capture a good portion of the impact of institutions (equations 2, 4, and 6). Of course, the much higher prices of equipment in many less-developed nations are not independent of institutions and policies. In the absence of protectionist and trade-distorting measures, all nations could import machinery at world prices (plus transport costs). Policies and institutions also influence the social rate of return on whatever equipment investment does take place. Noting the example of Stalinist Russia, deLong (1992) cautions that machinery investment leading to rapid growth is more likely to be generated by private firms and market allocation processes than by central planning.

In the absence of secure property rights, entrepreneurs must expend resources to protect their investments. In the presence of barriers to foreign trade and burdensome regulation of domestic trade, the menu of producer goods that entrepreneurs may choose to purchase is restricted. Availability of complementary inputs and essential spare parts is problematic. In the absence of a reliable provision of electricity and communications and transportation infrastructure, a sizable portion of private investment must be

---

[17]Analogous tests of investment in structures show a similar, but slightly weaker, relation to property rights and contract enforceability.

devoted to the purchase of generators and other costly substitutes.[18] Realization of the maximum social benefits from equipment investment will thus depend on the existence of (1) free and open markets, (2) secure rights to property, (3) a minimum of red tape, corruption and incompetence in the regulation of private business, (4) and provision of public infrastructure by government bureaucrats.

Table 4.4

Institutional Quality and Average Equipment Investment, 1975–1985

Institutional Measure	CIM		ICRG Index		BERI Index	
	Eq. 1	Eq. 2	Eq. 3	Eq. 4	Eq. 5	Eq. 6
Constant	-7.76	-1.40	2.48	2.58	-2.88	0.74
	(3.69)	(2.34)	(1.24)	(0.88)	(1.13)	(1.35)
Log 1975 GDP per capita	-0.09	0.68	-0.08	.68	-1.14	0.07
	(0.73)	(0.55)	(0.74)	(0.57)	(0.55)	(0.49)
Primary enrollment, 1960	-4.71	-.66	-2.35	0.36	2.55*	2.58**
	(2.56)	(1.35)	(2.17)	(1.13)	(1.23)	(0.83)
Secondary enrollment, 1960	4.88	0.76	2.80	-0.61	1.64	1.59
	(2.52)	(2.07)	(2.68)	(2.18)	(2.96)	(1.73)
Price of equipment investment goods		-5.89		-6.32		-4.77
		(0.95)		(1.09)		(0.96)
Institutional variable: CIM, ICRG, or BERI	19.36*	7.93	0.14**	0.07**	0.71*	0.19
	(6.49)	(3.90)	(0.04)	(0.02)	(0.12)	(0.16)
Adjusted R^2	.40	.69	.31	.69	.61	.78
N	58	58	61	61	37	37
Mean, dependent variable	5.2	5.2	5.2	5.2	5.4	5.4

Note: Dependent variable is equipment investment as a share of GDP (in %). Standard errors are calculated from White's heteroskedastic-consistent variance-covariance matrix. *Significant at .05 level, two-tailed test; **significant at .01 level.

[18]A survey of 179 businesses in Nigeria found that 92% owned their own electricity generators, an expense averaging 10% of total machinery and equipment expenditures for firms with fifty or more employees and 25% for smaller firms (World Bank 1994, 30).

DeLong and Summers (1991) calculated a 30 percent average social rate of return on machinery investment over the 1960–85 period. Our empirical investigations find that this return varies with institutional quality and openness to imports. For the full deLong-Summers sample and among the less-developed (i.e., non-OECD) nations, the growth effects of equipment decline significantly among nations with a higher black market currency premium (average over 1960–87). Among less-developed nations, the growth impact of machinery investment increases with CIM, ICRG, and with a subjective measure of independence of the judiciary (Humana 1986). The estimated benefits of equipment investment appear to be minimal for nations with sufficiently poor institutional quality and closed economies.

6   Policy Implications

The evidence reviewed in this chapter indicates that it is possible to find measures of the quality of some aspects of a country's economic institutions. While surely imperfect, these measures—contract-intensive money (CIM) and the political risk indicators—do seem to capture much of the international variation in the security of property rights, the enforceability of contracts, and the effectiveness of public bureaucracies in providing public goods and facilitating business activity. The evidence also indicates that these indicators help to explain differences in rates of economic growth and in investment, particularly why some poor countries experience rapid catch-up growth and others do not.

If these findings hold up under scrutiny and subsequent investigation, they contain some potentially important implications for our interpretations of the development process. Development should not be thought of as just the accumulation of physical and human capital and the adoption of superior technologies, important as these phenomena are. These accumulations and adoptions depend crucially on the institutional environment of the country and the incentives that it provides. In other words, the crucial problem lies not in the scarcity of capital but in residents' lack of incentives to invest in socially productive (but vulnerable) assets and in the lack of incentives of foreign businesses to transfer technology and managerial skills. The shortcomings of the financial system are not that the banks lack computerized check-clearing systems but that people do not trust the banks enough to put their money there. The problem is not so much the lack of resources for education and health as the absence of organizational structures and pricing policies for the delivery of these services.

students and vaccinate children, some individuals will be better off, but their income-producing capacity may improve little if the institutional environment of the country is poor. In any case, the aggregate performance of the country in growth and poverty alleviation will be little affected.

Economic policies have a great deal to do with why countries remain poor. Although there have been dramatic liberalizations and stabilizations in a number of countries in the last two decades, many countries' economies are still severely constrained by inflationary budget deficits, overstaffed public enterprises, exchange controls, restrictions on foreign trade and investment, agricultural price controls, and other violations of the standard World Bank–IMF–"Washington consensus" policy recommendations.

We have no quarrel with these policy recommendations—in fact, we think they are necessary parts of an overall strategy to help a country escape stagnation. But the changes need to go deeper, in two senses. First, the stabilization-liberalization-privatization package needs to find political support within the country. This is not to say that there has to be a consensus in favor of the package before it is launched—many successful reform efforts have found their political support after they have been initiated. But the society has to accept the new policies, and this is not simply a matter of changing directions at the top. Second, the reforms in most countries need to go well beyond getting the macroeconomics and the prices right. There needs to be change in the environment in which businesses operate. The institutional framework of a market economy needs to be put in place, including reliable supplies of public services, maintenance of physical infrastructure, freedom from excessive government regulation and interference, and arenas for the settlement of business disputes. This task requires far-reaching changes in government bureaucracies, in the expectations of businesspeople and government officials about how the other actors will behave, and in societal attitudes toward markets. The fact that these processes of institutional change are not well understood does not make the task of policy makers and donors any easier. But if the suggestive findings in the line of research represented here hold up under further scrutiny, the development community must gain a deeper understanding of these vitally important processes.

References

Barro, Robert J. 1991. "Economic Growth in a Cross Section of Countries." *Quarterly Journal of Economics* 106: 407–43.

Quarterly Journal of Economics 106: 407–43.

Barro, Robert, and Jong-wha Lee. 1993. "International Comparisons of Educational Attainment." *Journal of Monetary Economics* 32: 363–94.

Burrowes, Robert D. 1987. *The Yemen Arab Republic: The Politics of Development, 1962–86.* Boulder, Colo.: Westview.

Clague, Christopher. 1993. "Rule Obedience, Organizational Loyalty, and Economic Development." *Journal of Institutional and Theoretical Economics* 149: 393–414.

Clague, Christopher, Philip Keefer, Stephen Knack, and Mancur Olson. 1995. "Contract-Intensive Money: Property Rights, Contract Enforcement and Economic Performance." Working Paper 151 IRIS, College Park, Md.

deLong, J. Bradford. 1992. "Productivity Growth and Machinery Investment: A Long-Run Look, 1870–1980." *Journal of Economic History* 52: 307–24.

deLong, J. Bradford and Larry Summers. 1991. "Equipment Investment and Economic Growth." *Quarterly Journal of Economics* 106: 445–502.

Easterlin, Richard A. 1981. "Why Isn't the Whole World Developed?" *Journal of Economic History* 41: 1–19.

Fischer, Stanley. 1993. "The Role of Macroeconomic Factors in Growth." *Journal of Monetary Economics* 32: 485–512.

Gastil, Raymond D. 1987. *Freedom in the World.* Westport, Conn.: Greenwood.

Gurr, Ted Robert. 1990. *Polity II: Political Structures and Regime Change, 1800–1986.* 1st ICPSR ed.Ann Arbor. Mich.: Inter-University Consortium for Political and Social Research.

Humana, Charles. 1986. *World Human Rights Guide.* New York: Facts on File.

King, Robert G., and Ross Levine. 1994. "Finance and Growth: Schumpeter Might Be Right." *Quarterly Journal of Economics* 108: 717–37.

Keefer, Philip and Stephen Knack. Forthcoming. "Why Don't Poor Countries Catch Up? A Cross-National Test of an Institutional Explanation." *Economic Inquiry.*

Knack, Stephen. 1996. "Institutions and the Convergence Hypothesis: The Cross-National Evidence." *Public Choice* 87: 207–228.

Knack, Stephen, and Philip Keefer. 1995. "Institutions and Economic Performance: Cross-Country Tests Using Alternative Institutional Measures." *Economics and Politics* 7:207–27.

Economy of Agricultural Pricing Policy. Baltimore: Johns Hopkins University Press.

Kyriacou, G. 1991. "Level and Growth Effects of Human Capital: A Cross-Country Study of the Convergence Hypothesis." Working Paper 91-26 C. V. Starr Center, New York.

Macaulay, S. 1963. "Non-Contractual Relations in Business." *American Sociological Review* 28: 55–70.

McKinnon, Ronald. 1973. *Money and Capital in Economic Development.* Washington, D.C.: Brookings.

Murphy, Kevin M., Andrei Shleifer, and Robert W. Vishny. 1991. "The Allocation of Talent: Implications for Growth." *Quarterly Journal of Economics* 106: 503–30.

Nelson, Richard R., and Edmund S. Phelps. 1966. "Investment in Humans, Technological Diffusion, and Economic Growth." *American Economic Review* 56: 69–75.

North, Douglass C.. 1990. *Institutions, Institutional Change, and Economic Performance.* Cambridge: Cambridge University Press.

Olson, Mancur. 1994. "Who Gains from Policies That Increase Poverty?" Working Paper 137. IRIS, College Park, Md.

Psacharapoulos, George. 1993. "Returns to Investment in Education: A Global Update." Policy Research Working Paper 1067. World Bank, Washington, D.C.

Rosenberg, Nathan, and L. E. Birdzell. 1986. *How the West Grew Rich: The Economic Transformation of the Industrial World.* New York: Basic Books.

Stiglitz, Joseph E. 1992. "The Design of Financial Systems for the Newly Emerging Democracies of Eastern Europe." In *The Emergence of Market Economies in Eastern Europe*, Christopher Clague and Gordon Rausser. Cambridge: Blackwell.

Tornell, Aaron. 1993. "Economic Growth and Decline with Endogenous Property Rights." Working Paper 4354. National Bureau of Economic Research, Cambridge, Mass.

van Bastelaer, Thierry. Forthcoming. "The Political Economy of Food Pricing: An Extended Empirical Test of the Interest Group Approach." *Public Choice.*

Williamson, Oliver. 1985. *The Economic Institutions of Capitalism.* New York: Free Press.

World Bank. 1994. *World Development Report.* Washington, D.C.: World Bank.

5   Democracy, Autocracy, and the Institutions Supportive of Economic Growth

Christopher Clague, Philip Keefer, Stephen Knack, and Mancur Olson

There has long been intense interest in the relationships between democratic political institutions and economic progress. On one hand, there is the thesis associated with Lipset (1959) that economic growth (or a high level of per capita income) and the associated societal changes foster democratic political institutions. On the other, there is the question whether these democratic political institutions tend to promote or retard economic progress. Arguments can be advanced on both sides of this issue, and examples can be provided of successful and unsuccessful economic performance under both democratic and authoritarian forms of government. Recently, economists have developed an enhanced appreciation of the benefits for economic growth of the institutions of secure property rights and effective contract enforcement mechanisms. Chapter 4 reviews some recent evidence that these institutions are conducive to private sector investment and long-term economic growth. The main purpose of the present chapter is to explore the effects of the type of political regime (democratic versus authoritarian) on these property rights and contract enforcement institutions.

Given the varied and inconclusive results in the prior literature on the effects of regime type on growth, there is a need to distinguish among types of democracies and autocracies. This chapter takes one step in this direction by looking at the duration of political regimes and at the incentives that these create for political leaders. This focus on the duration of regimes arises naturally in an examination of property and contract rights, the beneficial consequences of which depend on the expectations regarding the behavior of politicians and judges.

A dictator who does not expect to last long and who wants to maximize his wealth has an incentive to appropriate whatever assets he can or, in short, to act as a roving bandit (for elaboration of this argument, see Olson, chapter 3 of this volume). Similarly, an autocrat who is threatened by a coup may take desperate measures to raise resources that can be used to buy political support. On the other hand, an autocrat who expects to remain in power for a long time, and perhaps even to bequeath his domain to his offspring, has an incentive to establish and then respect property rights for his subjects so that they will produce more output that the autocrat can tax. In contrast to the dictator, a democratic politician does not have the power to abrogate property rights, cancel contracts, and seize assets. It is in the very nature of a democratic regime that political leaders are constrained from repressing the political rights of opponents, and these same constraints may limit their power to abrogate property and contract rights, as well. Consequently, property and contract rights are likely to depend on the expected duration of the democratic regime itself, rather than on the expected tenure of a particular democratic chief executive. This chapter explores these issues by examining the effects of regime type and duration on property and contract rights.

Section 1 considers the relation of regime type and duration to property and contract rights and discusses some of the hypotheses that guide our empirical investigations. Section 2 reviews previous empirical literature on growth-democracy links. Section 3 contains a description of our data on regime type, regime duration, and property rights measures. Our empirical analyses are reported in section 4, while section 5 discusses what accounts for long-lasting democracies in the Third World.

1   Regime Type and Property Rights: Theoretical Considerations

Property rights are protection against arbitrary seizure of assets or other abridgement of their value by government officials and protection against encroachment by other private parties. Contract rights mean freedom to enter into contracts and protection against nonfulfillment of contracts by the government or other private parties.

At the theoretical level, there are conflicting arguments regarding the effects of autocracy and democracy on property and contract rights. A democratic political regime contains constraints on political leaders through electoral, legislative, and judicial institutions. The limits that these institutions place on arbitrary actions by political leaders, government officials, and judges imply that a rule of law is operative in the political sphere. That is, political leaders are not permitted to outlaw political organizations, limit freedom of speech and press, harass political opponents, or cancel elections. A political regime that respects the rule of law in the political sphere is likely also to respect it in the economic sphere. The same legislative and judicial institutions can be used to protect against arbitrary seizure of property or repudiation of contracts by the government.

Of course, the protection of property and contract rights in a democracy depends on the will of the electorate. It is logically possible to have a regime of democratic socialism, in which the rule of law is scrupulously adhered to in the political realm but in which there are only limited rights of private property and contract. Such a regime has never existed in history, perhaps for the reason that people have always perceived that some degree of property and contract rights are essential for their well-being. Still, some property and contract rights in a democracy may fail to be protected because of lack of popular support.[1]

An autocracy, by contrast, in a fundamental sense lacks a rule of law in the political sphere. Since the autocrat can act unilaterally to imprison opponents and to repress dissent, he can seize assets and repudiate contracts as well. But an autocrat may have incentives not to do so. If we follow Olson (chap. 3, this volume) in assuming that the autocrat seeks to maximize his tax theft, then he has a strong incentive to guarantee property and contract rights of private parties vis-à-vis each other. (In this respect, an autocracy is similar to a democracy.) These rights encourage investment, innovation, and growth, from which the autocrat can derive additional tax revenue. If the autocrat is secure in his power and has a reasonably long time horizon, it is also in his interest to convince his subjects that he will not himself abridge their property and contract rights, and while his promises may not be fully credible (since he has the power to break them), a record of not infringing on these rights is likely to build up confidence among his subjects.

It is obvious from casual observation that both democracies and autocracies are heterogeneous with respect to their protection of property and contract rights. Dictatorships in Taiwan and Chile have provided secure rights, while many in Africa and Central America have not. Similarly, property and contract rights are secure in rich Western democracies but not in some fledgling democracies of the Third World. Regimes may differ because of their states of economic development, and per capita income is one variable for which we control in the empirical work. Regimes also differ in the length of time that they have been in power.

Both democracies and autocracies are likely to be affected by the expected duration of the regime, which in turn may be influenced by the length of time it has been in existence. A newly installed autocrat normally faces a higher probability of being overthrown than one who has consoli-

---

[1]Election campaigns in India, for example, have often included promises by politicians to forgive debts.

dated his power. As the autocrat's time horizon lengthens, he faces a greater incentive to respect the property and contract rights of his subjects and to make efforts to secure the rights of private parties vis-à-vis one another. Thus we would expect that these rights would normally improve under autocracy as the autocrat remains longer in power.[2]

Similarly, newly established democracies may require time to consolidate the mosaic of institutions that characterize successful democratic polities. Executive branch adherence to the rulings of a supreme court, the education of voters, and the modalities of transparent administrative procedures do not emerge instantly. Rather, the multiple sources of authority that underpin successful democracies might in the early years, when decision-making procedures are underdeveloped and not well understood or accepted, create substantial uncertainties regarding property rights. Of course, duration is not the only factor that affects the solidity of democratic institutions. Some democracies of quite long duration have been replaced by autocracies (for example, Chile and Uruguay in the early 1970s and Turkey in 1980). One of the questions we examine here is whether property rights deteriorate in democracies that are perceived as failing.

The duration of a democratic regime is a straightforward concept—it is simply the number of consecutive years that a country has been a democracy. With regard to autocracies, however, the concept of regime duration is not so simple. Is there a new regime each time the leader himself changes? Or is there an autocratic group that may remain in power even while the person at the top is changed? Certain countries quite clearly fit one definition rather the other. There are *pure autocracies*, or cases of one-man rule, in which there are no rules of succession and no constraints on the dictator's freedom to change arrangements. At the other extreme are *institutionalized autocracies,* in which there are rules of succession and institutional constraints on the leader's power. Examples of the latter are Mexico under the PRI (the Institutional Revolutionary Party), Taiwan under Chiang Kai-shek and his son, some hereditary monarchies (Saudi Arabia, Kuwait, Morocco), and the communist regimes of the former Soviet bloc. In intermediate cases, a new leader comes into power peacefully and does not sharply break with the previous leader's arrangements, but there is

---

[2]There are cases of insecure autocrats who remain in power for long periods, despite facing repeated threats of being overthrown (Mobutu in Zaire is an example). If such cases could be identified, we would not expect property and contract rights to be well protected for these long-lasting dictators.

neither a strong political party constraining him nor the rules of a hereditary monarchy. In our empirical work, we employ two definitions: (1) the duration of the autocratic leader is the number of years the leader has been in power; (2) the duration of the autocratic group is the number of years the group has been in power, where we consider a new leader as part of the same group unless he comes to power through a coup d'état or is judged to represent a sharp break from the prior ruling group.

The issues that we address in this chapter should be distinguished from those in the recent literature on the political economy of economic policy reform (Nelson 1990; Haggard and Kaufman 1992; Bates and Krueger 1993; Williamson 1994; Haggard and Webb 1994). In this literature, the units of observation are episodes of successful or unsuccessful reform in macroeconomic, financial, foreign exchange, and trade policy. The present study is concerned with the state of contract and property rights, and observations are not limited to periods of attempted policy reforms. It would not be surprising if the effects of regime type and duration on economic outcomes differed in the two contexts. A theme of the policy reform literature is that democracies under "ordinary politics" (Balcerowicz 1994) might be less well equipped than autocracies to implement policy reform because of the blocking power of vested interests (see, for example, Haggard and Kaufman, 1992, chap. 6, on stopping inflation). When democracies have been successful in carrying out such reforms, the government frequently has been delegated substantial power in a time of crisis. "There is little substance to the claim that economic policy reform requires authoritarian government. But, on the basis of the evidence in the case studies, economic reform clearly leads to an increase in the power of the executive branch of the government and, in particular, of the financial units" (Bates and Krueger 1993, 462). The issue of whether democratic or authoritarian governments are more likely to implement policy reforms remains unsettled, but the point here is to draw attention to the fact that the considerations related to dramatic policy reform are not necessarily the same as those related to the maintenance of property and contract rights.

2   Recent Empirical Literature on Growth-Democracy Links

The Lipset proposition that growth or level of income favors the emergence or survival of democracy has often been supported by empirical studies (see the review in Diamond 1992). Recent studies embodying considerable statistical sophistication (in particular, using instrumental and lagged variables) come to the same conclusion (Burkhart and Lewis-Beck

1994; Helliwell 1994; Barro 1996). The literature is generally much less positive on the effects of democracy on growth. The three studies cited all find that democracy has either no influence or a negative influence on subsequent growth. On the other hand, a study by Bhalla (1994), also using instrumental variables, finds a positive effect of political rights on growth. The difference in results between Bhalla and the other authors seems to relate mainly to the choice of other independent variables.[3]

All four of these studies (as well as many others) make use of the Gastil measures of political rights and civil liberties: "Political rights are the rights to participate meaningfully in the political process. In a democracy this means the right of all adults to vote and compete for public office, and for elected representatives to have a decisive voice on public policies. Civil liberties are rights to free expression, to organize or demonstrate, as well as rights to a degree of autonomy such as is provided by freedom of religion, education, travel, and other personal rights" (Gastil 1989, 7). Gastil provides a checklist of rights under each category; the final scores are not a mechanical summary of the individual items but reflect the overall judgment of the raters. The Gastil measures include some rights that might be regarded as outcomes of political and economic processes rather than adherence to the procedures required for political democracy. For example, the civil liberties checklist includes "personal social rights, including those to property, internal and external travel, choice of residence, marriage, and family," "freedom from gross social inequality," "freedom from gross government indifference or corruption," and "socio-economic rights: including freedom from dependency on landlords, bosses, union leaders, or bureaucrats." The political rights checklist includes "recent shifts in power through elections," "significant opposition vote," and "informal consensus: de facto opposition power."[4] As explained below, our classification makes use of a purely procedural definition of democracy: basically, whether the political leaders

---

[3]We focus on these four studies because they make use of the most recent data on a large number of countries and because they pay careful attention to endogeneity problems. The earlier literature is also thoroughly inconclusive regarding the effects of democracy on growth. See, for examples, the review in Brunetti and Weder (1993).

[4]Barro uses only the political rights indicator, while the other three authors use the average or the sum of the two indicators. The two indicators are highly correlated; over the 1973–90 period, the correlation of annual figures was 0.896.

are chosen in competitive elections, whether the elections are fairly conducted, and whether freedoms of expression and association are respected.

Differences in the treatment of countries would arise in the following cases. A country might scrupulously respect the electoral laws and freedoms of speech and association and yet have a dominant political party (Botswana is an example). Or, a country with the same respect for electoral procedures and freedoms might still have government corruption, social inequality, and parts of the population dependent on landlords or union leaders (India and Jamaica might be examples). Conversely, an authoritarian regime may establish individual property rights, take steps to reduce social inequality, and, if it is not being threatened by critics, tolerate considerable freedom of expression and association. Because the Gastil measures incorporate outcomes for civil liberties associated with a "successfully functioning" democracy, it should be easier to find positive associations between the Gastil measures and property rights than between our procedurally defined democracy indicator and property rights. We plan to test this proposition in future work; we suspect, however, that the differences will not be dramatic. The simple Spearman rank-order correlations between our political regime indicator and the Gastil measures are quite high: 0.87 for political rights and 0.82 for civil liberties.

While the recent econometric literature (using mainly postwar data) does not support the hypothesis that democratic institutions are favorable to economic growth, if we step back in history we see that there has been a substantial connection between the institutions of representative government and individual rights of property and contract. To facilitate the collection of taxes, in preindustrial Europe kings acquiesced in the establishment of assemblies of nobles, and merchant-ruled towns set up their own representative bodies. The constraints on arbitrary action by rulers that were imposed by these assemblies and by independent judges greatly increased the security of contract and property rights. A particularly dramatic example is the establishment of parliamentary supremacy in England following the Glorious Revolution in 1688 (described in North and Weingast 1989). Further evidence is provided by the connection between nonabsolutist government and city growth in preindustrial Europe (deLong and Shleifer 1993).

Theoretical considerations help to explain why absolutism is inconsistent with secure property and contract rights (Grief, Milgrom, and Weingast 1994; Olson 1993). But there is nothing in the logic of separation of powers that requires that property rights be based on a broad franchise. These rights, however, rely on broad social acceptance, at least in the sense that the exercise of these rights does not meet with substantial resistance. In the eighteenth and early nineteenth centuries, social acceptance of property rights in this sense was compatible with representative institutions based on a very limited franchise, but there is virtually no country in the world today in which such an arrangement would not meet with resistance that would undermine these rights. Ironically, although the prevailing opinion in the early nineteenth century was that the extension of the franchise would undermine property rights, in fact the extension of the franchise in Western Europe and its British offshoots has been necessary for their preservation.

The close historical connection between the development of property and contract rights and the emergence of democratic political institutions poses problems for testing causal relationships. We believe, along with many others, that secure property and contract rights facilitate economic growth. Thus, a high level of income in a society today is an indication of good property rights institutions in the past, and, given the persistence of property rights, income is also a good predictor of current property rights. Moreover, many aspects of a political regime influence growth and hence, over time, the level of income: rule obedience, political legitimacy, bureaucratic competence, proclivity toward political violence, and social and economic inequality. These are also highly persistent over time. Hence, a high level of income in a society today also reflects a well-functioning regime in the past, and because of the persistence of these characteristics, it reflects the current political regime.

What makes our analysis possible is that independent forces produce changes in regime. In particular, there have been wars won by democracies (after which democracies were set up in countries that lacked them), and more important for our sample, there has been massive decolonization. But it remains true that current-period income contains a lot of information about the current state of property rights and political regime. This study uses some crude measures of political regime to try to detect the effect of regime on property rights, controlling for current income. Thus, the test is a demanding one.

3   Property Rights, Regime Types, and Regime Duration: The Data

3.1   Regime types

Our definition of democracy draws attention to the theoretical links between democratic institutions and property rights, as discussed in section

1. From our perspective, three important characteristics distinguish democracies from authoritarian governments: (1) the use of majority rule to select political leaders, (2) checks on the ability of majorities to expropriate the minorities, and (3) checks on decision makers placed either by voters or by other state entities, such as a legislature with respect to the executive. Such rules enhance the credibility of regime policies by establishing internal limits on future changes in property and contract rights. These considerations suggest the following procedural definition of democracy: in a democracy the chief executive and the legislature are both chosen in competitive elections, and the legislature is effective in the sense that it has considerable autonomy. In this definition, both presidential and parliamentary systems can be fully democratic. A regime falls short of full democracy if the elections are not fully competitive or if the executive's power is so predominant that the legislature does not provide an effective check on that power. The concept of democracy also includes political rights or freedoms such as free speech, the right to campaign freely, the right to form political parties, the right of peaceful demonstration, freedom from arbitrary arrest, and so forth. In our definition, these freedoms are implicit in the concept of competitive elections.

A full-fledged dictatorship, on the other hand, is a regime in which neither the chief executive nor the legislature is chosen in a competitive election or one in which the competitively elected legislature is rendered ineffective by a nonelected (or not competitively elected) executive.[5]

In our study, regimes are classified as much as possible on others' judgments, although in a few situations our own judgment is used to resolve ambiguities (see the appendix to this chapter). The basic sources of data on selection of the chief executive and effectiveness of the legislature are Gurr (1990) and Banks (1979). Our classification assigns a number from 1 to 5 to each country in each year, where these numbers have the following meanings:
1. Dictatorship
2. Almost dictatorship
3. Intermediate category
4. Almost democracy
5. Democracy

---

[5]The definitions of democracy and dictatorship refer exclusively to the characteristics of the national government. We do not attempt to characterize the selection of officials at the subnational levels.

These classifications are based on the variables executive competitiveness (XRCOMP) from Gurr and executive selection (EXSELEC) and legislative effectiveness (LEGEF) from Banks. Gurr and Banks provide two alternative judgments about the selection of the chief executive. Gurr's XRCOMP classifies countries into three categories with respect to how the chief executive is selected, loosely: (1) no elections or rigged elections, (2) dual/transitional, where there are two executives or there is a transition between selection and election, and (3) competitive election. Banks's EXSELEC provides essentially a two-way classification: the chief executive is either elected or not. Banks's LEGEF classifies countries into one of three categories with respect to the legislature: (1) no legislature or one that is rendered completely ineffective by domestic turmoil or by the actions of the chief executive, (2) a partially effective legislature, and (3) an effective legislature, elected under competitive conditions.

The five categories are derived from these variables in the following way. A full-fledged democracy is in the top category on all three variables, while a full-fledged dictatorship is in the bottom category on XRCOMP and LEGEF. An almost democracy falls short of the top rating on either XRCOMP or LEGEF, while an almost dictatorship is in the intermediate category on LEGEF. The other cases are classified in the intermediate category or are inconsistent (for example, because Gurr and Banks rate the chief executive differently, or because the legislature is rated as fully effective yet the chief executive was selected rather than elected).[6]

---

[6]Our conception of democracy is fundamentally consistent with those of Bollen (1990) and other political scientists who have adopted a procedural definition of democracy. There is a conceptual difference, though, between our scheme and those that add up the scores on different indicators. Such a methodology assumes that a characteristic contributes to the democratic nature of a regime independently of the level of other characteristics. However, the marginal productivity of an input (in this case, in producing democracy) usually depends on the level of other inputs. A dictator who tolerates freedom of the press during periods in which he feels secure in his position does not on that account become a more democratic ruler. Similarly, the fact that the ballots are counted honestly does not make a regime more democratic if important political alternatives are prevented from participating in the elections. As can be seen in the appendix of this chapter, our classification of regimes into the five categories does not yield a ranking identical to one obtained from a mechanical adding up of the scores on each of the three indicators.

The Gurr and Banks data are available only through 1986. Our judgment was used to update the variables in our regime codings to 1990, relying primarily on the *Europa Yearbook*. Only seven countries were changed classification between 1986 and 1990. As a check on our results from the Gurr-Banks scheme, we constructed a measure based on the classification of countries for 1988 provided by Hadenius (1992), which provides two equally weighted components: elections and freedoms. For consistency with our Gurr-Banks scheme, the comparison is made with Hadenius's elections component only. Ratings are the same for 100 of the 119 countries with data from both sources; in 11 cases, there are discrepancies of one category and in 8 cases, of two categories. The simple correlation of the two scores, treating them as interval scales, exceeds .90.[7]

3.2 Regime duration

Autocratic leader duration (AUTDUR) is defined as the number of consecutive years that the chief executive in an autocratic nation (in either classification 1 or 2) has been in power.[8] The variable is reset to 1 in any year in which the chief executive changes. The duration of the autocratic group (AUTGROUP) is not reset to 1 in cases in which the new leader comes to power by peaceful means and is not judged to represent a sharp break with the previous ruling group. AUTGROUP is reset to 1 whenever there is a coup d'état or when the new leader is clearly not associated with the old ruling group.

For democracies, two duration measures were created: DEMDUR refers to the number of consecutive years that a country has been a democracy (i.e., regime category 4 or 5), while DEXDUR is the number of years that the chief executive has been in office in a democracy. Thus, DEMDUR is reset to 1 in any year in which the country lapses from democratic status (i.e., fails to remain in either category 4 or 5), while DEXDUR is reset to 1 in any year in which the chief executive changes. The observations on property rights variables begin in 1969. In measuring duration of regimes, we go back no further than 1930. Since the regressions use the log of duration, little is lost by not carrying the regime types back before 1930.

---

[7]Details on the construction of the regime index using the Hadenius scores can be found in Clague et al. (1994).

[8]When a democratic leader becomes an autocrat, as Marcos of the Philippines did in 1972, AUTDUR is defined as the number of years that the autocratic leader has been in power, including his years as a democratic leader.

Our maintained hypothesis is that, for democracies, new leaders are constrained in their ability to alter the property and contract rights established in previous administrations. Consequently, investors are concerned with the expected longevity of democracy more than with the expected tenure of a leader. Autocrats, on the other hand, are relatively unconstrained in their ability to disregard previously established rights. This makes the tenure of individual autocrats, or of autocratic groups, more important to investors than the length of time that a country has been continuously ruled by autocrats.

Regime duration variables are employed as proxies for the expected future life of a regime. One check on the validity of this proxy is the correlation between duration and the likelihood of a coup. The probability of a coup among autocracies was calculated for 1948–82 as a ratio of the number of autocrats deposed by a coup in year t of their tenure to the number of autocrats with tenure greater than or equal to $t - 1$. The probabilities of both successful and unsuccessful coup attempts are quite high in the first five years of autocrat tenure, and they decline dramatically as tenure increases. The probability of a coup attempt (including a successful coup) is 32 percent for autocracies that are at most one year old, 20 percent for autocracies that are at most two years old, and falls below 10 percent for most tenures exceeding six years. These findings suggest that autocrat tenure is a reasonable approximation of regime stability. A similar calculation was made for democracies. Again, the probabilities of successful and unsuccessful coups tend to decline as the duration of democracy within a country increases.

3.3   Property rights, contract rights, and control variables

Property and contract rights are measured by the variables described in chapter 4: the index from International Country Risk Guide (ICRG), the index from Business Environmental Risk Intelligence (BERI), and contract-intensive money (CIM). Our sample period is 1969–90. CIM is available starting in 1969 for 104 countries; BERI starts in 1972 and includes 49 countries; ICRG is available only from 1982 and includes 101 countries. Given the dearth of empirical literature on the determinants of property rights, there are very few precedents to guide us on model specification. We include only (the log of) per capita income and time as control variables in our regressions. As explained at the end of section 2, income incorporates a good deal of information about past property rights and the past characteristics of the political regime, so that controlling for income makes for a demanding test of the effects of political regime variables on property rights.

4 Empirical Findings on Regime Type, Regime Duration, and Property and Contract Rights

Several types of regressions were run. In the first type, the observations were grouped by regime. A country with, for example, an autocratic ruler from 1960 to 1972, another autocrat from 1973 to 1983, and democracy from 1984 through 1990 would be represented in our sample by three regimes. For each regime, the dependent and independent variables are averaged over the years corresponding to that regime.[9]

Table 5.1 displays regressions of the three property rights variables, CIM, ICRG, and BERI, on the log of income, time, and a dummy for an autocratic regime. In this and all our regressions, we omit regimes in category 3. Thus, the democracies are the other regimes in the regression. The coefficient on the autocracy dummy is negative for all three dependent variables and is significant for the first two.[10] Holding income and time constant, an autocracy is expected to have a value of CIM 0.05 lower than a democracy; this amounts to a third of a standard deviation. Other things equal, an autocracy scores 6 points lower on the ICRG index, or about half a standard deviation.

The income coefficient is highly significant for all three dependent variables. As mentioned earlier, this variable probably captures a good deal of reverse causation, in that countries with good property rights tend to grow rapidly and to achieve high levels of income. The coefficient on time is significantly positive in the CIM regression. Time is probably capturing some secular improvements in banking technology as well as people's increased confidence in banks. The time coefficient is positive for the ICRG index and negative for the BERI index, reflecting the fact that ICRG

---

[9]Some regimes lasted less than one year while others lasted thirty or more years. Accordingly, we reran all the tests weighting observations by the square root of duration of the regime. Results on regime type and duration vary somewhat from OLS but not in a consistent direction, and they lead to similar conclusions. Furthermore, the error variance of the unweighted regressions is generally uncorrelated with regime duration. We therefore report OLS rather than WLS results in our tables.

[10]Since CIM is a monetary variable, it is possible that inflation and the real interest rate, as well as property rights, affect it. We have found in other work (Clague et al. 1995) that the property rights interpretation of CIM is robust to the inclusion of inflation and real interest rate variables.

scores tend to drift up over time, while BERI scores seem to reflect the relative positions of countries rather than absolute values for property rights.

Table 5.1

Regime Type and Property Rights
Cross-Sectional Regressions

	Dependent Variable		
Independent Variable	CIM	ICRG Index	BERI Index
Intercept	-0.057	-25.154	-7.023
	(0.067)	(9.255)	(2.245)
Log (income)	0.101*	5.567*	1.950*
	(0.008)	(0.779)	(0.198)
Time	0.0047*	0.610	-0.022
	(.0013)	(0.353)	(0.053)
Autocracy	-0.051*	-5.995*	-0.446
	(0.015)	(1.652)	(0.505)
Adjusted R^2	.50	.57	.50
N	240	137	93

Note: Table entries are regression coefficients, with White-corrected standard errors in parentheses. Autocracy dummy = 1 for regime types 1 and 2, = 0 for regime types 4 and 5. CIM = contract-intensive money. ICRG and BERI are property rights indexes and are described in chapter 4.
*Signicant at .05 or better, two-tailed test.

Next, we introduced duration variables into the regressions. In these regressions, the autocracies are separated from the democracies: there are two measures of regime duration for autocracies, AUTDUR and AUTGROUP, and two for democracies, DEMDUR and DEXDUR. In each regression, the log of one of these measures is included, along with income and time, as regressors. The coefficients on the duration variables are displayed in table 5.2. In the autocratic regimes, leader duration and autocratic group duration have positive coefficients for all three property rights variables: thus longer lasting regimes provide better property rights. Three of the six coefficients are significant at the 5 percent level. The *R*-squares tend to be a little higher for AUTGROUP regressions, indicating that perhaps this is the better variable for measuring duration. In democratic regimes, coefficients for regime duration (DEMDUR) are uniformly higher and more significant than those for leader duration (DEXDUR). The ICRG and BERI coefficients are significant at the 5 percent level. The fact that the coefficients are higher for DEMDUR than for DEXDUR is consistent with our hypothesis that property and contract rights depend on the expected duration of the democratic regime itself rather than on the expected tenure of the chief executive. All three DEMDUR coefficients are also uniformly higher than those for either of the autocratic regime duration variables, indicating that regime duration matters more for democracies than for autocracies.

The predicted values of CIM, ICRG, and BERI corresponding to selected values of income and duration are displayed in table 5.3. For short-duration regimes, autocracies tend to perform better than democracies, particularly at annual income levels below $2,500. Further, for long-duration regimes at an annual income level of $5,000, democratic regimes outperform autocratic ones. Since democratic regimes tend to last longer than autocratic ones, an appropriate comparison might be between a democratic regime of twenty-five years and an autocratic one of ten years, a comparison that favors democracies at both income levels. These calculations suggest a ranking of regimes in terms of their provision of property rights, and the best regime proves to be a lasting democracy (unless the country's income level is very low).[11] The worst regimes are short-duration ones, and among these, autocracies tend to perform better than democracies. Long-duration autocracies are in an intermediate position, being worse than long-lasting democracies but better than short-duration regimes.

These regressions support the hypothesis that democratic political institutions are favorable for property rights and that regime duration for both democracies and autocracies improves these rights. Another way of illustrating this conclusion is to employ countries as units of observation and put in a dummy variable for long-lasting democracies (LASTDEM). Annual

---

[11] At low annual income levels (say $500) the predicted values for democracies are very low for ICRG and BERI (although not for CIM). For what they are worth, these predictions say that very low-income democracies do not tend to provide good property rights, but these income values lie far from the mean income of democracies, and thus the predictions are of less-than-average reliability.

Table 5.2

Regime Duration and Property Rights:
Summary of Country-Regimes Cross-Sectional Regressions

Sample		Dependent Variable		
		CIM	ICRG Index	BERI Index
Autocrats	B	0.007	1.351*	0.240
(AUTDUR)	(standard error)	(0.008)	(0.524)	(0.154)
	Adjusted R^2	.34	.10	.31
	N	174	84	53
Autocratic groups	B	0.010	2.398*	0.486*
(AUTGROUP)	(standard error)	(0.009)	(0.433)	(0.165)
	Adjusted R^2	.30	.21	.36
	N	131	71	34
Democratic regimes	B	0.018	5.303*	0.854*
(DEMDUR)	(standard error)	(0.011)	(1.142)	(0.269)
	Adjusted R^2	.58	.81	.69
	N	66	53	40
Democratic leaders	B	.0087	0.764	0.416*
(DEXDUR)	(standard error)	(.0045)	(0.850)	(0.154)
	Adjusted R^2	.54	.69	.59
	N	248	111	157

Note: Table entries show coefficients and (White-corrected) standard errors for duration variables. The duration variable is the log of the number of years the regime lasts. Independent variables in addition to regime duration include the log of per capita income and time (= year − 1969). AUTDUR = autocratic leader duration. AUTGROUP = autocratic group duration. DEMDUR = democratic regime duration. DEXDUR = democratic leader duration. CIM = contract-intensive money. ICRG and BERI are property rights indexes and are described in chapter 4.
*Significant at .05 or better.

Table 5.3

Predicted Values of Property Rights Variables

| | Duration and Income Values | | | | | |
| | $2500 | | | $5000 | | |
	2 yrs.	10 yrs.	25 yrs.	2 yrs.	10 yrs.	25 yrs.
CIM						
Aut(G)	.720	.736	.746	.791	.807	.817
Dem(R)	.766	.795	.812	.806	.835	.852
ICRG						
Aut(G)	13.94	17.80	20.00	14.93	18.79	20.99
Dem(R)	6.30	14.83	19.69	11.05	19.58	24.44
BERI						
Aut(G)	6.57	7.35	7.79	7.08	7.86	8.31
Dem(R)	5.12	6.49	7.27	6.65	8.02	8.80

Note: Values calculated from regressions shown in table 5.2. Aut(G) = autocratic group, Dem(R) = democratic regime.

observations are grouped over 1969–90 for CIM, over 1982–90 for ICRG, and over 1973–90 for BERI (with deletions of years for which there were missing data). The independent variables are the log of income, time, and LASTDEM. The coefficients (standard errors) on LASTDEM in these three regressions were 0.058 (0.032) for CIM, 11.71 (1.93) for ICRG, and 2.38 (0.59) for BERI. Omission of the OECD countries does not much change the coefficients: 0.088 (0.041) for CIM, 6.75 (2.29) for ICRG, and 2.16 (0.79) for BERI.

All of these regressions, however, are subject to the qualification that they may be driven by unmeasured country characteristics. That is, the more favorable property rights in democracies may not be due solely to the democratic institutions but also to other country characteristics correlated with democracy. This is a fundamental limitation of these regressions. A way of overcoming this limitation is to run regressions on the annual observations, including country dummies to control for country-specific fixed effects, a procedure that exploits the time-series variation in the data.

Table 5.4 displays fixed-effects regressions of the three property rights variables on the log of income and the autocracy dummy, with country dummies and year dummies as additional regressors. In these regressions, the autocracy coefficient is influenced only by temporal variation in regime democracy or only autocracy type; that is, countries that experienced only a change in leadership rather than type of regime over the sample period do not influence the coefficient on the autocracy dummy. The autocracy coefficient in these regressions addresses the question, What is the effect of a shift into, or out of, the autocracy category? The autocracy coefficients are all positive, and two of them are significant. The positive signs indicate that a shift from democracy to autocracy is favorable to property rights, while a shift in the other direction is unfavorable to them. These favorable results for autocracy are the product of a relatively small number of countries that experienced shifts between autocracy and democracy during the sample period.[12]

Upon reflection, a temporary worsening of property rights and policies associated with a shift toward democracy is unsurprising. New democracies in recent years are hardly a random sample of all democracies. These "marginal" democracies exhibit a substantially worse income distribution, more ethnic tensions, and more political violence than that exhibited by countries that remained democracies throughout the 1970s and 1980s. Social conditions often subject these new democracies to extraordinary populist pressures, which autocrats in these same countries are (sometimes) better able to resist.[13]

---

[12]One-way shifts from autocracy to democracy during our sample period occurred in Pakistan (1988), Portugal (1976), Spain (1978), Dominican Republic (1978), Guatemala (1985), Bolivia (1986), Brazil (1985), and Peru (1980). One-way shifts from democracy to autocracy occurred in Lesotho (1970) and Sierra Leone (1973). Shifts in both directions occurred in Ghana, Nigeria, the Philippines, Thailand, Greece, Turkey, El Salvador, Argentina, Chile, Ecuador, and Uruguay.

[13]Keefer and Knack (1995) find that income distribution is a more important determinant of property rights and risk of loan defaults in democracies than in autocracies. Persson and Tabellini (1994) find that inequality is harmful to growth, particularly in democracies. One could alternatively interpret a significant interaction between democracy and inequality in growth equations as implying that democracy is beneficial to growth only where there exists a suitably egalitarian distribution of income.

Moreover, there are selection processes at work in the movements between autocracy and democracy that tend to impart a positive sign on the autocracy dummy in these fixed-effects regressions. Autocracies almost never replace democracies unless the latter are performing poorly—when their legitimacy in the eyes of the public is especially low. On the other hand, democracies are quite likely to replace economically successful autocracies. With the prominent exception of Argentina, autocrats giving way to new democratic regimes during our sample period generally chose to do so when the economic climate was favorable for a smooth transition to democracy. Given these selection processes, the autocracy coefficient in fixed-effects tests is conceivably capturing a regression-to-the-mean effect: autocrats succeeding democracies have more opportunity to improve the policy climate than do leaders of democracies succeeding autocrats. Finally,

Table 5.4

**Regime Type and Property Rights
Fixed-Effects Regressions**

Independent Variable	Dependent Variable					
	CIM	ICRG Index	BERI Index	Credit Risk	Currency Depreciation	Black Market Premium
Log income	0.089*	0.922	1.815*	35.054	-0.188*	-0.522*
	(0.008)	(0.960)	(0.217)	(1.760)	(0.017)	(0.070)
Autocracy	0.015*	0.173	0.446*	-0.148	-0.047*	-0.069
	(0.005)	(0.508)	(0.114)	(1.015)	(0.011)	(0.045)
R^2	.92	.97	.93	.97	.62	.53
N	1977	768	812	951	1828	1612

Note: Autocracy dummy = 1 for regime types 1 and 2, = 0 for regime types 4 and 5. Additional regressors include year and country dummies. CIM, ICRG, and BERI are defined in table 5.2. Credit risk is a rating of the riskiness of a country's foreign debt. Currency depreciation = inflation/(100 + inflation). Black market premium is the premium on foreign exchange.
*Significant at .05 or better.

Christopher Clague et al.

the coefficients on the autocracy dummy may be influenced by the short duration of democracy in many of the observations in countries that have changed regimes. Given results shown in table 5.2, it would not be surprising if newly established democracies failed to offer much protection for property rights. To address this question, we include duration variables in the fixed-effects regressions.

Table 5.5

Regime Duration and Property Rights: Fixed-Effects Models

Sample		Dependent Variable		
		CIM	ICRG Index	BERI Index
Autocrats	B	0.013*	0.499*	0.574*
(AUTDUR)	(Standard error)	(0.002)	(0.162)	(0.076)
	R^2	.89	.93	.82
	N	1082	394	275
Autocratic groups	B	0.014*	0.818*	0.992*
(AUTGROUP)	(standard error)	(0.003)	(0.215)	(0.100)
	R^2	.89	.93	.84
	N	1082	394	275
Democratic regimes	B	-0.016*	0.430	-0.366*
(DEMDUR)	(Standard error)	(0.002)	(0.481)	(0.061)
	R^2	.86	.98	.96
	N	895	374	537
Democratic leaders	B	-0.0012	0.112	-0.017
(DEXDUR)	(Standard error)	(.0015)	(0.169)	(0.038)
	R^2	.86	.98	.96
	N	895	374	537

Note: The duration variable is the log of the number of years the regime lasts. Independent variables in addition to regime duration include the log of income, year dummies, and country dummies.
*Significant at .05 or better.

These regressions are displayed in table 5.5. As before, the autocratic observations are separated from the democratic ones, and the three property rights variables are regressed on the log of income and the log of one of the duration variables, with country and year dummies as additional regressors. In the autocracy samples, all the duration coefficients are positive and significant, indicating that long-lasting autocracies provide better property rights than short-duration ones. Thus, these fixed-effects results reinforce the cross-regimes findings reported in table 5.2. Not being based on differences across countries, these fixed-effects results are not subject to concerns that they might be reflecting the influence of unmeasured country characteristics.[14]

In the sample of democratic leaders, the coefficients are quite insignificant, indicating that there is little connection between leader duration and property rights, as expected. The sample of democratic regimes, however, displays two (out of three) negative and significant coefficients on regime duration. These results are at first sight surprising, since they seem to say that property rights deteriorate as a democratic regime ages. This unexpected outcome is largely due to three countries in our sample in which long-standing democracies failed to manage the economy well and were replaced by autocracies that enacted extensive economic reforms. Subsequently, these autocracies relinquished power to new democratic regimes. Thus, our sample contains several years of a long-duration democracy with poor property rights, followed several years later by a new democracy with quite good property rights. The three countries that fit this pattern are Chile (autocracy 1973–88), Uruguay (autocracy 1973–84), and Turkey (autocracy 1980–87).[15] Their experience underlines the point that democratic regimes differ in their economic effectiveness. In the next section we attempt to explain why some work better than others.

---

[14]Reverse causation is a possible concern with these results in that autocratic regimes that perform well economically may have a tendency to last longer. In Clague et al. (1996), we address the reverse causation issue and conclude that our results are not primarily due to its effects.

[15]Removal of these three countries makes the coefficients on duration for both CIM and ICRG insignificant.

5   Long-Lasting Democracies in the Third World

We find that in comparisons across countries property rights and lasting democracy are positively associated but that shifts to democracy within a country are not associated (in the short run, at least) with improvements in property rights. These findings do not permit us to establish the direction of causation between democracy and property rights. We provide arguments in section 1 that democratic institutions are favorable to property rights, but it could also be argued that good property rights, by facilitating economic growth, enable democracies to last. This mechanism seems unlikely to account for the whole of the positive association between lasting democracy and property rights, because economic performance is only one determinant of whether democracies last, and its quantitative importance is in dispute. Probably a more weighty argument against inferring causation running from lasting democracy to secure property rights from our cross-section results is the possibility that other country characteristics influence both democracy and property rights. It is plausible that a low degree of social and economic inequality, and the absence of racial and ethnic divisions, are country characteristics conducive to both democracy and secure property rights. If this is the story behind our cross-section results, then we cannot make the argument that, if countries lacking such characteristics were to hold honest elections, they would develop into lasting democracies with secure property rights.

Let us look at the lasting democracies in the Third World to see if the story about the absence of cleavages rings true. There are nine Third World countries in our sample that have had uninterrupted democracy since 1969 (or since independence, if that came later): Barbados, Botswana, Costa Rica, India, Jamaica, Mauritius, Singapore, Sri Lanka,[16] and Trinidad and Tobago. (Two other lasting democracies that were poor in 1950 are Israel and Japan. We leave them out of the discussion on grounds that they are not considered to be part of the Third World, but their inclusion would not alter our conclusions.) These countries do not stand out for their lack of cleavages along economic, social, or racial lines. There are racial or caste divisions in all of them except Botswana and Costa Rica. Income inequality seems to be rather high in most of them (Singapore and perhaps Sri Lanka being ex-

---

[16]Sri Lanka actually had one year of interruption in 1977; India also had its "emergency" in 1975–76. In both cases, democratic institutions were quickly restored.

ceptions). All but Costa Rica have one distinguishing characteristic: they are former British colonies. This status is clearly not the whole story, for there are many former British colonies that have not enjoyed lasting democratic institutions. But there is a common element in their colonial history: they acquired practice in democratic electoral and judicial institutions while the British still monopolized coercion. Political parties and unions were allowed to form and to organize large sections of the population.

This observation of a connection between British tutelage and democracy does not resolve the questions of causation with which we began this section. It is still plausible that causation runs both ways between secure property rights and lasting democratic institutions and that both have been directly caused by British tutelage. What the examples do suggest, however, is that even very poor countries may enjoy lasting democracy if they get off to the right start. This proposition runs counter to the Lipset thesis that a reasonably high per capita income is necessary for the maintenance of democracy.[17]

The notion that democracy can exist and survive in poor countries with sharp racial, social, and economic cleavages seems counterintuitive, given that poverty and social cleavages impair the toleration needed for successful democracy. But this notion is consistent with an institutional interpretation of the behavior of political leaders. One way of thinking about the matter is as follows: what preserves democracy is the general knowledge that assaults on it will be resisted, and such resistance can be provided by organizations whose members believe they have a stake in continued democracy. That is, the survival of democracy does not depend on the benevolence of its leaders but on the calculation by them and by other political entrepreneurs that they cannot become autocratic rulers of the country. An NIE interpretation of the preservation of democracy stresses the consistency of behavior with self-interest, while recognizing that attitudes and values in the population, and organized interests in the political sphere, shape the incentives facing political entrepreneurs.

---

[17]For a recent interesting statistical model supporting Lipset, see Barro 1996. In Barro's model, the expected value of the Gastil political rights index in one decade is a function of the past level of the index, of income, and of some human capital variables. Countries with low income levels and high Gastil scores are expected to lose political rights as time passes.

6   Conclusions and Policy Implications

The findings from the statistical work reported in this chapter may be summarized as follows. First, there is rather solid evidence that long-duration autocracies provide better property rights than short-duration autocracies. This result is supported both by cross-section regressions (table 5.2) and by fixed-effects regressions (table 5.5). Unmeasured country characteristics cannot account for the latter result.

Second, there is cross-sectional evidence that long-lasting democracies provide better property rights than long-duration autocracies or short-duration regimes of either type. Fixed-effects regressions, however, do not indicate that replacement of autocracy by democracy improves property rights or that movements of regimes in the other direction make them worse. In fact, the results indicate the reverse: shifts in the direction of autocracy are associated with improvements in property rights.

The prospects for lasting democracy seem to depend on a variety of country characteristics, including the level of income, the degree of social and economic inequality, the degree of ethnic and racial tensions, qualities of the government bureaucracy, the presence or absence of the experience of British tutelage, and probably other country characteristics not currently known or measurable. Many country characteristics favorable to lasting democracy are also favorable to good economic policy and good property rights, even apart from their effects on democracy. Hence, it is difficult to nail down the causal effects of democracy on property rights and economic performance.

Theoretical considerations as well as historical evidence support the proposition that long-lasting democracy is favorable for property rights, and this chapter provides statistical evidence that is consistent with that proposition. Thus, we argue that democracy is likely to be beneficial for property rights in countries where it stands a good chance to last. For countries that, for one reason or another, lack the conditions needed for stable democracy, our data do not support those who claim that democracy is the key to improving the economic institutions favorable to economic growth. For a country for which stable democracy is not a feasible option, a durable autocracy with a leader who is rationally maximizing his long-term tax extraction may be, among the available political arrangements, the one most favorable to property rights.

Appendix: The Gurr-Banks Annual Scheme

The basic variables:

2.2 XRCOMP (Gurr 1990):
    0. Applies to situations in which power transfers are coded "unregulated" in variable 2.1 or involve a transition to or from unregulated
    1. The selection of chief executive (by hereditary succession, or rigged elections, or coups, or military designation, or repeated incumbent selection of successors)
    2. Dual/transitional: dual means two executives, one chosen by hereditary succession, the other by competitive election (Also used for transitional arrangements between selection and election)
    3. The election of chief executive (competitive election)

9.7 EXSELEC (Banks 1979):
    1. Direct election
    2. Indirect election
    3. Nonelective

9.12 LEGEF (Banks 1979):
    0. None
    1. Ineffective: either a rubber-stamp legislature, or domestic turmoil makes the implementation of legislation impossible, or the effective executive prevents the legislature from meeting or substantially impedes the exercise of its function
    2. Partially effective: the effective executive's power substantially outweighs but does not completely dominate that of the legislature
    3. Effective: significant governmental autonomy by the legislature

Classifications (see table 5A.1):
    1. Dictatorship (DI)
    2. Almost dictatorship (ADIC)
    3. Intermediate category (I)
    4. Almost democracy (ADEM)
    5. Democracy (DE)
    6. Empty (EM; category predicted to be empty)

Christopher Clague et al.

Table 5A.1: Definitions of Regime Classifications

#	XRCOMP			EXSELEC		LEGEF			DI	ADIC	I	ADEM	DE	EM
	0,1	2	3	1,2	3	0,1	2	3						
1	X				X	X			1					
2	X				X		X			1				
3	X				X			X						N
4		X			X	X					I			
5		X			X		X				I			
6		X			X			X						N
7			X		X	X								N
8			X		X		X							N
9			X		X			X						N
10	X			X		X			1					
11	X			X			X			1				
12	X			X				X						N
13		X		X		X				1				
14		X		X			X				I			
15		X		X				X				1		
16			X	X		X					I			
17			X	X			X					1		
18			X	X				X					1	

Note that EXSELEC becomes irrelevant in the classification of a dictatorship. If XRCOMP is judged not to be competitive, it doesn't matter whether the executive is elected or not. *Almost democracy* (ADEM) falls short of democracy in XRCOMP or LEGEF by one category. *Almost dictatorship* (ADIC) falls short of dictatorship in LEGEF by one category. In other words, an *almost democracy* is a regime of either of two types: (1) it has an effective legislature and an elected executive, but the elected executive may share power with a hereditary ruler or there may be a transitional arrangement between selection and election of the chief executive; or (2) the regime has a chief executive that is competitively elected, but that executive dominates the legislature to the degree that the legislature is only partially effective. An *almost dictatorship* differs from the genuine variety in that there is a legislature, which is partially effective. Like the true dictator, the almost dictator has not been elected by competitive vote.

Intermediate regimes: There are eighteen logically possible combinations of XRCOMP, EXSELEC, and LEGEF as displayed in table 5A.1. The intermediate combinations are five in number. Three of them (cases 4, 13, and 16) involve a totally ineffective legislature, with a chief executive that is either competitively elected or a dual/transitional case. The other two (cases 5 and 14) involve a partially effective legislature and a dual/transitional executive. All of these cases seem to be correctly classified as intermediate between almost democracy and almost dictatorship. The six cases in the EMPTY column are the ones that seem inconsistent. Four of the six cases (cases 3, 6, 9, and 12) involve a highly effective legislature combined with a chief executive that is not competitively elected or not elected at all. Case 7 has a competitively elected chief executive and a totally ineffective legislature. Case 8 has a competitively elected chief executive in XRCOMP and a nonelected chief executive in EXSELEC.

Table 5A.2

XRCOMP			EXECSELEC		LEGEF				
0,1	2	3	1,2	3	0,1	2	3	ADEM	ADIC
	X		X				X	1	0
		X	X			X		1	0
X	X			X		X		0	1

Updating Gurr-Banks: The data run through 1986. The annual data were extended to 1990 by Suzanne Gleason on the basis of the information in the *Europa Yearbook*. The countries in table 5A.3 were judged to have changed category between 1986 and 1990.

Table 5A.3
Regime Changes in Sample Period

Country	Year	Regime change
Lesotho	1990	1-3
Sierra Leone	1990	3-4
Pakistan	1988	1-5
Philippines	1986	1-4
Suriname	1987	1-5
Fiji	1987	5-1
Vanuatu	1989	5-1

References

Balcerowicz, Leszek. 1994. "Poland." In Williamson, ed., *The Political Economy of Policy Reform.*
Banks, Arthur S. 1979. "Cross-National Time Series Data Archive." Center for Social Analysis, State University of New York at Binghamton.
Barro, Robert. 1996. "Democracy and Growth." *Journal of Economic Growth* 1: 1–27.
Bates, Robert H., and Anne O. Krueger, eds. 1993. *Political and Economic Interactions in Economic Policy Reform.* Oxford: Blackwell.
Bhalla, Surjit. 1994. "Freedom and Economic Growth: A Virtuous Circle?" Paper prepared for Nobel Symposium Democracy's Victory and Crisis, Uppsala University, Sweden, August 27–30.
Bollen, Kenneth A. 1990. "Political Democracy: Conceptual and Measurement Traps." *Studies in Comparative Economic Development* 25: 7–24.
Brunetti, Aymo, and Beatrice Weder. 1993. "Political Sources of Growth: A Critical Note on Measurement." *Public Choice* 82: 125–34.

Burkhart, Ross, and Michael Lewis-Beck. 1994. "Comparative Democracy: The Economic Development Thesis." *American Political Science Review* 88: 903–10.

Clague, Christopher, Philip Keefer, Stephen Knack, and Mancur Olson. 1994. "Institutions and Economic Progress: A New Look at Democracies and Economic Growth." Paper prepared for the Eastern Economic Association Meetings, March.

———. 1995. "Contract-Intensive Money: Property Rights, Contract Enforcement, and Economic Performance." Working Paper 151. IRIS, College Park, Md.

———. 1996. "Property and Contract Rights in Autocracies and Democracies," *Journal of Economic Growth* 1: 243–76.

deLong, J. Bradford, and Andre Shleifer. 1993. "Princes and Merchants: European City Growth before the Industrial Revolution." *Journal of Law and Economics* 36: 671–702.

Diamond, Larry. 1992. "Economic Development and Democracy Reconsidered." In *Re-examining Democracy: Essays in Honor of Seymour Martin Lipset*, ed. Gary Marks and Larry Diamond. London: Sage.

Gastil, Raymond D. 1989. *Freedom in the World*. New York: Freedom House.

Greif, Avner, Paul Milgrom, and Barry Weingast. 1994. "Coordination, Commitment, and Enforcement: The Case of the Merchant Guild." *Journal of Political Economy* 102: 745–76.

Gurr, Ted Robert. 1990. *Polity II: Political Structures and Regime Change, 1800–1986*. 1st ICPSR ed. Ann Arbor, Mich., Inter-University Consortium for Political and Social Research.

Hadenius, Axel. 1992. *Democracy and Development*. Cambridge: Cambridge University Press.

Haggard, Stephan, and Robert R. Kaufman, eds. 1992. *The Politics of Adjustment: International Constraints, Distributive Conflicts, and the State*. Princeton: Princeton University Press.

Haggard, Stephan, and Steven Webb, eds. 1994. *Voting for Reform: Democracy, Political Liberalization, and Economic Adjustment*. New York: Oxford University Press.

Helliwell, John F. 1994. "Empirical Linkages between Democracy and Economic Growth." *British Journal of Political Science* 24: 225–48.

Keefer, Philip, and Stephen Knack. 1995. "Polarization, Property Rights, and the Links between Inequality and Growth." Working Paper 153. IRIS, College Park, Md.

Lipset, Seymour Martin. 1959. "Some Social Requisites of Democracy: Economic Development and Political Legitimacy." *American Political Science Review* 53: 69–105.

Nelson, Joan, ed. 1990. *Economic Crisis and Policy Choice: The Politics of Adjustment in the Third World.* Princeton: Princeton University Press.

North, Douglass C., and Barry R. Weingast. 1989. "Constitutions and Commitment: The Evolution of Institutions Governing Public Choice in 17th Century England." *Journal of Economic History* 49: 809–32.

Olson, Mancur. 1993. "Dictatorship, Democracy, and Development." *American Political Science Review* 87: 567–76.

Persson, Torsten, and Guido Tabellini. 1994. "Is Inequality Harmful for Growth?" *American Economic Review* 84: 600–21.

Williamson, John, ed. 1994. *The Political Economy of Policy Reform.* Washington, D.C.: Institute for International Economics.

6 Democratic Institutions, Economic Policy, and Development

Stephan Haggard

The relationship between regime type and economic development has long been a theme in the political economy literature, but the question has gained new salience with the global wave of democratization. Most new democratic governments have come to office facing daunting problems of short-term economic adjustment and long-term growth. This conjuncture of economic crisis and regime change raises the question of how the promotion of democracy and development can be most effectively combined.

Cross-national empirical evidence on the relationship between regime type and economic performance remains highly contested. Recent surveys by Sirowy and Inkeles (1990), Przeworski and Limongi (1993), and Helliwell (1994) find highly conflicting results and conclude that there is no strong relationship one way or another. There may well be a relationship between the protection of property rights and growth, but an established property rights regime should not be confused with democracy. There are also other features of political systems, such as their stability (Alesina 1994a, 1994b), that affect policy and growth, but these should not be confused with democracy, either.

Even if there were evidence that democracies outperformed autocracies (see chap. 5), we would still be interested in explaining the wide variation that exists *among* them. There are a handful of stable, developing country democracies (or semidemocracies) that have fared reasonably well in economic terms, including Costa Rica and Malaysia. There are other countries, such as India, where democratic rule has arguably contributed to sluggish, though not disastrous, performance. There are also a number of "populist" democratic governments, such as Peru under Alan Garcia, that pursued disastrous economic policies that ran directly counter to the interests of the constituents they purportedly served (Dornbusch and Edwards 1991).

Research is beginning to explore the effects that variations in democratic institutions might have on economic policy and performance; this

---

I wish to thank Christopher Clague, Joan Nelson, Robert Kaufman, and Matthew Shugart for their comments on this chapter and Ed Chan for research assistance. This work draws at a number of points on Haggard and Kaufman (1995).

chapter provides an introduction to some of this literature. I begin with an analysis of the political problems associated with initiating and sustaining growth-promoting policies, before digressing briefly to comment on interest group approaches to public policy. This theoretical approach—dominant among economists—carries pessimistic implications for democratic theory, since it suggests a trade-off between efficiency and civic association.

Fortunately, interest group analysis is highly misleading unless coupled with a careful analysis of the institutional setting in which groups operate. In the final three sections, I turn to the question of how variations in several core democratic institutions might affect the organization of interests and the policy process, examining the effects of parliamentary versus presidential rule, different party systems, and the constitution of executive authority. I pay particular attention to the way institutions generate incentives for the fragmentation and polarization of interests and the pursuit of particularistic electoral strategies by politicians. Though systematic cross-national evidence on the economic effects of democratic institutions is lacking, I draw examples from recent comparative studies on the political economy of policy reform in developing countries (Nelson 1990; Bates and Krueger 1993; Williamson 1994; Haggard and Webb 1994; Haggard and Kaufman 1995).

1   The Political Barriers to Economic Reform

For the newly emerging democracies of the developing and formerly socialist countries, the transition to the market involves a difficult set of economic reforms. Although there is no firm consensus on either the precise content of these reform measures or the speed and sequence with which they should be introduced, there is growing recognition of the necessity of stabilization and some "structural adjustment" and restructuring of property rights. Reequilibrating the balance of payments and stabilizing prices entail adjustment of the real exchange rate and control of fiscal and monetary policy, though more "heterodox" measures that include incomes policies and price controls may be appropriate under some settings. *Structural adjustment* refers to the complex of policies aimed at rationalizing the allocation of resources through the reform of trade and industrial policies and through the adjustment of relative prices. Though the state's role in this process remains contested, there is a growing consensus that some liberalization of both trade and domestic markets is required. Finally, there is the question of reforming the system of property rights, both by strengthening the incentives for private investment and by divesting or reforming state enterprises.

The precise political logic of these reforms varies from policy to policy, but recent work in political economy emphasizes three general political problems that recur regardless of the particular reform in question: collective action dilemmas, distributive conflicts, and the related problems of time horizon and credibility.

Collective action problems arise to the extent that economic policy has properties of a public good. Take, for example, the problem of stabilizing a persistent inertial inflation in a setting with extensive indexation, as in Brazil. Although some financial groups might derive speculative profits from high and volatile inflation, most groups would gain from greater price stability. However, the cooperative behavior needed to stabilize the price level might prove unobtainable since the risks of accepting deindexation are substantial if others are not making similar and simultaneous sacrifices.

Collective action problems also arise *within* political institutions. (Kiewit and McCubbins 1991; Geddes 1994). For example, legislators have a collective interest in effective fiscal management, since it affects overall economic performance and thus their reputations as incumbents. But legislators also have electoral concerns that tempt them to seek particularistic benefits for their constituents; if all legislators succeed in this strategy, perhaps through logrolling, then suboptimal policy will result.

The distributive implications of economic reforms constitute a second political challenge. In the collective action model, all parties would prefer a cooperative outcome but are blocked from it by incentives to cheat. In a distributive model, policy reform is supported by winners and opposed by losers, and the outcome is given by the balance of political power between the respective coalitions. Trade reform, devaluation, and price liberalization provide examples. Though these measures might increase both aggregate social welfare and the income of specific groups, they also typically encounter opposition from, respectively, import-competing interests, the nontraded goods sector, and those with access to goods at controlled prices.

In theory, a reform that generates a net social gain should also be politically viable. If the gains can be used to compensate the groups experiencing losses, it can be shown that it is always possible to construct a minimum winning coalition for reform. Yet it is pious to assume that such compensatory mechanisms exist, and there are thus good reasons why "losers" may prevail. One classic problem is that the costs of reform tend to be concentrated, while benefits are diffuse, producing perverse organizational incentives. Losers are usually well organized, while prospective winners face daunting collective action problems (Olson 1982). As

Fernandez and Rodrik (1991) point out, additional difficulties are introduced if we assume uncertainty about the outcome of the policy. Not only are prospective winners likely to be poorly organized, they may not even know who they are.

Both the collective action and distributive approaches to reform assume that policy is the result of conflicts among contending social groups or their political representatives. A third set of related problems arise if we examine the time horizons of government decision makers (Alesina 1987, 1994b). Again, politicians should be willing to undertake reforms that yield net social gains. Yet political constraints can lead the politician to discount future gains steeply, for example, because of impending elections or the fear of sparking demonstrations or riots. This does not mean politicians are irrational; it simply means that, given some set of institutional and political constraints, the time horizons over which they assess the political costs and benefits of reform may be "too short."

This final problem is closely related to problems of credibility and commitment that have been prominent in recent discussions of reform (Rodrik 1994). Politicians may commit themselves to reform but may also have an interest in reneging on that commitment when political pressures mount. If actors are forward looking and can see that there is an incompatibility in the incentives of the politician, they will discount policy pronouncements, thereby reducing their effect.

2   Socioeconomic Institutions: The Organization of Social Interests

The underlying assumption of the new institutionalist analysis is that institutions can either exacerbate or mute the three political dilemmas just outlined. Before turning to these questions of institutional design, however, it is important to address the question of the effects of interest groups on public policy. Interest group analysis—though often implicit—has been central to the way economists have approached the politics of economic reform and growth.[1]

---

[1]The distortionary effect of interest groups is at the heart of the Stigler–Peltzman and "capture" models of regulation (Peltzman 1976), the literature on rent seeking (Krueger 1974), and endogenous tariff theory (Nelson 1988). Important studies by political scientists (Bates 1983; Rogowski 1990; Frieden 1991) proceed along similar lines.

Such analysis poses a strong challenge to the goal of reconciling democracy with economic efficiency. This can be seen by examining one of the most influential statements of this approach, Olson's (1982) *The Rise and Decline of Nations.* Drawing on his earlier work, Olson argues that interest groups have difficulty in forming but that, if they do form, they will survive only through the provision of selective benefits to their members. The group could serve its members either by making society as a whole more productive, which would allow the income of the group to rise even if its share remained the same, or by obtaining a larger share of total output. Olson's pessimistic conclusion is that the second strategy typically dominates the first, with the result that efficiency and growth suffer. Only under the relatively rare circumstances in which "encompassing" organizations form is it possible—and then only possible (ibid., 52–53)—that interest groups will be a force for social good.

Fortunately, Olson's analysis—and the more general style of which it is exemplary—is incomplete in several important respects. Olson's analysis rests on the implicit counterfactual of an efficiently functioning market economy; onto this tabula rasa are written the policy distortions that result from interest group pressures. Yet the typical starting point for most new democracies is an economy characterized by numerous distortions that had their origins in the efforts of authoritarian rulers to build bases of support (Bates 1983).

In such a setting, an interest group that seeks a larger share of the social pie for itself does not necessarily reduce efficiency; to the contrary, responding to the demands of exporters, agricultural producers, the informal sector, and labor-intensive manufacturers would improve efficiency, aggregate social welfare, and probably the distribution of income as well. The problem is, thus, not that there are too many interest groups but too that there are too few, of the wrong sort, and facing too little effective competition from groups with divergent social interests.[2]

Olson's key insight is that this skewed distribution of interest organizations is endogenous to the logic of group formation; an efficiency-enhancing interest group is an oxymoron. However, the political-institutional analysis of interest groups suggests that this is only part of the story. Patterns of group organization are also a function of the survival and electoral strategies of politicians and of the institutional setting in which groups

---

[2]For a theoretical argument about why competition among pressure groups may serve to reduce rents, see Becker (1983).

operate. Thus the groups that democratic governments must confront often achieve the level of organization they do only through government leadership, support, and proscription of rival groups.

These observations are crucial for understanding the politics of economic reform. Olson's analysis suggests that interest groups typically constitute barriers to reform; these barriers must either be tolerated, finessed, or overridden. Yet, this provides a misleading picture of the way in which reform occurs under democratic auspices. Independence from interest group pressures may be a prerequisite for *initiating* reform, but reforms can only be *consolidated* under representative government if there are bases of electoral, legislative, and—ultimately—interest group support. As Waterbury puts it, reform must be seen as a process of coalition building (Waterbury 1989; see also Haggard and Kaufman 1992). Governments that seek to adopt reforms without building bases of organized support among the winners will fail, in part precisely because organized losers will operate through the political system to maintain the status quo. Thus, a crucial part of any reform strategy is not simply appealing to potential gainers but, where necessary, changing institutions so that beneficiaries have greater incentives to organize and more effective channels of representation (Shugart and Nielson 1994a, 1994b).

Under certain conditions, democratization itself constitutes an institutional change that is conducive to expanding the representation of those who gain from economic reform. For example, it has become a commonplace that economic policy under many African regimes has been characterized by urban bias (Bates 1983); despite their coercive powers, dictators nonetheless sought to mollify the more volatile urban sector. However, this concentration on urban areas was also partly a function of the absence of elections that would give politicians the incentive to seek rural votes. In his classic study of political order in changing societies, Huntington (1968, 448–61) notes that when rural majorities have been mobilized into electoral politics, policy undergoes a significant shift in orientation; such "ruralizing elections" occurred in Jamaica (1944), Turkey (1950), Senegal (1951), Ceylon (1956), Burma (1960), and Lesotho (1965).

The importance of building bases of political support for reform appears clear; somewhat more counterintuitive is the observation that successful reform may be facilitated by developing political relationships with *losers,* as well. This point can be illustrated by considering in more detail the issues surrounding the management of labor in the adoption of market-oriented policies, since more independent labor organization is almost always a concomitant of the transition to democratic rule.[3]

Organized labor typically faces losses in the initial phase of a standard adjustment program. Tight fiscal and monetary policies imply a reduction in aggregate demand and employment and hit directly at public sector employment and wages. Political models of inflation and stabilization often explicitly or implicitly have a labor-business conflict at their core (Alesina 1994a, 1994b). Trade and exchange rate policy also engage workers' interests. Trade liberalization places pressure on the import-substituting sector, and real devaluation hits nontraded goods producers (Rodrik 1994). Privatization also strikes at well-organized public sector workers. Thus, in a number of policy domains, we would expect organized labor to resist reform efforts.

If this assessment is correct, then getting labor to agree to temporary setbacks is a crucial aspect of managing adjustment. Under authoritarian regimes, labor is typically subject to a variety of controls, and this has arguably been one reason for their "success" in implementing stabilization efforts. In some new democracies, such as Turkey and Korea, controls on labor extended into the democratic period (Haggard and Kaufman 1995, chap. 7). If democratization is genuine, however, political liberalization is likely to lead to more extensive and active union organization and greater labor militancy. This happened in Spain, in Turkey after 1987, and in Poland, where labor led the fight against the communist government.

Whether labor resisted reform and was successful in doing so depended in part on its degree of organization and sectoral location, as an interest group model would predict. Devaluation and trade liberalization were more contentious and subject to reversal where labor found other allies opposed to adjustment or where labor was concentrated in strategic sectors of critical importance for the economy as a whole, such as the coal miners in Poland or in the state-owned enterprise sector.

There are other cases, however, with strategically placed unions (Mexico) or resurgent unions following democratization (Spain) in which labor did not constitute a block to stabilization and adjustment because of its relation to the government and political parties. Previous studies of Europe have found that corporatist arrangements (Katzenstein 1985) or close ties with governing social-democratic parties (Cameron 1984; Lange and Garrett 1985; Hicks 1988) integrate labor into the political system in ways that

---

[3]The following draws on the findings of a recent World Bank project (Haggard and Webb 1994).

provide the basis for compromise, enhanced policy credibility, and superior economic performance. Center-left governments in Spain and Poland secured labor acquiescence, at least in the short run; so, too, has the Concertacion in Chile, a coalition led by the Christian Democrats but with Socialist participation. By contrast, where labor had weak links with the government but strong ties with class-based leftist or populist parties, as in Turkey both before September 1980 and after 1987, reform proved more difficult.

The reason for the apparently anomalous result of social-democratic governments extracting concessions from labor is that they are more likely to enjoy trust and are, thus, better positioned to secure short-run restraint for promises of longer term gain; institutionalized labor-government relations solve both distributional and time-horizon problems. By contrast, right-of-center governments are less credible in promising long-term improvements for labor. As a result, labor is likely to be more demanding, and ironically, the government is more likely to resort to short-run concessions in the face of labor pressure, such as wage increases that outstrip productivity or expanded public employment.

These observations have been used to support the claim that adjustment can be facilitated under democratic auspices through corporatist institutions that provide a consultative forum between political leaders and major interest groups (e.g., labor and capital, ethnic groups). The essence of Concertacion is that the most important economic actors can either negotiate binding agreements on major policy variables directly, such as wages, investment, and prices, or provide credible support for bargains struck on key government initiatives, such as macroeconomic and industrial policies. The enthusiasm for this solution grows precisely out of a reading of the experience of the small European states, which have managed to combine social democracy, open economies, and comparatively good records with respect to both growth and inflation.

The question is whether this institutional solution is viable in the new democracies of Asia, Latin America, Africa, and Eastern Europe. The negotiation of binding agreements implies that all of the actors must be internally cohesive. For interest associations, this means the capacity to speak authoritatively for their memberships and to guarantee compliance. Most new democracies lack these conditions; again, it is the weakness rather than the strength of interest groups that constitutes the liability.

This discussion suggests several broad conclusions about the organization of interest groups in understanding reform in a democratic context. First, the expansion of the number of interest groups associated with the democratization process does not necessarily constitute a threat to growth-oriented policies; to the contrary, it may serve to offset rent-seeking interests organized under authoritarian rule. Second, close government ties to interest groups are not necessarily inimical to reform. The political mobilization of supporting interests is a critical component of moving from one policy equilibrium to another, establishing credible ties with "losers" may also be helpful. Third, corporatist arrangements along the lines of the small European democracies are not likely to constitute an option for most developing countries because of the weakness of interest group organization.

3   Parliamentary versus Presidential Rule

The most fundamental constitutional difference among democracies is between parliamentary and presidential systems of government.[4] The debate over the relative merits of these two systems has been particularly intense in Latin America, where presidentialism has been held responsible not only for the region's economic failures but for its long-standing history of political instability as well (Mainwaring 1989; Linz 1993a, 1993b; Linz and Valenzuela 1994; Horowitz 1993; Lijphart 1993; for contrary views, see Shugart and Carey 1992, 28–54; Mainwaring and Shugart 1994).[5]

Parliamentistas argue that the two core features of presidential systems—separate and independent election of the executive and legislature and fixed terms—pose significant difficulties for the stability and efficiency of democratic rule. Dual democratic legitimacy poses the greater problem. In parliamentary systems, at least in theory, there are clear lines of authority from voters, to ruling party or coalition, to cabinet, to bureaucracy. In presidential systems, by contrast, the lines of authority are complex and overlapping; rather than a clear division of powers, presidents and legislatures typically share them. As a result, there are more veto points over policy, particularly where legislative powers are further divided between two houses.

One result of this divided political authority is the tendency both to stalemates and to "bidding wars" between the branches. Executives with an

---

[4]This section draws on Haggard and Kaufman (1995) chap. 9.

[5]A theoretical literature has also begun to explore the policy and administrative consequences of parliamentary and presidential rule (Moe 1990; Weaver and Rockman 1993; Moe and Caldwell 1994; Palmer forthcoming).

independent electoral base and separate powers have fewer incentives to seek enduring coalitions, and independently elected legislators are less likely to cooperate for the purpose of making the president look good (Shugart and Carey 1992, 33). This is true even when the president's own party holds a legislative majority and will be still more marked when executives are limited to a single term or when the president's agenda includes difficult adjustment measures. Divided government (when the president and the legislative majority are from different parties) further exacerbates these problems, as can be seen with the failures of American fiscal policy in the 1980s (McCubbins 1991).

A second consequence of presidential rule advanced by Moe (1990) and Moe and Caldwell (1994) is bureaucratic inefficiency. Presidents, who have a national constituency, have an interest in efficient administrative structures that can serve as an instrument for implementing their programmatic agendas.[6] However, legislators in a presidential system are not in the business of creating effective government; they are in the business of making themselves popular and their jobs secure (Moe and Caldwell 1994, 175). They accomplish this by courting interest group backing and pursuing particularistic legislative concerns.

Moreover, in a presidential system with competing and overlapping centers of power, it is possible for legislators to protect their policies against future reversal by designing complicated rules that reduce the discretion of bureaucrats, such as decision criteria, procedures, timetables, personnel rules, and so forth. Given the independent institutional and electoral interests of legislators and the multiple veto points built into a system of divided powers, these structures become extremely difficult to eliminate once in place.

The separate electoral mandate for executives in a presidential system can complicate policy making in an additional way. In presidential systems with weak parties, direct elections open a clearer route for "outsiders" to gain executive power; where many candidates are in the race, there are also greater opportunities for leaders appealing to the extreme end of the political spectrum. If countries such as Brazil and Peru had parliamentary systems during the 1980s, it is unlikely that a Collor or Fujimori would have come to power or that leaders like Lula or Brizola would have been serious contenders for the Brazilian presidency. Because "outsiders" or "extremists"

---

[6]Though see Geddes (1994) on bureaucratic corruption in presidential systems.

can come to power without the backing of broadly based party organizations, they are poorly positioned to develop the legislative support required to sustain economic reform programs.

In parliamentary regimes, executive and legislative authority are fused. This central institutional feature of parliamentarism not only eliminates the problem of executive-legislative stalemate but also can enhance party discipline. Particularly in majoritarian systems, backbenchers have strong incentives to cooperate with the party leadership and to maintain party discipline, if for no simpler reason than that the fall of the government could lead to the calling of new parliamentary elections. As Cox (1987) demonstrates in his brilliant analysis of the emergence of party government in Britain, these arrangements have important implications for policy; political competition is structured to a greater degree around broad party programs than around the particularistic interests of individual legislators. Narrow interest groups, particularly geographically based ones, are less likely to have effective access to policy making. In such a system, it is also impossible for legislators to protect against future policy changes through complex and efficiency-reducing administrative engineering, since succeeding governments can undo the policies of their predecessors at will.

In parliamentary systems, executives are highly unlikely to be outsiders. Parliamentary leaders normally ascend to office as a result of extensive party and legislative experience. Moreover, since their tenure depends on their capacity to maintain legislative majorities, they must consult with supporters to retain those majorities, whether within their own parties or among coalition partners. For these reasons, they are also more likely to be able to forge coalitions to support their programs; this is taken by some to be a particular virtue of multiparty parliamentary systems (Lijphart 1993).

A second cluster of defects in presidential systems arises from the existence of fixed terms. It is extremely difficult to change governments when the legislature, but more particularly the president, has lost political support and exhausted leadership potential. Presidentialism served to prolong crises in Brazil and Peru, for example, where presidents Sarney, Collor, and Garcia outstayed their effectiveness. In Bolivia and Argentina in the 1980s, lame duck presidents were forced to resign before the expiration of their terms. Changes of government would arguably have come earlier and more smoothly under parliamentary rule.

There are, however, reasons to doubt that parliamentarism per se is inherently superior to presidentialism for undertaking and sustaining economic reform; much depends on the nature of the party system. A parliamentary system is not necessarily more conducive to consultation with affected parties. Where parties rule by absolute majority in a parliamentary system, or where majority coalitions are cohesive, prime ministers can acquire greater discretionary latitude than presidents, who must necessarily negotiate with legislatures to achieve their objectives. The potential for wide swings in policy is therefore increased.

Executive-legislative stalemates are possible in parliamentary as well as presidential systems, though they naturally take a different form. Under parliamentary systems with proportional representation, fragmentation of the party system and patronage demands from party leaders can create dangerous stalemates not only in making policy but in the formation of governments. The few empirical studies of this issue—all focusing on European parliamentary systems—suggest that stabilization is more difficult as the number of parties in the governing coalition grows larger because of the increase in the number of side payments required (Roubini and Sachs 1989a, 1989b; Schick 1993). Turkey in the late 1970s stands out as an example of a parliamentary system in which economic policy making was incoherent because of the difficulty of negotiating compromises within coalitions and the instability of governments themselves.

The political upheavals in Japan and Italy in 1993 show that pork-barrel politics and corruption can flourish just as well in parliamentary systems as in presidential ones, particularly where there are strong incentives to dispense patronage. Though such systems do not appear to have slowed growth in those two cases, the costs of patronage are arguably higher in the developing world.

Haggard and Kaufman (1995, chap. 9) review the economic exper-iences of twenty-four developing democracies in the second half of the 1980s. The sample is biased toward presidential systems because these tend to be more prevalent in the developing world than parliamentary ones.[7] The authors find no clear pattern differentiating presidential and parliamentary systems with respect to their capacity to manage the economy or undertake economic reform. Korea and Chile continued their high growth trajectories under presidential auspices, and the Philippines avoided the tragedies of a

---

[7]Parliamentary systems with proportional representation are rare in the developing world, and thus we have surprisingly little evidence as to how such systems would perform there. Those parliamentary systems that do exist in the Third World have largely been based on the Westminster model, usually as a result of a British colonial heritage.

number of Latin American cases. In Colombia and Costa Rica, presidential regimes instituted moderate adjustment policies and maintained positive growth rates. On the other hand, all of the cases of developing-country hyperinflation in the 1980s (Argentina, Bolivia, Brazil, and Peru) occurred under presidential or mixed-presidential systems. Performance in the Dominican Republic was highly erratic. The Venezuelan regime did not address major structural problems until the end of the decade; when it did, it experienced the most profound political upheaval since the inception of its contemporary democratic structure in 1958 and, partly as a result, reversed policy course in the early 1990s.

Multiparty parliamentary regimes in Thailand and Turkey sustained adjustments undertaken by their authoritarian predecessors. But Thailand's political system was only semidemocratic for most of the 1980s, and its successful adjustment was, arguably, in spite of the parliamentary nature of its democratic rule. The military's reentry into politics in the early 1990s was partly in response to the growing incoherence and corruption of democratic rule. Turkey performed reasonably well through the mid-1980s, but fiscal policy deteriorated in the late 1980s and early 1990s as the political system became more competitive, and the country experienced a crisis in 1994.

Economic performance was relatively good in a number of the pure Westminster systems, in which parliamentary rule is coupled with plurality voting rules in single-member districts. But the strong record with respect to inflation management probably has less to do with parliamentarism than other British institutional inheritances, such as strong currency boards. Moreover, most of these cases were small island economies in the Caribbean that do not provide particularly enlightening comparisons for large, middle-income countries. Trinidad and Tobago is the largest of these, but its record is not encouraging; the country experienced profound policy drift and seven straight years of economic decline in the late 1980s.

India's economic performance is mixed. Growth was higher than in the past, but budget deficits and inflation increased as well. Moreover, the country showed disturbing signs of increasing ethnic and regional polarization. It could be argued that these forces have been contained by the country's strong parliamentary heritage. Yet it is just as plausible to argue that it was the dominance of the Congress Party and federalism, rather than parliamentarism per se, that mattered in this regard.

This review does not imply complete agnosticism on the question of the effects of parliamentary versus presidential rule. However, it suggests that the effects of this fundamental constitutional choice are contingent on other components of institutional design, particularly the party system.

4   The Structure of the Party System: Fragmentation and Polarization

To understand the effects that party systems have on the initiation and consolidation of reform, it is important to consider the incentives facing individual politicians in more detail. Most incumbent politicians seek reelection and are, therefore, responsive to the interests of voters. Politicians' views of reform should thus reflect trends in public opinion among their constituents. They are likely to acquiesce to adjustment initiatives during honeymoons, oppose those elements of reform that cut against the interests of core constituents, and adopt more favorable views when—and if—the reforms yield results.

Party politicians, and particularly party leaders, must also respond to political pressures emanating from the competitive context in which they find themselves. The party system constitutes a critical determinant of politicians' behavior in this regard. First, politicians are engaged in a strategic interaction with adversaries; their positions with respect to reform and their willingness to compromise are a function not simply of their constituent base but also of the strategy and tactics of their political opponents. Second, party leaders must respond to competing factions, backbenchers, and organizational activists within their own ranks. How politicians respond to these pressures is a function of two features of the party system: the number and the ideological distribution of parties and the internal politics of party organization.

4.1   Alternative party systems: Fragmentation and polarization

A number of features of party systems are salient for understanding political behavior and resulting policy outcomes, but fragmentation and polarization have received the most sustained attention (Mainwaring and Scully 1994). Fragmentation is typically defined by the number of effective parties (Sartori 1976, 185ff.; Powell 1982, 80–84). Polarization is defined by the ideological distance between the extreme parties in the system (Sartori 1976, 132–37; Cox 1990). Fragmentation can be measured easily, but it is notoriously difficult to gauge the extent of ideological distance among parties, even in the advanced industrial states. The problem is compounded in developing countries, where party cleavages do not always fall along a clear left-right dimension. Several indicators to point to polarization, however. One is the presence of left and populist parties that have historically mobilized followers around anticapitalist or antioligarchic protests. It is also useful to consider the strength of "movement parties" that exhibit the sectarian characteristics of a social movement and rest on strong solidaristic and exclusivist loyalties among party activists; the Italian fascists constitute an historical example, as do the Peronists at several points in their history.

Nonpolarized party systems, by contrast, are characterized by a low level of ideological distance among parties, typically meaning that left and populist parties are weak or nonexistent. Nonpolarized systems rest on "pragmatic" parties, in which ties between leaders and followers are largely instrumental and rest on shared interests in obtaining political office rather than strong ideological commitments.

Fragmentation should create impediments to the coordination required both to initiate and sustain policy changes. More cohesive systems, by contrast, generate the stable electoral and legislative support that is a prerequisite for consolidating economic reform (Weaver and Rockman 1993; Shick 1993). However, fragmentation alone says nothing about the under-lying preferences of the contending political forces in the system or the extent of cleavage among them. We expect that reform will be more difficult in polarized systems in which strong left, populist, and movement parties compete, both because of their effects on partisan conflict and because of their influence on the stance of interest groups, particularly the labor movement and the urban popular sector, which includes lower-middle-class, white-collar workers and portions of the informal sector.

The principal effect of fragmentation on the conduct of policy is the difficulty it poses for coordination within the ruling coalition, between executive and legislative branches, and among levels of government. In parliamentary systems based on proportional representation with high proportionality, a multiplicity of parties increases the difficulty of forming and sustaining coalition governments. The division of cabinet posts among contending parties that is required to form such coalitions can undermine the capacity of central authorities to undertake the coordinated implementation of reform programs; policy becomes a logroll. When such governments are formed, small coalition partners can hold veto power over policy decisions (Roubini and Sachs 1989a, 1989b). Israeli politics exhibits these characteris-tics in the extreme.

Analogous problems can exist in presidential systems. As Main-waring (1989) argues, party fragmentation in presidential systems com-pounds the chances that executives will become politically isolated and powerless to pursue their agenda. The incentives for small parties to cooperate with the government are weaker than in a parliamentary system, since there is no ability to threaten early elections, and the temptations to legislative blackmail are correspondingly greater.

The effects of fragmentation on policy making will also depend on whether the system is simultaneously polarized. This can be seen by comparing economic policy and performance in Thailand and Brazil. Thailand in the late 1980s had a highly fragmented party system but showed no signs of polarization. In the absence of strong left or populist parties, the principal coordination problems centered on the struggle for pork. With multiple contenders and weak party organizations, there were few constraints on politicians in the competition for patronage and pork-barrel expenditures and limited incentives to cooperate around reforms that provide public goods. To the extent that Thailand did escape this trap, it was due to enduring features of the executive and the bureaucracy (Doner and Laothamatas 1994).

Coordination becomes even more difficult when the centrifugal pressures in fragmented systems are compounded by strong ideological polarization or sectarian tendencies. Parties in such systems are more likely to engage in programmatic bidding wars, both to differentiate themselves from opponents and to maintain the allegiance of relatively narrow constituencies. For similar reasons, fragmented and polarized systems amplify the distributional demands coming from antiadjustment interest groups. These two consequences are particularly marked when there are splits among populist or left parties, which then compete among themselves for support of labor unions and other popular sector groups. This characteristic was particularly true of Peru during its first two posttransition governments.

The combination of polarization and fragmentation also affects economic management by exacerbating political business cycles (Alesina 1987). Not only do elections in such systems invite opportunistic behavior and encourage the delay of adjustment efforts, but the combination of an unstable and volatile party landscape with deep partisan antagonisms increases the uncertainty surrounding elections due to the potential for large policy swings between successive governments. Argentina, Bolivia, Brazil, and Peru all experienced profound economic collapse in the run-up to elections.

In cohesive party systems, competition is organized among a small number of large parties. At the time of its transition to democracy, the Philippines had probably the most cohesive party system among new developing country democracies; the transitional election was fought between two blocs, consisting of pro-Marcos and anti-Marcos forces. In subsequent elections, the weakness of party organizations and the tendency to personalism and fragmentation emerged more clearly, but these tendencies were constrained by the centripetal incentives associated with single-member electoral districts for the lower house. Chile, Korea, and Taiwan also showed low levels of fragmentation, as all three moved toward the formation of broad-based political blocs. Korea even evolved "past" a two-party system toward a dominant party model, along Japanese lines. Argentina and Uruguay were also relatively cohesive, although the Uruguayan case is complicated by institutionalized competition within the major parties, which had important implications for its adjustment efforts in the late 1980s and early 1990s. Turkey also constitutes an ambiguous case. At the time of the transitional election in 1983, the country had less than three effective parties, but this was the result of a military ban on full party participation. By the late 1980s, the Turkish party system had become both more fragmented and more polarized, which helps explain the growing incoherence of economic policy.

What are the effects of a cohesive party system with a low degree of polarization on the conduct of economic policy? First, we would expect politicians to crowd the center and to avoid strong programmatic appeals that would differentiate them sharply from their competitors. Where the median voter opposes reform, or where the party is captured by powerful interests, stalemate is certainly possible. Party leaders in cohesive, nonpolarized settings can be expected to resist reforms when these threaten patronage opportunities or remove protection from core constituents. If there are strong interest group and electoral forces arrayed against reform, then a cohesive, nonpolarized system would militate against radical market-oriented reforms in favor of a more incremental approach.

But broad-based, catchall parties also have advantages with respect to initiating and sustaining reform. Given the tendency for such parties to move toward the center, we would expect cohesive, nonpolarized systems to generate strong organized support for the initiation of reform in crisis situations in which voters are disaffected with the policy status quo. In opposition, catchall parties will naturally seek to discredit the policies of the government. But when things are going well, they are less likely to press for the wholesale reversal of government initiatives; when things are going badly, they are less likely than leftist or movement parties to gravitate toward radical, polarizing solutions or to back strikes, demonstrations, and protests that complicate the ability of governments to act.

A small number of large parties also has a moderating influence on the way interests are aggregated. In countries with cohesive party systems, interest groups are forced to operate in an encompassing coalition, in which diverse interests are represented and among which compromises must be struck. Unlike both fragmented and polarized systems, politicians operating in such systems are not as closely linked to, or dependent on, specific economic interests. This has the effect both of facilitating the organization of support and of diffusing opposition.

Given these incentives, the combination of a cohesive yet polarized system is unlikely. There are fewer opportunities for strongly ideological or movement parties to operate in a system with a small number of parties; most cohesive systems are not polarized. As we would also expect, the left and movement parties that have resurfaced in more cohesive systems have had strong incentives to move toward the center. The exception that proves the rule is Turkey, which did become more polarized over time. However, this was partly the result of lowering the barriers to political entry and allowing more parties to compete; the system became more polarized as it became more fragmented.

Chile and Argentina do combine a low level of fragmentation with the presence of parties with strong populist and socialist legacies. By around 1990, both the Chilean socialists and the Peronists, once highly sectarian, had taken on many properties of pragmatic catchall parties. When compared to movement parties in more fragmented systems, those in cohesive systems have a strong incentive to broaden their appeal and deemphasize traditional solidarities.

The behavior of left and movement parties operating in a cohesive party system depends on whether these parties are in or out of power. Incentives for left and populist parties to resist reform are strongest when they are in the political opposition and adjustments are initiated by their rivals. Movement parties in opposition are much more likely than catchall parties to launch a "principled" opposition to adjustment initiatives, with broad appeals to egalitarian and nationalist values. They are also more inclined to back these appeals with support for labor activism and social protest.

The case of Argentina demonstrates that this behavior has an important effect on the position of more moderate groups within both the government and opposition. Militant opposition by the Peronists increased the electoral risks of initiating reforms or of continuing their implementation, even when these seemed important for averting more severe economic difficulties. In short, cohesive but polarized party systems can come to resemble fragmented and polarized systems under some circumstances.

The policy orientation of left or populist parties can change substantially, however, if they are incorporated into the government; this observation may be important for understanding the politics of "reformed" communist parties in the former socialist countries. This outcome is much more likely to occur in consolidated, than in fragmented, systems. In fragmented systems, the movement of some left or populist groups toward the center is likely to be resisted by other factions that can gain through militant appeals to narrow constituencies. Consolidated systems, by contrast, provide opportunities for left or populist parties to gain office by extending their appeal beyond their core constituencies and demonstrating their capacity for moderation; there is space to move toward the center. Left parties in power have an additional advantage in cohesive systems, which I already noted in the discussion of interest groups: their links with organized labor and other groups disadvantaged by reform may actually make it easier for them to gain trust and to negotiate compensatory agreements that permit reform to move forward.

4.2   Internal party organization

At several points in the foregoing discussion, issues of intraparty organization have necessarily entered into the analysis. For example, in discussing the parliamentary-presidential debate, it was noted that legislators in a presidential system have a tendency toward particularism. However, this might be due to the lack of party discipline rather than presidentialism per se. How precisely do the incentive structures *within* parties affect the propensity to provide public goods and coherent economic policy?[8]

The key variable is the relative strength of the party leadership vis-à-vis the individual politician. Where party leaderships are strong, there is greater prospect of enforcing programmatic discipline on followers and less likelihood that programs will be dominated by geographic or other constituent interests. Party strength is likely to be reflected not only in intraparty organization but also in the design of legislative institutions themselves. Strong parties are more likely to favor rules and institutions that further buttress party discipline, such as strong oversight or control committees, extensive agenda-setting and committee assignment powers for party leaders, and weak policy committees.

The strength of the party leadership depends on the extent to which electoral rules encourage politicians to cultivate a personal reputation. Where

---

[8]The following draws extensively on Shugart and Nielson (1994a 1994b) and the analysis by Ramseyer and Rosenbluth (1993) of the Japanese electoral system.

politicians have incentives to cultivate the personal vote, they are more likely to develop narrow constituent bases of support and to press for particularistic policies at the expense of party platforms. As Shugart and Nielson (1994b, 18) put it, "in personalistic systems, party programs are constantly being scavenged by individual politicians for their idiosyncratic interests—they seek to break up national policies into localized or issue-specific parcels in appeal to narrow groups." These particularistic policies take the form of patronage, pork, and the drafting of statutes that are cast in general language but that are, in fact, designed to appeal to narrow constituent—and even individual!—bases of support. The growth of American tax expenditures provide an example of the last stratagem (Shick 1991).

A number of interrelated rules affect the extent to which party control is centralized. First, party leaders must control access to the ballot and the order in which candidates are elected. Such control, exercised through closed-list rules on nomination procedures, allow party leaders to screen out undesirable mavericks. For those with secure positions on the party list, closed lists may encourage complacency. However, they are also likely to encourage loyalty to the party platform if one exists because a politician's position on the ballot is determined by the party leadership. A more open and decentralized nomination procedure weakens party control. In an open-list system, the electorate effectively orders the ballot. Open lists allow entrants to free-ride on the party label while simultaneously encouraging them to curry a personal reputation for the provision of particularistic goods.

A closely related feature of the electoral system that determines politicians' behavior is whether they are competing against members of their own party. In some systems with multimember districts, members of the same party are in competition with each other. As the size of the district increases, and the individual politician is competing with more members both of the opposition and her own party, this competition becomes more fierce. Of course, the party label is of no use in competition with members of one's own party; the only way to conduct such rivalry is by stressing personal traits that differentiate the candidate. In effect, politicians are encouraged to pursue what Ramseyer and Rosenbluth (1993) call a "niche" strategy. These strategies might be subtly ideological: politicians from the same party may emphasize different aspects of the party platform. Nonetheless, it is usually easier to secure niche support on the basis of instrumental promises to followers and the provision of personal services than it is by standing up for the public good.

A third feature of the electoral system is whether voters choose parties or candidates. If voters choose parties, then the politician has little incentive to differentiate himself from the party platform; his fate rises or falls with the party's. If the voter chooses individual candidates, there are, again, incentives to cultivate a personal vote.

Fourth is the control of campaign finance. Where individual politicians have responsibility for raising their own campaign money and, consequently, control their own purses, there is an incentive to cultivate a personal reputation. Donors in such settings typically provide candidates with money for the purpose of realizing particular objectives.

It is important to underscore that centralized control is certainly not a guarantee of good economic policy. Centralized parties might well have ideological platforms that are hostile to economic reform. The distribution of private goods is also of use to politicians even in a centralized system (Geddes 1994). Party leaders still have an interest in maintaining the loyalty of both legislators and voters and will use patronage and pork to that end. Venezuela, for example, has highly centralized party institutions, but they have been riddled with corruption and patronage.

However, the distribution of private goods through centralized monitoring mechanisms, either the party's or the legislature's, may have a salutary effect in the reform process (Shugart and Nielson 1994a, 1994b). The distribution of a certain amount of patronage and pork provides a mechanism for building support, including among previously excluded groups, and of partially compensating losers. The key issue is guaranteeing that pork is distributed in a relatively efficient way. One way of achieving this is through electoral reforms that reduce intraparty competition, such as the formation of single-member districts. However, control may also be exercised by delegating greater authority to the executive.

5   The Constitution of Executive Authority

A centralized executive authority plays a pivotal role in overcoming the collective action problems and distributive conflicts associated with the initiation of comprehensive economic reforms. In the early phase of a reform, key decisions about the design of policy and the political and legislative strategy are usually taken by the president or prime minister on the basis of counsel from a hand-picked team of advisers. The executive's ability to act aggressively is partly a function of conjunctural factors. In democratic systems, honeymoons provide new governments with the opportunity to take new initiatives. Economic conditions can also generate strong pressures for policy change and a willingness to expand the discretionary authority of the executive.

In addition to these conjunctural determinants of executive power, institutions have also been explicitly designed either to buttress central authority or to insulate decision making from political interference. In analyzing the powers of the executive, it is important to distinguish between those powers that belong to the executive by constitutional right and those that are explicitly delegated (Shugart and Carey 1992, chap. 7). In presidential systems, the former typically include a veto (of varying scope and with differing provisions for legislative override) that provides some check on legislative power. Presidential authority also typically includes certain legislative or decree powers that grant presidents more direct control over the policy agenda. These powers can be extremely important for the conduct of economic policy. In Korea, the president introduces the budget, and the legislature has no power to increase spending; it may only shift expenditures between categories and reduce spending. In Brazil, presidential authority to issue "urgent" laws was used by the Collor administration to initiate reform legislation, though not always successfully.

These powers must be distinguished from those that are explicitly delegated to the executive by the legislature. Prime ministers and their cabinets in parliamentary systems are typically quite powerful; they can legislate more or less at will. However, this power results from their backing by a majority in parliament, either of the dominant party or a coalition. Similarly, in presidential systems, legislators may delegate quite substantial decree powers to the president on a temporary basis. Such powers were important in the initiation of reforms in Argentina and Peru but would not have been possible without ultimate congressional backing.

Another feature of the executive that can have important implications for the conduct of economic policy is the delegation of decision-making authority to specialized agencies *within* the executive. Such delegation can substantially alter the political calculus, and even the very organization, of interest groups. Perhaps the best-known examples are the creation of independent central banking institutions (Cukierman, Webb, and Neyapti 1992) and quasi-judicial structures for the adjudication of certain trade policy issues. In both cases, the establishment of independent agencies limits the access of groups to decision making or alters the way in which they exercise influence. The establishment of quasi-judicial procedures for the management of unfair trade practices may provide access for aggrieved parties with protectionist intent, yet they are also demand that petitioners demonstrate that their cases are in conformity with statute. Such a process differs fundamentally from a lobbying relationship with a legislator.

Though constitutional arrangements and processes of delegation can strengthen the hand of the executive by expanding the discretionary power to initiate policy or by insulating decision making from short-term political pressures, such mechanisms do not necessarily provide an effective basis for policy coordination and the management of distributive conflict over the long run. To the contrary, strong executive discretion can weaken the incentives for party, legislative, and interest group leaders to support policy initiatives (Shugart and Carey 1992, 174–93). Legislators with limited influence over policy are likely to distance themselves from the chief executive, particularly during times of economic distress; this is especially true in presidential systems and where parties are weak.

Efforts to insulate decision making can also backfire. The purpose of such institutional arrangements is to offset threats from the opposition to policy continuity and coherence, particularly in countries with long histories of polarization and social conflict over economic issues. However, as both Turkey and Thailand demonstrate, an insulated executive is not sufficient to prevent opposition to reform as barriers to political contestation fall, and it may itself become the focus of the opposition. To the extent that both executive power and the insulation of agencies are the result of delegation, both can be reversed—though only at some cost. Such processes of delegation may run particular risks in weakly institutionalized democracies. Take for example the recent tendency in Latin America for legislators to grant executives substantial powers for the purpose of undertaking economic reform measures, a process Bresser Pereira, Maraval, and Przeworski (1993) label "decretism." First, it is not clear that the decisions taken under such conditions are necessarily optimal or even politically sustainable, since they avoid consultation with affected parties. Second, there is also the question of whether they will lead to a plebiscitarian political style and the atrophy of representative institutions.

Nonetheless, the process of delegation is central in all democratic systems; modern democracy would be impossible without it. Thus, the issue is not whether or not to delegate but how delegation can be structured to maximize both efficiency and accountability. This is probably the area of institutional design where outside donors can have the greatest influence. The transition to the market involves the creation of new, or the strengthening of old, regulatory institutions: from rules and laws governing industrial relations, to environmental agencies, to the oversight of financial markets. There are two competing conceptions of how such institutions can be strengthened and given more independence. One is to increase their capacity. This technocratic strategy has some merit. By increasing salaries, attracting high-quality personnel, and injecting greater expertise through training, agencies gain political weight. The foreign link itself constitutes an important resource.

The record of the recent past suggests that such a technocratic strategy is inadequate by itself. For agencies to sustain themselves over time, they must also build on bases of constituent support. For example, recent research on central banks reveals that these institutions gain "independence" not through statute but by maintaining close relationships with those politicians and interest groups favorable to the conduct of stable monetary policy (Lohmann 1994; Maxfield 1994). The task for institutional design is therefore to consider how new policy-making bodies can enfranchise and strengthen the hand of proreform groups that have previously been underrepresented not only within the party system more broadly but also within the state itself.

6   Conclusions

Research on the relationship between institutions and economic policy and performance is in its infancy, and it is thus important to retain caution and humility when drawing policy implications. It is dangerous to think that all political barriers to effective economic reform and governance can be overcome through institutional engineering. Moreover, institutional design itself is not exogenous to politics. Nonetheless, this survey suggests some findings that may be useful for those involved in the design and reform of institutions.

It is, first, important to underscore some general analytic principles. Most analyses of economic policy focus on the distribution of underlying preferences or the organization of interest groups. I argue, by contrast, that the organization of interests and their influence is contingent on institutions, as are the incentives facing the politicians who constitute the ultimate decision makers with respect to economic reform.

Given a particular distribution of interests, what institutions are conducive to economic reform? This depends to a certain extent on the distinction between initiating and consolidating reform. The initiation of reform is facilitated by institutions that expand executive discretion. In presidential systems, these include constitutionally entrenched or delegated powers. In parliamentary systems, executive power is tied directly to the structure of the party system. Rules that limit the number of parties also limit the need for coalitions and, thus, expand executive independence.

A central theme of this chapter is the importance of building bases of support for reform over the longer run; the key issue is how such support is organized. One solution that meets Olson's (1982) demand for encompassing organizations is corporatism. However, it is not clear that such a solution is likely in most developing countries—nor, if it were feasible, whether it would be desirable to bypass fragile democratic institutions through direct corporatist bargaining.

I place particular attention on the interaction between basic constitutional choices—presidential versus parliamentary rule—and the party system. In a democratic system, parties serve as the key link between politicians and constituents, and the party system establishes the incentives for partisan competition. Electoral rules that provide low barriers to political entry encourage the fragmentation and polarization of the political system, factors that make coordination difficult. These problems are compounded by incentives to politicians to cultivate the personal vote and, thus, particularistic policies.

It is again worth emphasizing that institutions are not the end of the story; preferences matter. Getting the institutions right, however, increases the likelihood that reform will succeed and, thus, that underlying political preferences will shift in a proreform direction.

References

Alesina, Alberto. 1987. "Macroeconomic Policy in a Two-party System as a Repeated Game." *Quarterly Journal of Economics* 102: 651–78.

———. 1994a. "Macroeconomics and Politics." In *Macroeconomics Annual.* Cambridge: MIT Press.

———. 1994b. "Political Models of Macroeconomic Policy and Fiscal Reforms." In Haggard and Webb, *Voting for Reform.*

Bates, Robert. 1983. "The Nature and Origins of Agricultural Policies in Africa." In *Essays on the Political Economy of Rural Africa*, ed. Robert Bates. Berkeley: University of California Press.

Bates, Robert H., and Anne O. Krueger, eds. 1993. *Political and Economic Interactions in Economic Policy Reform.* Cambridge: Blackwell.

Becker, Gary S. 1983. "A Theory of Competition among Pressure Groups for Influence." *Quarterly Journal of Economics* 98: 371–400.

Bresser Pereira, Luiz Carlos, Jose Maria Maraval, and Adam Przeworski. 1993. *Economic Reforms in New Democracies*. New York: Cambridge University Press.

Cameron, David. 1984. "Social Democracy, Corporatism, Labor Quiescence, and the Representation of Economic Interests in Advanced Capitalist Society." In *Order and Conflict in Contemporary Capitalism*, ed. John H. Goldthorpe. Oxford: Clarendon.

Cox, Gary W. 1987. *The Efficient Secret*. New York: Cambridge University Press.

——. 1990. "Centripetal and Centrifugal Incentives in Electoral Systems." *American Journal of Political Science* 34: 903–35.

Cukierman, Alex, Steven B. Webb, and B. Neyapti. 1992. "The Measurement of Central Bank Independence and Its Effect on Policy Outcomes." *World Bank Economic Review* 6: 353–98.

Doner, Richard F., and Anek Laothamatas. 1994. "Thailand: Economic and Political Gradualism." In Haggard and Webb, *Voting for Reform*.

Dornbusch, Rudiger, and Sebastian Edwards. 1991. *The Macroeconomics of Populism in Latin America*. Chicago: University of Chicago Press.

Fernandez, Raquel, and Dani Rodrik. 1991. "Resistance to Reform: Status Quo Bias in the Presence of Individual-Specific Uncertainty." *American Economic Review* 81: 1146–55.

Frieden, Jeffry. 1991. "Invested Interests: The Politics of National Economic Policies in a World of Global Finance." *International Organization* 45: 425–51.

Geddes, Barbara. 1994. *Politician's Dilemma*. Berkeley: University of California Press.

Haggard, Stephan, and Robert Kaufman, eds. 1992. *The Politics of Adjustment: International Constraints, Distributional Conflicts, and the State*. Princeton: Princeton University Press.

——. 1995. *The Political Economy of Democratic Transitions*. Princeton: Princeton University Press.

Haggard, Stephan, and Steven B. Webb, eds. 1994. *Voting for Reform: The Politics of Adjustment in New Democracies*. New York: Oxford University Press.

Helliwell, John F. 1994. "Empirical Linkages between Democracy and Economic Growth." *British Journal of Political Science* 24: 225–48.

Hicks, Alexander. 1988. "Social Democratic Corporatism and Economic Growth." *Journal of Politics* 50: 677–704.

Horowitz, Donald L. 1993. "Comparing Democratic Systems." In *The Global Resurgence of Democracy*, ed. Larry Diamond and Marc F. Plattner. Baltimore: Johns Hopkins University Press.

Huntington, Samuel. 1968. *Political Order in Changing Societies*. New Haven: Yale University Press.

Katzenstein, Peter. 1985. *Small States in World Markets: Industrial Policy in Europe*. Ithaca: Cornell University Press.

Kiewit, Rodrik, and Matthew McCubbins. 1991. *The Logic of Delegation*. Chicago: Chicago University Press.

Krueger, Anne O. 1974. "The Political Economy of the Rent-Seeking Society." *American Economic Review* 64: 291–303.

Lange, Peter, and Geoffrey Garrett. 1985. "The Politics of Growth: Strategic Interaction and Economic Performance in the Advanced Industrial Democracies, 1974–1980." *Journal of Politics* 67: 792–827.

Linz, Juan J. 1993a. "The Perils of Presidentialism." In *The Global Resurgence of Democracy,* ed. Larry Diamond and Marc F. Plattner. Baltimore: Johns Hopkins University Press.

———. 1993b. "The Virtues of Parliamentarism." In *The Global Resurgence of Democracy,* ed. Larry Diamond and Marc F. Plattner. Baltimore: Johns Hopkins University Press.

Linz, Juan J., and Arturo Valenzuela. 1994. *The Failure of Presidential Democracy*. Baltimore: Johns Hopkins University Press.

Lijphart, Arend. 1993. "Constitutional Choices for New Democracies." In *The Global Resurgence of Democracy*, ed. Larry Diamond and Marc F. Plattner. Baltimore: Johns Hopkins University Press.

Lohmann, Susanne. 1994. "Federalism and Central Bank Autonomy: The Politics of German Monetary Policy, 1960–1989." Department of Political Science, University of California, Los Angeles.

Mainwaring, Scott. 1989. "Presidentialism in Latin America." *Latin American Research Review* 25: 157–79.

Mainwaring, Scott, and Timothy R. Scully. 1995. "Party Systems in Latin America." In *Building Democratic Institutions: Party Systems in Latin America,* ed. Mainwaring and Scully. Stanford: Stanford University Press.

Mainwaring, Scott, and Matthew Soberg Shugart, eds. Forthcoming. *Presidentialism and Democracy in Latin America*. New York: Cambridge University Press.

Maxfield, Sylvia. 1994. "The Politics of Central Banking in Developing Countries." Yale University.

McCubbins, Matthew D. 1991. "Party Politics, Divided Government, and Budget Deficits." In *Parallel Politics: Economic Policymaking in Japan and the United States*, ed. Samuel Kernell. Washington, D.C.: Brookings.

Moe, Terry M. 1990. "Political Institutions: The Neglected Side of the Story." *Journal of Law, Economics, and Organization* 6: 213–53.

Moe, Terry M., and Michael Caldwell. 1994. "The Institutional Foundations of Democratic Government: A Comparison of Presidential and Parliamentary Systems." *Journal of Institutional and Theoretical Economics* 150: 171–95.

Nelson, Douglas. 1988. "Endogenous Tariff Theory: A Critical Survey." *American Journal of Political Science* 32: 796–837.

Nelson, Joan, ed. 1990. *Economic Crisis and Policy Choice: The Politics of Adjustment in the Third World*. Princeton: Princeton University Press.

Olson, Mancur. 1982. *The Rise and Decline of Nations*. New Haven: Yale University Press.

Palmer, Matthew S. R. Forthcoming. "Towards an Economics of Comparative Political Organization: Examining Ministerial Responsibility." *Journal of Law, Economics, and Organization*.

Peltzman, Sam. 1976. "Toward a More General Theory of Regulation." *Journal of Law and Economics* 19: 211–40.

Powell, G. Bingham. 1982. *Contemporary Democracies: Participation, Stability, Violence*. Cambridge: Harvard University Press.

Przeworski, Adam, and Fernando Limongi. 1993. "Political Regimes and Economic Growth." *Journal of Economic Perspectives* 7: 51–69.

Ramseyer, Mark, and Frances M. Rosenbluth. 1993. *Japan's Political Marketplace*. Cambridge: Harvard University Press.

Rodrik, Dani. 1994. "Credibility of Trade Reform: A Policy Maker's Guide." *World Economy* 12: 1–16.

Rogowski, Ronald. 1990. *Commerce and Coalitions*. Princeton: Princeton University Press.

Roubini, Nouriel, and Jeffry Sachs. 1989a. "Government Spending and Budget Deficits in the Industrial Countries." *Economic Policy* 4: 100–132.

———. 1989b. "Political and Economic Determinants of Budget Deficits in the Industrial Democracies." *European Economic Review* 33: 903–33.

Sartori, Giovanni. 1976. *Parties and Party Systems*. New York: Cambridge University Press.

Shick, Allen. 1991. "The Surprising Enactment of Tax Reform in the United States." In *Parallel Politics: Economic Policymaking in Japan and the United States*, ed. Samuel Kernell. Washington, D.C.: Brookings.

————. 1993. "Governments versus Budget Deficits." In Weaver and Rockman, *Do Institutions Matter?*

Shugart, Matthew, and John M. Carey. 1992. *Presidents and Assemblies*. New York: Cambridge University Press.

Shugart, Matthew, and Daniel Nielson. 1994a. "Liberalization through Institutional Reform: Economic Adjustment and Constitutional Change in Colombia." Graduate School of International Relations. University of California, San Diego.

————. 1994b. "A Liberal Dose: Electoral Reform and Economic Adjustment in the Wake of the Debt Crisis." Paper prepared for the annual meeting of the American Political Science Association, New York, September.

Sirowy, Larry, and Alex Inkeles. 1990. "The Effects of Democracy on Economic Growth and Inequality." *Studies in Comparative International Development* 25: 126–57.

Waterbury, John. 1989. "The Political Management of Economic Adjustment and Reform." In *Fragile Coalitions: The Politics of Economic Adjustment*, ed. Joan Nelson. New Brunswick: Transaction.

Weaver, R. Kent, and Bert A. Rockman, eds. 1993. *Do Institutions Matter? Government Capabilities in the United States and Abroad*. Washington, D.C.: Brookings.

Williamson, John, ed. 1994. *The Political Economy of Policy Reform*. Washington, D.C.: Institute for International Economics.

III PARTICIPATION AND LOCAL INSTITUTIONS

7   Investing in Capital, Institutions, and Incentives

Elinor Ostrom

In the summer of 1991, two buildings stood in different parts of the village of Wereng, located about fifty kilometers south of Jos, the capital of the Plateau state in Nigeria. Both were constructed to provide health care to local residents. Given the incidence of malaria, measles, and malnutrition in this village, the 550 families living in Wereng desperately needed convenient and low-cost health care.

One building was located outside the village on a steep hill overlooking the high flatlands, where the remains of a once active tin-mining industry lay in heaps here and there. This government dispensary was a large and substantial structure built in 1977, with a full front porch, a large reception area, a spacious examination room, and a dispensary. The front door was open, and my colleagues and I entered to find it virtually empty.[1] No patients, no doctor, no nurses, and no dispenser were to be seen. Even more startling, there was no furniture in the entire building except for a table and a bench in the examination room and a dilapidated set of shelves in the dispensary. Other than a few bowls and jars, nothing was on the shelves.

Financial support for this project from the Ford Foundation (under grant number 920-0701), from the U.S. Agency for International Development (to the Decentralization: Finance and Management Project), and from the Workshop in Political Theory and Policy Analysis is gratefully acknowledged. The Decentralization: Finance and Management (DFM) Project is sponsored by the Office of Economic and Institutional Development of the Bureau for Research and Development (RD/EID/IDM) of the U.S. Agency for International Development (USAID). Associates in Rural Development (ARD) is the prime contractor for the DFM project under USAID contract number DHR-5446-Z-00-7033-00 with subcontracts to the Metropolitan Studies Program of the Maxwell School of Citizenship and Public Affairs at Syracuse University and the Workshop in Political Theory and Policy Analysis at Indiana University.

[1]My colleagues were Dele Ayo, Kenneth Hubbell, and Tina West. We were part of a team that studied "The Experience in Nigeria with Decentralization Approaches to Local Delivery of Primary Education and Primary Health Services," a report that is drawn on extensively in this introduction. Further details of health care in Wereng can be found in Ayo et al. (1992). The study in Nigeria was part of a larger study including Ghana and Côte d'Ivoire (see Garnier et al. 1992; Fiadjoe et al. 1992).

Within a few minutes of our arrival, the dispenser greeted us and spent several hours with us telling us about his background and why the dispensary was empty.

A much smaller building, located in the center of the village, was owned and operated as a private clinic and dispensary. When we arrived there, several villagers were waiting to see the "doctor." After seeing his patients, the pharmacist also told us his background, the encouragement he had received to set up a clinic in this village, and why his dispensary was the best stocked among the four regions we had visited in Nigeria.

The contrasts between the two dispensaries in Wereng were striking. In terms of physical capital, the government building represented a major investment. Its design, like many other government dispensaries we saw during the summer, was the standard plan for a village of this size. The materials were provided by the Plateau state government. The justification for such large buildings was that it would be easier to upgrade them at a later time to provide additional services. The building had been constructed by "volunteers" from the village, who were promised better health care in return for their labor.

The building housing the private dispensary had been constructed by the owner in 1987 from locally available building materials. Although much smaller than the public dispensary, it had a small reception area, a laboratory (with a microscope to examine blood and stool samples), a room for inoculations and injections, another for consultations and a room with a single bed for patients staying overnight. The owner planned to add a new room with additional beds. Apart from being licensed to sell drugs, the owner was apparently not supervised by the local or state government. His building contained a wide variety of medicines available at a modest markup over the price he paid for them in the nearest larger town.[2] The chief of the village told us that local residents considered the services provided by the private clinic superior to those provided by the government dispensary. Residents would go for free consultations to the government dispensary only for minor problems, such as a cold or a runny nose.

Why the difference? Why did the privately owned dispensary have patients, furniture, medical equipment, and medicines, while the government facility had few if any of these? Could it be that the proprietor of the clinic had better training and that patients were willing to pay to visit him rather

---

[2]The owner showed us medicine for hookworm that he had purchased at N7.50, for sale in his clinic at N8.50, a markup of 13 percent.

than obtain doubtful free advice from a poorly trained functionary? We had already visited one village where the "doctor" in a government dispensary was actually hired and paid as the custodian and had learned his skills observing medical workers for many years. The government dispenser in Wereng was, however, actually quite well trained.[3] Thus, differences in human capital (the education and training of the two pharmacists) and in physical capital (the two buildings) did not account for the difference in services. Obviously, other factors accounted for the differences.

The financial constraints facing all Nigerian governmental agencies in 1991, due to the effects of structural adjustments, in part caused the lack of supplies on the shelves of the government dispensary, but they could not account for the absence of furniture.[4] Neither could these constraints explain why, in 1987, ten years after the public dispensary had opened, villagers would encourage the setting up of a private clinic where they would have to pay for services. Further, the fact that one clinic was private and the other was a government facility affected the incentives of the two dispensers: one got paid (when government paychecks were actually issued) whether or not the villagers were satisfied with his services; the other was remunerated only if the villagers valued his services. But attributing the success primarily to private ownership is too quick an answer and not all of the story.

Local residents were not involved in any of the decisions as to where the government dispensary should be located, how large it should be, what materials should be used in its construction, or even whether it should be built or not. Their only participation was the manual labor of constructing the building. Decisions about what hours the facility would be open, what services would be available, and when medicines and drugs would be sent were made elsewhere, with no input from the village. Decisions about who should be assigned to this post and how their performance was to be reviewed were also made elsewhere. Prior dispensers had not wanted the assignment in Wereng, far from their families and other opportunities, but

---

[3]The government dispenser had received a grade 2 teaching certificate and had taught primary school for three years. After this, he attended the School of Health Technology in Jos for three years. At the time of our visit, he was studying to be certified as a community health officer—the highest primary health care certification.

[4]The previous dispenser left the facility with no furniture except the dilapidated shelves and without handing over official papers. The village chief had given the new dispenser the table, and the church had given him the bench.

the present occupant had actually requested a transfer to Wereng; his family land was located there, and he could engage in farming to augment his low salary. While he was happy with this assignment, his satisfaction came from his opportunity for private gain rather than from serving the residents of Wereng.

In contrast, the chief of the village and local residents were involved in all major decisions in setting up the private clinic. The owner contacted the chief of the village about the possibility of moving to Wereng to establish the clinic. The chief interviewed him and discussed this possibility with the ward heads. To assist him in establishing a clinic, the village sold him a good plot of land at a low price. Similarly, he was allowed to buy a piece of nearby land at a reasonable price to set up his own farm. He would give surplus food from his own farm to malnourished villagers, and local residents would bring him their own surpluses either for his own use or to be given to those in need. The private clinic is, thus, tied into a network of relationships, even though it is privately owned and must earn sufficient income to cover costs. Analytical models of arms' length market exchanges do not include the type of reciprocity found between this private clinic and villagers.

The government facility, on the other hand, is hardly linked to the village at all. Analytical models of government service provision assume that public services will not be provided by private enterprises (or at least not at the quality and quantity desired). However, in this case, the government facility produced no services, while the private clinic was busy serving patients and had medicines on its shelves ready to dispense. Village residents were highly supportive of the private clinic and considered its presence a great asset to their community, while they considered the government facility as worth little to them. A fundamental lesson from this case is that physical facilities do not operate or maintain themselves automatically, nor is the allocation of trained personnel sufficient. Social capital in the form of local institutions is a necessary complement for physical and human capital to have a lasting impact (Clague, chap. 1, this volume).

1   The Meaning of Physical, Human, and Social Capital

All forms of capital are created by spending time and effort in transformation and transaction activities.[5] Investment in capital involves

---

[5]Transformation activities take physical inputs and transform them into physical outputs, which may then be used in either further transformation activities

making intertemporal decisions. Human and social capital may be developed as a by-product of other activities, while physical capital investment is usually a more conscious investment activity.

1.1 Physical capital

Physical capital is the stock of material resources that can be used to produce a flow of future income (Lachmann 1978). Physical capital exists in a wide variety of forms, including buildings, roads, waterworks, tools, cattle and other animals, automobiles, trucks, and tractors, to name just a few. "People form capital when they withhold resources from present consumption and use them instead to augment future consumption [or production] possibilities" (Bates 1990, 153). The origin of physical capital is the process of spending time and other resources constructing tools, plants, and facilities that can, in turn, be used in producing other products or future income.[6] The construction of the government dispensary in Wereng was such a process. Funds that could have been used to supply current needs were used instead to purchase building materials. Time that villagers could have used for other purposes was devoted to constructing the facility.

The construction of physical capital involves establishing physical restraints that (1) create the possibilities for some events to occur that would not otherwise occur (e.g., channeling water from a distant source to a farmer's field), and (2) constrain physical events to a more restricted domain (e.g., holding water in a channel rather than allowing it to spread out). Thus, physical capital opens up some possibilities while constraining others. A well-constructed building creates the possibilities of storing medicines and

---

or consumption. Transaction activities are the relationships among the individuals involved that take time and energy to accomplish the transformation activities. See Ostrom, Schroeder, and Wynne (1993) for a detailed discussion of the transformation and transaction costs involved in the provision and production of goods and services.

[6]Cattle have frequently been a major form of capital accumulation in Africa. Fielder (1973, 351) notes that the Ila of Zambia often say that: "Cattle are our bank." Fielder continues, "By this . . . they mean a deposit account where their property is saved and where it will increase in value the longer it stays there. Cattle are regarded very much as shares and investments in capitalist societies. . . . There is no mystery about it at all: the investment is a very sound and highly rational one, and every Ila, educated or otherwise, is imbued with its sense from the time he herds his father's cattle as a small boy" (352).

providing health care protected from the elements. It also implies that patients travel to the facility rather than that medical assistance travels to the patient.

The intention to construct useful physical capital is not always fulfilled—as is obvious in Wereng. Physical capital may not generate an improved flow of future services. An empty building represents a failed investment decision. Physical capital may even have a dark side and generate more harm than benefits. Investments in a power generation plant or other forms of infrastructure may produce more negative externalities than the benefits generated.

1.2   Human capital

Human capital is the health and acquired knowledge and skills that an individual brings to an activity. The forms that human capital take also differ: a college education is a different type of human capital than the skills a cabinetmaker acquires through apprenticeship training. Human capital is formed consciously, through education and training, and unconsciously through experience.

Both pharmacists in Wereng had invested their own time and energy in educational and training programs that increased their skills. Public treasuries had also invested in their human capital since education is highly subsidized in Nigeria. Both pharmacists had also learned how to farm to provide their families with a reliable source of food. In one case, the prior investment increased the services provided to others, while in the other case it did not. Human capital can be used for destructive purposes as well as productive ones; organizational skills can be devoted to the establishment of legitimate, commercial enterprises or to creating a gang that preys on innocent people.

1.3   Social capital

Social capital is the shared knowledge, understandings, institutions, and patterns of interactions that a group of individuals brings to any activity (Coleman 1988; Ostrom 1990; Putnam 1993). In any coordinated activity, participants accomplish far more per unit of time devoted to a joint activity if they draw on capital resources to reduce the level of inputs needed to produce the joint outcome. They can be far more productive, with whatever physical and human capital they draw on, if they can agree on a broad form of coordination and commit themselves credibly to a sequence of future actions. This agreement can be based on mutual learning about how to work better together or on one person agreeing to follow someone else's commands regarding this activity. It can be based on the evolution or construction of a set of norms or rules for how this activity will be carried out repeatedly over time and for how commitments will be monitored and sanctions imposed.

Social capital takes many forms. Putnam (1993) identifies social capital as involving networks, norms, and social beliefs that evolve out of processes that are not overtly investment activities. Family structure is considered a form of social capital. Bates (1990), for example, summarizes major research on the Luo and Kikuyu of Kenya, the Bambara of Mali, and East African pastoralists and clearly demonstrates that different types of lineage groups create different types of property rights and access to flows of future incomes. He points to the costs to individual families of belonging to extended lineages and the benefits that they obtain by spreading risk in those environments where ecological or economic variation is high.

Patterns of trust and reciprocity are another form of social capital. When individuals learn to trust one another so that they are able to make credible commitments and rely on generalized forms of reciprocity rather than on narrow sequences of specific quid pro quo relationships, they are' able to achieve far more than when these forms of social capital are not present. "In a reciprocal relationship, each individual contributes to the welfare of others with an expectation that others will do likewise, but without a fully contingent quid pro quo" (Oakerson 1993, 143). Thus, investments made in building trust and reciprocity can produce higher levels of return in the future, even though individuals are not fully conscious of the social capital they are constructing.

Both evolved and self-consciously designed rule and monitoring systems are forms of social capital. Thus, the crafting of institutions—sets of rules to allocate benefits from a physical facility and to assign responsibility for paying its costs—is a way to invest in social capital (Ostrom 1990, 1992). The rules used by individuals to structure their patterns of relationships may enhance or retard the creation of other forms of social capital and also affect the level and impact of human and physical capital (see Clague, chap. 2, this volume; Olson, chap. 3, this volume). As discussed below, rules relate to patterns of activities at several levels, from day-to-day operational activities all the way to constitutional activities that create and recreate the general patterns of authority in a society. The rules that individuals find productive depend upon the norms and patterns of reciprocity that already exist. Similarly, patterns of trust and reciprocity depend largely on existing rules. Oakerson (1993, 154) points out that modifying the structure of constitutions within a society is one technique for affecting the level of reciprocity—particularly, that between rulers and those who are ruled.

> To begin to modify a general constitution in which serious asymmetry exists, what needs to be done is to raise the price of rulership. To do this, one must find ways of introducing new elements of symmetry in order to leverage greater reciprocity from rules. Success will depend upon a capacity to sustain such relatively autonomous organizations as private businesses, labor unions, churches, and local governments, which are able to constrain the decisions of rulers. . . . Only the development of countervailing structures of authority and power can introduce greater reciprocity into the general constitution of a society in which serious political asymmetries exist.

Norms and *rules* are both considered forms of social capital, but they do not share all attributes (Crawford and Ostrom 1995). The norm of reciprocity implies some levels of symmetry among those who engage in long-term reciprocal relationships. Other norms, however, are not based on symmetric relationships. The norm of deference to elders or to those with more status or authority is based fundamentally on a concept of asymmetric relationships. The norm of retribution can trigger quite destructive and escalating patterns of conflict and violence. Rules imply asymmetries between those assigned authority to monitor and enforce them and those subject to the rules. Rules also contain a reference to a sanction that can be enforced if nonconformance to a rule is observed by such an authority.

All forms of social capital are based on patterns of relationships, whether these patterns are constructed consciously or unconsciously. Consequently, there are important analyses to be undertaken of all forms of capital formation, maintenance, and dissolution. Other analyses will need to focus on specific forms of capital such as family structure, gang structure, and patterns of entrepreneurship. To create social capital in a self-conscious manner, individuals must work with one another to find better ways of achieving outcomes. In Wereng, the chief and the members of his ward council tried to find ways of reducing the costs of setting up a private clinic. Land was provided at a subsidized price in the middle of the village, where health care could be easily provided to villagers as part of their everyday activities. The owner and the villagers give and take food surpluses as part of reciprocal relationships that supplement the quid pro quo relationships that must also be present for the owner to make a living.

Informal norms may be established without as much collective, self-conscious thought as is involved in creating new rules or establishing new entrepreneurial opportunities. Individuals facing a particular problem in a specific location and time decide to handle it in a particular manner. That decision seems to fit other situations that come along. After some repetition, the initial decision becomes a norm that most individuals in that community follow when they face this type of decision. While the group may never have discussed the establishment of the norm, the consideration of how best to act in this situation was made by many separate individuals as they faced similar situations over time.

Like physical capital and human capital, social capital opens up some opportunities while closing others. A decision to establish majority rule as the decision rule for making particular collective choice decisions, for example, opens opportunities that did not previously exist. Voting does not exist in nature, and the opportunity to vote is created by rules. A rule that forbids a farmer from growing a particular water-intensive crop—rice during the dry season, for example—restrains activities to a more limited set than previously available. A rule that villagers must construct health facilities changes the allocation of time from one activity to another.

2   Sustaining Social Capital over Time

Simply agreeing on a set of rules is, however, rarely enough to create social capital. Working out exactly what these rules mean takes time. If those learning how to use a set of rules do not trust one another, further investments are needed in extensive monitoring activities. Appropriate sanctions for nonconformance must be developed. Conditions under which exceptions to rules can be made without endangering the basic ordering principles must be discovered and discussed. Conflict over rule interpretation and adjustment will occur, which may destroy the process of building capital if no facilities for conflict resolution are available. The time it takes to develop workable rules, known to all relevant parties, is always substantial. If this is the first time a set of individuals has attempted joint activities, the time needed and the level of contestation involved in the process will tend to be higher than in settings where the same individuals have worked well together in the past.

Part of learning through experience is what happens when things go wrong. In all practical affairs, many things can go wrong. Everyone may not have received the same information about joint objectives, processes to be followed, and how one process feeds into another. Some may do their part, while others fail to perform. Some may want to interpret a rule in a way that is harmful to the interests of others. There may not be fair and objective conflict resolution processes available. Conflict may destroy prior lessons about how to work together and may reinforce prior doubts about the reliability and trustworthiness of some participants.

Social capital may enhance the outcomes of a few without any impact on others, or advantages to the few may come at the expense of others. Alternatively, the advantages to a few may generate positive benefits for others. Social capital can also have a dark side: cartels and organized crime are networks of relationships that lower overall productivity while generating disproportionate benefits for a few beneficiaries. A system of government based upon military command and the use of instruments of force can also destroy other forms of social capital while building its own.

2.1 Differences between social and physical capital

While social capital shares many characteristics with physical capital, it differs from physical capital in several respects. Many of these differences are due to the importance of shared cognitive understandings that are essential for social capital to exist and to continue from one generation to another.

First, social capital differs from physical capital in that it does not wear out with use but rather with disuse. Social capital may, in fact, improve with use as long as participants continue to keep prior commitments and maintain reciprocity and trust. Mutual understandings and ways of relating can frequently be used to accomplish entirely different joint activities at much lower start-up costs (Putnam 1993). It is not that learning curves for new activities disappear entirely. Rather, one of the steepest sections of a learning curve—learning to make commitments and to trust one another in a joint undertaking—has already been surmounted. The fungibility of social capital is, of course, limited. No tool is useful for all tasks. Social capital that is well adapted to one broad set of joint activities may not be easily molded to activities that require vastly different patterns of expectation, authority, and distribution of rewards and costs than those used in the initial sets of activities.

If unused, social capital deteriorates rapidly, just as individuals lose human capital when they do not exercise their skills. When several members of a permanent group must all remember the same routine in the same manner, however, the probability that at least one will forget some aspect of the routine increases rapidly over time. In addition, some individuals enter and others leave the groups. If newcomers are not introduced to the established pattern of interaction (through job training, initiation, or other ways), social capital dissipates. Eventually, no one is quite sure how they used to get a particular joint activity done. Either the group has to pay most of the start-up costs all over again, or it forgoes the joint advantages achieved at an earlier time.

Second, social capital is not as easy as physical capital to find, see, and measure. The presence of physical capital is usually obvious to onlookers. Health centers, schools, and roads are simple to see. Social capital, on the other hand, may be almost invisible unless serious efforts are made to inquire about the ways in which individuals organize themselves and the rights and duties that guide their behavior—sometimes with little conscious thought. Even when asked, local residents may not fully describe the rules they use.[7] If external agents of change do not expect that villagers have developed ways of relating to one another that are productive in the setting in which they live, those who are trying to help may easily destroy social capital without knowing what they have done. If past social capital is destroyed and nothing takes its place, well-being can be harmed by such external "help."

Consequently, social capital is harder than physical capital to construct through external interventions. A donor can provide the funds to hire contractors to build a road or a health facility. Building sufficient social capital, however, to make an infrastructure operate efficiently requires knowledge of local practices that may differ radically from place to place. Organizational structures that facilitate the operation of physical capital in one setting may be counterproductive in another. Local knowledge is essential to building effective social capital.

Third, the creation of a "strong" state may reduce the capabilities of other institutions to build social capital. When national governments declare that they will provide all education and health services in a country and close down schools and hospitals run by religious groups, they destroy an immense stock of social capital in short order. Rarely can this be replaced rapidly. Creating dependent citizens rather than entrepreneurial citizens reduces the capacity of individuals to generate capital.

---

[7]Yoder (1994, 39) warns those interested in helping farmers that they must probe deeply and in nonthreatening ways to get adequate information on the rules used to allocate water and maintenance duties. "Intimidated by the higher status of officials, they may fail to communicate the details of the rules and procedures they use to operate and maintain their system."

Elinor Ostrom

2.2 Capital and development

Development efforts have focused on physical capital and, to a lesser extent, on building human capital through education and training. Much less effort has been devoted to learning about indigenous social capital, which can be drawn on effectively to enhance the other investments. The importance of social capital (with notable and successful exceptions) has been overlooked, a problem in primary health care and education in many developing countries. It is also a major problem in Asia with regard to irrigation, which can make a major difference in crop yields per unit of effort or land.

The difficulty of sustaining collective action over the long term, when contributions are costly and benefits are hard to measure and dispersed over time and space (Olson 1965), has led many to presume that only interventions from state agencies could provide adequate infrastructure in developing countries. Further, where technical knowledge and economies of scale are involved, it has often been presumed that this external force should be a large, centralized government. If collective action did occur at a local level, it was feared that it would be undertaken by those who already have substantial assets and power, exacerbating the differences between the haves and the have-nots in rural areas of developing countries (Pant 1984). The central government has been seen as the agent of change that can break the control of wealthy landowners, who obtain a disproportionate share of whatever suboptimal collective action is undertaken. In many countries in Asia, almost all irrigation facilities are provided by and, in principle, operated by government agencies. Recent research on the performance of large government agencies in the supply and governance of irrigation in Asia, however, provides strong evidence that most large irrigation systems that lack active farmer participation perform inadequately (Ascher and Healy 1990; Uphoff 1986; Chambers 1988).

Making large investments in irrigation efficient is difficult for many reasons. While central agencies may be involved in the design of engineering works, farmers may be doing much of the day-to-day upkeep of these systems. Farmers are rarely consulted by design engineers when new investments are being contemplated (Pradhan 1989b; Uphoff 1986; Tang 1992). Educated engineers presume that uneducated farmers do not know enough about hydrology and engineering to be consulted. Consequently, engineers do not learn from local farmers many of the local details about soil conditions, water velocity, and shifting watercourses that are important to make "improved" engineering works operate better than the "primitive" systems they replace. Irrigation engineers have also paid little attention to the distribution of water rights that existed prior to the construction of new systems (Coward 1980).

Unless an agency allocates substantial personnel to the operation and maintenance of an irrigation system, it is the farmers who must make these systems work after the engineers have reconstructed them. Even when a government agency reconstructs a system that had been built and operated by farmers and takes on the further task of operation and maintenance of a rebuilt system, it is the farmers who bear all the risk of growing crops dependent on a supply of water over which they now have no control. Insufficient emphasis has been placed on the incentives that officials of government agencies and farmers face after a new irrigation system is constructed or an existing system is reconstructed. The presumption has been that making a physical system easier to operate and maintain would automatically enable farmers to produce agricultural products more effectively.

Improving the physical structure of an irrigation system may change the relationships among participants within an irrigation system and destroy extant social capital that has been slowly constituted to cope with the day-to-day operation and maintenance of a system. External interventions to improve the physical attributes of farmer-organized irrigation systems have been known to lead to the demise of farmers' organizations that had successfully managed even large and complex systems prior to their "improvement."

3   Irrigation System Performance in Nepal

While many development policies have been based on a presumption that national governments need to solve collective action problems where farmers cannot do so, evidence from recent studies of irrigation systems in Nepal is not consistent with this view (Ostrom and Gardner 1993; Benjamin et al. 1994; Lam 1994, Ostrom 1994). Yield data are available for 108 systems in the Nepal Irrigation Institutions and Systems (NIIS) data base, created by colleagues associated with the Workshop in Political Theory and Policy Analysis at Indiana University and the Institute of Agriculture and Animal Science in Rampur, Nepal.[8]   Of these, 86 farmer-governed

---

[8]Data were compiled from detailed case studies (including, among others, Pradhan 1989a; Svendsen and Small 1990; Laitos et al. 1986; Martin and Yoder 1983; Shivakoti 1991, 1992; Yoder 1986; Curtis 1991) and supplemented by field

systems average six metric tons a year per hectare; the 22 agency-managed systems average five metric tons per hectare ($p = .06$). Systems organized by the farmers also tend to achieve higher crop intensities. A crop intensity of 100 percent means that all land in an irrigation system is put to full use for one season, or partial use over multiple seasons amounting to the same coverage. A crop intensity of 200 percent is full use for two seasons; 300 percent is full use for three seasons. The cropping intensity achieved at the tail end of irrigation systems in the three major agricultural regions of Nepal—the hills, the river valleys, and the Terai—are arrayed in table 7.1. In all regions, including the flat Terai where both agency and farmers' systems tend to be large, the average tailend cropping intensity achieved on farmer-managed systems is greater than on agency-managed systems.

Table 7.1

**Tailend Cropping Intensity
by Type of Governance Arrangement and Terrain**

Terrain	N	Farmer-Managed Irrigation Systems		Agency-Managed Irrigation Systems		p
		%	Number	%	Number	
Hills	46	238	40	155	6	.00
River valleys	26	205	17	182	9	.31
Terai	46	250	40	208	6	.06
All systems	118	237	97	182	21	.00

One of the basic reasons for the difference in performance, controlling for size and type of region, between farmer-organized and government-organized irrigation systems is the incentive structure. Incentives are the positive and negative outcomes that actors expect from actions taken within a set of working rules given a relevant physical and social setting. Incentives include financial rewards and penalties but are not limited to them. Rules

---

visits to many of the systems in early 1992 and the summer of 1993 (see Benjamin et al. 1994).

that affect how individuals are recruited, monitored, and rewarded are among the important sources of incentives. The internal values of individuals and the general cultural values shared by individuals in a community are also a source of incentives. Engineers and irrigators, for example, will be influenced by professional and cultural values as well as by the pay and work policies of the agencies for which they work. Thus, incentives are the result of how different forms of social capital interact within the sociophysical setting.

3.1   Incentives in agency-managed irrigation systems

Currently, most professional staff on government irrigation systems in Nepal are employed within a civil service system with only two levels: gazetted and nongazetted.[9] The former is the higher civil service whose appointment, promotion, and transfer are published in the Nepal *Gazette*. In the Department of Irrigation, staff above the rank of section officer belong to the gazetted level. Almost all officials in this group have a baccalaureate degree in engineering, and it is these officials who are responsible for managing irrigation systems. Below the gazetted officials are junior staff, who work near the field doing accounting and administrative work. Education requirements at the nongazetted level include a minimum ten years of education or the equivalent; recruitment is also through open examinations. (Staff employed to do manual labor do not have civil service status.)

Promotion in the Department of Irrigation is largely based upon seniority, the evaluation of superiors, and qualifications. Only four grades exist in both the gazetted and nongazetted levels, and because of this shallow range of grades, promotion is slow. Officials spend an average ten to fifteen years in the same position. Several features of the civil service system affect the behavior patterns of irrigation officials (see Lam 1994).

First, the results of civil service examinations and formal qualifications are the two major criteria for the recruitment and career advancement of irrigation officials. Neither criterion is relevant to ability to work with farmers, knowledge about irrigation systems, and success in solving the day-to-day problems of an irrigation system. From the perspective of officials, their jobs and status derive from their profession rather than whether they can serve farmers well.

---

[9]This section draws on Ostrom, Lam, and Lee (1994).

Second, farmers do not participate at all in the hiring of irrigation officials. Farmers have no say even in the hiring of the lowest level government employees with whom farmers will have the most frequent contact. For farmers, Department of Irrigation officials are a group of strangers who have many resources but who know almost nothing about the people and the agricultural systems in a particular locality.

Third, promotion, as a motivational tool, is rendered ineffective by the length of time it takes. For an official, outstanding performance might pay off only after a long time, if at all. For officials whose discount rates are high, short-term comfort may be preferable to long-term career advancement through hard work. Why work when the payoff is so remote? If civil servants can observe that good evaluation is not accompanied by an appropriate reward, they are not likely to treat evaluations seriously. Why should a civil servant strive for excellence in any matter if evaluations do not have a major effect on future returns?

Fourth, seniority has effectively become the most important criterion for promotion, while evaluation has been increasingly abandoned by superiors as a motivational tool. When seniority becomes the basic criterion for promotion, there is little incentive for officials to be actively involved in solving farmers' problems. Individual initiative and creativity are discouraged. Such a situation becomes even more perverse when local politics affect the promotion decision. Facing an incentive structure in which pleasing politicians instead of hard work pays off, officials have a strong temptation to assist politicians in their rent-seeking activities.

Fifth, corruption pervades the day-to-day operation of the many government offices and takes many petty and far-from-petty forms. The most serious corruption in the use of public funds comes from large government contracts. Politicians try to bring government contracts to their districts as a way of winning political support but also as a way of receiving "commissions." Contractors provide a percentage of the contract in "commissions" to the appropriate field representative of the government, who, after taking his cut, passes on the rest up the bureaucratic hierarchy to the higher level government officials who arranged the commissions in the first place. A contractor describing the system concluded by saying that "in Nepal, only corruption is on an organized basis!" (Benjamin 1989, 259). There is a strong incentive for civil servants in many countries to join the bandwagon of corruption. A civil servant working in an agency where corruption is widespread will find that the only options open are to cooperate in the corruption, be isolated by colleagues, ask for a transfer, or quit. If he does not cooperate, he will likely be harassed by his coworkers or transferred by superiors anxious that their share of the illicit proceeds arrive as promised. The pressure to conform is strong. And, given the low salary levels of civil servants, forgoing the income associated with "accepted" practices is also extremely difficult.

Sixth, professional engineers have undertaken higher education in order to gain the status associated with the profession. Building things is where the status is in engineering. Being assigned to operation and maintenance is considered undesirable in terms of both status and the financial support given to the division: funding is weak and such assignments provide few opportunities for personal income enhancement. Officials may find themselves engulfed in conflict with village factions and dissatisfied farmers.

Seventh, civil servants usually wish to invest in the health and education of their children and to live an urban lifestyle away from the village settings from which many have come. Operation and maintenance assignments in remote areas are considered highly undesirable unless they are related to an active construction phase of a project. Officials assigned as resident engineers tend to spend as much time as possible in Kathmandu with their families, who live there permanently and, further, they try to arrange for transfers to headquarters.

Given the absence of intrinsic or extrinsic rewards to government officials for keeping an irrigation system in good condition or for encouraging agricultural productivity, it is not surprising that most systems constructed by the government of Nepal and maintained by engineers assigned to operation and maintenance activities are not adequately maintained. The only strong incentives for government officials are those related to the construction of new facilities rather than the upkeep of old ones. Construction of modern irrigation systems with permanent headworks and lined canals has been for many engineers a source of professional pride (and sometimes a source of personal income).

3.2   Incentives in farmer-organized irrigation systems

In contrast to agency systems, farmers tend to operate their own systems relatively effectively and achieve higher agricultural productivity. In government systems, someone other than farmers determines the design of the physical system, what boundaries to use to determine who receives water, how water should be allocated, how responsibilities for maintenance should be determined, and how rule infractions should be monitored and enforced. In farmer-governed systems, farmers not only have a voice in most of these decisions, they make most of them.[10] The persons chosen to be officials on farmer-governed systems are usually themselves farmers. Those who allocate water are employed only as long as they are considered efficient and fair in the conduct of their duties. Officials are often paid in grain at the end of the season. If the system operates well, the amount of grain to be shared is greater. Thus, incentives for those who operate farmers' systems are tied very closely to overall productivity. Collective action problems are overcome by rules crafted by the farmers themselves (Ostrom 1992; Tang 1992; Lam 1994).

3.3   Investments in physical capital and performance

During the past three decades, substantial investments have been made in modernizing the physical capital of irrigation systems in Nepal. The presumption has been that the primitive irrigation systems that farmers had built could be improved substantially by constructing modern, permanent headworks and by lining the canals with concrete; in areas where farmers depend entirely on rain to water their crops, plans were made to construct new agency systems with extensive physical hardware. Analysis of the NIIS data base, however, does not provide evidence that these investments are associated with higher performance.

A multivariate analysis (Ostrom and Gardner 1993) finds that the difference in water availability at the head and at the tail of irrigation systems is significantly affected both by physical variables and by the type of governance. Holding other variables constant, the presence of a permanent headworks (usually constructed and financed by external sources) is associated with the largest difference in water availability between the head and tail of systems. Systems governed by farmers showed smaller differences.

A later study (Lam 1994, 221) finds that Nepali irrigation systems with permanent headworks have significantly lower performance, controlling for terrain and size of system, than systems without permanent headworks, on three dimensions: the physical condition of the canals, water delivery, and agricultural productivity. All three measures are significantly lower for irrigation systems where there are differences in water availability between the head and tail sections of the canal (Lam 1994, 224). On the other hand, the cost of maintaining such systems, in the form of labor days, is lower. Only 2 days per household per year are devoted to maintenance on systems

---

[10]For a more detailed analysis of farmers' incentives, see Ostrom (1994).

with permanent headworks, while about 5⅓ days per household per year are devoted on systems with at least partial lining (but without permanent headworks) and 8½ days per household on those systems without lining or permanent headworks (Lam 1994, 222; $p = .02$).

Thus, the cost of maintaining systems where investments in physical capital have been made in the form of permanent headworks and at least partial linings is less than the cost of maintenance on those unlined, farmer constructed and operated systems with only mud, rocks, and trees for headworks. In this regard, the investment in physical capital has reduced the operating costs of running these systems, as expected. However, this is only an intermediate benefit and is not associated with increased agricultural productivity. The reduction in labor time with permanent headworks provides a clue as to why and how these investments in physical capital are associated with reduced, rather than increased, agricultural productivity.

Physical structure affects the nature of the relationships among individuals and can increase or decrease the difficulties involved in developing adequate social capital to make physical structures operate efficiently. In irrigation systems, the relationships among farmers are affected by the physical fact that headenders can obtain water before tailenders. When farmers are growing rice, they can hardly obtain too much water. Headend farmers prefer to take as much water as they can get whenever it is available so that they do not risk reduced crop yields due to water stress. Further, having standing water on their fields decreases the amount of labor needed for weeding. Thus, "natural" asymmetries exist in the physical relationships among headenders and tailenders. To gain effective economic returns from the operation of irrigation systems in rice-growing regions, these asymmetries must be overcome through social organization that gets water to the tailend of the system. Since the marginal benefit of having standing water on the fields of headenders is much less than the marginal benefit of getting more water to the tailend of the system, efficiency requires that tailend farmers obtain reliable rights to sufficient water for crops other than those planted during the monsoon season. They also need to be able to hold headend farmers accountable for getting that water to them.

In farmer-organized systems, tailenders meet often with headenders to bargain over the rules they will use for water allocation and resource mobilization. In those systems where the resources needed for maintenance are substantial, tailend farmers have substantial bargaining power. They can refuse to contribute resources (primarily their labor) unless the headenders make credible commitments to allocate sufficient water to them so that their investment in maintenance is worthwhile. Thus, institutions resulting from bargaining over the rules is affected by the relative symmetry or asymmetry of the participants.

External intervention to "improve" existing irrigation systems can disrupt the relative bargaining power of tailenders. Since many external interventions do not require farmers to pay back the investments made in modernizing the physical capital, these "gifts" can be disruptive. Without any need for resources from tailenders, headenders can ignore their interests and take a larger share of the benefits. It is particularly tragic that investments made in a very poor country have reduced, rather than improved, agricultural productivity.

3.4   An intervention that worked

Based on a detailed understanding of these processes and a deep awareness of the sophistication of many farmer-governed systems in Nepal, Prachandra Pradhan and Robert Yoder designed an intervention strategy that overcame many of the perverse incentives that typify prior efforts. This project is funded by the Ford Foundation and designed by the Water and Energy Commission/Secretariat, Nepal, and the International Irrigation Management Institute in Nepal (WECS/IIMI). Because of their long-standing research and action program in Nepal (Yoder 1986; Pradhan 1989a, 1989b), these two researchers became aware of highly successful farmer-governed irrigation systems, which had survived for long periods of time and had achieved agricultural yields far above average. Poor roads and communication networks made farmers in one area virtually unaware of what farmers in other areas were capable of doing. Farmers in many areas could also effectively utilize modest levels of new physical capital.

Under the WECS/IIMI project, a preassessment of 119 farmer-organized irrigation systems in the Indrawati basin in the Sindhu Palchok district identified 19 irrigation systems that had at least some level of operating organization and that could substantially benefit from better alignment of canals, new materials for aqueducts, and modest lining of the canals. To obtain external aid, the farmers had to agree to the following conditions:[11]

---

[11]My thanks to Robert Yoder for reviewing a draft of these conditions and supplying me with a carefully revised list of conditions.

—The farmers would form a water-users organization to identify existing and future users and to develop a plan for water allocation approved by all identified water users.

—The farmers would prepare an initial plan for improvements to the system and for its future operation and management.

—The farmers would determine the requirements for unpaid labor and set the rates for paid labor (within guidelines set by the project). Money saved by lower labor rates could be used for further improvements.

—The organization would appoint a management committee to assist the field engineer in carrying out the site investigation, design work, and day-to-day implementation.

—The farmers would keep records of their expenditures and of decisions made at meetings, records that were to be available to anyone who asked to see them.

The project hired engineers, who listened to farmers and who stressed the design of improvements that the farmers themselves could operate. The designs were shown to the farmers, who made suggestions for improvements. The farmers had to sign off on the designs, so there was a considerable amount of time and effort put into learning from the farmers about how the existing systems operated and blending the knowledge brought by the design engineers with the farmers' knowledge. Once agreement was reached on how each improvement would be designed, the farmers ranked the improvements into first-, second-, and third-level priorities. The farmers were told that funds allocated to their system would be equal to the amount estimated as necessary for the first-priority improvements. They could decide to contribute part of the labor (generally done by reducing the labor rate) and take other measures to save money and use the savings for second- and third-priority improvements. Many of the systems were able to construct all of the desired improvements because of the resources that the farmers themselves contributed.

The project also offered a farmer-to-farmer training program, which was among the more ingenious aspects of this project. Farmer representatives were taken from the systems in the project area to irrigation systems in other districts (similar in terrain) where farmers had designed particularly effective governance structures. The farmer representatives (1) attended an annual meeting of one of these systems, (2) toured the entire length of the farmer-governed system, discussing why the farmers had used different kinds of weirs (mechanisms to divide water among branches of the canal) and how these were related to water rights, and (3) participated in a special session in which they could question the local farmers about the patterns of association that had evolved in the successful systems. In other words, the program enabled farmers who had developed successful social capital in one setting to impart that knowledge to other farmers from a similar setting. Given that the visiting farmers could tell rapidly that the farmers in the systems they were visiting were doing much better than they were, the visiting farmer representative took this training program very seriously. This was not a college graduate telling them about principles learned from a textbook; it was a group of similarly situated farmers telling them how they had been more successful in achieving collective action through their own investment in rules that had been tested in their local circumstances.

The proof of the effectiveness of this development project takes two forms (WECS/IIMI 1990; Lam and Shivakoti 1992). The first is in increased land productivity (tables 7.2 and 7.3). The second is in the difference in the social capital constructed by the farmers. A survey was conducted one year later to ascertain what governance and management differences could be observed (Yoder 1991). In all nineteen systems, farmers indicated a stronger sense of ownership. Leadership had changed in eleven of the systems but was now clearly defined in all nineteen systems. Nine of the systems reported changes in the rules they had developed for operation and maintenance, and formal meetings with recorded minutes continued after project completion. "In all systems there has been more cooperative effort to maintain the canal during the monsoon" (Yoder 1991, 13). The variety of rules adopted, ways of handling maintenance responsibilities, and ways of monitoring conformance indicate that farmers did not simply copy something an official showed them but struggled to develop their own workable systems. The project encouraged the slow development of rules rather than the rapid passage of rules that will not work. The farmers have also had to learn how to enforce their own rules. Farmers in several systems branched out, growing crops that they could not have grown before when their irrigation was unpredictable.

Table 7.2

Irrigable Area and Cost of Improvements to FMIS in Sindhupalchok

System	Existing Command Area (ha)	Expansion Command Area (ha)	Total Irrigable Area (ha)	Project Grant (NRs)	Cost per Irrigable Hectare (NRs)
Chhahare	126	37	163	126,615	777
Naya Dhara	55	55	110	139,720	1,270
Besi	65	20	85	119,839	1,410
Dhap & Subedar	30	35	65	85,000	1,308
Soti Bagar	19	11	30	150,699	5,023
Dovaneswar	2	10	12	74,807	6,234
Magar	100	43	143	160,805	1,125
Siran Tar	18	6	24	136,789	5,700
Majha Tar	71	16	87	114,321	1,314
Ghatta Muhan	23	10	33	124,321	3,767
Bhanjyang Tar	21	14	35	65,178	1,862
Tallo Jhankri	18	13	31	91,707	2,958
Chholang Khet	23	14	37	116,066	3,137
Chapbot	12	5	17	71,630	4,214
Baghmara	3	6	9	44,433	4,937
Siran Baguwa	18	19	37	57,488	1,554
Majha Baguwa	13	20	33	113,541	3,441
Tallo Chapleti	8	15	23	78,065	3,394
Total	625	349	974	1,871,024	
Average cost/ irrigable ha					1,921
Consultant & supervision				1,192,747	
Tools supplied				82,182	
Farmer training				55,000	
Average cost of supervision/ha					1,356
Total cost of improvement/ha					3,286

Source: WECS/IIMI (1990, 29); Lam and Shivakoti (1992).

Table 7.3

Area Growing Irrigated Crops in Winter Season Immediately before and after Assistance and Headend and Tailend Cropping Intensities

System	Potato		Oilseed		Wheat		Vegetables		Head Intensity		Tail Intensity	
	Pre	Post	Pre	Post	Pre	Post	Pre	Post	Pre	Post	Pre	Post
Chhahare	0.2	2.5	n/a	n/a	n/a	n/a	0.1	1.6	200	167	200	192
Naya Dhara	n/a	n/a	n/a	n/a	n/a	n/a	n/a	n/a	200	200	200	200
Besi	n/a	n/a	n/a	n/a	n/a	n/a	n/a	n/a	200	235	200	235
Subedar	0.2	0.4	3.0	12.0	6.0	15.0	0.2	0.4	250	270	250	270
Dhap	0.2	0.4	3.0	12.0	6.0	15.0	0.2	0.4	250	290	250	250
Soti Bagar	0	0.6	0.2	2.5	6.0	15.0	0.2	0.4	150	215	150	215
Dovanswar	0	0.5	0	0	1.0	2.0	0	0.2	300	200	300	200
Magar	0.5	2.5	0	1.0	n/a	n/a	0.5	1.3	190	194	190	200
Siran Tar	0.5	0.8	3.5	3.5	n/a	n/a	0.2	0.5	255	200	255	250
Majha Tar	0.8	3.0	2.5	3.0	3.0	15.0	0.5	1.5	300	230	300	230
Ghatta Muhan	0.3	0.8	0.6	1.3	10.0	10.0	0.5	1.0	271	290	271	270
Bhanjyang Tar	0.4	0.4	0.5	1.5	3.0	6.0	0.5	0.6	260	300	260	220
Tallo Jhankri	n/a	n/a	n/a	n/a	n/a	n/a	n/a	n/a	200	270	200	270
Chholang Khet	0	4.6	2.0	3.5	63.0	63.0	0	1.5	220	235	220	220
Chapbot	n/a	n/a	n/a	n/a	n/a	n/a	n/a	n/a	270	300	270	270
Baghmara	n/a	n/a	n/a	n/a	n/a	n/a	n/a	n/a	300	300	300	300
Siran Baguwa	2.5	5.5	3.5	8.5	10.0	15.0	0.5	1.5	300	295	300	285
Majha Baguwa	0	5.0	0	7.5	0	20	0	2.0	280	300	280	300
Tallo Chapleti	n/a	n/a	n/a	n/a	n/a	n/a	n/a	n/a	250	300	n/a	300

Source: WECS/IIMI (1990, 29); Lam and Shivakoti (1992).

Further social capital formation is in the making. Some farmers from the more successful systems have set up a consulting firm and are holding training sessions, thus greatly augmenting their income. The Institute of Agriculture and Animal Science is planning to develop an association of farmer-governed irrigation systems and publishes a Nepali-language newsletter that highlights developments of interest to self-organized farmers and describes the successful farmer-governed associations.

4   Conclusion

When farmers select their own officials to govern and manage an irrigation system they own and operate, officials' incentives are closely aligned with the incentives of farmers in the system. System performance is linked to farmers' evaluation made of officials' performance. Similarly, when villagers invite a pharmacist to open a private clinic in their community, the clinic's performance is linked to the evaluation the villagers make of the services and goods provided. For most national government systems, no such linkage is present; where the revenue paid to an irrigation agency or a health clinic is not linked to taxes placed on the value of a crop yield or to the health of a community, the agency's budget is not even loosely linked to system performance. Nothing offsets the dependency of citizens on insulated officials where fees are not an important source of revenue to the units' operating and maintaining systems and where the hiring, retention, and promotion of employees are in no way connected with the system's performance. The incentives of farmers, villagers, and officials weigh more than the engineering of physical systems in determining performance.

The difficulties of sustaining long-term collective action are substantial, but the benefits of creating local organizations and selecting locals as leaders who are rewarded for their performance can offset these difficulties. Instead of assuming that collective action is impossible, we are better advised to assume that it is possible, even though difficult. What is needed is sufficient local autonomy to invest in the social and physical capital involved in building systems and monitoring performance.

Donor agencies should think about investing in those countries and sectors within countries where self-organizing activities already exist. Funds that only bolster political careers and build little at the ground level are a poor investment from a donor's perspective. Further, since the likelihood of success of any project or reform effort is always less than unity, investing in a larger number of smaller projects makes more sense—in terms of impact—than investing in large projects, some of which are very likely to fail. The record of large infrastructure projects funded by donors during the past forty years has been less than distinguished. It is hard for donor agencies to accept the notion that some projects will fail and that mega-projects are particularly suspect, given their own incentives to "move the money." But as the volume of money available to donor agencies is reduced, the need to spread risk across a wider array of projects becomes even more important. It makes more sense to invest in those projects where the recipients invest some of their own capital. In such settings, an infusion of external monetary capital and the construction of physical capital to complement social capital may cumulate to a substantial degree.

Social capital is created and maintained by the very process of working together. It can be eroded by a lack of attention to the way a physical structure affects the relationships among participants, to the kind of trust and reciprocity that exists, or to the rules that individuals themselves have developed regarding the allocation of inputs and the distribution of benefits. Social capital is definitely destroyed by the lack of sanctions for breach of prior commitments. Universal rules imposed without regard to local conditions will also undermine social capital. Rapid changes in population or in the relative prices of important inputs are major exogenous shocks to existing social capital that may or may not be overcome depending on the creativity and autonomy of local public and private entrepreneurs. Major changes in agricultural prices or new opportunities for labor away from remote villages also challenge the viability of the institutional arrangements that have been constructed over time. Such exogenous shocks, however, are less likely to threaten institutions in areas where arenas for communication and joint problem solving have already been established. Once participants learn they can solve some problems effectively by adjusting their own rules and procedures, their capabilities for adjusting in the future are far better.

References

Ascher, W., and R. Healy. 1990. *Natural Resource Policymaking in Developing Countries.* Durham: Duke University Press.

Ayo, D., K. Hubbell, D. Olowu, E. Ostrom, and T. West. 1992. *The Experience in Nigeria with Decentralization Approaches to Local Delivery of Primary Education and Primary Health Services.* Burlington, Vt.: Associates in Rural Development.

Bates, R. H. 1990. "Capital, Kinship, and Conflict: The Structuring of Capital in Kinship Societies." *Canadian Journal of African Studies* 24: 151–64.

Benjamin, P. 1989. "Local Organization for Development in Nepal." Ph.D. diss. University of North Carolina, Chapel Hill.

Benjamin, P., W. F. Lam, E. Ostrom, and G. Shivakoti. 1994. *Institutions, Incentives, and Irrigation in Nepal.* Burlington, Vt.: Associates in Rural Development.

Chambers, R. 1988. *Managing Canal Irrigation: Practical Analysis from South Asia.* New Delhi: Oxford and IBH Publishing.

Coleman, J. 1988. "Social Capital in the Creation of Human Capital." *American Journal of Sociology*, suppl. 94: 95–120.

Coward, E. W., Jr., ed. 1980. *Irrigation and Agricultural Development in Asia: Perspectives from the Social Sciences.* Ithaca: Cornell University Press.

Crawford, S., and E. Ostrom. 1995. "A Grammar of Institutions." *American Political Science Review* 89: 582–600.

Curtis, D. 1991. *Beyond Government: Organizations for Common Benefit.* London: Macmillan.

Fiadjoe, F., D. Green, C. Schwabe, and T. West. 1992. *Decentralization: Improving Governance in Sub-Saharan Africa—Ghana Case Study.* Burlington, Vt.: Associates in Rural Development.

Fielder, R. J. 1973. "The Role of Cattle in Ila Economy." *African Social Research* 15: 327–61.

Garnier, M., A. B. Noel, C. Schwabe, and J. Thomson. 1992. *The Experience in Ivory Coast with Decentralized Approaches to Local Delivery of Primary Education and Primary Health Services.* Burlington, Vt.: Associates in Rural Development.

Lachmann, L. M. 1978. *Capital and Its Structure.* Kansas City: Sheed Andrews and McMeel.

Laitos, R., et al. 1986. "Rapid Appraisal of Nepal Irrigation Systems." Water Management Synthesis Report 43. Colorado State University, Fort Collins.

Lam, W. F. 1994. "Institutions, Engineering Infrastructure, and Performance in the Governance and Management of Irrigation Systems: The Case of Nepal." Ph.D. diss. Indiana University, Bloomington.

Lam, W. F., and G. Shivakoti. 1992. "A Before and After Analysis of the Effect of Farmer-to-Farmer Training as an Intervention Strategy." Technical report. Workshop in Political Theory and Policy Analysis, Indiana University.

Martin, E. D., and R. Yoder. 1983. "Review of farmer-managed irrigation in Nepal." Paper prepared for the Water Management Issues Seminar, APROSC, Kathmandu, July 31–August 2.

Oakerson, R. J. 1993. "Reciprocity: A Bottom-Up View of Political Development." In *Rethinking Institutional Analysis and Development: Some Issues, Choices and Alternatives*, ed. V. Ostrom, D. Feeny, and H. Picht. San Francisco: Institute for Contemporary Studies Press.

Olson, M. 1965. *The Logic of Collective Action.* Cambridge: Harvard University Press.

Ostrom, E. 1990. *Governing the Commons: The Evolution of Institutions for Collective Action.* Cambridge: Cambridge University Press.

———. 1992. *Crafting Institutions for Self-Governing Irrigation Systems.* San Francisco: Institute for Contemporary Studies Press.

———. 1994. "Constituting Social Capital and Collective Action." *Journal of Theoretical Politics* 6: 527–62.

Ostrom, E., and R. Gardner. 1993. "Coping with Asymmetries in the Commons: Self-Governing Irrigation Systems Can Work." *Journal of Economic Perspectives* 7: 93–112.

Ostrom, E., W. F. Lam, and M. Lee. 1994. "The Performance of Self-Governing Irrigation Systems in Nepal." *Human Systems Management* 13: 197–207.

Ostrom, E., L. Schroeder, and S. Wynne. 1993. *Institutional Incentives and Sustainable Development: Infrastructure Policies in Perspective.* Boulder, Colo.: Westview.

Pant, N., ed. 1984. *Productivity and Equity in Irrigation Systems.* New Delhi: Ashish.

Pradhan, P. 1989a. *Increasing Agricultural Production in Nepal: Role of Low-Cost Irrigation Development through Farmer Participation.* Colombo, Sri Lanka: International Irrigation Management Institute.

———. 1989b. *Patterns of Irrigation Organization in Nepal.* Colombo, Sri Lanka: International Irrigation Management Institute.

Putnam, R. 1993. "The Prosperous Community: Social Capital and Public Life." *American Prospect.* Spring: 35–42.

Sengupta, N. 1991. *Managing Common Property: Irrigation in India and the Philippines.* New Delhi: Sage.

Shivakoti, G. P. 1991. "Effects of Public Intervention in Farmer-Managed Irrigation Systems in Nepal." Paper prepared for the second annual meeting of the International Association for the Study of Common Property, Winnipeg, Canada.

————. *Variations in Intervention, Variations in Result: Assisting FMIS in Nepal.* London: ODI Irrigation Management Network.

Svendsen, M., and L. Small. 1990. "Farmers' Perspective on Irrigation Performance." *Irrigation and Drainage Systems* 4: 385–402.

Tang, S. Y. 1992. *Institutions and Collective Action: Self-Governance in Irrigation.* San Francisco: Institute for Contemporary Studies.

Uphoff, N. 1986. *Improving International Irrigation Management with Farmer Participation: Getting the Process Right.* Boulder, Colo.: Westview.

WECS/IIMI (Water and Energy Commission/Secretariat, Nepal, and International Irrigation Management Institute). 1990. *Assistance to Farmer-Managed Irrigation Systems: Results, Lessons, and Recommendations from an Action-Research Project.* Colombo, Sri Lanka: International Irrigation Management Institute.

Yoder, R. D. 1986. "Farmer-Managed Irrigation Systems in the Hills of Nepal." Ph.D. diss. Cornell University.

————.1991. "Peer Training as a Way to Motivate Institutional Change in Farmer-Managed Irrigation Systems." Paper prepared for Workshop on Democracy and Governance, Washington, D.C., September 19.

————. 1994. *Locally Managed Irrigation Systems.* Colombo, Sri Lanka: International Irrigation Management Institute.

8   Social Capital and Technical Change: The *Groupements Naam* of Burkina Faso

Melinda Smale and Vernon Ruttan

During the 1970s, in the most environmentally degraded region of Burkina Faso, one of the poorest countries of sub-Saharan Africa, farmers constructed earthen dikes to harvest water and retain soils across an estimated 60,000 hectares (150,000 acres). In the following decade, finding that porous, stone dikes were more effective and durable, they covered thousands of hectares with stone dikes—despite an estimated labor input of up to two hundred person-hours per hectare (Sanders, Nagy, and Rama- swamy 1990; Critchley 1991). Although the labor cost of dike construction to individual farmers is likely to be prohibitive, the water-retention technology enhances the private profitability of a recommended technical package of improved sorghum seed and modest levels of fertilizer (ICRISAT 1985; Sanders, Nagy, and Ramaswamy 1990). A traditional method that was improved by Yatenga farmers and members of the nongovernmental organization Oxfam, the stone dikes have been in large part diffused by the *groupements naam* (Harrison 1987). The *groupements naam* are mutual assistance groups derived from the traditional age-set associations of Mossi culture.

The contour dike construction by the *groupements naam* illustrates a fundamental theme of the New Institutional Economics—that social capital, in the form of institutions that affect economic behavior, may be a more important explanatory factor than physical or human capital in economic development.[1] Certain cultural endowments of the Mossi contributed to the successful formation of an indigenous development organization—a specific form of social capital. Membership in the indigenous development organization provides incentives for farmers to implement a costly technical innovation that enables them to raise the yields of their staple food. Although human capital, in the form of a charismatic leader, and physical capital, in the form of some inputs provided through access to

[1]Ostrom (Chap.7) defines physical capital as the stock of material resources that can be used to produce a flow of future income. She defines human capital as the acquired knowledge and skills than an individual brings to an activity. Social capital is the shared knowledge, understandings, institutions, and patterns of interactions that a group of individuals brings to any activity.

international donors, were important factors in the development and diffusion of contour dikes, the cultural endowments of the Mossi are arguably key.

The story also generates several hypotheses that are related to applications of the New Institutional Economics. First, specific cultural endowments can facilitate the formation of indigenous development organizations. Although culture is viewed most frequently in the economic development literature as an impediment, cultural endowments such as the tradition of the strongly disciplined, self-reliant *naam* groups may facilitate cooperative arrangements.[2] The New Institutional Economics suggests that, while policies and incentives matter most in determining the path of economic development, the incentives faced by individuals are strongly influenced by cultural norms (see Clague, chap. 2, this volume). Cultural norms can affect the time it takes to develop the set of mutually agreed upon and enforceable rules that serve as the foundation for social capital (see Ostrom, chap. 7, this volume).

Second, such indigenous development organizations can increase the adoption by farmers of new technologies. In the example presented here, the rules of conduct and function in the indigenous development organization facilitated the construction of water-retention infrastructure. This infrastructure, in turn, enhances the private profitability of a proposed seed-fertilizer innovation. This hypothesis bears on the study of collective action and its applications. Third, foreign institutions are less likely to be successfully transferred than "renovated" institutions.[3]

The following sections outline the cultural endowments of the Mossi that were recognized by the founder of the *groupements naam* movement as instrumental to their formation, summarizes how economists, political scientists, and anthropologists explain the existence of similar mutual

---

[2] The role of culture in the literature on economic development has been critically reviewed by Ruttan (1988).

[3] Fetini (1993) defines three archetypal models of institutional development: innovation, adaptation, and renovation. Renovation consists of building a new institution from an existing—but no longer functional—institution. Fetini characterizes some aspects of the farmers' group movement in the Sahelian region of Africa, and in particular that of the *groupements naam*, as institutional renovation.

assistance groups, describe features of the institution-building process and how the *groupements* may have facilitated technical innovation, and discuss issues affecting the continuity and replicability of the movement and whether the example provides any clear implications for donor assistance.

1   The *Kombi-Naam* Cultural Endowment

Those endowments most clearly instrumental in the formation of today's *naam* groups are expressed in the operation of the *kombi-naam*, one of the traditional mutual assistance organizations of the Mossi who inhabit the Yatenga province of Burkina-Faso.[4]   Here, the term cultural endowment refers broadly to the dimensions of culture, including religion and ideology, that have been transmitted from the past.[5]

The *kombi-naam* was a temporary association of young men and women from the same age group, reestablished spontaneously in each generation when they gathered to choose leaders and designate annual group activities. They worked in common fields, provided labor in the fields of those who demanded, or were in need of, special assistance, and were remunerated in kind according to the nature of the labor and the means of the household employing them. Certain other vital community tasks were collectively and cheaply completed by the youth association. At the close of the year, to mark the dissolution of that particular realization of the *kombi-*

---

[4]The description of the *kombi-naam* is drawn from Ouedraogo's (1990) account, which he based on interviews with elders who had been courtiers of the last king of Yatenga. Ouedraogo is the founder of the *groupements naam* movement. A similar description is found in a manuscript by Skinner (n.d.), who is a scholar of Mossi society.

[5]There are many definitions of culture in the anthropological literature. One of the more helpful and contemporary perspectives is that the basis of culture is the means of preserving order (Gans 1985). In economist North's (1990) framework, culture is the socially transmitted body of teachings, knowledge, and values that generate the informal constraints on individual choice sets that humans devise to shape their interaction. In political scientist Ostrom's (1992) view, "culture is in large part made up of the norms and codes of behavior that have evolved to counteract opportunistic behavior."

naam, they organized a festival to which the youth of other villages was invited.

Several features of the *kombi-naam* may be said to compose the basis of the social capital upon which B. L. Ouedraogo sought to build the *groupements naam* movement. First, membership and internal leadership cut through the hierarchy to include individuals from all socio-occupational sets, including minorities and servile groups. Strict sexual mores were enforced, to encourage young men and women to learn mutual respect in a cooperative work environment. For a moment in time, all villagers of that generation were "equal." The second special feature was the method for selecting leaders. In contrast to Western definitions of democracy as majority rule, Ouedraogo describes the traditional election as an exercise in "qualitative democracy." Consensus was achieved when unanimity emerged from a long process of discussion and mutual concessions. A third special feature is that the *kombi-naam* leadership included some dignitaries who represented institutions of the greater traditional society. The link between youth and elders mediated intergenerational tensions in a society in which age confers status. The content of the cooperative work activities, such as cleaning the village mosque, increased positive intergenerational contact.

The signal feature of the *kombi-naam*, for our purposes, is the tradition of rigorous discipline and the denial of opportunism to which the young people freely consented, given that unanimity had been achieved for certain key decisions. As late as the 1960s, Hammond (1966, 91) observed that "the young people set to work without supervision after the leader and farmer have agreed upon a price . . . work is performed collectively and profits shared equally."

Other related facts about the historical evolution of the *kombi-naam* may also be of importance. The concept of *naam* is a dominant leitmotiv in the lives of the Mossi of Burkina Faso (Skinner 1964; Izard 1985a, 1985b). Literally, *naam* means chieftainship (Ouedraogo 1990), sovereignty or power (Izard 1985b), or the power first possessed by the ancient founders (Skinner 1964). Philosophically, the Mossi refer to it as that "force of God that enables one person to dominate others" (Skinner 1964, 13). Many of the key economic, political, religious, and social institutions of the Mossi are patterned around *naam* and are designated by titles derived from that word (Izard 1985b; Skinner 1964).

What limited the potential of the *kombi-naam* as an development organization? First, the experience in equality, self-reliance, community service, and mutual assistance lasted only one year. Membership in each realization of the *kombi-naam* was only temporary. There was no time for individuals to reap long-term benefits from a current investment in mutual assistance. Youth carried into adulthood the sense of having participated, but the titles and active solidarity were embodied only in the *kombi-naam* institution. Servants then undertook their hereditary occupation as servants, and young women prepared to become wives and mothers in a patriarchal society. Second, the *kombi-naam* accumulated no capital. At the close of the year, its earnings were exhausted in one ceremony.

2   Theoretical Explanations for the *Kombi-Naam*

In general, mutual assistance groups and solidarity networks are a common feature of traditional societies but not necessarily of societies in transition. Anthropologists, political scientists, and economists have long debated why such groups exist and how effective they are. For political scientists, the focal question has been under what conditions voluntary cooperation exists without their imposition by a coercive state. Economists have often phrased the same question in terms of the contradiction between altruism and the pursuit of self-interest.

Scott (1976) explains the existence of mutual assistance and solidarity networks in southeast Asia through the "subsistence ethic" of peasants, which reflects, in a "moral economy," the overriding common need to organize against food crises. Opposing Scott's view, Popkin (1979) argues that collective action often fails because of the opportunistic behavior of peasants who have no incentive to organize cooperative strategies. Posner (1980) reconciles the views of Scott and Popkin by arguing that mutual assistance systems can be sustained in the long run by the existence of a lasting relationship between self-interested members. Similarly, anthropologists have long recognized that gift giving is a form of commodity exchange that, as compared to an impersonal exchange of goods in a market, establishes a durable personal relationship between donor and recipient (Mauss 1954; Gregory 1982). Posner's argument is formalized in work by Kimball (1988) and others. Related literature, models, and arguments are exhaustively reviewed by Platteau (1991) and Fafchamps (1992).

Political scientists and economists rely largely on the game theoretic approach to present the formal explanation for the existence of mutual assistance groups and cooperation. They solve Olson's free-rider problem

(1965) by showing that in repeated, rather than in one-shot games, there is no dominant strategy. Wealth- or utility-maximizing individuals find it worthwhile to cooperate with other players when the game is repeated, when they possess complete information about other players' past performance, or when there is a small number of players. Building on the extensive literature and expanding the game theoretic approach, Fafchamps (1992) demonstrates how key observed features of mutual assistance groups and solidarity networks can be explained through the theory of repeated games. Using a different approach with game theory, Ostrom (1990) demonstrates simply that a contract enforced by unanimous approval of the rules, such as in Ouedraogo's "qualitative democracy," can result in a cooperative equilibrium in which agents share costs and returns from common property.

The use of game theory in this context has also been criticized. When game theory is used as the construct for explaining why mutual assistance groups exist, the analysis focuses on how cooperation results from the optimal meeting of game-derived demand functions, rather than the institutionalized incentives that individuals have to participate (Ellsworth 1988) or how the costs of transacting are altered by different institutional structures (North 1990). As Fafchamps (1992) argues, the theory of repeated games does not explain how specific organizational structures or mutual assistance associations are chosen. The elements needed to build such a theory, says Fafchamps, would include culture, political institutions, and historical events. For the purposes of this chapter, although game theory can be used to explain the existence of the *kombi-naam*, it tells us little about whether the *kombi-naam* can evolve as an institution that supports technical innovation. Game theory can be used to demonstrate why a particular institution assures a stable equilibrium but cannot explain why that institution (and not another) evolved historically.

Mutual assistance groups and solidarity networks can also be viewed as special cases of risk-pooling insurance mechanisms in which villagers organize vertically (as in patron-client relationships) or horizontally (as in the original *kombi-naam*) to protect themselves against famine and other disasters. In land-abundant, semiarid countries with simple technology, a high covariance of risk in crop or livestock output helps to explain the lack of formal insurance mechanisms and the need for geographically extensive social institutions or private capital accumulation in the form of grain stocks or livestock (Binswanger and McIntyre 1987). For example, analysis by Nugent and Sanchez (1993) highlights the role of tribes in the transhumant (long-distance herding) activities of semiarid regions. As population density increases, however, the propensity to rely on such extensive social institutions as insurance mechanisms can be expected to decrease because of the reduced cost of the infrastructure and access to economic activities with less covariation (Binswanger and McIntyre, 1987). Although the *kombi-naam* were organized horizontally, the only risk they were designed to cover, or could cover effectively, was uncorrelated and specific, such as providing labor to assist the sick or needy.

3   Renovating the *Kombi-Naam* as a Development Organization

Bernard L. Ouedraogo, the charismatic leader of today's *naam* movement, initiated a process of building a community development institution from the traditional *kombi-naam*.[6] In his own words, he and his co-workers sought "development without damage" (*développer sans abîmer*) (Ouedraogo 1990, 13). The process of renovation occurred in several stages. First, public education programs designed to provide basic instruction to village children were reorganized as training programs for young farmers (*formations des jeunes agriculteurs*, or FJAs). The FJAs were then broadened to include postschool farmer youth groups (*groupements des jeunes agriculteurs*, or GJAs). In 1967, the GJAs were then "grafted" onto the *kombi-naam* by redefining rules of function and organization.

As in the *kombi-naam*, the GJA-*naam* groups maintained close ties with village elders. To gain acceptance in a village, the GJA-*naam* groups provided assistance to village elders, retaining an honorary presidential post for elders (usually a former soldier who had traveled), and in return obtaining land-use rights from elders, borrowing their plows and oxen. As in the *kombi-naam*, membership in the GJA-*naam* was open to individuals of all ethnic and socio-occupational groups. Leaders were selected through a consensus process similar to that used in the *kombi-naam*, although the leadership functions were defined in new ways. The general functions of the GJA-*naam* groups were newly defined as educational, political, recreational, and economic.

---

[6]Much of this section is drawn from Ouedraogo (1990).

Ouedraogo recognized that, as noted above, temporary association and an inability to accumulate capital were inherent features of the *kombi-naam* that needed to change before the traditional institution could be used as a development tool by the community. Solving the capital accumulation problem in the economic function of the GJA-*naam* entailed convincing members that the earnings—formerly exhausted at the annual festival—could be more usefully directed toward collective savings and investment. According to Ouedraogo, this was no easy task.

The effort to prolong the life span of the *naam* groups seems to have been reinforced by concurrent changes in resource endowments. Those who joined the GJA-*naam* in the 1960s remained members well into adulthood in the 1970s. Ouedraogo and others (Gentil 1986; Pradervand 1989) contend that the 1967–85 period of low rainfall, which included the severe droughts of 1967–73 and 1982–84, contributed to the proliferation of the *naam* groups. To reclaim degraded land through the construction of dikes, dams, reservoirs, and other public works, villagers needed cooperative, collective action. In terms of the induced innovation framework, a change in resource endowments (the drought) increased the demand for an institution that supported collective action, and cultural endowments (the *kombi-naam*) facilitated cooperative arrangements by reducing the cost of consensus.

The *naam* groups of today are a federation of associations of varying size and composition, including young and old, men and women. Crudely, the "renovation" of the *kombi-naam* extended the payback period for investment in mutual assistance and diversified its portfolio.

4   *Groupments Naam* and Technical Innovation

In the Sahelian and Sudanian climatic zones of sub-Saharan Africa, the principal production constraints are lack of soil moisture and low soil fertility. Land degradation has caused even further deterioration in soil quality. High capital and maintenance costs have deterred investments in conventional, large-scale irrigation projects over the past two decades (Matlon 1987). Other water conservation or retention techniques are potentially important, particularly in degraded Sudanian regions like Yatenga. In such areas, rainfall is low and irregular, and soil encrustation leads to infiltration problems. Water retention techniques can reduce runoff and help exploit rainfall by increasing the effectiveness of nutrients, especially when combined with improvements in soil fertility.

Sorghum and millet are the staple cereals in the Sahelo-Sudanian zones of Burkina Faso. Based on the record of nearly a decade of research on new technologies in Burkina Faso, Sanders, Nagy, and Ramaswamy (1990) conclude that only with increased soil moisture and moderate fertilizer application (organic or inorganic) are improved sorghum varieties more attractive than traditional varieties in terms of yield potential, profitability, and risk. Increasing soil moisture when the nutrient levels remain low does not generate large increases in yield; applying fertilizers without an assured water supply is risky since the response to fertilizer depends on the availability of water at critical stages of plant development. As these scholars portray it, technical change in the Sahel is a staged process, depending on initial soil conditions and expected rainfall; the adoption of technologies to improve water retention and soil fertility is the precondition for the productivity increases associated with change in plant varieties (See also Sanders and Ramaswamy 1992).

Using the induced innovation framework, Sanders, Nagy, and Ramaswamy (1990) also argue that, with the Sahelian drought, changes in resource endowments spurred the demand for technical innovation. As soil resources declined through depletion and erosion, and as nonfarm employment opportunities (even through migration to the south) grew less rapidly than rural population, farmers were induced to adopt yield-increasing, labor-intensive technologies such as contour dikes and organic fertilizer. Sanders, Nagy, and Ramaswamy (1990) report that the region of most rapid adoption of water retention and soil fertility technologies is Yatenga, even though the estimated rates of return to the technologies are higher in other, less-degraded regions. They explain this anomaly by hypothesizing that, unless farmers are pressured by soil deterioration and falling labor-land price ratios, the implicit returns on these large labor inputs are too low to interest farmers (8). In other words, changes in relative returns to factors, rather than the absolute level of returns, encouraged the adoption of new technologies. As suggested here, however, there may also be cultural reasons why diffusion was more rapid in Yatenga.[7]

---

[7]Depending on the location, conservation activity, and time, reports differ about whether public financing of the Food for Work project was used to compensate labor. Much of the work, particularly in the early years of the *naam* movement, appears not to have been externally financed.

One of the more effective dike (alternatively, *diguette*, bund, contour ridge, or contour line) techniques has its genesis in Mossi methods. Based on fieldwork in western Burkina Faso, Savonnet (1958) identifies and describes in detail four techniques for soil erosion and water control among the Mossi and other ethnic groups. These and other techniques used historically by the Mossi are also reported in Reij (1989). According to Reij and Critchley (1990), some techniques have fallen into disuse. The efficiency of stone and earthen lines was limited, principally because contours were not accurately measured and other construction details such as stone placement and line spacing needed improvement.

Harrison (1987) calls the process of dike improvement in Yatenga "barefoot science." When Oxfam began work on an agroforestry project in Yatenga in 1979, one of their fieldworkers brought the concept of water harvesting from a visit to the Negev desert in Israel. In emphasizing that their priority was food production rather than agroforestry, farmers helped shift the design of the project. The farmers and the Oxfam project director set to work improving the simple stone contour line. One improvement involved placing large foundation stones preceded by smaller stones to act as a permeable water filter (Critchley 1990). But accurate contours are impossible to gauge by eye on the slight slopes (2–3 %, according to Reij, Mulder, and Bergemann 1988) in Yatenga. Aside from questions of spacing, breadth, and depth, the key was the development of a simple hose pipe water level that costs six dollars to make, can be mastered by illiterate villagers in a day or two, and ensures correct alignment of the contours (Wright 1985; Harrison 1987). The *naam* groups subsequently adopted the technique and diffused it as rapidly (Younger and Bonkoungou 1985; Harrison 1987).

In the short term, the contour dikes improve crop yields in two ways. First, controlled rainfall runoff improves infiltration, increasing water absorption by crops and land. Second, fertilizer (usually manure) and other organic material applied behind the dikes is much more effective since it is less likely to be washed away. The organic matter also attracts termites, which bore into the ground and aerate the soil. Over the longer term, the dikes control erosion and increase soil quality.

The evidence on the economic rate of return to contour dikes is positive but patchy and inconclusive. According to Sanders and Rama- swamy (1992), the yield effects of contour dikes combined with organic fertilizer placed behind the dikes are "small but the diffusion is impressive" (249). In 1985, ICRISAT evaluated a package of stone dikes, tied ridges, a low dose of fertilizer, and an improved sorghum variety. On farmers' fields, where only the package was evaluated, the yield difference was 67 percent in the first year in the Sahelian (less favored) zone. ICRISAT calculated that a break-even sorghum yield increment of only 155 kg would assure a return of 15 percent on labor and cash investment, which was exceeded by over two-thirds of farmer participants in the Sahelo-Sudanian zone.[8] On researcher-managed fields in the Sahelian zone, the yield increment from stone dikes alone was 40 percent in the first year. Oxfam's data are less controlled but generally show statistically significant yield increases with stone contours on farmers' fields, with the highest differential occurring in dry years (Wright 1985).

Using ICRISAT's cost data and some of the lower yield differentials in Wright's data, Younger and Bonkoungou (1985) estimate an internal rate of return to the Oxfam project (excluding the diffusion outside of the project zone by the *naam* groups) of about 40 percent. For a new hectare of land, the rate of return they calculate is 147 percent (excluding sunk research and development costs).

Institutions such as the *naam* groups, however, affect the calculation of rates of return to investment in technologies such as the contour dikes, large-scale dams, and water retention infrastructure. As North (1990, 5) argues, institutions affect the costs of exchange and production through determining transaction and transformation costs. Rate-of-return calculations do not capture the external effects of dike construction by one farmer on other farmers' fields or the possible cost-reducing effects of construction by a *naam* group as compared to construction by an individual. Dikes are a divisible but lumpy technology. The only portion of the benefit that is measured in conventional rate-of-return analyses is the private benefit to the farmer of planting a fertilized, improved cultivar behind the dike.

---

[8]CIMMYT usually recommends using a discount rate of 50% for technologies that are familiar to the farmer and up to 100% for technologies unknown to the farmer. In either case, a 15% discount rate is generous in that it does not incorporate risk and uncertainty factors. On the other hand, all data came from the first year of application only—understating the rate of return for the package over time, as the effects of the contour dikes on soil quality cumulate.

5   The Continuity and Replicability of the *Groupements Naam*

Supporters, critics, and Ouedraogo himself question the potential for continuity of the *groupement naam* movement and its replicability in other regions of sub-Saharan Africa. As concerns the replicability of the institution, the *naam* movement and similar farmer organizations are widespread in the Sahel, and particularly in Senegal and Burkina Faso. Gentil (1986) cites a number of factors that are likely to be related to the evolution of successful farmers' movements. The first is the openness of the political climate. The governments of Senegal and Burkina Faso have been relatively tolerant of trade union activity, multipartyism, and a free press. He notes, however, that most successful groups serve at least some government interests. For example, the economic activities of farmers' groups in Senegal have never threatened the cash crops that are the lifeline of the Senegalese economy. Charismatic leaders also seem to play a crucial role. A unifying ideology, a "hostile" external force, or a major obstacle to overcome help to rally support and enforce cohesion.

Both economic and political issues affect the potential for continuity in the *naam* movement. Critics most often question its economic viability. The basic organization of savings and credit in *naam* groups is simple: all earnings are deposited in a bank account and distributed in three unequal parts, depending on the needs of the group. The first part is seed money for a revolving fund or for repaying bank loans. The second, smallest, part is an expense account for funding annual harvest festivals. The third part is for expansion of activities through purchase of factors of production or for livestock and tool replacement. To draw individual loans from the account, such as consumption credit, is prohibited.

To secure the necessary seed capital for *naam* groups, its creators insisted that, in the first phase, capital should be self-generated, "so that potential supporters and detractors of the organization could take it seriously" (Fetini 1993). In 1976, to meet the challenges of training farmers in both technical spheres and in project development, and to relieve key constraints on scientific know-how (human capital) or physical capital in projects they identified, Ouedraogo and a colleague (Bernard Lecomte) established an umbrella organization, the 6-S (*Se Servir de la Saison Sèche en Savane et au Sahel*), that includes the *groupements naam* and other local and international nongovernmental organizations across the Sahel. Although the 6-S expands the capital base of the *naam* movement, a large proportion of funds are provided as reimbursable loans.

Central to the financial functioning of the 6-S is the notion of *fonds souples* (flexible funds), as contrasted to project aid. Initially, modest funds are made available to the *naam* federation without earmarking them for specific end uses. The funds are distributed only when a group shows sufficient initiative and are increased only as the group demonstrates management ability. When a group's project becomes profitable, the funds are reimbursed and the money is recycled to the project of another group. At the level of the 6-S, the funds are disbursed as grants, but they are used as a 70 percent reimbursable loan by *naam* recipients. That 70 percent, when repaid, is placed in a revolving fund to be extended to poorer *naam* groups. Funding diminishes or ceases when groups demonstrate enough efficiency to attract other donors (Fetini 1993).

As *naam* groups proliferate and as the range of their commercial activities expands, some groups and some activities are clearly more successful than others. Ouedraogo (1990) stresses the significance of the villagers' acceptance of the revolving fund concept, of which they were originally suspect. He relates how the concept was explained to villagers and how, in the ideology of the *naam* movement, they are constantly reminded of how their actions relate not only to their own group but also to the potential of other groups. The concept of repayment with interest and the prohibition on giving credit or food to the needy from the group account have been difficult, but usually not insuperable, problems. In some cases, more flexible arrangements have been developed, which suggests that these requirements are not rigid.

Naam groups engage in a portfolio of activities, only some of which generate cash income. Their commercial activities include the purchase, installation, and operation of grain mills, the constitution and regulation of village grain banks, livestock production, artisanry, vegetable production on irrigated plots operated by the collective, and petty trading. Some observers (Beaudoux and Nieuwkerk 1985; Gentil 1986) express reservations about their economic performance.

The very breadth of *naam* activities may also be a key to their success in adopting and diffusing agricultural technology. In many failed efforts at community action in similar activities (agricultural experimentation and terrace building), were organized for a too limited set of tasks, with transactions costs not compensated by the specific activity. The lesson to be learned may be that, in encouraging one community-based activity, it is better to base the work within existing institutions and to ensure that the institutions have a life beyond that particular activity (R. Tripp, personal communication).

But Ouedraogo (1990) and others further emphasize that commercial activities are in some sense of lesser importance to the long-term vitality of the group than the community and social activities that lend the group its fundamental cohesion. Ouedraogo describes water retention work as one of the principal activities of a *naam* group, although he classifies it as a "community" rather than an "economic" activity. In his survey of several hundred groups, Buisrogge (1989) was startled to find that, among the identified future intended activities of these groups, most were public works. He expected greater interest in profit-making enterprises, for which incentives are obvious. He explains his finding by recognizing that, for many of the villages beset by drought and youth out-migration, community action is a question of survival. To maintain viable communities, it is necessary to retain the population. Questions of environment and soil fertility, for example, are foremost.

Political viability seems more likely to prove a real issue than economic viability. Assembling data from across West Africa, Gentil (1986) describes the current farmers' movement as consisting of three types of groups: (1) groups promoted by a nonstatal apparatus, such as a church or nongovernmental organization, (2) groups initiated by farmers but linked closely to a charismatic, nonfarmer, leader, and (3) groups initiated and sustained by farmers and farmer leaders. He claims that a large proportion of the groups are created and dissolved within a short period of time. He describes many of the groups as artificial and entirely dependent on external organizations.

Some groups have clearly been initiated by, and derive their strength from, village communities. Pradervand (1989) refers to the 6-S as the first international organization run by peasants. Harrison (1987, 282) writes that in the 6-S, professionals and experts take up their proper roles of training and technical and financial backup, but that "the heart of the *naam* is . . . in the villages." But the unique qualities of groups like those of the early *naam* movement may succumb to externally driven development fads and fashions. Certainly the *naam* federation of today is likely to include more "collective opportunists" than in the early years before government acceptance and the establishment of the 6-S. The *naam* movement was officially recognized in

1978 by the government of Burkina-Faso, and *naam* groups were then federated and linked to a broader national structure. Most of the groups in Buisrogge's survey (1989) were formed around 1974–77, when the government began to pursue specific community development policies.

A remarkable aspect of the *naam* movement is how its leaders have been able to work effectively with revolutionary regimes in Burkina Faso as well as in other parts of West Africa (Skinner, n.d.). A more philosophical question is, however, the extent to which the views of *naam* farmers, rooted in their own experience and localities, can continue to mesh with those of national politicians and international development organizations. Ouedraogo himself (1990) concludes that the future of the federation in the 6-S, in terms of retaining a sense of village base and control, is unsure. As the scale of the *naam* bureaucracy and the involvement of its leaders with national politics and donor culture increase, how will the institution evolve?

Another interesting dynamic in the development of the *naam* movement is its relation to the national government and what that means for the structure of political power. Through the *naam* movement, a substantial portion of the labor-intensive work involved in constructing infrastructure and of the costly work of on-farm research and demonstrations is being transferred from the state to its poorest citizens. One might hypothesize that some "enlightened" governments may choose to use farmers' groups to shift the burden of development costs back onto rural communities. Some governments may find it in their interest to co-opt successful farmers' groups to consolidate their own political bases. The case of farmer groups in Bakel, Senegal, detailed by Adams (1981), demonstrates that at least some associations, perceiving government recognition as potentially exploitative, resist assimilation.

The political role of donors and other development organizations in such an environment is also at issue. For example, Skinner (n.d.) is suspicious that the development community, unwilling and unable to obtain or use effectively the tremendous resources necessary to assist Africa, may have simply decided to turn the problems over to Africans (NGOs and farmers' groups). Yet another possibility is that movements such as the *naam* groups will eventually be co-opted by international NGOs. Over the past few decades, a proliferation of NGOs have gradually assumed the tasks of community development (and more) from bilateral development assistance institutions. Yet some have expressed concern that many of them may be repeating the same errors (Ward 1989).

6   Conclusions

The water retention work of the *groupements naam* of Yatenga, Burkina Faso, illustrates a point that is basic to the themes of the New Institutional Economics. Culture affects economic outcomes by influencing the formation and composition of the social capital that conditions economic behavior. In the case of the *groupements naam,* specific cultural endowments of the Mossi in Yatenga appear to have facilitated the formation of a development organization through the "renovation" of a traditional institution. The rules of conduct and function embedded in the social capital of the new institution seem to have provided special incentives for communities to undertake costly public works in water retention infrastructure. This infrastructure, in turn, has enhanced the profitability and risk characteristics of a recommended technical package of improved sorghum seed and fertilizer relative to traditional varieties. Cultural endowments, therefore, appear to have played a role in raising the potential for technical change in staple food production.

The implications for donor assistance are not so clearly mapped. One obvious implication may be that the lower the level of direct involvement, the better. Another, suggested by the success of the flexible funds approach, is that project-based funding may be damaging for the development of indigenous social capital. Conventional rate-of-return analyses are too limiting and project life cycles are too short to use as bases for evaluation. The story also suggests that donors should not always assume that institutions must be transferred or built anew—some "renovated" institutions can be progressive.

One hypothesis about how donors might encourage the development of similar institutions is suggested only peripherally in this account. The *groupements naam* have survived several regimes in Burkina Faso and are part of a transnational federation of farmers' groups that spans the Sahel. Government tolerance of the movement may have played a role in its longevity. However, it is also possible that government tolerance is mistaken for government weakness. An alternative hypothesis is that movements such as the *groupements naam* flourish precisely when national governments use them as a means of consolidating their rural power base.

References

Adams, A. 1981. "The Senegal River Valley." In *Rural Development in Tropical Africa,* ed. J. Heyer, P. Roberts and Gavin Williams. New York: St. Martin's.

Beaudoux, E., and M. Nieuwkerk. 1985. *Groupements paysans d'Afrique: Dossier pour l'action.* Paris: L'Harmattan.

Binswanger, H. P., and J. McIntyre. 1987. "Behavioral and Material Determinants of Production Relations in Land-Abundant Tropical Agriculture." *Economic Development and Cultural Change* 36: 73–100.

Buisrogge, P. 1989. *Initiatives Paysannes en Afrique de l'Ouest.* Paris: L'Harmattan.

Critchley, W. 1990. "Catch the Rain." *CERES* 125: 41–5.

———. 1991. *Looking after Our Land: Soil and Water Conservation in Dryland Africa.* Oxford: Oxfam.

Ellsworth, L. 1988. "Mutual Insurance and Non-Market Transaction among Farmers in Burkina-Faso." Ph.D dissertation, Department of Agricultural Economics. Madison: University of Wisconsin, 1988.

Fafchamps, M. 1992. "Solidarity Networks in Preindustrial Society: Rational Peasants with a Moral Economy." *Economic Development and Cultural Change.* 41: 148–74.

Fetini, H. 1993. "Institutional Deficiencies and Indigenous Responses—A Case of Institutional Renovation and Diffusion: The *Groupements Naam* and the 6-S NGO in the Sahel." World Bank, Washington, D.C.

Gans, E. 1985. *The End of Culture: Toward a Generative Anthropology.* Berkeley: University of California Press.

Gentil, D. 1986. *Les Mouvements Coopératifs en Afrique de l'Ouest: Interventions de l'État ou Organizations Paysannes?* Paris: L'Harmattan.

Gregory, C. A. 1982. *Gifts and Commodities.* New York: Academic Press.

Hammond, P. B. 1966 *Technology in the Culture of a West African Kingdom.* New York: Free Press.

Harrison, Paul. 1987. *The Greening of Africa: Breaking through in the Battle for Land and Food.* London: Paladin Grafton.

ICRISAT (International Crops Research Institute for the Semi-Arid Tropics) 1985. *Annual Report of ICRISAT/Burkina Economics Program.* Ouagadougou: ICRISAT.

Izard, M. 1985a. *Yatenga Précolonial: l'Ancien Royaume du Burkina.* Paris: Karthala.

————. 1985b. *Gens du Pouvoir, Gens de la Terre.* Cambridge: Cambridge University Press.

Kimball, M. S. 1988. "Farmers' Cooperatives as Behavior Toward Risk." *American Economic Review* 78: 224–32.

Matlon, P. J. 1987. "The West African Semi-Arid Tropics." In *Accelerating Food Production in Sub-Saharan Africa.* Ed. J. W. Mellor, C. L. Delgado, and M. J. Blackie. Baltimore: Johns Hopkins University Press.

Mauss, M. 1954. *The Gift.* Glencoe, Ill.: Free Press.

North, D. C. 1990. *Institutions, Institutional Change and Economic Performance.* Cambridge: Cambridge University Press.

Nugent, J. B., and N. Sanchez. 1993. "Tribes, Chiefs, and Transhumance: A Comparative Institutional Analysis." *Economic Development and Cultural Change* 42: 87–113.

Olson, M. 1965. *The Logic of Collective Action.* Cambridge: Harvard University Press.

Ostrom, E. 1990. *Governing the Commons: The Evolution of Institutions for Collective Action.* Cambridge: Cambridge University Press.

————. 1992. *Crafting Institutions for Self-Governing Irrigation Systems.* San Francisco: Institute for Contemporary Studies Press.

Ouedraogo, B. L. 1990. *Entraide Villageoise et Développement: Groupements Paysans au Burkina Faso.* Paris: L'Harmattan.

Platteau, J.-P. 1991. "Traditional Systems of Social Security and Hunger Insurance: Past Achievements and Modern Challenges." In *Social Security in Developing Countries,* ed. E. Ahmad, J. Dreze, J. Hills, and A. Sen. Oxford: Clarendon.

Popkin, S. L. 1979. *The Rational Peasant: The Political Economy of Rural Society in Vietnam.* Berkeley: University of California Press.

Posner, R. A. 1980. "A Theory of Primitive Society, with Special Reference to Law." *Journal of Law and Economics* 23: 1–53.

Pradervand, P. 1989. *Listening to Africa: Developing Africa from the Grassroots.* New York: Praeger.

Reij, C. 1989. *Indigenous Soil and Water Conservation in Africa.* Sustainable Agriculture Programme, Gatekeeper Series 27. London: International Institute for Environment and Development.

Reij, C., P. Mulder, and Louis Begemann. 1988. *Water Harvesting for Plant Production.* Technical Paper 91. Washington, D.C.: World Bank.

Ruttan, V. W. 1988. "Cultural Endowments and Economic Development: What Can We Learn from Anthropology?" *Economic Development and Cultural Change,* suppl., 36: 247–271.

Sanders, J. H., J. G. Nagy, and S. Ramaswamy. 1990. "Developing New Agricultural Technologies for the Sahelian Countries: The Burkina Faso Case." *Economic Development and Cultural Change* 39: 1–22.

Sanders, J. H., and S. Ramaswamy. 1992. "Impacts of New Technologies in Burkina Faso and the Sudan: Implications for Future Technology Design." In *Proceedings of a Workshop on Social Science Research and the CRSPs.* INTSORMIL Publication 93-3. Lexington: University of Kentucky.

Savonnet, G. 1958. "Méthodes employées par certaines populations de Haute-Volta pour lutter contre l'érosion." *Notes Africaines* 78: 38–40.

Scott, J. 1976. *The Moral Economy of the Peasant: Rebellion and Subsistence in South East Asia.* New Haven: Yale University Press.

Skinner, E. P. 1964. *The Mossi of the Upper Volta.* Stanford: Stanford University Press.

———. [n.d.] "Traditional Institutions and Economic Development: The Mossi *NAAM.*" Columbia University.

Ward, H. G. 1989. *African Development Reconsidered: New Perspectives from the Continent.* New York: Phelps-Stokes Institute.

Wright, P. 1985. "Water and Soil Conservation by Farmers." In *Appropriate Technologies for Farmers in Semi-Arid West Africa,* ed. H. W. Ohm and J. G. Nagy. Purdue: Office of International Programs in Agriculture, Purdue University.

Younger, S., and E. G. Bonkoungou. 1985. "Burkina Faso: The Projet Agro-Forestier—A Case Study of Agricultural Research and Extension." In *Successful Development in Africa,* ed. R. Bheenick. EDI Development Policy Case Series, Analytical Case Studies 1. Washington, D.C.: World Bank.

9 Focus on People's Participation: Evidence from 121 Rural Water Projects

Deepa Narayan

The UN International Drinking Water Supply and Sanitation Decade (1980–90) promoted community participation as a way of reaching the poor. The expectation was that, where markets do not function and where, in Hirschman's (1970) terminology, "exit" options are few, the exercise of "voice," or participation, can induce collective action and improve the accountability and performance of public sector agencies. The UN Decade generated hundreds of small and large water projects that have been documented and evaluated. However, individual case studies do not offer convincing evidence that people's participation makes a difference in project performance and, hence, is worth financial investment, nor do they provide useful guidance on policies or procedures for project implementation agencies or financing institutions such as the World Bank.

1 The Study

Could a way be found to distill and combine the experience of so many case studies? Could the existing material be sorted and sifted analytically to study whether participation affects project success, what benefits it brings, and when it works best? This task was attempted through a combination of content analysis and statistics, building on an approach pioneered by Essman and Uphoff (1984) and further developed by Finsterbusch and Van Wicklin (1987). The results are unambiguous. Participation is shown to be one of the most significant factors contributing to project effectiveness, the maintenance of water systems, and economic benefits, even after taking into account the effects of eighteen other factors commonly associated with project success. It was also the most important factor contributing to local capacity building, including individual and organizational empowerment.

The chapter represents the view of the author and should not be attributed to the World Bank, its affiliated organizations, its Board of Executive Directors, or the countries they represent. This study was financed by the World Bank Participatory Development Learning Group and by the UNDP–World Bank Water and Sanitation Program.

1.1   Methodology

The study went through three distinct phases. In the first phase, more than four hundred documents on completed rural water supply projects were assembled from around the world and reviewed for their relevance. There were two criteria for inclusion: (1) the primary purpose of the project had to be the provision of physical facilities (as opposed to policy improvements, for example), and (2) the report had to have sufficient information to allow coding. On this basis, 121 projects were selected. During the second phase, two coders independently reviewed the case studies and assigned ratings to 149 variables. The ratings were of course subjective, but intercoder reliability was higher than 0.88 on the key variables. While there was some halo effect, it did not substantially affect the results.[1] The coders' results were then subjected to initial statistical analysis (correlations, factor analysis, and data quality tests). In the third phase, approximately 50 variables were chosen to test the effect of participation through multivariate analysis. Throughout the process, quantitative methods were balanced by qualitative analysis, for example through in-depth reviews of the 20 projects that scored highest in effectiveness and the 20 scoring highest in participation.

1.2   The characteristics of projects

The 121 projects selected were located in forty-nine developing countries in Africa, Asia, and Latin America. They were generally quite large in size: 31 percent cost more than $10 million (the largest was $110 million), 32 percent cost between $3 and $10 million, and 37 percent were below $3 million. They were implemented and financed by governments, NGOs, and external support agencies, for the most part in the 1980s. Technologies ranged from hand-dug wells to piped systems (fed by both gravity and by boreholes with motorized pumps). Just under half of the projects included sanitation and some primary health care activities as well as water supply itself.

1.3   What is participation?

For the purposes of this study, participation is defined as a voluntary process by which people, including the disadvantaged, influence or control the decisions that affect them. The essence of participation is exercising voice and choice. Participation is viewed as a means to defined ends, which

---

[1] For detailed discussion of methodology, see Narayan (1994) and Isham, Narayan, and Prichett (1994).

in this case includes improved and sustainable water systems and the local capacity to solve problems and keep systems functioning into a changing future. A priori, there is no assumption about the most appropriate form or intensity of participation. Participation imposes transaction costs on beneficiaries and agencies, and thus intense forms of participation naturally decline over time as goals are met. Participation is therefore a dynamic process that changes in character and intensity over time, taking different forms during different stages of the project cycle and beyond. Most projects included referred to community participation or made it a specific project component, but only a handful treated beneficiary participation as a guiding principle. Only 21 percent of the projects scored high in overall client participation; 17 percent scored high on women's participation. Thus, in many cases intentions did not translate into practice.

2   Client Participation and Project Effectiveness

The measurement of participation includes the extent to which beneficiaries were involved in decision making during the project cycle, from design to maintenance. Information sharing and consultation with beneficiaries were not heavily weighted on the participation index. Gender differences were also taken into account. Factor analysis shows one measure, overall beneficiary participation (OBP), to be the best single indicator, and hence it was used in the analysis. The correlation between OBP and women's participation was high, and the pattern of relationships for the two was similar. Multivariate regression analysis was used to test the contribution of OBP to overall project effectiveness (OPE) and a range of other project outcomes, after controlling for eighteen other determinants of project outcomes. Table 9.1 reports the coefficients and *t*-statistics for the three models tested.

Model 1 tests the effect of beneficiary participation on project effectiveness, a linear regression (ordinary least squares). Nonparticipatory determinants were then added to the bivariate model: model 2 included seven direct nonparticipatory determinants, such as GNP/capita and total project costs. Model 3 adds eleven other determinants that could have a direct impact on outcomes or an indirect impact through beneficiary participation. There are five subcategories: appropriateness of technology, external agents (e.g., support of host government), client characteristics,

Table 9.1

Water System Outcomes as a Function of Overall Beneficiary Participation

Dependent Variable	Model 1[a]	Model 2[b]	Model 3[c]
Overall project effectiveness			
Partial correlation	0.62****	0.28****	0.24***
t-statistic	10.6	5.3	3.7
N	121	77	68
Percentage of water systems in good condition			
Partial correlation	0.54****	0.30**	0.29*
t-statistic	6.4	3.1	2.4
N	98	64	60
Overall economic benefits			
Partial correlation	0.53****	0.27****	0.26***
t-statistic	10.3	4.1	3.6
N	120	77	68
Percentage of project's target population reached			
Partial correlation	0.29****	0.17*	0.25**
t-statistic	5.3	1.9	2.5
N	118	76	68
Environmental benefits			
Partial correlation	0.21****	0.23**	0.23*
t-statistic	3.9	2.8	2.3
N	115	74	67
Equality of access			
Partial correlation	0.23****	0.26*	0.17
t-statistic	3.9	2.8	2.3
N	115	74	67

[a]OBP alone (bivariate).
[b]OBP plus seven direct determinants.
[c]OBP plus seven direct plus eleven direct/indirect determinants.

*Significant at .05; ** significant at .01;***significant at .001;****significant at .0001

Table 9.2

**Nonwater System Outcomes as a Function
of Overall Beneficiary Participation**

Dependent Variable and Outcome	Model 1[a]	Model 2[b]	Model 3[c]
Community Empowerment			
Partial correlation	0.77****	0.59****	0.55****
t-statistic	15.6	8.2	6.7
N	121	77	68
Water system task capacity building			
Partial correlation	0.77****	0.70****	0.63****
t-statistic	14.9	8.3	6.3
N	121	77	68
Extent local organizations strengthened			
Partial correlation	0.99****	1.01****	0.98****
t-statistic	17.1	10.0	8.1
N	109	71	63
Net effect on local leaders			
Partial correlation	0.24****	0.26**	0.26**
t-statistic	4.6	3.0	2.4
N	106	70	64

[a]OBP alone (bivariate).
[b]OBP plus seven direct determinants.
[c]OBP plus seven direct plus eleven direct/indirect determinants.

*Significant at .05; ** significant at .01;***significant at .001;**** significant at .0001

external climate (political, social, economic, and geological), and quality of management. The results establish that overall beneficiary participation is a significant determinant of overall project effectiveness even in the presence of eighteen other factors that affect of project outcomes. The practical significance of this finding is indicated by focusing on the size of the coefficient, which hovers around 0.3. This means that, controlling for all other inputs, increasing beneficiary participation from low to high levels (from 2 to 7 on the input scale) increases project effectiveness by about 1.5

times (from a mean of 4.8 to 6.3) on the output scale. In other words, increasing participation from low to high levels moves a project from a medium rating to a highly effective category.

Beneficiary participation also contributes significantly to the proportion of water systems in good condition, overall economic benefits, percentage of target population reached, and environmental benefits. Equality of access to facilities share this characteristic, although to a lesser extent. The only other factor to emerge as important is the availability of spare parts and repair technicians. However, as project experiences attest, without beneficiary participation in decision making, in most situations sustainability is not achieved even when spare parts and skilled repair technicians are available. These factors make a difference only when there is community interest and demand for these services.

2.1   Capacity-building outcomes

Participation contributed not only to more effective projects but also to building human capacity for organization and management. Without local management capacity, sustainable operation and maintenance are impossible to achieve. The study finds that beneficiary participation in decision making resulted in overall community empowerment, increased skills in the management of water resources, and strengthened local organizations. In addition, it has a net beneficial effect on leaders, who gain in respect and status.

In summary, beneficiary participation in decision making results in more effective rural water projects and empowered local people and organizations.

2.2   Tracing causal paths (proximate determinants)

It is hypothesized that beneficiary participation influences final outcomes by affecting the outcomes at each project stage (design, implementation, construction, and maintenance), the proximate determinants. A series of multivariate regressions were conducted to test these relationships (tables 9.3 and 9.4). The following findings resulted.

1. *The impact of overall beneficiary participation is greater than participation during any particular stage.* The coefficients are less significant when the project is broken down into stages (table 9.3, column 3) than for overall beneficiary participation across all stages (table 9.1, column 3). Participation should be viewed as a holistic evolutionary process, in which beneficiaries have to be involved in decision making from the beginning to the end. The approach of many public sector agencies, which build systems

Table 9.3

Impact of Participation in Particular Stages
on Proximate Determinants of Project Performance

Dependent Variable	Model 1[a]	Model 2[b]	Model 3[c]
Beneficiary participation in design			
Quality of design			
Partial correlation	0.26****	0.12	0.14
t-statistic	3.6	1.7	1.5
N	113	72	64
Beneficiary participation in construction			
Effectiveness of construction			
Partial correlation	0.20***	0.13	0.13
t-statistic	3.3	1.7	1.6
N	117	76	67
Beneficiary participation in operations and maintenance			
Effectiveness of O&M			
Partial correlation	0.39***	0.08	0.05
t-statistic	6.5	1.4	0.7
N	119	77	68

[a]Participation alone (bivariate),
[b]Participation plus seven direct determinants,
[c]Participation plus seven direct plus eleven direct/indirect determinants.

*Significant at .05; **significant at .01; ***significant at .001; ****significant at .0001

without any community consultation and then hand systems over to communities with great ceremony—expecting them to take care of and pay for the operation of the systems, is doomed to failure.

2. *Overall beneficiary participation is the most important factor in determining overall quality of implementation* (table 9.4). Large rural water projects consist of hundreds of subprojects. The quality of implementation includes the design of these subprojects within an overall framework. This finding supports the emerging consensus that, to achieve lasting

Table 9.4

Impact of Overall Beneficiary Participation (OBP)
on the Proximate Determinants of Project Performance

Dependent Variable	Model 1[a]	Model 2[b]	Model 3[c]
Quality of design			
Partial correlation	0.46****	0.12	0.16
t-statistic	6.9	1.3	1.3
N	118	76	68
Quality of implementation			
Partial correlation	0.53****	0.17**	0.21**
t-statistic	9.3	2.7	2.7
N	121	77	68
Effectiveness of construction			
Partial correlation	0.30****	0.18	0.11
t-statistic	4.6	1.8	0.9
N	120	77	68
Effectiveness of operations and maintenance			
Partial correlation	0.49****	0.14*	0.11
t-statistic	7.4	2.0	1.1
N	121	77	68
Maintenance after one year			
Partial correlation	0.43****	0.16*	0.18
t-statistic	6.6	2.0	1.8
N	117	75	66

[a]OBP alone (bivariate).
[b]OBP plus seven direct determinants.
[c]OBP plus seven direct plus eleven direct/indirect determinants.

*Significant at .05; ** significant at .01; ***significant at .001; ****significant at .0001

development impact, much more attention has to be paid to quality of implementation.

3. *Beneficiary participation is significant to the quality of the overall project design but only in the bivariate model* (table 9.4). When the effects of eighteen other factors are considered, the importance of this participation

declines considerably. Direct and high levels of beneficiary participation in macro project design may not be as important as consultation with beneficiaries through social assessment surveys and the incorporation in project design of lessons learned from pilot projects. The study does not measure the involvement of other stakeholders. The direct involvement and commitment of a different set of stakeholders may be more important in macro project design than the direct involvement of a large number of beneficiaries.

4. *The quality of project design is positively related to the attention paid to ensuring the availability of spare parts and repair technicians.* On the other hand, this quality is significantly and negatively related to the complexity of project design, as measured by the number of activities that had to be completed, the complexity of the technology, and the number of organizations that had to be coordinated. This suggests that, in view of the difficulties in eliciting beneficiary participation and the central importance of such participation in project effectiveness, it is better to stagger project objectives; for example, water first, sanitation later.

5. *Beneficiary participation contributed to the effectiveness of operation and maintenance, and maintenance after one year.* It has less influence on the effectiveness of construction when the effect of all the other input factors is taken into account (table 9.4). The findings on operation and maintenance once again highlights the importance of availability of spare parts and the presence of skilled technicians.

Statistics tell only a partial story. To understand more fully the factors contributing to project effectiveness, an in-depth review was conducted of the twenty projects that scored the highest in project effectiveness. Nongovernmental organizations were overrepresented in this sample, with 50 percent of these projects executed by NGOs, even though such projects constituted 15 percent of the total sample. Although not necessarily more participatory, NGOs have greater autonomy than most government departments and have the advantage of being less bureaucratic and more flexible. Secondly, over 90 percent of these projects were executed by agencies other than ministries of public works and engineering departments.

In summary, multivariate and case analyses establish the importance of beneficiary participation in determining rural water project effectiveness, the empowerment of local people, and local management capacity. It also establishes that, thus far, few projects have achieved beneficiary participation in decision making. Hence, it is important to understand the conditions under which beneficiary participation occurs.

Table 9.5

Determinants of Overall Beneficiary Participation

Independent Variable	Overall Participation
Prior commitment	
Partial correlation	0.19**
t-statistic	2.5
Extent clients organized	
Partial correlation	0.23*
t-statistic	2.1
Use of local knowledge	
Partial correlation	0.2
t-statistic	2.5
Participation a goal	
Partial correlation	0.2*
t-statistic	1.9
Autonomy of project or agency	
Partial correlation	0.17
t-statistic	1.8

*Significant at .05; **significant at .01; ***significant at .001; ****significant at .0001

2.3   Factors determining beneficiary participation

Whether people participate or not in a project is influenced by beneficiary characteristics (such as needs and interests) and agency characteristics (such as client orientation, rules, and regulations). Once again, multivariate regression analysis was used to sort out which of twelve beneficiary and agency characteristics are important. The variables included in the regression for client characteristics are commitment prior to implementation, the organization of beneficiaries, the extent such organization was based on traditional collectives, the skills and knowledge of beneficiaries, the quality of leadership, and dependance on charismatic leaders. The key agency/project design characteristics were consensus on objectives, implementation flexibility, autonomy of projects, the extent participation was made a goal, the use of local knowledge, and the extent to which the project was driven by physical targets (table 9.5). The two significant beneficiary characteristics are commitment made in advance of construction or "demand" and the degree of organization of beneficiaries.

Demand orientation

The commitment of beneficiaries—or more appropriately, clients—prior to delivery of any hardware inputs is the critical feature of demand orientation. While many projects proclaim a demand orientation, relatively few consistently maintain responsiveness to demand throughout their lives. Project case analyses reveal several consistent patterns with important implications for policy and project design. First, demand or felt need cannot be assessed on the basis of objective criteria, such as quality or quantity of available water or morbidity. Second, community expression of demand translates into community commitment, including payment of capital as well as recurrent costs. Third, it is not sufficient to measure demand for water; what is important is establishing demand for a specific service level. For example, in India, while communities are unwilling to pay small amounts for communal hand pumps, they are willing to pay higher amounts for yard pipe connections. If project offerings do not match the service level desired, participation is not elicited. Fourth, unless demand or commitment is used as the primary community selection criterion, community interest and motivation are not tapped and agency strategies continue to be supply driven. Fifth, although project strategies are diverse, all projects use some form of community self-selection into project activities.

Beneficiary organization

The second important beneficiary characteristic is the ability of users to organize themselves to undertake action. Although the forms of organizations vary widely, they are characterized by internally owned rules and regulations and sanctions commonly known and accepted by members. Qualitative analysis shows that the existing stock of social capital that results in norms of reciprocity and trust is more important than written rules imposed by outsiders. Although local leaders and elites play lead roles in many projects, their contribution does not emerge as statistically significant

Agency characteristics

When beneficiary participation is induced by outside agencies, agency characteristics become particularly important. The single most important agency characteristic is the extent to which achieving beneficiary participation is a goal that is monitored, evaluated, and rewarded. Agencies that induce participation are characterized by client orientation, responsiveness during implementation, and the yielding or sharing of decision making with communities. Thus when managers make achieving participation a goal, they utilize local knowledge in designing projects; the participation goal also assists in setting priorities, evolving strategies, and allocating resources to the training of staff and to local capacity building. The relative autonomy of project agencies to pursue these goals is also important.

Gender differences

Effective women's participation is difficult to achieve, even though many projects state their intention to do so. Overall, 17 percent of the projects achieved meaningful women's participation. While there is a high correlation (association) between overall beneficiary participation and women's participation, there are significant differences in the factors influencing the two. In other words, achieving high levels of beneficiary participation does not necessarily lead to high levels of women's participation. An analysis of the twenty most participatory projects reveals that only half of them are also high in women's participation. Given the fact that in most rural cultures, women are disadvantaged compared to men in education, income, health, and access to public life, it is not surprising that, even in a sector closely related to their daily lives, women are not reached and empowered unless specific strategies are developed and resources are allocated to do so.

2.4   Intermediate steps in the participatory process

Participation is an organic process that cannot be meaningfully broken down into components except for analytical purposes. One can plan or design for participation, but whether it actually takes root depends on factors in implementation. Participation is circular, iterative, evolutionary, and infinitely varying, with several things happening simultaneously. Yet if agencies want to facilitate participation, it is useful to identify some intermediate steps toward achieving participation. The intermediate steps most highly correlated with participation are local control and ownership, agency responsiveness to feedback, user investment in capital costs, and user attention to field agents.

Multivariate analyses reveal that the degree of local control and ownership is influenced by the organization of clients, whether the organization is based on a traditional collective, the knowledge and skills of clients, or the broad-based leadership qualities of clients. It is not determined by the presence of charismatic leaders. The most important agency factor influencing local control is the agency's autonomy in decision making.

2.5   The management challenge

Success in rural water supply projects depends heavily on beneficiary participation; this, in turn, depends on beneficiary demand and on degree of organization and agency factors, such as their participation commitment, autonomy, and use of local knowledge. Clearly, the challenge facing the sector is institutional and not technological, although the availability of spare parts is important.

The creation of effective and sustainable rural water supply systems for which community groups take responsibility and which continue to function after projects are completed, requires a fundamental shift from a supply- to a demand-based participatory approach. The demand-based approach requires working with hundreds of communities, each different and each evolving at its own pace. The central management challenge is to manage uncertainty and ambiguity and to build local management capacity and ownership rather than to focus on construction. This, in turn, implies radical changes in planning, implementation strategies, and indicators of success. Managers must move away from a controlling, master plan, approach to a learning process approach. The learning process approach is marked by experimentation, responsiveness to clients, clarity and consensus on objectives, and monitoring of key process and outcome indicators. Decision making and control are delegated to communities, with no attempt at early standardization of how, when, and where implementation will proceed. Instead, agencies disseminate information and provide technical assistance to support community initiative.[2] The reinvention of agencies to support community-based development requires the following:

1. The community must have a felt need for the service; there must be a commonality of interest. The agency must respond to demand and know what people want, using the following mechanisms:
   —Assessment of demand
   —Community self-selection
   —Information campaigns
   —Outreach
   —Social analysis to identify and understand key actors, their power, interests, and needs

---

[2]From Narayan (forthcoming).

2. The community is to control and have authority over resources, decisions, and rule making. The agency lets go of control over implementation details; spells out the framework for interaction and negotiation with communities, through the following mechanisms:
    —Definition of objectives and indicators of success to support achievement of local control
    —Reorientation of staff and performance criteria

3. The community is assumed to have the needed capacity and skills and the ability to mobilize financial resources for long-term survival. The agency puts local empowerment and capacity building high on its agenda.
    —Institution of a capacity-building process
    —Resource investment in training
    —New funding mechanisms that reach communities quickly
    —A focus on strategies for groups to achieve financial self-sufficiency
    —Phase in payment of outreach workers by community groups

4. Every community is assumed to be unique. The agency plans for diversity and encourages local adaptation.
    —Use a learning process approach
    —Short planning horizons
    —Implementation plans modified by feedback from monitoring and evaluation

5. If the poor and marginal, including women and indigenous groups, are left out of community planning, the agency must focus on reaching them.
    —A focus on poor and marginal is reflected in objectives, institutional mechanisms, targeting strategies, and indicators of success.

The central challenge in adopting participatory approaches on a large scale is reversing control and accountability from centralized agencies to community groups. A new generation of large-scale rural water supply projects financed by the World Bank have been designed to put community groups in the center. This has involved putting in place new processes and institutional arrangements. For example, the Sri Lanka Rural Water Supply Project will be implemented by a new unit within the Ministry of Housing and Construction, with full financial control and autonomy in approval of subprojects and disbursement of funds. Community groups have to apply for inclusion in the project, either directly or through NGO intermediaries after information about the project is disseminated widely through the mass media. During project preparation, rather than drawing up detailed engineering designs for the total project area, a limited number of technical designs are developed to gauge unit costs for different technological options in different parts of the country. The application forms that community groups submit include community assessment of need, land and water surveys, technical design, and financial commitment.

Similarly, in Nepal, rather than working through the Ministry of Public Works, an autonomous water fund is being created. The board of directors will consist of representatives from NGOs, the private sector, and government. The primary responsibility of the board is to prequalify intermediaries, consulting firms, NGOs, or the local government to work as partners with community groups to develop sustainable water systems. Thus the fund encourages competition among potential providers of water services.

Since institutional reform is radical, all these projects are using pilot projects or a process of gradual expansion, feeding lessons learned every year into the planning cycle for the next year. Thus, the Rural Water and Sanitation Project for Low Income Communities in Indonesia, through NGO involvement, tested proposed institutional mechanisms alongside project preparation in sixty-two "starter villages" and monitored the process intensively. The centerpiece of the entire project are village action plans, initiated and formulated by village groups, which then form the basis of negotiation and planning with the technical agencies. The project has set an upper limit for funds available to communities in different hydrogeological zones; the higher the service level desired, the higher the proportion contributed by communities.

3   Conclusion

It is clear that beneficiary participation in decision making is critical in project effectiveness, the maintenance of water systems, environmental effects, community empowerment, and strength of local organizations. The bad news is that, so far, relatively few externally supported projects have achieved meaningful beneficiary participation. Even fewer have empowered women. The good news is that, in developing countries, policy change and project design are beginning to shift to enable new partnerships to emerge between community groups, NGOs, the private sector, and government engineering agencies.

References

Essman, Milton J., and Norman T. Uphoff. 1984. *Local Organizations: Intermediaries in Rural Development.* Ithaca: Cornell University Press.

Finsterbusch, Kurt, and Warren A. Van Wicklin III. 1987. "The Contribution of Beneficiary Participation to Development Project Effectiveness." *Public Administration and Development* 7: 1–23.

Hirschman, Albert O. 1970. *Exit, Voice, and Loyalty: Responses to Decline in Firms, Organizations, and States.* Cambridge: Harvard University Press.

Isham, Jonathan, Deepa Narayan, and Lant Pritchett. 1994. "Does Participation Improve Project Performance? Establishing Causality with Subjective Data." Policy Research Working Paper 1357. World Bank, Washington, D.C.

Narayan, Deepa. 1994. "The Contribution of People's Participation: Evidence from 121 Rural Water Supply Projects." ESD Occasional Paper 1. World Bank, Washington, D.C.

———. (Forthcoming). "Designing Community Based Development." ENV Technical Paper. World Bank, Washington, D.C.

10   Participation and Development

Vernon Ruttan

The issue of democratization and political development has been a consistent theme in development thought and in development assistance policy. In this chapter I review the evolution and role of participation in both thought and practice. I then turn to the lessons that might be drawn from earlier experience for contemporary efforts to strengthen the role of participation in development assistance programs.

1   Development Thought

When development economics emerged as a subdiscipline in the 1940s and early 1950s, there was a pervasive view among economists that the late industrializing countries required strong, authoritarian state institutions to mobilize the resources required for growth.[1] Democracy was a "luxury" that poor states could not afford. This view drew on and was reinforced by the apparent success of centralized planning in Stalin's Russia.

The theme that late-industrializing countries benefit from the evolution of strong state institutions with the capacity to intervene directly and to participate in economic activities is a pervasive theme in Gerschenkron's studies of European economic history (1962, 77–79, 1968, 257–80). A major organizing principle in Gerschenkron's work is the continuing tension between change and continuity in history. Industrialization occurs in rapid "spurts" along the lines suggested in the "takeoff" or "big push" views of economic development. The more backward the economy, the more likely that industrialization would occur "discontinuously as a sudden great spurt."

In the case of the early-industrializing countries, it was sufficient for the state to pursue policies aimed at creating a suitable environment, through an appropriate legal framework and the supplying of physical infrastructure, for the growth of industrial enterprise. But in the more backward economies of Russia and of Eastern and Southern Europe, "successful industrialization

---

I am indebted to Christopher Clague and Melinda Smale for comments on a draft of this chapter.

[1]In this section I draw on Ruttan (1991).

requires more than simply introducing the institutional framework that suffices for the purposes of industrialization in an advanced country." The state must have the power to pursue "forced draft" industrialization—to extract surpluses from a reluctant peasantry and to direct capital into industrial development.

Gerschenkron displays considerable caution in drawing the implications of his analysis for development policy. Other scholars who share Gerschenkron's historical perspective are less reticent. De Schweinitz (1964) argues that, while economic growth and democracy are complementary in the advanced Western economies, this relationship is reversed during the early stages of modern economic development. The Euro-American route to democracy is closed to countries undergoing industrialization now. The impulse for industrialization must come from the center of political power and spread outward into society rather than, as was the case in the West during the nineteenth century, coming from society itself. If developing countries are to grow economically, they must limit democratic participation in political affairs—"Justice must take a back seat to growth objectives" (de Schweinitz 1964, 277).

Bhagwati (1966) is even more explicit; he insists that "socialist countries, such as the Soviet Union and mainland China, have an immense advantage: their totalitarian structure shields the government from the . . . reactionary judgments of the electorate. The Soviet government's firm control on expansion of consumption over the last few decades could hardly ever be attempted by a democratic government. Another advantage of the socialist countries is their passionate conviction and dedication to the objective of economic growth—which contrasts visibly with the halting and hesitant beliefs and actions of most democracies" (203).

I cite de Schweinitz and Bhagwati not to criticize their work from the vantage of the late twentieth century but to emphasize the pervasiveness of the view that authoritarian regimes, whether capitalist or socialist, were more effective than democracies at mobilizing resources for development. The belief that authoritarian regimes are conducive to economic growth was pervasive not only among students of economic and political development but also among the political elites and enterprise managers in developing countries, as well as among the officers and technocrats in the international financial institutions and assistance agencies (Freeman 1985).

It was not until later that efforts were made to rigorously test the strong-state hypothesis against historic experience. During the 1970s and 1980s, Adelman and Morris pursued an exceedingly ambitious research agenda designed to explore the role of "initial institutions" on the pace and structure of economic development (Adelman and Morris 1967, 1973; Morris and Adelman 1988). Their methodology was empirical rather than theoretical. A variety of statistical methods was employed to identify configurations of economic and political change and for grouping closely related variables for different country types and groups. An attempt was made to capture the role of political institutions by variables measuring (1) the domestic economic role of government, (2) the socioeconomic character of political leadership, (3) the strength of national representative institutions, (4) political stability, and (5) foreign economic dependence and colonial status.

The Adelman-Morris results for the 1850–1914 period are consistent with the perspective of the "modernization" school in sociology and political science. "At critical junctions . . . political institutions mattered greatly. With rare exceptions, economic growth and its benefits did not diffuse far where domestic landed elites aligning with foreign export interests dominated the political process. In all countries undergoing substantial industrialization, domestic commercial and industrial classes had or gained significant power in national leadership. In more politically diverse country groups— for example, land-abundant dependent countries—economic growth spread far only when landed elites no longer dominated domestic economic policies" (Morris and Adelman 1988, 211).

The emergence of a legal system that strengthened property and market institutions was important for market expansion, industrial development, and agricultural development. In their earlier book, which focuses on more recent economic history, Adelman and Morris were not able to discover the close association between political and economic development that was revealed in their analysis of the 1850–1914 period. There was no systematic association between form of the political system and performance of the economic system. Indeed, the most striking pattern that emerges from their empirical analysis is the progressive differentiation and separation of the social, economic, and political spheres. The social elites lost control over both economic and political resources. Command over political and economic resources was no longer in the same hands. Furthermore, this differentiation emerges relatively early in the development process.

It is difficult to discover broad agreement among economic historians and development economists who have given explicit attention to political development. It does appear, however, that there would be fairly general assent to the proposition that authoritarian regimes in which command over economic and political resources was relatively undifferentiated characterized the societies from which currently developed market economies emerged. Furthermore, in these societies the emergence of capitalism preceded the emergence of democracy.

2   Development Assistance

Democracy and development were important objectives of the original Point Four legislation and of the Alliance for Progress (Ruttan 1996). The 1963 Foreign Assistance Acts contained language encouraging popular participation in development projects. The 1966 act was more explicit. "In carrying out programs authorized in this chapter [Title IX], emphasis shall be placed on assuming maximum participation in the task of economic development . . . through the encouragement of democratic, private, and local institutions."[2] The 1973 "new directions" legislation added a concern for human rights to the emphasis on democracy. In the summer of 1982, President Reagan, in a speech to the British Parliament, committed the United States to "fostering the infrastructure of democracy, a free press, unions, political parties which allows a people to choose their own way to develop their culture. . . . It is time we committed ourselves to assisting in democratic development" (Reagan 1982). Building democracy was identified by the Clinton administration as one of the leading issues in its foreign assistance strategy (Task Force to Reform A.I.D. 1993).

An important theme in the democratization agenda has been the design of local institutions of governance to empower communities to mobilize their own resources for development. We are now experiencing the third cycle of such concern. Programs organized under the rubric of *community development* were a major focus of U.S. development assistance during the 1950s and early 1960s. During the 1970s this concern was recycled under the rubric of *integrated rural development.* The theme emerged again in the early 1990s as *participation.* It may be useful to remind ourselves what has been learned from programs carried out under the earlier efforts.

2.1   Community development
In the first development decade after World War II, community development became a major focus of development assistance (Mosher 1976; Holdcraft 1978; Morris 1981).[3] From its inception, community development included both economic and political development objectives.

---

[2]Cited in Braibanti (1969, 15).

[3]This section draws on Ruttan (1975, 1984).

development included both economic and political development objectives. It held forth the promise of both building grassroots democratic institutions and contributing to the material well-being of rural people—"without revolutionary changes in the existing political and economic order" (Holdcraft 1978, 14).

Community development was viewed as a process that (1) involves the direct participation of people in the solution of their common problems, (2) employs the democratic process in the joint solutions of community problems, and (3) activates or facilitates the transfer of technology to the people of a community for more effective solutions of common problems. The process by which community goals were to be realized was itself important. The community development process was "rooted in the concept of the worth of the individual as a responsible, participating member of society. . . . It was designed to encourage self-help efforts to raise standards of living and to create stable, self-reliant communities with an assured sense of social and political responsibility" (Holdcraft 1978, 16).

A project initiated in 1948 in the Etawah District of Uttar Pradesh, India, served as a model and inspiration for many other community development projects and programs (Mayer, Marriott, and Park 1958; Korten 1980). The Etawah project employed multipurpose workers at the village level workers to initiate self-help approaches to increasing agricultural production and strengthening rural infrastructure. In 1952 the Indian government adopted the Etawah model as the basis for a major national rural development effort. When the program was extended on a national scale, however, the government did not have the technical or bureaucratic capacity "to adopt the painstaking approach to developing a participative administrative structure able to respond to bottom-up initiatives which had been the key to the Etawah project's success" (Korten 1982, 3).

The community development movement expanded rapidly during the 1950s. By 1960 more than sixty nations in Asia, Africa, and Latin America had launched national or regional community development programs. But by the mid-1960s community development was being deemphasized by both development assistance agencies and national governments. Support declined because of disillusionment on the part of both political leaders in the developing countries and officials of assistance agencies with the effectiveness of community development in meeting economic or political development objectives. Community development programs were criticized for failing to improve either agricultural productivity or the economic and social well-being of rural people. The criticism was also made that failure to reform the community power structure led to local gains generated by the programs. A related criticism, seldom stated explicitly, was that when programs were successful they set in motion political forces that were not easily controlled by the central authorities.

The global food crises, triggered by the crop failures in South Asia in the mid-1960s, shifted the attention of both national governments and development assistance agencies away from community development to a narrower focus on programs designed to enhance agricultural production. This shift was reinforced during the late 1960s as the potential of the new seed-fertilizer technology became apparent. The bilateral and multilateral assistance agencies redirected their support for institution building toward attempts to strengthen agricultural research, extension, credit, and input supply systems.

2.2   Integrated rural development

After a decade of relative neglect, rural development again emerged near the top of the development policy agenda in the early 1970s. A major symposium entitled "Agricultural Institutions for Integrated Rural Development" was convened in Rome by the FAO in 1971. In 1973 the president of the World Bank pledged his organization to direct its resources toward improving the productivity and welfare of the rural poor in the poorest countries (McNamara 1973).[4] Integrated rural development became an increasingly important focus of bilateral and multilateral development assistance.

The integrated rural development approach drew on a complex of often mutually contradictory intellectual and ideological perspectives.[5] One was a perception that even rapid growth of income in rural areas did not ensure either the availability of—or equitable access to—social services and amenities. A second influence was the emergence of systems thinking about institutional design and program implementation. The recognition that rural development involves a large number of interrelated activities was interpreted to imply that integrated program implementation could contribute to the achievement of rapid and measurable gains in agricultural production and rural welfare. A third influence originated in the growing disillusionment with technocratic and bureaucratic approaches to rural development.

---

[4]For a history of the evolution of poverty-oriented rural development programs at the World Bank, see Ayres (1983, 93–147).

[5]See reviews by Lele (1979); Mosher (1976); Montgomery (1979); and Cohen (1980).

Bureaucratic approaches were increasingly viewed as an instrument of control. This perspective led to a reemphasis on the local participation and resource mobilization themes of the earlier community development movement.

Complementarity among the sectoral components of development was a common assumption of both the bureaucratic and populist approaches to development programs in the 1970s. This comprehensive, or integrated, approach distinguished the new programs from the more traditional programs designed to increase agricultural production, improve rural education, build farm-to-market roads, supply health services, or promote family planning. But widely different definitions of integration were employed. By some definitions, the integrated delivery of materials (seeds and fertilizer), credit, and extension, as in the Pueblo Project in Mexico, was sufficient.

The village development program pioneered by the Bangladesh (formerly Pakistan) Academy for Rural Development at Comilla was one of the models that received particularly widespread attention (Raper 1970; Haq 1973; Khan 1974; Stevens 1974).[6] The academy was established in 1959 as a training center for public officials responsible for rural development activities in Comilla villages. The program involved three elements: (1) developing a two-tiered village and *thana* (or township) cooperative system; (2) inducing cooperation among public agencies in labor-intensive resource development efforts, particularly irrigation, drainage, and roads; and (3) developing the capacity of local government to coordinate and direct the efforts of departments responsible for civil administration and development (agriculture, water, health, education, and others).

The Comilla program was clearly successful when evaluated in terms of the diffusion of more productive agricultural technology, the mobilization of local resources for village improvement, and the development of cooperative institutions. The cooperatives proved capable of generating modest savings and of partially replacing traditional moneylenders as a source of credit. They also became effective channels of technical information about rice production practices, health practices, and farm and cooperative management between the villagers and the technicians located at the *thana* center. Many of the cooperatives also proved capable of (1)

---

[6]For a critical review, see Khan (1979). The Pueblo Project in Mexico also exerted a major impact on the design of production-oriented rural development projects (Redclift 1983; Swanberg 1982).

at the *thana* center. Many of the cooperatives also proved capable of (1) managing capital investments, such as tube wells, (2) handling the distribution of inputs, such as fertilizer, insecticides, and seeds, and (3) organizing services, such as tractor plowing. Roads, irrigation, and drainage were improved. In areas where such changes occurred, the value of farm output increased, the incomes of owner and tenant cultivators grew, and land values rose in response to the greater productivity and higher incomes. And the experience gained in the Comilla *thana* had an impact on rural administration and development in a number of other *thanas* in East Pakistan. After independence, the government of Bangladesh announced that the Comilla project would be used as the model for a national rural development program. However, the program that was actually implemented could be described more accurately as a cooperative development program than a rural development program.

The Comilla experience and similar experiences in other countries have led some observers to question why it is so easy to identify a number of relatively successful, small-scale or pilot rural development projects but so difficult to find examples of successful rural development programs or programs in which pilot projects have made the intended transition into general practice (Caiden and Wildavsky 1974; Ruttan 1975). Part of the reason is that when the programs are extended on a national scale they become mechanisms for imposing centrally mandated programs on communities rather than instruments that enable communities to mobilize their own development resources. Another reason is the dilution of technical and logistical support, which was abundantly provided at the pilot program stage. Assistance agency personnel often failed to understand the difference between decentralized administration and decentralized governance— between locating the administrative offices of central ministries at the provincial or district level and strengthening the fiscal and administrative capacity of local government.

2.3   Basic needs

In 1973 the Congress instructed the U.S. development assistance agency to direct its efforts toward meeting the basic needs of the poorest people in the developing countries (United States Congress 1973). In 1974 the UN World Food Conference adopted a declaration calling for the eradication of hunger and malnutrition by 1985 (United Nations 1975). This was followed by specific program design proposals by the International Labour Organization (ILO) at the 1976 World Employment Conference (International Labour Office 1976). These proposals and their program

Bank, and the U.S. Agency for International Development (Chenery et al. 1974; Ghai et al. 1977; Streeten and Burki 1978; Crosswell 1978; Streeten et al. 1981).[7]

The basic needs approach represents a radical departure from conventional development strategy. "The evolution from growth as the principal performance criterion, via employment and redistribution, to basic needs is an evolution from abstract to concrete objectives, from a preoccupation with means to a renewed awareness of ends, and from a double negative (reducing unemployment) to a positive (meeting basic needs)" (Streeten and Burki 1978, 413). Meeting the basic needs of the poor is, in this view, the central focus of development policy and planning. Growth objectives are replaced by consumption targets. And the consumption targets are translated into specific program goals—"a life expectancy of 65 years or more . . . a literacy rate of at least 75 percent . . . an infant mortality rate of 50 or less per thousand births . . . and a birth rate of 25 or less per thousand population" (Grant 1978, 9).

What impact did the basic needs perspective have on the organization of rural development programs? In the case of World Bank–supported projects, the effect was to include more nonagricultural social services. World Bank projects begun since the early 1970s in East Africa were more complex in design and objectives than earlier projects—they involved many more activities in the productive and social service sectors than was considered feasible at earlier stages (Lele 1979, 234). Lele also notes that their targets were often more ambitious than could be supported with existing technical and administrative capacity and that successful projects were difficult to replicate when governments and donors attempted to expand them into national programs.

A second problem that development assistance agencies have faced in their attempts to incorporate basic needs objectives into rural development programs has been reconciling (1) a commitment to the objectives of mass participation in local decision making and the building of institutions capable of mobilizing local resources for development with (2) the achievement of measurable improvements in basic needs indicators within the relatively limited time span between program initiation and evaluation.

---

[7]Within the World Bank there were two major doctrines on poverty alleviation: (1) the "redistribution with growth" school associated with Hollis Chenery, and (2) the "basic human needs" school associated with Mahbub ul Haq and Paul Streeten (see Ayres 1983, 76–91).

the relatively limited time span between program initiation and evaluation. A frequent result is that the participation and mobilization goals have been supplanted by bureaucratic approaches to program delivery (Uphoff and Esman 1974; Uphoff, Cohen, and Goldsmith 1979; Soedjatmoko 1978; Cernea 1979).

There is, of course, a danger in overemphasizing the conflict between efficiency in program design and delivery and local mobilization of economic and political resources for development. This is one of the most difficult problems for any society to resolve. Indeed, the capacity of a society to resolve this conflict is one of the relatively sure indicators of political development.

2.4 Lessons of experience

The basic human needs orientation represented a major shift. The community development programs of the 1950s had placed major emphasis on energizing rural communities for self-help. The rural development programs of the 1970s placed more emphasis on achieving greater equity in the distribution of the gains from economic growth between urban and rural areas and between economic and social classes within rural areas. The result was a shift in program focus from the mobilization of community resources to the delivery of program inputs and services.

By the early 1980s the new basic needs and integrated approaches to development came under severe scrutiny. The decline of integrated rural development and basic needs programs did not reflect a retreat on equity goals as much as a growing recognition that the programs, particularly in Africa, were not solving one of the most fundamental rural problems—achieving a reliable food surplus (Eicher and Baker 1982). Thus the reasons for the decline in emphasis on the new direction in programs of the 1970s were similar to those that led to the decline of community development in the early 1960s.

But the number of families whose level of consumption falls below even the most basic of the basic needs in poor countries continues to grow. The need for services to support agricultural production and an improvement in the quality of life in rural areas has not disappeared. It is useful, therefore, to attempt to draw the lessons that might be learned from this experience.

A clear inference from the literature on rural development is that efficient delivery of bureaucratic services to rural communities depends on effective organization at the community level. Rural communities, operating through either the formal structure of local government or informal or voluntary institutions, must be able to interact effectively with the central institutions charged with responsibility for the delivery of services to local communities. These community organizations must be able to interact effectively in the establishment of priorities. They must be able to provide feedback to the agency management on program performance. And they must be able to mobilize sufficient political resources to provide incentives for effective bureaucratic performance (Montgomery 1979; Friedmann 1981; Korten 1982).

Many rural development pilot projects have been successful because of their relatively intense use of human resources devoted to organization, management, and technical assistance. When attempts are made to generalize the pilot projects as the model for a national or regional rural development program, the intensity of human resource input cannot be sustained. Further, access to the higher levels of government and the administrative freedom to tailor programs precisely are frequently sacrificed to administrative convenience when projects are generalized. A highly centralized administration of national programs makes it difficult to carry out the experiments with program content and delivery methods that are essential if rural development programs are to meet the diverse needs of rural areas.

This attempt to interpret recent development experience leads to five generalizations with respect to program ideology and design, which are essential to the viability of any large-scale rural development effort. First, a rural development program must be organized around activities and services that have relatively well-defined technologies or methodologies and objectives. It is important to rural communities that the technologies, methodologies, and services needed to improve rural welfare become simultaneously available but not necessarily administratively integrated. Second, program activities must be organized to use the relatively low-quality (and inexperienced) human resource endowments that are available in rural areas. They must be extensive rather than intensive in their use of high-cost human capital. Third, the effective implementation of the program, to a substantial degree, depends on the development of the institutional capacity to mobilize the limited political and economic resources available. In societies in which rural administration is organized with a strong control orientation, the political and economic conditions necessary for rural development will rarely be met. Fourth, welfare in the rural areas of most developing countries remains at least as much a problem of the level of output per person as of distribution. New sources of income growth must continue to be sought in both technical and institutional change. Fifth, given the severe constraints on the availability of high-quality technical and administrative manpower, premature transitions from a pilot project to a national program are counterproductive for the development of a viable program. The human resources needed for the program can be expended only gradually through formal training and pilot program experience.

Developing countries have also been slow to encourage the development of local institutions that would enable rural people to mobilize their own economic and political resources. There is increasing evidence that the success of rural development programs in strengthening rural infrastructure or meeting the basic needs of the poor depends on the development of local representative institutions. But the strengthening of local governance is often viewed as a threat to political stability rather than as a resource for development by the national political leadership and the central bureaucracies. These attitudes have sometimes been reinforced by the staffs of development assistance agencies, who often have little historical insight into the evolution of rural development institutions in the currently developed countries. The result is a widening of the disequilibrium between the potential for reducing the worst features of poverty in rural areas and the realization of that potential.

3   Conclusion

The strengthening of democratic institutions has traditionally ranked relatively high, at least at a rhetorical level, among the objectives of U.S. foreign assistance policy. With the end of the Cold War, there have been renewed calls "to promote freedom and democracy around the world." As noted earlier, building democratic participation in development was among the four major initiatives listed in early pronouncements by Deputy Secretary of State Wharton and AID Administrator Atwood. But U.S. commitment to political development has, like commitment to economic development, often faltered when confronted with short-term strategic considerations.

In the case of economic development, both sector development and policy reform efforts have been able to draw on a powerful body of economic thought—primarily neoclassical economic theory—that provides the analytical tools to address issues of development practice and the design of economic reform. The application of these tools, even when used with skill and sensitivity, has not represented a guarantee against failure in project, program, or policy design. There is no similar body of theory that can serve as a guide in the design of a program to strengthen the institutions of governance or of a program to achieve a liberal political order (Krueger, Michalopoulos, and Ruttan 1989; Ruttan 1996).

One of the few guides available is the empirical generalization, noted earlier, that political liberalization is more sustainable when it is preceded by a successful program of economic liberalization. The generalization is sufficiently strong to support a conclusion that a poor country is fortunate if economic liberalization runs sufficiently ahead of political liberalization to generate economic growth at the same time that political reforms are being put into place. This generalization is clearly consistent with recent East Asian experience. The East Asian tigers—Korea, Taiwan, Hong Kong, and Singapore—certainly cannot be classified as liberal democracies, nor can the second echelon of rapidly growing economies in the region—Thailand, Malaysia, and Indonesia. They have, however, developed political systems capable of sustaining policies consistent with economic growth. And that economic growth seems to be inducing effective demands for modest political liberalization.

References

Adelman, Irma, and Cynthia Taft Morris. 1967. *Society, Politics, and Economic Development: A Quantitative Approach.* Baltimore: Johns Hopkins University Press.

———. 1973. *Economic Growth and Social Equity in Developing Countries.* Stanford: Stanford University Press.

Ayres, Robert C. 1983. *Banking on the Poor: The World Bank and World Poverty.* Cambridge: MIT Press.

Bhagwati, Jagdish. 1966. *The Economics of Underdeveloped Countries.* New York: McGraw-Hill.

Braibanti, R., ed. 1969. *Political and Administrative Development.* Durham: Duke University Press.

Caiden, Naomi, and Aaron Wildavsky. 1974. *Planning and Budgeting in Poor Countries.* New York: Wiley.

Cernea, Michael M. 1979. "Measuring Project Impact: Monitoring and Evaluation in the PIDER Rural Development Project—Mexico." Working Paper 332. World Bank, Washington, D.C..

Chenery, H., M. S. Ahluwalia, C. L. G. Bell, J. H. Duloy, and R. Jolly. 1974. *Redistribution with Growth.* London: Oxford University Press.

Cohen, J. M. 1980. "Integrated Rural Development: Clearing out the Underbrush." *Sociologia Rurales* 20: 195–212.

Crosswell, Michael. 1978. "Basic Human Needs: A Development Planning Approach." Discussion Paper 38. Agency for International Development, Washington, D.C.

de Schweinitz, Karl. 1964. *Industrialization and Democracy*. Glencoe, Ill.: Free Press.

Eicher, C. K., and C. K. Baker. 1982. *Research on Agricultural Development in Sub-Saharan Africa: A Critical Survey*. International Development Paper 1. East Lansing: Department of Agricultural Economics, Michigan State University.

Freeman, John R. 1985. *The Politics of Indebted Economic Growth*. Denver: Graduate School of International Studies, University of Denver.

Friedmann, John. 1981. "The Active Community: Toward a Political-Territorial Framework for Rural Development in Asia." *Economic Development and Cultural Change* 29: 235–61.

Gerschenkron, Alexander. 1962. *Economic Backwardness in Historical Perspectives*. Cambridge: Harvard University Press.

———. 1968. *Continuity in History and Other Essays*. Cambridge: Harvard University Press.

Ghai, D. P., A. R. Kahn, E. H. L. Lee, and T. Alfthan. 1977. *The Basic-Needs Approach to Development: Some Issues Regarding Concepts and Methodology*. Geneva: International Labour Office.

Grant, J. P. 1978. *Disparity Reduction Rates in Social Indicators: A Proposal for Measuring and Targeting Progress in Meeting Basic Needs*. Monograph 11. Washington, D.C.: Overseas Development Council.

Haq, M. N. 1973. *Village Development in Bangladesh*. Comilla: Bangladesh Academy for Rural Development.

Holdcraft, L. E. 1978. "The Rise and Fall of Community Development in Developing Countries, 1950–65: A Critical Analysis and an Annotated Bibliography." Rural Development Paper 2. Michigan State University, East Lansing.

International Labour Office. 1976. *Employment, Growth and Basic Needs: A One-World Problem*. Geneva: ILO; New York: Praeger, 1977.

Khan, A. H. 1974. "The Comilla Projects—A Personal Account." *International Development Review* 16: 2–7.

———. 1979. "The Comilla Model and the Integrated Rural Development Programme of Bangladesh: An Experiment in 'Co-operative

Capitalism.'" In *Agrarian Systems and Rural Development*, ed. Dharam Ghai, Azizur Rahman Khan, Eddy Lee, and Samir Radwan. New York: Holmes and Meier.

Korten, David C. 1980. "Community Organization and Rural Development: A Learning Process Approach." *Public Administration Review* 40: 480–511.

Korten, Frances F. 1982. "Building National Capacity to Develop Water Users' Associations: Experience from the Philippines." Working Paper 528. World Bank, Washington, D.C.

Krueger, Anne O., C. Michalopoulos, and V. W. Ruttan. 1989. *Aid and Development*. Baltimore: Johns Hopkins University Press.

Lele, Uma. 1979. *The Design of Rural Development: Lessons from Africa*. Baltimore: Johns Hopkins University Press.

McNamara, Robert S. 1973. Address to the Board of Governors. International Bank for Reconstruction and Development, Washington, D.C.

Mayer, Albert, McKim Marriott, and Richard L. Park. 1958. *Pilot Project, India: The Story of Rural Development at Etawah, Uttar Pradesh*. Berkeley: University of California Press.

Montgomery, J. D. 1979. "The Populist Front in Rural Development: Or Shall We Eliminate the Bureaucrats and Get on With the Job?" *Public Administration Review* 39: 58–65.

Morris, Cynthia Taft and Irma Adelman. 1988. *Comparative Patterns of Economic Development, 1850–1914*. Baltimore: Johns Hopkins University Press.

Morris, Jon R. 1981. "Managing Induced Rural Development." International Development Institute, Indiana University.

Mosher, Arthur T. 1976. "Thinking about Rural Development." Agricultural Development Council, New York.

Raper, A. F. 1970. *Rural Development in Action: The Comprehensive Experiment at Comilla, East Pakistan*. Ithaca: Cornell University Press.

Reagan, Ronald. 1982. Address to Members of the British Parliament, Westminster, June 8.

Redclift, M. 1983. "Production Programs for Small Farmers: Plan Pueblo as Myth and Reality." *Economic Development and Cultural Change* 31: 551–70.

Ruttan, Vernon W. 1975. "Integrated Rural Development Programs: A Skeptical Perspective." *International Development Review* 2: 129–51.

————. 1984. "Integrated Rural Development Programmes: A Historical Perspective." *World Development* 12: 393–401.

————. 1991. "What Happened to Political Development?" *Economic Development and Cultural Change* 36: 265–92.

————. 1996. *U.S. Development Assistance Policy: The Domestic Politics of Foreign Economic Assistance*. Baltimore: Johns Hopkins University Press.

Soedjatmoko. 1978. "National Policy Implications of the Basic Needs Model." *Prisma: Indonesian Journal of Social and Economic Affairs* 9: 3–25.

Stevens, R. D. 1974. "Three Rural Development Models for Small-Farm Agricultural Areas in Low-Income Nations." *Journal of Developing Areas* 8: 409–20.

Streeten, P. and S. J. Burki. 1978. "Basic Needs: Some Issues." *World Development* 6: 411–21.

Streeten, P., with S. J. Burki, M. ul Haq, N. Hicks, and F. Stewart. 1981. *First Things First: Meeting Basic Human Needs in the Developing Countries*. New York: Oxford University Press.

Swanberg, K. G. 1982. "Institutional Evolution: From Pilot Project to National Development Program—Pueblo and Caqueza." Discussion Paper 132. Harvard Institute for International Development.

Task Force to Reform A.I.D. and the International Affairs Budget. 1993. "Preventive Diplomacy: Revitalizing AID and Foreign Assistance in the Post-Cold War Era." U.S. Department of State.

United States. Congress. House of Representatives. Committee on Foreign Affairs. 1973. *Mutual Development and Cooperation Act of 1973*. Hearings, 93 Cong., 1 sess. Washington, D.C.: GPO.

United Nations. 1975. *Report of the World Food Conference, Rome, 5–16 November 1974*. New York: UN.

Uphoff, N. T., and M. J. Esman. 1974. *Local Organization for Rural Development: Analysis of Asian Experience*. RLG 19. Ithaca: Rural Development Committee, Center for International Studies, Cornell University.

Uphoff, N. J., J. M. Cohen, and A. A. Goldsmith. 1979. *Feasibility and Application of Rural Development Participation: A State-of-the-Art Paper*. RDM 3. Ithaca: Rural Development Committee, Center for International Studies, Cornell University.

IV IMPLEMENTING INSTITUTIONAL REFORM IN FORMERLY COMMUNIST SOCIETIES

11 Missed Policy Opportunities during Mongolian Privatization: Should Aid Target Policy Research Institutions?

Peter Murrell

One vital element of the institutional profile of developed economies is the set of organizations that provides policy-relevant information-gathering and research, contemporaneous with events. This chapter employs the term *policy* to denote the wide spectrum of government measures—the creation of laws, the building of new institutions, regulations, etc. When an important policy change is on the agenda, new information assails lawmakers, regulators, and government bureaucrats. The research departments of interest groups offer their analyses; scholars pursue historical and comparative parallels; think tanks publicize counterproposals. Democratic process and open debate compel the policy maker to use this information.

Almost the converse story could be told concerning Mongolia's privatization. Policy wandered along a path largely unmapped by society, even in retrospect. Production and analysis of basic information could have been immensely important to the privatization process, leading to new policy proposals. Instead, politicians and bureaucrats labored under misguided impressions, focusing on extraneous issues while problems accumulated for want of easy corrective measures. The missed opportunities were not a result of political pathologies, nor of conceptual problems in formulating corrective policies, nor of the cost of correction. Rather, problems arose because nobody systematically examined events and evaluated consequences. Informational feedback was weak enough that policy makers could safely ignore newly arising problems, the political opposition lacking sufficient knowledge about events to force the government to undertake new policies.[1] The absence of institutions providing informational feedback is a key characteristic of the society in which IRIS has provided technical assistance, taught, and conducted research over the last five years.

This observation is relevant in two ways to the foreign aid process. First, when domestic sources of information are scarce, it is difficult to identify productive targets of assistance. The foreign aid process is hampered

---

[1]Informational feedback refers not only to events occurring over time, but also between simultaneous but separate events. See section 3 for more details.

in the same way that domestic politicians are handicapped. (As argued in section 1, research by donors is a poor substitute for domestic research capacity.) Second, foreign assistance might aim to create a capacity for information gathering, research, and analysis. This capacity is a neglected institution with significance both for economic policy and for strengthening democratic processes. In the West, the public goods problem of information production has been attenuated by the growth of a self-perpetuating educational and research establishment, the development of competing interest groups that monitor policy, and the gradual accretion of independent government agencies. In countries emerging from the Soviet bloc, these elements of society are either missing or lack the independence to play the role of investigator, critic, and generator of alternative policy proposals.

A subtext of this chapter is a view of reform and development derived from the author's observations of transition processes. This view emphasizes informational problems, as does the New Institutional Economics. However, the New Institutional Economics stresses information asymmetries, the coordination and incentive problems that they present, and the institutional solution to these problems. Somewhat slighted is the problem of information generation, particularly in its public goods aspects. This is the emphasis of the present chapter, as discussed in section 1.

Section 2 introduces the reader to Mongolia and pertinent aspects of its privatization program. Section 3 describes the character of the Mongolian policy-making environment, emphasizing characteristics common to other transition countries. Sections 4–9 explore various facets of Mongolia's privatization program, each section pinpointing information that might have affected policy formulation and implementation, had it been brought to the fore.

Apart from providing empirical evidence for the main thesis of the chapter, sections 4–9 provide a characterization of the way in which privatization proceeds in a society with few complementary institutions. This characterization shows that privatization in a country such as Mongolia results in a structure that has little in common with a Western private sector. Nevertheless, it is surely the image of a modern private sector that allowed privatization per se to become a strong, early focus of aid policies in former socialist countries, in contrast to the realities of the changes that were actually occurring. This observation returns us to the main theme of the chapter, the need for reforming economies to have a capacity to develop accurate images of the changes generated by new policies.

Before proceeding with the argument, it is necessary to present a caveat on the interpretation of the following. Readers should bear in mind that the following sections focus on flaws and failures in order to diagnose ills and their causes. The purpose is not to catalog the healthy parts of the body politic. Thus, this chapter is not an overall evaluation of the privatization process in Mongolia, which in fact might be viewed as successful relative to privatization programs in analogous countries.

1   The Embedding of Policy Analysis Institutions

The central vision underlying this chapter is of socioeconomic mechanisms as information-generating and information-processing devices. With informational processes central to economic success, then aid programs should consider supporting mechanisms that enhance and use knowledge. Indeed, such support is already present in aid policies. For the long-term, there are varied efforts in the educational field. For the short term, there are models of laws, strategies of reform, and analyses of specific policies, largely originating in Western countries. These, however, are necessarily incomplete, because information cannot be bestowed on a country in the same way that food and antibiotics are donated. The usefulness of information is contingent on its fit with the environment.

A country's socioeconomic framework develops in a gradual process of incremental change.[2] Each new institution interacts with a larger preexisting structure. Therefore, the effectiveness of each new institutional brick crucially depends on its fit with the existing institutional foundation. As a consequence, if it is to be effective, the generation of information on the effects of existing policies and on the formulation of new policies needs to reflect the deep characteristics of a society. To know how a policy will work, one must understand the concurrent processes occurring in the economy. A model imported from the West is useful only to the extent that it provides a disciplining pedagogical device, not a magic key that will fit any door. Thus, North (1990) emphasizes the path dependence and unpredictability of institutional development. The path dependencies arise because, in the short-run, culture defines the way people process and utilize information. In Mongolia, for example, measures for the deregulation of prices functioned less well than measures for the regulation of prices because of the surrounding cultural environment (Murrell, Korsun, and Dunn, 1992).

---

[2]This is a view of socioeconomic development that follows from Popper (1971). See Murrell (1992).

To be most productive, the organizations that analyze proposed policies and monitor their results must be embedded within a society, able to reflect the deeper features of that society. The embedding of such organizations facilitates the absorption into their work of the cultural and historical aspects of the functioning of existing institutions. Moreover, domestic organizations can frame the presentation of their analysis in terms that are likely to be appreciated within the existing cultural and political milieu. Of course, modern skills of analysis are necessary, but they must be combined with an indigenous capacity that is able to come to grips with the complexity of the local environment.

By creating an indigenous capacity for informational feedback on policy, an additional public good is generated. As the underlying factual and analytical content of policy discourse improves, there will be a consequent enhancement in the quality of argumentation used in open public debates.[3] Blatantly specious arguments will be squeezed from public discourse, weeding out the worst elements from the set of contemplated policies. Logic and facts are powerful weapons against ideology, symbolism, and political chicanery.

One can imagine a typical counterargument to the above. A critic of this chapter's thesis would object to its naiveté about politics, arguing that politics determines policy and that little change occurs simply by raising the quality of information. Such arguments have been all too prominent in Western analysis of the transition process. Nevertheless, as argued in sections 4–9, the experience of Mongolia does little to support those who place the greatest stress on rent seeking and coalitions that block change. While these elements of policy formulation have been present in Mongolia, the following argues that purely political pathologies have been far less important than the politics of rational ignorance, combined with the historical legacy of a system in which there was no interest in and no capacity for production of information on the effects of policy.

---

[3]The effects of a general improvement in the quality of debate are already clear in Mongolia. Debates on stabilization and liberalization are carried on in completely different terms in 1995 than they were in 1991, with consequent improvements in policy. As the society moves to more technical reforms, however, such as those on corporate governance, the same level of improvement will not arise simply from general experience of the market; higher levels of technical capacity will be needed.

2 Privatization in Mongolia

Mongolia's peer group is the set of smaller, less-developed, former Soviet republics. In 1921, Mongolia followed Russia's turn to communism, and in the years that followed the Soviet model was implanted so thoroughly that Mongolia became known as the de facto sixteenth republic. However, the very fact of de jure independence meant that Mongolia began its reforms early, with political ones beginning in 1990 and economic reforms in early 1991.

The initial economic conditions were not auspicious. In the first months of 1990, Mongolia was still under Soviet hegemony, receiving aid equal to 25 percent of gross domestic product and conducting 95 percent of its trade within the CMEA.[4] Previously, there had been only a small amount of decentralizing reform, the private commercial sector accounting for only 2 percent of national income. The Mongolian constitution still had state ownership as its fulcrum, and the notion of privatization was just entering the political vocabulary.

After the country's first free elections in mid-1990, the old Communist Party formed a coalition government with new reformist parties. The most influential of these parties was formed around a core of young economists, whose leader, Ganbold, became first deputy prime minister in charge of economics. A month after the new government's formation, this group persuaded Prime Minister Byambasuren to commit Mongolia to an ambitious privatization program. By April 1993, over 75 percent of large enterprises had completed all steps of the privatization process, these enterprises accounting for over 80 percent of assets in the large-enterprise sphere.

The progress on privatization stood in stark contrast to developments on other reforms. Liberalization, legal and institutional reform, and macroeconomic stabilization proceeded in fits and starts. Even now, liberalization is incomplete, with price and trade controls recently reintroduced for important goods.[5] Legal reform stopped at the passing of statutes, with implementation receiving little attention. While macroeconomic stabilization shows short-run successes, long-term prospects remain

---

[4]For the disastrous effect of these legacies on economic outcomes in the early post-Soviet years, see Boone (1994) and Denizer and Gelb (1994).

[5]The time of writing is November 1995.

uncertain, with the government engaging in an inflationary burst of domestic credit expansion during 1995.

Turning to the privatization program itself, in January 1991 the government established the Privatization Commission, whose staff had considerable power, and the Stock Exchange, which performed a key role in the smooth privatization of large enterprises. The basic components of the radical reformers' program made their way into law in May 1991. Privatization would be comprehensive and fast. "Small privatization" would encompass small enterprises, mostly in the trade and service sectors, livestock, and eventually housing. "Large privatization" would focus on all large enterprises. Agriculture was the last of the three distinct programs. This chapter focuses on the nonagricultural portion of large privatization, which was aimed at more than four hundred enterprises in industry, transportation, and distribution.[6]

On the supply side, large privatization was centralized. Enterprises had little discretion—every enterprise would be sold for vouchers on the Stock Exchange. Before sale, each enterprise was corporatized shortly after the approval of its privatization plan. At that time, control shifted into the hands of the general director, the workers, and the Privatization Commission, as putative representative of future shareholders.

On the demand side, the process was highly decentralized. Markets determined the allocation of shares among individuals, as each citizen used a set of seven nontradeable vouchers dedicated to large privatization. Enterprises were sold on the Stock Exchange for vouchers only, using a nationwide network of brokerage houses. The brokerages also run mutual funds, providing an alternative for citizens unwilling or unable to choose particular enterprises.

3   Two Pertinent Features of the Mongolian Policy-Making Environment

Comparing informational processes across economic systems, a curious paradox emerges. Market systems, built largely by spontaneous action, have a host of organizations that catalog and analyze economic processes. Centrally planned systems, purportedly built by design, relied on

---

[6]Kraay (1992) gives the early background to privatization from an adviser's perspective. For an overview of private sector development, see Hahm (1993).

ideology much more than economic analysis. In Mongolia, there was no tradition of reflective economic analysis, in either research institutes or universities. To be sure, practitioners—planners or price setters, for example —understood the mechanics of their small piece of the world. But their tools were description, cladistics, and ideology, rather than modern methodologies. The role of economics was thoroughly consistent with Ruttan's (1984) observation that social science knowledge is least in demand in societies dominated by ideology. Mongolia's stock of such knowledge was way below equilibrium levels in 1990.

On the advent of reforms, this analytical gap applied especially to knowledge of the market economy. Parodies of the market appeared, rather than analyses, from the supposed ubiquity of speculators and exploitation, on the one hand, to the mystical belief in the invisible hand, on the other. This lack of knowledge has been critical in framing the intellectual and informational atmosphere surrounding policy debates (Murrell, Dunn, and Korsun, forthcoming). Additionally, without a domestic capacity for analysis, there was no feedback on the effects of policy. There was virtually no systematic monitoring of outcomes, in order to understand whether midcourse corrections were needed.

The lack of temporal informational and analytical feedback was matched by a similar disconnect between simultaneous, but separate, activities. The "departmentalism" of the old system continued in the new. Thus, developments in corporate law refused to acknowledge the special nature of the privatization process. Other laws made unjustified assumptions about the state of the judicial system. Undoubtedly, the lack of an analytical approach to public policy and the absence of an independent policy research community to point out lapses were both instrumental in allowing departmentalism to continue.

The second conspicuous characteristic of the policy-making environment was that politics had a limited role in the formulation of the large privatization program, despite heated debates. Early in the reform process, privatization became the touchstone of progress and received a high level of commitment. The debate about privatization during 1991 was not about whether it would occur or about whether it would be fast, but about small details. Urban workers demonstrated to demand a larger role, but were easily mollified with token concessions. The general directors, although given only the same token concessions, proved to be a compliant group in readying enterprises for privatization. Even the massive fall in the standard of living, caused by the collapse of the USSR and the CMEA, produced only a hiccup in the progress of privatization. When conservatives in late 1991 tried to use the general discontent to question aspects of the privatization program, they had no effect on outcomes.

The significance of the unimportance of politics lies in the interpretation of the policy episodes reviewed below. These episodes are best understood as results of a flawed policy-making process, with the flaws most notably arising from shortcomings in information and analysis. Political economy models provide few insights.

4   The Development of Corporate Law

The first year of reform saw the development of a rudimentary corporate law, to be called the Economic Entities Law. The law was based upon textbook examples of European laws, aided by the knowledge of recent Hungarian experience but filtered through perceptions derived from socialist experience. The law's drafters remained aloof from the realities of the enterprise sector. There was no attempt to study the real needs of enterprise governance at the time.[7] As one drafter said to us: "Even when writing the law I could not understand what relations I was regulating."[8] Moreover, because of departmentalism, the drafting of the law was divorced from developments in privatization itself. This was doubly important because the law gave legal status to the new entities created by privatization and because the law was the only statute relevant to corporate governance when state entities became independent.

The status of bodies mediating between shareholders and permanent management provides an example of the consequence of such a confused legal environment. In the Economic Entities Law, there was no equivalent to a board of directors. The only outside influence on the general director and the workers (besides shareholders' meetings) was a "control council," a curious hybrid between the monitoring units of the old centralized administrative system and a German-type supervisory board. These control councils were to comprise outsiders, the law barring employees from membership. However, 51 percent of privatized enterprises surveyed in 1993 were in violation of this stipulation. Elementary research on the

---

[7]Interview with Suvdaa, lawyer for the Union of Production Cooperatives, October 1991.

[8]Interview with a member of the Working Group on the 1991 Economic Entities Law, May 27, 1995.

decisions of privatizing enterprises could have uncovered this phenomenon, but there was no attempt to gather data systematically. Hence, when amendments were made to the Economic Entities Law, in mid-1993, there was no redress of this problem, since there was no general awareness of it. Enterprises remained in a legal purgatory, leaving a tangled web for the future. Because illegalities come to light mainly in crises, a past illegality makes it all the more difficult for courts to resolve efficiently the disputes that come before them.[9]

The fact that there is no conjuncture between statute law and events on the ground is especially critical in a civil law country such as Mongolia, where judges seek guidance from above rather than interpreting the law. Disputes over corporate property are put on hold by the lower courts, pending clarification of the law from above.[10] Of course, a new law might address the problem and the early reformers did have a strategy of drafting simple, amendable laws.[11] Unfortunately, there is no informational feedback to force drafters of new laws to take events into account. In preparing a new company law, drafters did not systematically evaluate the workings of the old law.

The Mongolian Economic Entities Law and its successor Company Law are not a priori faulty. Rather, their problem is the lack of fit with the Mongolian environment. Corporate law does not work, a fact obvious to those who have to deal with the law, primarily companies and the judiciary. But law drafters do not take such views into account because there is no systematic fact-finding process that inserts itself into decisions on policy. Thus, top policy makers and law drafters erroneously believe that the new law will solve the problems of corporate governance.[12] A domestic research capability could make a large difference by uncovering pertinent information and inserting this information into the policy process.

---

[9]Korsun and Murrell (1994, 1995b) checked compliance with just two features of the Economic Entities Law, on the holding of shareholders' meetings and on whether control councils had employee members. Two-thirds of sample enterprises openly admitted violating one of these two features.

[10]Interview with a district court judge, September 1994.

[11]Interview with Zholjargal, head of Stock Exchange, July 23, 1993.

[12]A view expressed by a leading official at the IRIS Roundtable on corporate governance, Ulaanbaatar June 1, 1995.

5   The Development of the Privatization Law

The Privatization Law of May 1991 was a symbolic statement that privatization was definitely going to happen. Debate on the law was conducted in symbolic terms, driven hardly at all by an understanding of likely consequences. This was so even on small details for which repercussions were predictable. Systematic analysis of the logic of privatization procedures would have greatly helped lawmakers, but there was no organization with the skills, incentive, or mandate to do such analysis, apart from those few individuals with a stake in quick implementation of privatization. The lack of information and analysis allowed symbolism to dominate. An example of the consequences of the tenor of debate appears in the matter of whether employees should get preferential ownership rights. The relevant part of the law, passed over the opposition of the program designers, did give some preferential rights. The designers saw this as a defeat. But there is double paradox here, one not broadly understood in Mongolian society.

First, because of the mechanics of the share selling process, the preference turned out to be trivial. The workers gained little from the measures introduced by the parliament (Korsun and Murrell 1994). Second, employees did not need such measures. They have as much control now, and their ownership share is as large, as if they had been given real preferential rights.[13] Meanwhile, the public and many government officials believe the symbolism and do not focus on the real reasons that the institutions of corporate governance have been ineffective.[14]

The emphasis on symbolism—the voucher market, the speed of privatization—facilitated by the absence of an analytical capacity meant that there was no debate on the relation between the ultimate objectives of the privatization program and its structure. For example, attention to corporate governance issues might have meant that the privatization law was better integrated with corporate law. The Stock Exchange might have been allocated statutory powers to supervise enterprise compliance with measures to protect outside shareholders. Of course, many problems would have

---

[13]This was a result of employees' decisions in using their vouchers and of lacunae in governance procedures. Later sections clarify this matter, but full details appear in Korsun and Murrell (1994).

[14]This misplaced emphasis still appeared among contributors to the IRIS Roundtable on corporate governance, Ulaanbaatar, June 1995.

remained given that policy analysis works imperfectly everywhere. But in Mongolia, the absence of such analysis meant that ideology and symbolism had no natural enemy.

6 The Process of Privatization

Laws and resolutions contained nothing that mandated how companies should be governed before privatization. Departmentalism had produced a major gap at the intersection of privatization and the governance of enterprises awaiting privatization. This gap was crucial because of the length of the privatization process: the median enterprise waited over two years between the announcement of privatization and the final sale of its shares.

In this void, there was general reliance on the Economic Entities Law, inappropriately so since this law was not designed for the privatization process. A clause dictated that a "constituents' assembly" of shareholders should meet in new companies to adopt a corporate charter and to elect the company's administration. This assembly should take place within thirty days of the last sale date for shares. In 75 percent of enterprises, this last-sale date was interpreted as occurring when the Privatization Commission created the shares, holding them on behalf of future owners. This curious interpretation was probably technically inconsistent with the law and certainly inconsistent with its spirit.

The constituents' assemblies were attended by workers, management, and a staff member of the Privatization Commission, ostensibly representing future outside shareholders. The absence of a corporate governance framework specific to privatization facilitated bargaining between management and workers to establish control over the enterprise. For example, one general director was able to insert into his company's charter a provision limiting any single individual's ownership to 5 percent of the company's shares. Similarly, government officials were elected to the control councils of many enterprises in which government had no ownership stake. These results were surely not welcomed by new outside shareholders.

Corporatization and privatization stretched over a lengthy time period. The pertinent information could have been generated and made public in the first months of implementation of privatization. Then, there would have been the possibility of quick corrective action, affecting the large majority of state enterprises waiting to be privatized. But the absence of any independent informational input into public policy debate meant that elementary results of the privatization process were never monitored. The society lacked informational feedback from events to public policy, which might have put pressure on the few officials aware of how implementation was proceeding.

7   The Residual State Share

An important decision concerned whether the state would retain a stake in enterprises and, if so, of what size. The more conservative members of government wanted a significant share. The radicals, who were implementing privatization, wanted minimal state involvement. In practice, the implementers had a great deal of decision-making latitude and usually chose the size of the residual government share. Rather surprisingly, then, the state retained stakes, ranging from 15 percent to 80 percent in 41 percent of the enterprises that were privatized.

These results were an unintended consequence of a sequential privatization that was largely unmonitored. When government officials were alerted to the size of this share, they were often surprised. They would probably be startled to know that there was a systematic (but seemingly unconscious) pattern to the decisions. Korsun and Murrell (1994) show that the state tended to keep a share in enterprises most likely to be vulnerable in the future. Thus, the government was left with a crucial role in the privatized sector, one that the privatization program had not envisaged and one that decision makers did not want.

One reason for this outcome was the poverty of informational feedback during privatization. Undoubtedly, information on the state share was easily available and known by those making privatization decisions. But these actors had no interest in communicating the plain facts to the policy-relevant community.[15] Perhaps a different result would have occurred had there been policy analysts ready to insert the information into public debate, simultaneously articulating its significance to a broader audience.

---

[15]Here, the explanation for events is at least partially political, political motives surely being behind the nonrevelation of information. But the political problems might have been alleviated by increasing the capabilities for the production of information and analysis.

8 Employee Ownership

The radical reformers continuously stressed the egalitarian aspects of the privatization program—the fact that each citizen would acquire the same share of the country's assets. Thus, they fought against those advocating the entitlement of workers to their factories. Parliament did give a concession to employees, who were allowed to purchase shares at a price of a hundred voucher-currency units in a pre-public offering. Since the median share price turned out to be seventy-six, this amounted to a concession in only a minority of cases. Had all employees exercised their preferential right, this arrangement would have resulted in an employee ownership of 13.6 percent, well below the radicals' unofficial maximum of 20 percent. However, employees could forgo participation in the preferential scheme and play the market, using their vouchers on the Stock Exchange as did other citizens.

Few employees used their preferential rights, acquiring only 4.3 percent of enterprise shares in this manner. For a while, this figure became official data on the size of employee ownership. However, employees used their own and their families' vouchers on the Stock Exchange to buy shares in their own enterprises. Evidence of this phenomenon can be found only by doing basic research through enterprise surveys. The survey of Korsun and Murrell (1994) generates estimates of employee-plus-family ownership of 44.6 percent of enterprise shares on average. This is more than ten times greater than the estimate announced by government officials and more than twice the unofficial target for the ceiling on employee ownership.

Thus, the implementation of privatization and the development of corporate governance policy labored under a misconception for a lengthy time. The facts were there to find but were never collected. Had the facts been known, perhaps there could have been some strategic shifts in policy. But a prerequisite for such shifts would have been systematic investigation of ownership data, allowing policy makers to understand that ownership patterns had taken an unexpected turn. Policy makers had no interest in such an investigation and there were no independent institutions capable of generating the information and forcing policy makers to react to it.

9 Increasing the Power of Outsider Shareholders

A disappointing element of policy has been the delay in passing a securities law, which would legalize cash trading of those shares originally bought through vouchers. The Stock Exchange was ready to conduct this secondary trading in early 1993. Yet the passage of a law and its implementation took more than two years, until August 1995.

Few plausible reasons have been offered for the slow implementation of secondary trading, except for vague concerns over increasing inequality and Chinese ownership. These concerns fade in significance compared to the costs of the delay in improving the governance of enterprises. The lack of influence of outsider shareholders and the dominance by insiders is clearly evident from survey data (Korsun and Murrell 1994). However, the realization of this situation came to the attention of the policy community only slowly.

In the meantime, the mutual funds, created within brokerage houses by the Stock Exchange, might have served a role of concentrating ownership. However, these state-controlled funds were the poor cousins of the privatization process. They were given little publicity. Entry into the mutual fund market was blocked. Thus, only 2 percent of shares are currently held by mutual funds.

The solution to the problem of lackluster mutual funds would have required more than the mere uncovering of facts. Here, the generation of information on the creation of solutions would have been important. A research community aware of international events might have provided the relevant information. The Czech and Russian experience with mutual funds could have been highly instructive, for example. The importance of free entry into the mutual fund market was fundamental in these two countries. Knowledge of this fact and the logistics of implementation might have done much to change the outcome of the Mongolian privatization process. But there were no domestic organizations that could have inserted these facts into the public debate.

The present structure of corporate governance reflects many of the factors described above. Shareholders' meetings are stacked in favor of insiders, and general directors dominate the nomination of boards. Proxy procedures do not give outsiders a fair chance to affect decisions. Voting methods at meetings often rely on head counts, ignoring representation by numbers of shares. As a result, the emerging picture of corporate governance evidences little outsider influence. Insiders appear the real winners, with the general directors as powerful as they ever have been (Korsun and Murrell 1995b).

An obvious way to begin to address present problems of corporate governance is to create a workable system of shareholder proxy voting, but no law or regulation facilitates this procedure, and, in any case, the country's communications and transportation are poor. It is difficult to argue that this situation is simply a result of power politics, since time and time again over the last years political events have shown that the urban workforce and the old corps of general directors are not a strong lobby. However, the lack of basic information on the workings of corporate governance might be a central cause of the present unsatisfactory situation. There was no study of the workings of shareholders' meetings before the drafting of the new Company Law began. Not surprisingly then, the new law ignores the lack of outsider representation in companies and, if anything, makes such representation less likely. Had there been domestic organizations that monitored the governance of companies and had enough influence to insert the information into the public policy arena, then this law would surely have been constructed very differently.

10   Conclusions

Mongolian privatization and related public policy measures developed on a trajectory that was largely unaffected by informational feedback from the new environment created by privatization. Policy did not react to events. A prime cause of the unresponsiveness of policy was the absence of institutions that could generate, and insert into the political arena, policy-relevant information and analysis. In the less-developed reforming socialist economies, there is nothing equivalent to the policy analysis apparatus that exists in the West. This very fact is a challenge for the future, an opportunity for foreign aid to help develop an analogous capacity in postsocialist countries, together with those reforms in the policy process that allow such a capacity to affect events.

This chapter has been one-sided, focusing on the benefits of policy analysis organizations. It provides evidence for such benefits by highlighting the problems arising from poor informational feedback during one critical policy episode. It has not addressed the cost of creating such organizations. Nevertheless, the relatively high level of general education in the postsocialist countries implies that one of the basic inputs into policy analysis is already present in comparative abundance.

References

Boone, Peter. 1994. "Grassroots Macroeconomic Reform in Mongolia" *Journal of Comparative Economics* 18: 314–28.

Denizer, Cevdet, and Alan Gelb. 1994. "Mongolia: Privatization and System Transformation in an Isolated Economy." In *Changing Political Economies: Privatization in Post-Communist and Reforming Communist States,* ed. Vedat Milor. Boulder: Rienner.

Hahm, Hongjo. 1993. *Mongolia: Development of the Private Sector in Transition Economies.* Discussion Paper, 223. Washington, D.C.: World Bank.

Korsun, Georges, and Peter Murrell. 1994. "Ownership and Governance on the Morning After: The Initial Results of Privatization in Mongolia." Working Paper 95. IRIS, College Park, Md.

Korsun, Georges, and Peter Murrell. 1995. "The Effects of History, Ownership, and Pre-Privatization Restructuring on Post-Privatization Governance." Working Paper 147. IRIS, College Park, Md.

Kraay, Aart. 1992. "A Workable Privatization Program—Lessons from the Mongolian Experience." Harvard University.

Murrell, Peter. 1992. "Conservative Political Philosophy and the Strategy of Economic Transition." *East European Politics and Societies* 6: 3–16.

Murrell, Peter, Karen Turner Dunn, and Georges Korsun. forthcoming. "The Culture of Policy Making in the Transition from Socialism: Price Policy in Mongolia," *Economic Development and Cultural Change.*

North, Douglass C. 1990. *Institutions, Institutional Change, and Economic Performance.* Cambridge: Cambridge University Press.

Popper, Karl. 1971. *The Open Society and Its Enemies.* Princeton: Princeton University Press.

Ruttan, Vernon. 1984. "Social Science Knowledge and Institutional Change." *American Journal of Agricultural Economics* 66: 549–59.

12 Implementing Legal Reform in Transition Economies

Charles Cadwell

In Russia, the focus of this chapter, most prices are freely set, state control of economic decisions has collapsed in broad parts of the economy, money has value, and there have been democratic elections. At the same time, the establishment of the rule of law has been elusive. In the wake of the December 1995 parliamentary elections, the future direction of reform is not clear.

Lawyers and economists from the West have played an active part in advising reformers across the former Soviet Union and in Eastern Europe.[1] This chapter draws on that experience as well as on others to address the very practical question of how outsiders can interact with reformers to promote reforms that are implemented, sustained, and of broad impact. At the beginning of the postcommunist transitions, there was no model to follow; hence much of the assistance was patterned on mechanisms used elsewhere or was developed in an ad hoc fashion. This chapter suggests that we have learned much from developments so far that can improve the effectiveness and sustainability of ongoing efforts in the region and elsewhere. The same learning can of course also inform reformers themselves as they move forward.

The need to develop and implement functioning legal institutions is increasingly recognized, even by those commentators who, early on, emphasized shocking society with macroeconomic, trade, and price reforms and changed ownership structures as the main reform steps. However, even if there is agreement that certain institutional arrangements are a priority,

I appreciate the helpful criticisms of both economist colleagues and fellow lawyers, including Peter Murrell, Christopher Clague, Leonid Polishchuk, David Fagelson, and Lane Blumenfeld. This essay is improved on account of their suggestions, though shortcomings remain my responsibility.

[1]At the University of Maryland's IRIS Center, we have been fortunate to be able to conduct research on the transition and to work with reformers in Russia, Ukraine, Armenia, Poland, Kazahkstan, Lithuania, Bulgaria, Macedonia, the Kyrgyz Republic, and Mongolia as well as in many other countries outside the region. Our work has been supported by a variety of sponsors, mainly the U.S. Agency for International Development.

there are no clear theories of how one develops such institutions. Section 1 describes some characteristics of the reform process that illuminate missing foundations of the rule of law. Section 2 draws some lessons from that experience to suggest how outsiders can contribute, suggesting an approach that moves beyond the traditional "technical" assistance, in which a small group of outside experts huddles with a tight group of experts from a key ministry.

1   The Reform Process and the Establishment of the Rule of Law

Numerous examples of law development illustrate the difficulty of the transition.[2] These include

—limitations flowing from the training and experience of those involved in developing and implementing reform or from the interests of opponents

—limitations flowing from unfamiliarity with the democratic policy process and the unfinished development of that process.

These difficulties are compounded by the outcome of the December 1995 parliamentary elections, in which communists garnered 22.3 percent of the seats, and the uncertain prospects for reformers in the June 1996 presidential elections. However, courts are functioning and governmental bodies are subject to a degree of political control. The privatization of major portions of Russian industry occurred largely within established procedures. Despite widespread reports of crime and corruption, commerce is growing.

---

[2]Lawyers who have reviewed the process of law reform in the former Soviet Union provide detailed analyses of the substance of various legal regimes (land law, energy law, telecommunications, etc.). These usually describe the limitations to the effectiveness of the proposed solutions,   including unclear or conflicting governmental responsibility, scarcity of trained personnel, and lack of capital assets or technology upon which implementation depends.   The recommendations of these authors are of reduced practical use since their implementation depends on the prior alleviation of these limitations. In short, these analyses typically describe the end state of legal reform but not the path to get there. Springer (1994) provides a summary of several such articles.   Others have taken considerable effort to account for the political and institutional context in crafting their advice (see Black, Kraakman, and Hay 1994).

1.1 The debate over reform and the uneven capability for reform

Still powerful old interests

The demise of central control and the nominal privatization of many firms has not changed the reality that these firms and their workers are still part of large and politically active organizations with existing relationships to ministries, banks, and local and national administrators. These firms are better able to make their needs and views heard than any of the new or yet-unformed entities that will have a much greater stake in successful reform. Frydman and Rapaczynski 1994, 175) suggest that privatization has simply effected a "transfer of valuable resources from the control of . . . state bureaucrats . . . to others, and one of the primary effects . . . is to enfranchise the new owners and make them more powerful, not only in the economic, but also in the political sense."[3]

In a vacuum caused by government disorganization and undeveloped constitutional or other norms about appropriate political and legal processes, these existing interests are likely to do relatively well (Orlov 1995). Privatization weakens but does not eliminate the claim on state support. If the new owners were true outsiders, the lack of relationships to government would increase their incentive to make difficult business decisions about production, workforce size, marketing, and so forth. The acceptance of the current privatization scheme by workers and managers reflects their understanding of this point.

This does not mean that Russia would be better off and that there would be more respect for law if privatization had not occurred, but the expectation that change of formal relationships would quickly lead to demand for public provision of stable legal rules has been overly optimistic.

The demand for new public goods has been slow in emerging. Listen to the description of a key reform leader, Yegor Gaidar: "A significant proportion of entrepreneurs, particularly at the local level, consists of people connected in one way or another with the former and current nomenklatura, who have signed up for nomenklatura capitalism and can conceive of nothing else for themselves" (Gaidar 1995, 18).

---

[3]The power of these new owners, both managers and workers, is likely to be such that requests for intervention will undermine the system of property rights that is the ultimate aim of the program (Frydman and Rapaczynski 1994, 183).

Lawyers, economists, and implementers

For seventy years, judges and lawyers were subjugated by a set of ideas about economics, and their resulting distrust of economic arguments about legal rules has been a drag on the legal reform process. While legal drafters express commitment to market reform, and their work reflects significant change from the existing code, their backgrounds and training limit their ability to think systematically about the economic implications of legal rules. The preferred method is to use their considerable knowledge of formal Western legal rules to modify the formal Russian legal rules. This "technical" approach has much to recommend it in terms of taking into account the existing understanding and practices of Russian law. It suffers in that the framework that then drives legal thinking is the structure and logic of the Civil Code, not an integrated vision of the way legal rules interact with economic activity.[4]

On the implementation side of legal reform, the existing cadre of judges and officials has no training and little else in their backgrounds that prepare them to interpret new commercial rules for a market economy. An exception may be judges involved in international arbitration who have been exposed to market concepts related to contracts, credit, banking, transportation, and insurance. Attempts to alter the curriculum at law schools will not have an effect for years to come. Beyond the matter of training, there are dozens of areas in which judges have no practical experience. Areas of concern that have been expressed to us include prosaic matters of administering courts, cases, and parties. Ideas about the complementary interaction of law and commerce are often entirely new.[5]

As work on the code began in 1993, there was considerable debate about whether there should be a single code or whether it would be more effective to proceed with a series of targeted reforms—a securities code, a law on sales, a company law, and so on. Lawyers tended to favor a code, economic reformers a series of narrower reforms. The development of a

---

[4]Kovacic (1995) describes the commercial, political, and public institutional context for reform of competition policy. The description and the lessons drawn are highly compatible with the examination of political organization and processes here.

[5]A fall 1994 IRIS workshop for arbitration court judges was enthusiastically received, especially the portion dealing with economics and the law. However, it elicited the following comment from one participant: "This is great information; unfortunately our colleagues in Russia will never get it."

narrow piece of legislation could presumably be accomplished with a smaller group and would require less expertise. However, it would also tend to lead to more inconsistencies with existing provisions or other new enactments. This would in turn lead to implementation responsibilities that overlapped and conflicted with existing authority, creating confusion among practitioners and judges who need to deal with the inconsistencies.

Even if the judiciary consisted of the most talented individuals in Russia, they would face a difficult time providing clarity on new and old laws, decrees, and rules. The new Civil Code and other laws are far from perfect. For example the fifty-three sections of Part I of the Civil Code contain many provisions on property and contract freedom that are inconsistent with markets.[6] Many of these provisions reflect political battles that were lost or not taken on as the code was pressed on a fractious duma. Others reflect choices made by the drafters, others simply oversight.

Despite these obstacles, the courts are working to implement the code. For example, a February 1995 Supreme Court decree lays out guidelines for interpreting the code during the transition period. The decree provides guidance on how preexisting contracts or disputes will be handled, how the court would handle gaps left until Part II of the code is effective, and how various statutes of limitation will be applied. However, this guidance is not likely to fill the more critical gaps in training, experience, or substantive legal provisions, especially in courts of first instance.

1.2   Unformed and unfamiliar mechanisms of democratic debate

Elections in Mongolia, Russia, Hungary, Bulgaria, Lithuania, Estonia, and Poland suggest that a pace of radical changes not supported by the public is not politically sustainable. Much progress can be made during windows of opportunity that Balcerowicz calls times of "extraordinary politics" (Balcerówicz and Gelb 1995, 26). Poland made considerable progress during such a time; Yegor Gaidar implemented many changes that are largely irreversible. But the ability to see these programs through has been slowed by uneasy and uncertain electorates.

---

[6]For a discussion of the difficult soil in which Russian application of Western ideas is being implemented, see the discussion of privatization in Frydman and Rapaczynski (1994). Chapter 6 reviews the faults of early assumptions that simply reducing the role of the state would permit markets to flourish or that privatization would alter the incentives of special interests regarding the policy process.

The highly developed mechanisms that exist in other democracies for proposing ideas, conducting public debate, and adapting to public reaction are not well developed in the transition societies. While even under communism, advancing a particular policy required that support be won by persuasion and the organization of interests, the targets and methods of such persuasion have changed. Use of the media, coordination of complementary interests, use of economics and technical expertise in the political process, and processes of compromise and conciliation are all new tools in the new environment. The effect of the lack of mechanisms for channeling information to policy makers in Mongolia is described by Murrell (chapter 11, this volume).

The routines of communication about policy, plans, and their execution that exist among the branches and levels of government in established democracies are not in place in Russia. While there are many ad hoc communications, there are no routine or formal mechanisms. Information that would inform many debates does not exist or is of poor quality. The applied economic skills needed to analyze it are in short supply. There is a profusion of analytic centers attached to the government and the presidency, but their roles are not clear.

Federal separation of powers or conflict of powers?

The problems of political debate are not simply ones of unfamiliarity, they reflect an incomplete redistribution of political authority. The locus of initiative for steering and designing the reform process is disputed, even after the elections and the adoption of the current constitution in December 1993. Ordeshook (1994) describes these formal contradictions in some detail, highlighting the conflicting incentives to support the rule of law that the constitutional arrangements build into the relationships between the president and the duma and between the center and the regions.[7] Both the legislature and the president can legislate (the duma through legislation, the president through decree). Each can veto actions of the other. Ordeshook (1994) suggests that constitutional arrangements provide several opportuni-

---

[7]There are contradictions inherent in the U.S. Constitution as well, but decades of working with the document have allowed for the development of mechanisms to overcome the contradictions. Examples of these mechanisms include the role of the court in reviewing legislative acts and the existence of "independent" regulatory agencies as arms of the Congress with both executive and judicial functions.

ties for executive-legislative confrontation, while the electoral system gives duma leaders elected from party lists an incentive to claim the same national mandate as a nationally elected president.[8]

The organization and management of the executive

Divided authority is not only an interbranch problem. While policy disputes within the executive branch are a part of most government, and while their resolution often delays the promulgation of important legislation (consider, for example, health care reform by the Clinton administration), in Russia policy freelancing has been taken to new heights. For example, after the announcement of the Russian government's budget in January 1994, the *Washington Post* carried a lengthy story quoting by name several cabinet ministers to the effect that the budget would be disastrous for this or that sector of Russian society. Few chief executives in Western democracies would tolerate this level of public dissent by ministers. Even after presidential resolution of intragovernment disputes, senior executive branch officials nonetheless feel free to carry the fight to the duma.

Observers describe two executive branches, one headed by the president and one by the prime minister (see, for example, Malia 1995). The initiative for policy may rest in one or the other. Officials in ministries have their own connections to the president or to his advisers, connections that allow them to compete with officials on the president's staff. The number of decrees declaring who is in charge of a particular policy is but the superficial sign of more turbulent currents. Responsibilities assigned in this environment are not fixed.

The likelihood that authority will continue to be disputed has been increased by many new laws providing that implementation or enforcement is the responsibility of several ministries or levels of government at the same time. While there are occasions in which one might want bureaucracies to compete, such as when they compete for exclusive jurisdiction over a

---

[8]Legislatures in which representatives have a primary interest in their own districts do not give rise to the same type of competition for ownership of a national mandate. Parliamentary systems in which the executive is a creature of the parliamentary majority obviously solve the problem in a different fashion. In Russia, the arrangements borrow a little from both approaches, creating a problematic "middle" path.

particular transaction,[9] overlapping implementation exacerbates the uncertainty that the adoption of legal rules aims to reduce. Especially when the level of societal agreement on basic economic norms is low, this dispersion adds to the chaos. For example, a draft law on prices prepared by duma staff authorized the enforcement of price regulations by several ministries and levels of government (Alexeev et al. 1994).[10]

The problems of inconsistent formulation and dispersed implementation affect both Russian and foreign consumers of law. One observer suggests that conflict and confusion over authority may be the main source of problems of contract enforcement rather than problems with the contract norms themselves (Rubin 1994, 28).

Competing visions of the federation

Another characteristic of the Russian reform context is the unfinished redistribution of power between the center and the regions. The problems inherent in the constitutional and other arrangements between the center and the regions can be summarized by four observations: (1) the lengthy and detailed enumeration of shared and exclusive powers in the constitution for *oblasts*, *krais*, and other subnational units does not in fact clarify areas of unique capability, ensuring that there will be competition and confusion,[11] (2) the acceptance of special tax arrangements and other

---

[9]The effects of monopoly in the area of legal dispute resolution on development in France, compared to that in England where legal systems faced competition from other jurisdiction, are discussed in Greif and Kandel (1993, 8). They describe the relative efficiency of the British contract enforcement mechanisms as stemming from the ability of private parties to select venues for resolving for their disputes. In Russia, the problem is not that branches compete for jurisdiction but rather that assertions of jurisdiction do not bar others from claiming it as well.

[10]For discussion of similar problems in Mongolia, see Kovacic and Thorpe (1994) and Murrell, Korsun, and Dunn (1992). In Peru, different ministries have issued conflicting decrees with no attempt at reconciliation. The consequences are described in Keefer (1992).

[11]At an IRIS workshop with the authors of regional constitutions, not one of the representatives of the federal government or the various regions could identify a power granted to the regions by the constitution that was not also granted to the federal government. This was in response to a question concerning the scope of Articles 71, 72, and 73 posed by Peter Ordeshook.

privileges for some regions suggests that all the constitutional provisions are negotiable, (3) the development of local constitutions apparently requires approval of the center,[12] and 4) apparent federal control of electoral processes suggests that party decentralization or duma activity respective of regional autonomy will be minimal (Ordeshook 1994, 13).

The development of local constitutions by regions and republics is occurring with a similar lack of framework for a federal system. In the drafts and in those that have actually been adopted, there is wide variety in the mechanisms for defining and then implementing executive and legislative responsibility in a way that shares power (Lysenko 1995) and in their treatment of subregional units (which are guaranteed "equal rights" with regional governments as subjects of the Russian Federation by Article 5 of the federal constitution).

Ad hoc arrangements continue: A 1995 privatization decree purports to establish a process but postpones the decision of who owns the several thousand properties. The cost of not deciding "process" issues is paid again and again, without a pattern emerging that could be formalized into constitutional or other regularizing provisions. In failing to take account of the incentives built into political arrangements or in leaving the battles for a later day, the designers of Russia's new democratic arrangements have dispersed and confused the roles of various levels and organs of government, leading to a continuation of the uncertainty and shortened time horizons for any potential investors.[13] Old methods of making administrative decisions and executive decrees largely continue.

One outcome of the confusion at the federation level and among the levels of government is that any of several arms of the state continue to have the ability to violate property rights, while none has organized yet to effectively protect them. Private interests with their own enforcement mechanisms, or access to state enforcement, have eliminated the state's

------

[12]Interview with Leonid Smirniagin, member of the Presidential Council and chief of the Regional Branch of the Analytical Center of the President of the Russian Federation, October 1994. Although it would be reasonable to expect the center to resolve conflicts with the federal constitution, there are no areas of clear local constitutional discretion.

[13]A general review of the functions of constitutions in the transition environment is found in Elkin, Kaminski, and Sunstein (1993). However, suggestions for achieving the consensus required to adopt such constitutional arrangements are outside the scope of their article.

monopoly on violence. According to one observer of Russian commodities markets, the emergence of these private enforcers not only undermines the use of state mechanisms, it also discourages the development of private arbitration (Frye 1995). For our purposes, it suggests that attention to isolated legal reforms, in the absence of a resolution of fundamental issues related to the location and nature of state power, ought to be undertaken both with modest ambition and options in mind that take into account this limitation.

2   Implications for Assistance

Decisions about whether and how to interact with any of these reforms is a complicated issue for any donor, involving decisions about self-interest, a conception of how the local political and economic developments will unfold, and a view of effective or permissible ways to influence any of the events. Since this activity is "assistance" of some sort, some level of agreement from the host country government is also a part of the mix. The multiplicity of sources of inspiration for particular programs can lead to oversold expectations, local suspicion, inattention to important local interests, and it must be allowed, better and faster adoption of useful reforms.

The characteristics of the reform process in Russia described in section 1 are not all unique to Russia and exist in varying degrees in many other situations. They do suggest that, as outsiders attempting to support particular developments or to influence others, we need to be realistic about the extent to which our effort will alter the course of events.

2.1   The reforms to support

The key institutions of a market economy are property rights, mechanisms for enforcement of contracts, and reliable and peaceful ways of organizing political debate. Functioning securities markets, credit markets, and private distribution systems are built on these basic institutions. For example, lacking basic contract enforcement institutions or property rights, complicated trading rules and computer systems will be difficult to implement.[14] Spending scarce resources to renovate and outfit a building for the Mongolian Stock Exchange may have had some symbolic value, but its main

---

[14]See Greif and Kandel (1993) for a description of the lack of attention to contract enforcement among reform advocates.

effect may have been to deflect the attention of key people toward a secondary institution.

From the need to deal with basic institutions and from the confused political process, two related lessons arise. The first is that the concepts of secure property rights and impartial contract enforcement will come up in any of dozens of specific policy areas. It is difficult, if not impossible, to determine in advance which area will provide the best opportunity. Land law, company law, privatization, insurance, banking, and dozens of other areas all share a reliance on fundamental ideas about the incentives created by private property and the economics of contracts. It is less important which of these initiatives is the vehicle than it is that the assistance result in local understanding of ideas and concepts that underlie the experience of successful market economies. Ensuring that the interaction between donor and recipient communicate these concepts and understanding will ensure that a cadre of articulate local experts can participate more capably in any legal issues that may arise. This means that the mix of experts and the agenda for interaction ought to be different from what might be indicated by purely "technical" assistance. It means that the choice of which particular policy to focus on will be subject to some opportunism on the donor's part: given that basic ideas can be advanced in any of several areas, which local initiative is the most promising vehicle?

The second lesson is that a key contribution of outsiders can be to focus on implementation. If it is important to have a registry system to go along with a collateral law, then thinking about implementation will lead one to think not only about the structure of the law itself but also about where the registry is located, how firms and lenders interact with it, and a host of other practical and legal issues. Identifying these issues earlier may lead to different conclusions about where responsibility for policy development and implementation ought to be lodged, and it may force attention on budget issues and identify beneficiaries who can help support the proposed law. In short, a focus on implementation can help overcome the divided responsibility currently limiting progress in several areas of law.

2.2 Benefits for new and small firms

The interests of existing large firms will not be neglected during the transition. Less likely to benefit from decisions made at the center are new and small firms. The importance of new and small firms may be found in patterns of economic growth. In Poland, while the privatization of large firms has proceeded haltingly, growth has nevertheless been dramatic and its benefits widely dispersed as thousands of new small firms have been formed and grown. It is not necessary to agree that small or new firms will always play a dominant role in job generation to recognize their importance in the transition process.

In market economies, the "creative destruction" of firm entry and exit is an important source of growth (Davis, Haltiwanger, and Schuh 1996). In Korea, for example, 80–90 percent of the gross national product in the 1970s was accounted for by factors of production that were engaged in activity different from that of the early 1960s (Krueger 1992). In formerly socialist economies, the number of firms to be privatized is finite, and the number of those firms that will survive is smaller. Yet the economic activity upon which growth will be based will occur in thousands of firms and organizations that do not even exist today. To provide benefits to wide numbers of individuals and firms, there must be clear institutional arrangements and enforcement of contracts, coupled with a searching attack on regulatory barriers to entry. A reform process centered on government interaction with existing firms is not likely to spread the benefits of reform widely and provide positive incentives to new entities.

Thus, in delivering assistance it is useful to organize activities in ways that illustrate competitive processes, increase access for newcomers, and demonstrate transparency. This will both improve the product at hand and transmit important policy development "technology." A recent example of such a process is the World Bank's selection of sites for a large housing loan facility. Many cities have been invited to compete for access to this facility. The basis for the competition is a variety of policy measures and a commitment to implement steps that create more open markets in related support and service sectors. As an outside entity, the Bank can be credible in establishing clear and transparent rules, impartially applying them, and deciding with known criteria. These same efforts can be made in allocating space in coveted foreign-based workshops or access to assistance-supported equipment or other resources.

2.3   Local participation

As the discussion earlier suggests, it is not at all clear who is best placed to advance reform. Not only do personalities change, but the roles of whole ministries or branches of government are not well defined. In addition, given the basic constitutional malarrangements that limit the ability of any particular actor to make a reform "stick," the likelihood that a particular counterpart will be the best one over the course of the interaction is greatly reduced. This suggests that whenever possible (since host governments control the structure of assistance to a degree), donors should avoid creation of counterpart monopolies for the receipt of technical assistance.

There are other reasons to avoid creating a counterpart monopoly, which go to the process of reform. Ministries or other bureaus with nominal charge of a particular issue often see things through the "old lens of command and control," leading them to develop their ideas in secret and to keep proposals from public discussion as long as possible. There is no reason for donors to participate in this approach. Instead, donors can contribute to broadening of public debate, especially among the idea elites who lead opinion in democracies: journalists, academics and researchers, and officials in competing centers of power.

Acting on this approach in Poland, IRIS located its assistance effort for developing a collateral law in Warsaw University and later in the American Studies Center, in a deliberate effort to avoid creating a counterpart monopoly.[15] Choosing to lodge assistance in only one of the competing bodies would have alienated the others, all of whom have a voice in the ultimate reform. The result in Poland has been that the ministries of finance and justice, the central bank, the law professors who serve as civil code guardians, and the banking community have jointly developed a proposed reform that enjoys broad support. In effect, assistance in Poland has contributed to the organization of a coalition with an encompassing interest that has overcome the narrower concerns of particular factions or industries. The process has demonstrated alternative, more open, and informal patterns of discussion, debate, and compromise.

In Mongolia, in discussions with key officials on how to structure assistance on economic policy reform, we were pressed hard to cede designation of participants to a single government ministry that would dictate on this issue. Our insistence on a broader approach led us to include key people from the private sector, the parliament, political parties, and academia. The current prime minister, who attended and benefited from the first workshop, would never have made the list had the process been monopolized. The participation of legislators, economists, and officials helped bridge substantive and semantic gaps that existed even within that narrow policy community in a small country. This approach requires that outsiders understand local thought processes and context, though not necessarily that they trim their advice as a result of this understanding.

---

[15]For a description of the changes in Polish secured lending rules, see Dwight and Reichenbach (1993).

In Russia, IRIS was directed to work with a particular player in the civil code reform effort—a group that included representatives of most key ministries, the duma, and the Supreme Arbitration Court. This group was charged with the main responsibility for the draft code. Efforts to encourage them to open their process to broader public discussion have met only modest success. Further, a contest with other executive branch interests has slowed the introduction and adoption of the new code. Hindsight suggests a better approach: avoid a "client" relationship with a particular counterpart and organize activities that make expertise available to a range of interests. To do otherwise snares the donor "technical experts" deeply in local political matters.

It could be argued that such client relationships are necessary to build the trust of officials such that they will share information and strategies. While it is probably true that counterparts will be more open with advisers who they feel share a partisan perspective and that proposals can be developed more quickly and easily by smaller, closed groups, opportunities to spread ownership and build indigenous capacity will have been lost. An assistance process that contributes to closed policy development fails to develop the broader political support needed to pass and implement new rules. The progress of privatization policy may be an example of this.

A participation strategy developed by the U.S. Agency for International Development acknowledges this goal but notes that assistance must help to "build the degree of social consensus [particularly among the poor] that . . . [is needed] . . . to carry out and sustain changes in policy or social and economic programs" (Atwood 1994). Our experience suggests that it is unrealistic to expect poor people or small-business owners to participate in the rewriting of a civil code, even though it is their interests that are most at stake. (Large, politically connected entities have less need for the rule of law; they can obtain administrative recourse or enjoy bargaining advantages.) Efforts to involve diverse and, as a result, encompassing interests may be the closest substitute for direct involvement of the impoverished.[16]

---

[16]A January 1995 World Bank paper on the Bank's own legal technical assistance contains many pertinent lessons consistent with our own at IRIS related to the importance of local ownership of reform efforts, long-term commitment by donors, broad participation, and understanding local conditions. These recommendations tend to be aimed at Bank participation, not participation by others in technical assistance. Nonetheless, non-Bank donors and providers of technical assistance may have different views with respect to the utility of

Beyond the value of broader participation as a way of improving the substance of change and building support for it, an additional benefit may be the training function of involvement in the process. Judges who have helped to develop new commercial laws are better placed to spread capability for implementation. A final point in thinking about whom to work with: it is dangerous to assume that participation is beneficial if it means simply helping existing interests get organized. If the interests are narrow, the outcome is likely to be so as well.

2.4 What kind of assistance?

A sustainable reform of legal institutions occurs as laws are implemented and as they come to affect the behavior of firms and individuals. For this evolution to occur, not only must the formal rules be appropriately fashioned, a variety of actors need to understand and accept them. Since it is not realistic to support the detailed operation of the various bureaucracies, it is essential to build capability among local individuals and organizations. This effort is more likely to succeed if it is launched at the beginning of assistance than after the adoption of new laws.

This concern drives choices about counterparts; it also suggests that assistance is much less technical than it is educational. The mix of skills and ideas needed for this task reaches beyond standard economics or the arcana of Western legal mechanisms. In some respects, it is less important which particular policy is the focus of assistance than which sets of ideas about that policy are communicated.[17] If new laws on land, securities, and price

---

recommendations such as those suggesting that the Bank take the lead in coordinating multilateral and bilateral legal technical assistance or that legal assistance be in accord with the Bank's noninterference in politics. Because of the Bank's self-limitation as to topics, required relationship to loan or grant activity, and the limited range of assistance, it may not be best situated to coordinate particular legal reforms. Further, the political aspects of reform may well be the most fundamental ones to worry about. (The question of who owns property is intensely political and needs resolution before privatization.) Nongovernmental providers of technical assistance can provide important capability to those involved in political processes. Bilateral donors, with fewer internal governance constraints on the nature of involvement in particular countries, can take these issues on more directly.

[17]Kovacic and Thorpe (1994) describe how assistance on development of an antimonopoly law was conducted in a fashion that transferred key ideas

regulation are developed without communicating basic concepts concerning property and its incentives for economic activity, or without attention to how they will be implemented in that society, then the assistance—no matter how good in a narrow technical sense—will be ineffective.

Even if armed with a clear understanding of theory and of Western examples, advocates of particular reforms will face issues, interests, and objections that are unique to their situation. To carry their own reforms forward, local implementers of reform need to understand their implications and their interaction with other policies. Implementers will benefit strongly from attention to the process and the incentives inherent in the scheme for which they have responsibility. While the slogans of market economics are simple to grasp, the implications for real policy development are not always straightforward.[18]

Others have made the point that solutions need to be compatible with the capability for implementation ("keep it simple") and that rules that require decades of interpretive experience ensure, at best, chaotic implementation by businesspeople, officials, and judges (see Kovacic 1995; Black, Kraakman, and Hay 1994). This line of reasoning suggests that progress will not unfold in a straight line nor occur quickly. As a result, sustained interaction between donors and recipients will be important. We have found greater success with the presence of long-term advisers who can identify suitable moments for interaction and provide local context for senior experts and day-to-day support for the variety of counterparts. These persons should be thinking not only about the substance of their particular reform project but also about the structure and process of decision making. In Mongolia, it was only after considerable examination of this type of issue that the

---

about the organization of incentives related to the substance and implementation of a law, how this information supported the development of a law that enjoyed informed local support and how the lack of sustained interaction nonetheless limited the effectiveness of otherwise productive assistance.

[18]An alternative argument might be, "Set up the new tools. They'll use them, make a few mistakes, and learn how eventually." This approach presumes that the new tools or rules will be attended to. In Mongolia, from the center, price decontrol appeared to be working well but, at the local level, price regulators continued their prior activity. In late April 1995, local Ulaanbaatar administrators announced new meat price controls and the establishment of a price commission to address a broader range of goods. Meat is again in short supply.

existence of a "Main Department" in the government was discovered, performing many of the functions of the prior Politburo but out of the sight of most donor experts and officials. An example of successful application of this model is our experience in providing assistance on the Mongolian antimonopoly policy. The interaction of our long-term adviser with key policy leaders on other issues led to a very focused and productive interaction, which would not have resulted from any detailed project design or a two-year project-planning exercise. In addition, there is considerable value to ensuring that top outside experts are prepared to have frequent and repeated exchanges with counterparts, both in person and through fax, e-mail, or return visits.[19]

While assistance such as short-term training and study tours are helpful if conducted as a part of longer term interaction, IRIS experience in Russia, Poland, Nepal, Chad, and Mongolia suggests that, absent sustained interaction, one ought to have limited expectations about the effect of such activities. As frustrating as it is for us to host study tours that generate much interest but only a brief exchange without a chance to plumb the details of issues, it is similarly frustrating for local officials and others to host a series of short-term "development tourists."

3   Conclusion

While there are differences among economists and other experts concerning the best set of measures and the best pace or sequencing of reform, our work suggests that there are ideas that are important to share widely among the policy-making elite and, eventually, a broader public. These ideas include an appreciation of the role of the state in both protecting and violating property rights, the incentives inherent in various political arrangements, and a sense of the economic forces in the transition period. The reform process, to be sustained, needs to tackle this understanding gap, not ignore politics. Assistance to the reform process, if the reform is to be sustainable, will a unifying goal of increasing indigenous research and advocacy capacity.

---

[19]See Kovacic and Thorpe (1994) on the costs of not providing for outside expertise over the course of law development and implementation.

References

Alexeev, Michael, Charles Cadwell, William Kovacic, Noreen McCarthy, Peter Murrell, and Robert Thorpe. 1994. "Comments on Draft Law on Fundamentals of Pricing Policy." Paper prepared for the Russian State Duma, Committee on Economic Policy. IRIS, College Park, Md.

Atwood, Brian. 1994. "Statement of Principles on Participatory Development." U.S. Agency for International Development, Washington, D.C.

Balcerowicz, Leszek, and Alan Gelb. 1995. "Macropolicies in Transition to a Market Economy: A Three-Year Perspective." In *Proceedings of the World Bank Annual Conference on Development Economics, 1994.* Washington, D. C: International Bank for Reconstruction and Development.

Black, Bernard, Reinier Kraakman, and Jonathan Hay. 1994. "Corporate Law from Scratch." Paper prepared for the World Bank Conference on Corporate Governance, December.

Davis, S., J. Haltiwanger, and S. Schuh. 1996. *Job Creation and Destruction.* Cambridge: MIT Press.

Dwight, Ronald, and Leigh Anna Reichenbach. 1993. "Seeking Security in Poland." *Central European,* June: 48-49.

Elkin, Stephen, Bartlomeij Kaminski, and Cass Sunstein. 1993. "Communism, Constitutionalism, and the Transition to Market-Based Democracy." Working Paper 93. IRIS, College Park, Md.

Frydman, Roman, and Andrzej Rapaczynski. 1994. *Privatization in Eastern Europe: Is the State Withering Away?* Budapest: Central European University Press.

Frye, Timothy. 1995. "Contracting in the Shadow of the State: Private Arbitration Courts in Russia." In *The Rule of Law and Economic Reform in Russia.*

Gaidar, Yegor. 1995. "You Cannot Escape or Hide from Elections. You Have to Win Them." *Izvestiya,* April 7, 1995. FBIS-Sov-95-072, April 14, 1995.

Greif, Avner, and Eugene Kandel. 1993. "Contract Enforcement Institutions: Historical Perspective and Current Status in Russia." Working Paper 92. IRIS, College Park, Md.

Keefer, Philip. 1992. "Credibility, Rent-Seeking and Political Instability." Working Paper 31. IRIS, College Park, Md.

Kovacic, William. 1995. "Designing and Implementing Competition and Consumer Protection Reforms in Transitional Economies: Perspectives from Mongolia, Nepal, Ukraine and Zimbabwe." Paper prepared for DePaul Law Review Symposium on Cultural Conceptions of Competition: Antitrust in the 1990s, Chicago, February 3.

Kovacic, William, and Robert Thorpe. 1994. "Antitrust and the Evolution of a Market Economy in Mongolia." Working Paper 97. IRIS, College Park, Md.

Krueger, Anne. 1992. "Institutions for the New Private Sector." In *The Emergence of Market Economies in Eastern Europe,* ed. Christopher Clague and Gordon Rausser. Cambridge: Blackwell.

Lysenko, Vladimir. 1995. "The 'Little Constitution' Does Not Dispute the 'Big One.'" *Rossiyskiye Vesti,* April 18, 1995. FBIS-Sov-95-081-S, April 27, 1995.

Malia, Martin. 1995. "The Nomenklatura Capitalists." *New Republic,* May 22: 17–24.

Murrell, Peter, Georges Korsun, and Karen Dunn. 1992. "The Culture of Policymaking in the Transition from Socialism: Price Policy in Mongolia." IRIS Working Paper 32. Forthcoming in *Economic Development and Cultural Change.*

Ordeshook, Peter. 1994. "Institutions and Incentives: Prospects for Russian Democracy." IRIS Working Paper 115. IRIS, College Park, Md.

Orlov, Dmitry. 1995. "The Battle of the Titans 'Under the Carpet.'" *Rossiyskiye Vesti,* February 25, 1995. FBIS-Sov-95-048-S, March 13, 1995.

Rubin, Paul. 1994. "Growing a Legal System in the Post-Communist Economies." *Cornell International Law Journal,* 27: 1–47.

Springer, Susan. 1994. "Law Reform in the Republics of the Former Soviet Union—Annotated Bibliography." George Mason University.

V IMPROVING GOVERNMENT PERFORMANCE

13 The Reform of Tax Administration

Vito Tanzi and Anthony Pellechio

Few, today, would question the idea that a principal determinant of a country's economic success is the quality of the country's institutions and policies. Because institutions are the vehicles that carry policies, the existence of good institutions is a necessary, if not a sufficient, condition for the implementation of good policies. This is true in many areas of economic policy, but it is especially true in taxation, where the distinction between policy and administration may become artificial. In some cases, tax administration becomes tax "policy" because it can distort and change the objectives that the policy makers want to pursue through tax policy and can, thus, greatly influence the structure of taxes and lead to unintended results.

In spite of the obvious importance of the topic, there is a remarkably limited literature on tax administration. The reason for this may be that those who work in tax administration often do not have the time, the interest, or the background to write about it. Furthermore, when they do write, they normally limit themselves to an evaluation of the tax administration of the country in which they operate. In other words, their writing tends to be country-specific and, as a consequence, to lack universality. On the other hand, those who venture to write in a more general way often lack the detailed knowledge necessary to make their writing useful. Very few individuals have had the opportunity to observe closely the workings of the tax administration of several countries. Exceptions are individuals working for the Fiscal Affairs Department of the International Monetary Fund, who have over many years assisted many countries with tax administration reform. This chapter draws from the experiences of these people and from various (confidential) reports prepared at the request of ministers of finance.

A country's tax system can be described statistically, statutorily, and also in terms of its effectiveness. A statistical description allocates actual tax revenue to statutory tax bases and provides an impression of the revenue importance of various tax bases and tax rates; a statutory description is found

The views expressed are strictly those of the authors. They should not be interpreted as official IMF positions. This chapter has been much influenced by discussions with Milka Casanegra de Jantscher, to whom the authors owe a great debt. Comments received from Christopher Clague on a draft of this chapter are much appreciated.

in the tax codes, laws, and regulations. An effective description is the one based on economic reality, taking into account all the distortions brought about by tax evasion, tax avoidance, misapplication of laws, abuses on the part of tax officials, and so forth. It is the description needed for the kind of tax analysis undertaken by economists. In a country where the tax administration functions optimally and where tax laws and regulations are unambiguous, there will not be a significant distinction between statutory and effective tax systems. In such a country, a tax on income would in fact be a tax on a correctly defined and measured concept of income, and the tax law would provide a good indication of the tax effectively collected from income.[1] Tax administration would not distort the intention of the tax law. Equally, the statistical description would provide a faithful account of the initial impact of the tax system on particular tax bases. A sales tax would in fact be a tax on sales; an income tax would be one on income.

Unfortunately, tax administration does not function optimally. In some cases, it can be so inefficient as to distort completely the intention of tax laws. Inefficient tax administration (1) reduces tax revenue, (2) creates unintended distortions, or nonneutralities, in the tax system, which means that taxes affect markets in ways not intended by legislators, and (3) introduces inequities through the tax system, for example between honest citizens and tax evaders. In other words, poor tax administration will change the way taxation affects the traditional objectives of government policy, namely, allocation of resources, redistribution of income, and stabilization. In this case and in terms of its effect on the economy, tax administration becomes indistinguishable from tax policy, and a tax policy that is, in addition, arbitrary and capricious.

The causes of inefficient tax administrations can originate in the tax laws, in the political system, and in the tax administration itself. First, laws can be exceedingly complex and opaque, requiring from taxpayers information and attention that is difficult to provide. Tax laws have often become legislative jungles, represented by exceedingly complex tax codes, through which only a few can find their way. (In many countries the tax laws may not even have been compiled in a code.) When interpretation can vary between those who administer taxes (or even among them) and those who

---

[1]This discussion ignores the issue of tax shifting.

pay them, administrative problems are bound to arise.[2] At times, the laws may be clear but the incentives for taxpayers may be wrong. For example, in some countries, the penalties for delaying the payment of taxes are so low that taxpayers do not bother to send the tax payments at the time they fall due, creating tax arrears and administrative problems. For them, borrowing from the government becomes the cheapest source of credit. Second, those who make the laws may write them in ways that protect themselves, or those associated with them, against high tax liabilities. A small clause in the drafting of the particular law, which may not attract attention at the time the law is passed, may create a particular and well-targeted loophole. In our work at the IMF we have found that those who propose the laws and those who have to approve them may not be able to separate their role as taxpayers from their role as policy makers. The view that policy makers will pursue the public interest regardless of the impact that the laws will have on them as taxpayers is often naive, especially for taxation. Public choice considerations are especially relevant in this area. Third, a lack of tax administration resources, lack of professionalism, and lack of a clear strategy all contribute to inefficiency.

One often hears that, to improve its effectiveness, tax administration needs a significant increase in its budget and, particularly, in its personnel. There is no question that there are cases in which this is true. However, tax administration is notoriously inefficient in the way it uses its available resources (both personnel and money). Personnel are often assigned to tasks that have very low productivity, while important functions go unattended. A reallocation of resources away from traditional tasks and toward more productive ones can improve tax administration even when total resources available do not change. However, this requires both a clear strategy for reform and the flexibility to make the necessary changes.

Lack of professionalism often results from a tradition in which (1) there are no rewards for taking the initiative and for doing a good job, (2) routine determines the tasks carried out, (3) salaries are low and undifferentiated between good and bad workers, (4) tax inspectors are not above accepting favors or even bribes from taxpayers in exchange for preferential treatment, and (5) political influence in tax administration is not rare. (For

---

[2]For example, at this moment in Italy, there are more than three million cases of litigation between taxpayers and tax administration concerning the proper tax liability. Each case must be resolved by commissions. This will require many years. The Italian situation is far from unique.

example, political interference may influence the selection of taxpayers to be audited.) When tax inspectors' salaries are low, their temptation to take bribes or favors from taxpayers grows and society becomes more predisposed to condone this behavior. This is particularly so when tax administration decisions are seen as responding to political pressure. At times, cynicism lowers the resistance to accepting bribes.

Motivating tax inspectors whose salaries are low to fulfill their public function in an ethical manner is a common problem. However, an appropriate, effective incentive structure for rewarding tax inspectors whose efforts can improve tax collection and compliance has proven elusive.[3] Some countries have adopted schemes in which a portion of the revenue from the collection of delinquent taxes and penalties is awarded as a bonus to the tax inspector responsible for collection. However, in some cases, this has produced perverse results: tax inspectors have purposely not informed taxpayers of their tax obligations so that violations take place, penalties collected, and bonuses paid. In some of these countries, it is impossible for a taxpayer to obtain a copy of the tax laws and, especially, tax regulations. Sometimes, taxpayers pay as much in penalties as in taxes, creating the suspicion of collusion between the tax inspector and the taxpayer to raise the tax inspector's income through penalty bonuses and to lower the taxpayer's total payment of taxes and penalties. The design of incentive structures to improve tax inspectors' job performance is a constant challenge in tax administration.

Lack of a clear strategy for reform is probably the most important reason that tax administration continues inefficient practices, although the lack of a strategy may be symptomatic of a lack of political commitment to reform. Such a strategy must be simple, must consist of few basic steps, and must not require unavailable resources. This strategy rarely consists of copying what other, and often different, countries are doing. This issue is taken up more directly in the next section, along with other essential elements of tax administration reform.

To a certain extent, the causes of inefficient tax administration can originate in the economy itself or in the culture of the country. For example, the American system of administering taxes depends much on the mail

---

[3]However, major tax administration reforms have often been accompanied by higher salaries for the personnel of tax administrations. Peru and Argentina are good examples.

system. Such a system would have difficulties in a country where the postal service is unreliable. A country with an atomistic structure of production will have greater difficulty in establishing good tax administration than a country where industries are more concentrated.[4] And to some extent, the history of a country, and especially the way taxpayers view the government, may have some effect on their propensity to evade taxes and, thus, on tax administration. However, in our view, this aspect is often exaggerated. Given the right institutions and incentives, taxpayers tend to behave in the same way regardless of where they reside. For example, following many years of poor tax administration and low compliance, Argentina, after reforming its tax structure, overhauled its tax administration. Tax administration reform encompassed a massive campaign to inform the public of their tax obligations and the consequences of noncompliance as well as higher salaries but less secure jobs for tax administrators. The ratio of tax revenue to gross domestic product rose in Argentina from 14.7 percent in 1989 to 20 percent in 1993, in spite of the elimination of almost 4 percent of GDP in highly distorting taxes. Similar experiences are found in Chile, Peru, Mexico, Uganda, Ghana, and other countries. These experiences indicate that, given the right incentives and institutions and the necessary political support, the efficiency of tax administration can be improved.[5]

1   The Elements of Tax Administration Reform

Tax administration reform does not just happen. It must be made to happen. To be successful and durable, it requires six essential elements:

—An explicit and sustained political commitment
—A team of capable, hard-working officials assigned full time to
    tax administration reform
—A well-defined and appropriate strategy
—Relevant training for staff

---

[4]The atomistic structure of the Italian economy has been blamed for the poorer tax administration and the higher tax evasion in Italy as compared to, say, the United Kingdom, where the productive structure is much more concentrated.

[5]In Argentina and Peru, Presidents Menem and Fujimori strongly supported the fight against tax evasion. President Menem made several Saturday speeches to condemn tax evasion and to urge Argentine taxpayers to comply with their tax obligations.

—Additional resources for tax administration or at least the reallocation of existing resources

—Changes in incentives for both taxpayers and tax administrators

1.1   Political commitment

Reform of tax administration, and tax reform in general, requires time as well as the explicit commitment of the government. When we talk about the government, we are really talking about one, or perhaps a few, powerful political figures who have the stamina, the interest, and the vision to push reform through and to stay with it perhaps over several years. These individuals become the mentors of reform; they must be willing to assume the responsibility for failure (and allowed to claim some "property rights" for success). Usually, they must be willing to spend some of their political capital to launch the reform because the benefits are typically widespread and delayed in time, while the costs are concentrated and occur early. These costs rise when losing groups are politically powerful and well organized.

Two important implications follow from the above. One is that such a process will be started and continued only when a government has a long time horizon; the rate of discount that the government will use to make the benefit-cost evaluation of reform will often be determined by how long it expects to remain in power: a government that is on its way out is unlikely to show much interest. The second implication is that a government that remains in power but whose members keep changing will have less chance of accomplishing a major reform. Successful tax administration reform is characterized by the involvement over an extended period of time of a powerful political mentor, who provides the reform with a face and a "trademark." Examples of strong political leadership in successful reforms can be found in Argentina, Bolivia, Chile, Ghana, Mexico, Peru, and Singapore. In Argentina, both President Menem and Minister Cavallo adopted the reform and provided the needed political support to Carlos Tacchi and Ricardo Cossio, who were directly responsible for carrying it out. In Bolivia, the mentor was Ramiro Cabezas, who, as minister in charge of revenue, created a new tax department while reforming the tax system in a revolutionary way. In Mexico, Francisco Gil-Diaz was the main actor, with the full support of President Salinas and Minister Aspe. In Peru, Minister Bolañas provided the needed political support.

1.2   Planning team

Major administrative reforms cannot be a part-time or an occasional activity for those responsible for them. Obviously, ministers of finance, with their many commitments and heavy demands on their time, cannot provide the day-to-day attention tax administration reform needs. Such reform requires the full-time commitment of a working group to plan the strategy, determine the sequence of the needed changes, and follow, on a daily basis, the steps to be taken. These individuals cannot have other major operational distractions. They must be fully committed and totally immersed in a process that is likely to be time-consuming. They are responsible for keeping the relevant minister or ministers fully informed through regular briefings.

Effective teams have comprised individuals who know the workings of the current administration but are not an operational part of it. When this is not the case, these individuals tend to be too concerned about the shifts in status and power that reform inevitably brings to the current administrative structure. In all the countries where reform has been successful, there has been a substantial pruning of the tax administration workforce in order to get rid of corrupt or inefficient individuals. This pruning requires strong political support and a relaxation or reform of civil service rules. In extreme cases, where the existing administrative structure is so corrupt or so inefficient as to be beyond reform, a new tax administration must be put into place. This has happened in Peru and Uganda.

1.3 Strategy

The reform of tax administration will not be successful unless it conforms to a well-defined plan or strategy. For example, a recent report lists literally hundreds of faults with the tax administration of a large developing country but it does not provide a sense of which faults are most problematic and which should be eliminated first. In other words, it provides no strategy and no sequence of steps to be undertaken. No wonder that the tax administrators of the country were baffled as to what to do.[6] There are also examples in which foreign advisers essentially suggested strategies that were simply the tax administration procedures of the home countries of these advisers. Local conditions, particular characteristics of the statutory tax systems, local customs, and other limitations were ignored.

No strategy is mechanically implementable in all countries; each strategy has to be adjusted to local conditions. Whichever strategy is chosen, it must be simple, must specify priorities and sequencing, and must be flexible enough to deal with unanticipated events. In some cases, the

---

[6]As that country's current attempt at reform is being carried out by the existing bureaucracy, not by a planning team, it is unlikely to be successful.

strategy can be gradual; in others, it must be more drastic. Which is preferable depends on the country's specific economic and other conditions. At times, administrative reform must be accompanied by reform of the tax system mainly because of the need to simplify the latter. In fact, reform of the tax system often precedes or accompanies reform of administration.

The possible approaches are essentially two: extensive and targeted. The extensive approach is the one implicit in the report on the country referred to above. It attempts to improve tax administration by changing everything at the same time. The targeted approach starts with improvements in well-defined area, which could be seen as a pilot project, and progressively enlarges the successful area. The discussion in the second section of this chapter suggests the main elements of the targeted approach. Of course, the specific application has to be fitted to the conditions of the particular country. It is this approach that the International Monetary Fund has found more promising and more likely to succeed.

1.4 Staff training

One area where large resources have been wasted has been training. To be effective, training must be aimed at achieving a precise objective. If one wants to win a marathon, one must train specifically for it. General athletic training, while of some benefit, will not help much with the specific objective of winning the marathon. The same is true for tax administration. One must train people to develop the skills necessary to implement the well-defined strategy. General training in tax administration is too unfocused to be of much use. For this reason, the benefit of exposing tax administrators to administrators of more advanced countries is limited unless this training conforms with the strategy chosen by the reforming country. Faced with a different environment and conditions, those who are exposed to general training soon go back to their old habits.

Thus, training is an integral part of the strategy for tax administration reform, but it must *follow* the decision regarding strategy and must be closely linked to it. In other words, tax administrators must learn the tools required by the chosen strategy, and the training must teach or sharpen those tools.

1.5 Reallocation of resources

A prevalent view is that tax administration reform requires considerable additional resources, which often are not available to the country. These additional resources are in the form of personnel and materials, especially computers. One is often told that without heavy spending on computers and without large additions to personnel no administrative improvements are possible. The refrain is often heard that, with more personnel, there would be more auditing and more controls in general and, thus, better tax administration.

The introduction of computer technology is, in fact, often a basic ingredient for substantive administrative reform. However, one mistake often made is to think that simply buying computers and making them available to the administrators is sufficient to improve tax administration. Tax administration offices of the world are full of expensive computers that are accumulating dust because no one has the vaguest idea what to do with them. Alternatively, when these computers are used, it is often to perform electronically many of the same useless or low-productivity tasks previously done by hand. In other words, the computers are not used to introduce a new strategy. Unfortunately, donor countries, and even international institutions, have occasionally pushed countries to spend large amounts of resources on tools that have proved to be of limited, if any, value. The basic principle must be the same as that for training: the purchase of the computers must *follow*, not precede, the development of a specific strategy. Computers, and the right kind of computers, must be acquired to serve well-defined objectives and to perform useful tasks.

In the area of personnel, similar considerations apply. Traditional tax administrations generally use their personnel and resources poorly. Often, a large share of personnel is occupied with trivial, mechanical, and highly unproductive tasks, while useful tasks are starved for resources. (In other cases, the misallocation of resources may be on a regional basis.) The reason for such misallocation is that today's allocation may reflect yesterday's needs. Other times it reflects past political pressures to provide employment for certain individuals. An example of poorly used resources is using a large proportion of available personnel to receive payments, when banks could perform this function much more efficiently and cheaply. Often administrative or union rules prevent reallocation of personnel.[7] Furthermore, because of low salaries, it is difficult to attract the kind of personnel that can bring a new vision to the tax administration.

Tax administration reform must relax some of these constraints. It must allow firing. It must allow hiring of new personnel. It must allow

---

[7]The minister of finance of a large country once remarked that he did not have the power even to move a security guard from one entrance of the ministry to another. It is not surprising that, in that particular country, problems of tax administration remain important.

salary differentiation and the provision of adequate salaries. It must allow the transfer of individuals from less productive to more productive functions or even from one location to another. Tax administration must be like a firm that, given a budget and subject to some constraints, must maximize a product—in this case, revenue. This maximization may require a massive reallocation of resources. A good example is the transformation of the tax administration from an organization based on the type of tax and taxpayer to an organization based on the key functions of tax administration. With enough flexibility and with a proper strategy, such reform may not require new resources. Before new resources are budgeted, it is important to ascertain that the resources available are being put to their best use.[8] For example, the shifting to the banking system of the function of receiving tax payments is likely to release personnel, who could then be used to strengthen other functions, such as auditing.

1.6   Changes in incentives

Successful tax administration reform has almost always included incentives to encourage both better compliance by taxpayers and more efficient and more honest performance by tax administration employees. Taxpayers who complied with the tax laws were assured a more courteous and less harassing relationship with tax collectors. Those who did not faced more certain and heavier penalties. More efficient and honest tax administration employees were compensated with higher salaries and faster promotions. Less efficient or less honest employees faced dismissal or more severe punishments. For tax evaders, penalties such as the temporary closing of their shops or places of business have proved successful in several countries, including Argentina and Peru. These penalties could be applied administratively and, thus, quickly. For corrupt officials or large-scale tax evaders, jail sentences have been applied in some countries for the first time. In some countries (e.g., Mexico) the application of these measures created the need to protect the main official responsible for the reform from threats by affected citizens.[9]

---

[8]However, the need to replace "dead wood" or "corrupt wood" with new personnel may require some new resources. In some major tax policy and tax administration reforms, it has been to get rid of existing organizations and replace them with new ones. Reflecting this, in Peru the average age of the staff of the national tax administration is now only twenty-eight years.

[9]There is almost no economic literature that analyzes incentives for tax administrators. This should be a fertile area for research.

2   Reforming Tax Administration

A country's tax administration represents an institutional arrangement by which citizens fulfill their tax obligations to the government. Tax administration should strive to be both effective and efficient. It is effective when a high level of citizen compliance is attained. Efficiency is achieved when administrative cost per dollar of tax revenue is minimal. Governments must not pursue efficiency at the expense of effectiveness; measures to improve effectiveness and efficiency in a systematic manner are presented in the following two subsections.

2.1   Measures to improve effectiveness

Goal of voluntary compliance

The primary goal of tax administration should be to achieve the highest possible voluntary tax compliance among taxpayers. Toward this end, tax administration should minimize the cost of complying. It should also be clear that compliance costs, at least in terms of time spent interacting with the tax administration, will increase if taxpayers do not fulfill their obligations properly. The procedures should reflect a logical sequence of actions undertaken by the tax administration to employ its scarce resources in the most efficient manner to process collections, identify instances of noncompliance, and take appropriate action.

Adoption of the principle of self-assessment

The resources devoted to tax collection can be minimized by empowering taxpayers to assess and pay their own tax liabilities according to prescribed procedures. A strategy to reform tax administration should take advantage of the fact that, given clear instructions, simple procedures, and sufficient encouragement, taxpayers can calculate and pay their tax liabilities on their own. The principle of self-assessment (and self-payment) is the foundation of modern tax administration. Self-assessment permits tax administrations to administer effectively tax collection with high ratios of taxpayers per tax official, and it should be a basic principle guiding tax administration reform.

Fundamental need for taxpayer education

The principle of self-assessment implies that a fundamental requirement for increasing voluntary compliance is taxpayer education. Taxpayers must receive clear and concise information describing what is taxable, when taxes apply, how to calculate their tax liabilities, and what they are required to do to pay their taxes. Also, forms and procedures for calculating and paying taxes should be simple. Given this, taxpayers who take full advantage of the opportunity to self-assess their tax liabilities and follow instructions and procedures for paying these liabilities will employ minimal resources of their own and of the tax administration. An example of the importance of taxpayer education can be found in countries that have successfully introduced value-added taxes in recent years, for example, New Zealand, Spain, Thailand, and Trinidad and Tobago. Most of these countries have allocated a large amount of resources, including the time of senior government officials, to the task of explaining the tax and the obligations of the taxpayers.[10] The countries that have not done so have had much less success with this tax.

Prompt detection of problems with tax filing and paying

A critical step in tax administration is the prompt detection of taxpayers who fail to submit tax returns (stopfilers) and taxpayers who fail to calculate correctly their tax liability on their tax return or make timely payment (delinquent taxpayers). A key role of tax administration is to ensure that, if the taxpayer fails to comply, something is going to happen—a notice will be sent, significant interest and penalties will be applied, and other actions will be taken. It is important to convey the impression that Big Brother is watching. Given the need for an accurate, up-to-date registry to detect stopfilers and delinquent taxpayers, tax administration reform should address whether there is a problem with nonregistration. This can include surveys in which tax officials go door to door within a district and check all businesses to see if they are properly registered. Another option is to examine the records of registered taxpayers to detect suppliers or customers who are not registered taxpayers. To detect stopfilers and delinquent taxpayers, a system for returns processing and accounting should be developed that quickly and accurately records taxpayers' transactions with the tax administration. Whether this system is based on manual ledgers, computers, or other means depends on many factors, including the customary business practices and relative costs of labor and capital, in a specific

---

[10]In Thailand, the permanent secretary in the Ministry of Finance and other senior personnel spent many months meeting with large groups of taxpayers to explain how the tax worked and the taxpayers' obligations.

country. The nature of the system is not as important as the fact that it constitutes an efficient system for processing returns and detecting noncompliance.[11]

Improvement of audit coverage

Noncompliance extends beyond stopfiling and delinquency to encompass fraudulent actions by taxpayers to understate their tax liability in ways that cannot be detected in the collection process. In a modern tax system, it is critical for taxpayers to believe that if they engage in such fraudulent actions there is a reasonable chance they will be caught and appropriately penalized. Also, it is important that taxpayers be confident that their competitors are paying the same taxes so they may compete fairly. This requires that an effective audit program be carried out by the tax administration.

Taxpayer compliance depends to a significant degree on their belief in the effectiveness of the audit program. Further, the chance of being audited will appear greater, and compliance will be higher, if the details of the audit program are not known. It is important that taxpayers believe that a larger percentage of taxpayers is audited than is actually the case. This suggests a rationale for the tax administration not to disclose information regarding its audit selection strategy and the number of taxpayers to be audited. Instead, the tax administration should promote the view that a variety of factors may lead to an audit. Toward this end, the tax administration should show taxpayers that it has both the information and the capacity to detect violations.

An audit plan represents a strategy to detect violations efficiently. The plan should reflect an analytic approach to increasing the probability of detection. Specific strategies would likely vary from year to year. For example, one year it may be decided to conduct a wide audit of taxpayers in the same or similar business, say restaurants. In another year, more audits might be conducted than usual on wholesalers. (Such a strategy has recently been announced by the Italian government.)

Application of adequate penalties

The tax system can be expected to function smoothly and to yield anticipated revenues only if adequate penalties are imposed for violations

---

[11]The Fiscal Affairs Department of the IMF has delved in great detail into the development of such systems in its technical assistance on tax administration.

that strike at the heart of the tax system, such as failure to file returns and to pay taxes on time. It is important that interest provisions for late tax payments compensate the government for the time that the taxpayer has use of the government's revenue. The total interest cost for late tax payment should exceed the interest rate for borrowing money—it should be less costly for the taxpayer to borrow to pay taxes rather than to delay paying taxes as a way to obtain cheap financing from the government. In addition, if registration and other requirements critical for a smoothly functioning tax system are adopted, adequate penalties should be applied for violations of these requirements as well.

The theoretical literature on tax evasion often concludes that, if penalties are high enough, audit coverage can be limited (Cowell 1990; Allingham and Sandmo 1972). The literature suggests that there is a trade-off between administrative expenditure and size of penalties. However, when penalties are high and audits are rare, penalties are unlikely to be fully enforced. (In this case, the penalty system violates one of the fundamental criteria of taxation, namely horizontal equity: tax evaders that get caught are highly punished, while those who are not caught escape the penalty.) Furthermore, taxpayers can appeal these sentences and delay the application of the penalties for years. Thus, penalties lose their deterrent effect. In many countries, it has proven more effective to apply smaller but highly visible penalties—such as the closing of shops for a few days or a few weeks, as was done very effectively in Argentina, Chile, and Peru—than high penalties (see Tanzi and Shome 1993).

2.2   Measures to improve efficiency

Within the overall strategy outlined above for enhancing effective-ness, tax administrations can adopt a number of measures to focus their scarce resources most efficiently for revenue collection and enforcement. The following measures should be regarded as options, as it is unlikely that it would be useful or possible to pursue all of them. The appropriate options for a particular country depend on its circumstances.

Establishment of large-taxpayers unit

The establishment of a large-taxpayer unit can be an effective initial step toward modernizing tax administration. It represents a targeted strategy for improving tax administration. This special unit, possibly made up of an elite group of better trained and less corruptible officials, would monitor the collection of taxes from large taxpayers, who although not large in number account for the major part, sometimes as high as 90 percent, of tax revenue from VAT and corporate income taxes.[12] Such a unit can virtually guarantee the timely collection of most tax revenue and the prompt identification of stopfilers and delinquent taxpayers so that appropriate action, including the imposition of penalties, can be taken. A large-taxpayer unit can significantly reduce errors in tax declarations and minimize delays in the collection of substantial amounts of revenue due to errors, late filing, and other violations. Such a unit would focus initial reform efforts on the adoption of more efficient procedures for large taxpayers, rather than those for small taxpayers, whose revenue generation is not substantial.

A large-taxpayers unit would serve as a model for tax administration for other taxpayers. Some form of monitoring large taxpayers has been adopted in more than twenty-five countries, both industrial and developing. In many countries, large-taxpayer units were introduced as pilot projects. Successful pilots can demonstrate to the tax administration—which, as a bureaucracy, tends to resist change—that it is possible and advantageous to modify procedures and systems. In many countries, once these modern practices were tested by the large-taxpayers unit, they were applied to progressively larger groups. For example, Argentina developed these new practices for a group of less than 1,000 taxpayers and has expanded them to apply to more than 200,000 taxpayers. A large-taxpayers unit may include not only the collection function but also the audit function, since detection of evasion is important for the same reasons that monitoring of compliance is. In addition, large taxpayers usually have a high volume of transactions and complex operations. They frequently have several branches of operations and even branches outside the country. They have highly skilled accountants and lawyers and may use forms of evasion that are difficult to detect, such as transfer pricing. These characteristics of large taxpayers often make it necessary to establish separate monitoring units with highly specialized staff.

Adoption of a threshold for tax registration

In a modern economy, it is not feasible to collect all major taxes from every economic enterprise. The accurate computation of tax liability by a taxpayer, and its control by the tax administration, requires that the taxpayer be able to maintain books and records at a certain minimum standard. Furthermore, it is not necessary that every enterprise be liable for taxes that

---

[12]These large taxpayers also account for a sizable share of income taxes withheld at source.

apply to some enterprises. For example, the objective of the value added tax is to tax the value of goods and services consumed by individuals. This tax is collected from enterprises on the basis of their value added (and also on imports) as a matter of convenience. In effect, although such enterprises are specified as "taxpayers" in the VAT law, they are acting as "tax collectors." The operation of the VAT system is not undermined if small-scale enterprises—which despite their numbers account for only a small proportion of the value of goods supplied to final consumers—are exempt from liability for the tax.

Imposition of an alternative tax on small taxpayers

With the threshold proposed above, most small enterprises engaging in cash transactions would not be liable, in principle, to pay VAT on their sales and would not receive credit for VAT already paid on their purchases. Every country finds it difficult to appropriately tax the income (or value added) of small traders in an appropriate manner; to assess the true level of income reasonably accurately, when most transactions are not recorded, can absorb considerable resources, and the revenues generated by this use of the tax administration's limited resources are likely to be small.

Three solutions to this dilemma have been adopted by various countries. One is to levy an annual license fee on small traders, as a rough substitute for the VAT, income tax, or both. Different license fees are often set for different types of business. Such fees need to be set at a level high enough to act as a reasonably fair substitute for income tax or VAT but not so high as to discourage enterprise. Another approach is a presumptive tax, under which the taxable income of the small business is computed indirectly on the basis of certain objective indicators such as the value of goods for sale, the number of employees, total wages paid, and the amount and type of physical assets. Estimating taxable income on a presumptive basis can, however, require considerable effort on the part of the tax administration (Tanzi 1991, chap. 13; Tanzi and Casanegra 1986). The third approach relies on withholding tax on the purchases of these small traders. In many countries, imports by traders who are not registered for the VAT, and sales of goods to such traders by registered enterprises, are subject to a special withholding tax—typically, 2 percent of the value of the purchase. Traders who believe that the amounts withheld by their suppliers exceed the liability on their value added have the option of registering for the VAT and submitting returns showing their actual VAT liability.

Use of final withholding

Withholding taxes on income when it is earned is widely used for collecting revenue with minimal use of administration resources. A popular mechanism is wage withholding, commonly known as pay as you earn (PAYE), in which employers are the withholding agents for personal income tax on the earnings of their employees (Van der Heeded 1994). This shifts the tax administration's monitoring responsibilities from a large number of individual taxpayers to a much smaller number of employers, thus achieving a more efficient focusing of administrative resources.

With the same efficiency gains, taxes can be withheld on sources of income other than wages by collecting from the payer rather than the payee. This includes payments of interest by banks, dividend payments by companies to stockholders, and interest and dividend payments by mutual funds. This process is facilitated when the taxes withheld become final taxes, as when a schedular approach is followed for taxing personal incomes.

Use of banks

Banks have a natural role in the administration of taxes. Banks are accustomed to receiving payments and handling money, and they are well equipped for the task of receiving tax payments. The main tax administration services provided by banks entail the receipt of payment forms, the receipt of money from taxpayers in payment of taxes, the batching of payment forms and balancing with monies received, the deposit of these monies into the proper tax accounts, and the submission of payment forms to the tax administration. In some countries, banks are also responsible for processing tax returns combined with payment forms; this system has substantially improved the efficiency of collection. The responsibility for maintaining an accurate record of taxpayers' transactions and for enforcing the collection of taxes remains, however, with the tax administration.

2.3 Organizational considerations

The measures discussed above for improving the effectiveness and efficiency of tax administration strongly influence its organization. Once the tax administration determines its key functions, an organizational structure should be adopted to support these functions. The discussion in the previous two subsections suggests the following five principal functions:

—*Taxpayer education.* Staff responsible for educating and assisting taxpayers distribute printed material that explains tax regulations, and they respond to inquiries from taxpayers. This important function has often not received the attention it deserves. As mentioned earlier, Spain, New Zealand, and Trinidad and Tobago provide good examples of successful taxpayer education.

—*Registration, accounting, and return processing.* Staff in this function are responsible for data entry and for declarations and payments processing. For instance, if a taxpayer uses the wrong tax rate, a computer can detect the error and automatically send a letter asking for payment at the correct rate. After the data have been verified, they are stored in a central record of all taxpayer transactions with the tax administration.

—*Collection enforcement.* This function focuses on collection of taxes from stopfilers and delinquent taxpayers. Basically, all compliance control except inspection is centralized in this function. Much of the information that is needed is provided by the accounting and processing department.

—*Audit.* To detect underreported taxes, staff in this function usually audit taxpayers' files and records at tax administration offices or business activities and records at the taxpayer's premises. By this point, routine checks have already been performed by the accounting and processing department.

—*Legal services and appeals.* Staff in this function take cases to court, defend tax authorities against legal appeals, and provide advice as to which actions are legal and which are not.

With a functional organization working as outlined, the work flow is more specialized and better supports a self-assessment system. The main objective is to identify the exceptions, that is, instances of noncompliance. The major part of the staff concentrates on the exceptions as well as on auditing to check compliance. Such an organization entails a strategic element of self-checking among staff, whereby the work in one function serves as a control on another. In other words, the organizational structure itself becomes a self-enforcing measure.

3   Conclusion

Given the right conditions, much progress in efficient tax administration can be achieved in a relatively short period of time. However, reform of tax administration usually requires years. Section 2 of this chapter outlines the main ingredients for a flexible strategy that has proved successful in a growing number of countries. This is a strategy in which foreign advisers can be useful provided that they have clear ideas and relevant multicountry experience.

The experience of several countries in recent years proves that tax administration can be reformed and can be made more efficient. However, these successful experiences have almost always occurred in countries that met several or all of the conditions outlined in section 1 and that, additionally, made concrete efforts to reform their economies. Tax administration cannot be an institutional island, reforming itself independently from the rest of the economy. Its reform will be facilitated—or indeed made possible—by a general change of attitude on the part of policy makers to welcome a greater reliance on market forces while, at the same time, they attempt to stamp out corruption and cronyism and to modernize the workings of the public sector.

If the rest of the economy is not being reformed and if attitudes about the role of the public sector and of the market are not changing, it will be difficult to reallocate resources within the administration or to create incentives for both taxpayers and the tax administration to improve compliance. If populism remains strong, or if union rules and other constraints continue to restrict policy actions, some of the essential elements of the reform will not be there.

References

Allingham, M. C., and A. Sandmo. 1972. "Income Tax Evasion: A Theoretical Analysis." *Journal of Public Economics* 1: 323–38.

Cowell, Frank A. 1990. *Cheating the Government: The Economics of Evasion.* Cambridge: MIT Press.

Tanzi, Vito. 1991. *Public Finance in Developing Countries.* Aldershot, England: Edward Elgar.

Tanzi, Vito, and Milka Casanegra de Jantscher. 1986. "The Use of Presumptive Income in Modern Tax Systems." In *Changes in Revenue Structures: Proceedings of the Forty-second Congress of the International Institute of Public Finance.* Detroit: Wayne State University Press.

Tanzi, Vito, and Parthasarathi Shome. 1993. "A Primer on Tax Evasion."
    IMF Staff Papers 40: 807–28. Published in 1994 in *Bulletin for
    International Fiscal Documentation* 4: 328–37.
Van der Heeded, Koenraad. 1994. "The Pay-As-You-Earn Tax on Wages—
    Options for Developing Countries and Countries in Transition."
    Working Paper 94:105. International Monetary Fund, Washington,
    D.C.

14 Information and Incentives in Institutional Reform

Robert Klitgaard

In the World Bank report *Governance* (World Bank 1994), there is a boxed passage entitled "The Importance of Institutions: Evidence from the East Asian Miracle Economies." What aspects of institutions would you guess it highlights? The first of four points concerns "competent, honest, and realistically paid bureaucracies." The opposite, in other words, of many government institutions in developing countries, whose poor performance constrains economic, social, and political development.[1] Presumably, such bureaucracies are everywhere sought. So the question becomes, how are they attained? According to the box, the East Asian countries have succeeded because, among other things, they have "merit-based recruitment and promotion, incentive-based compensation, and clearly defined, reward-oriented career paths."[2] The opposite, in other words, of seniority-based promotion, pay based solely on position, and vague career paths only weakly linked with rewards—characteristics of most bureaucracies in developing countries.

So, does a clear recommendation emerge? Not quite. The rest of the report hardly mentions incentives. Civil service reform is a key topic, but "better pay and motivation" here means slightly higher base salaries for smaller numbers of public servants. In another box the report does state that

---

[1] I take as stylized facts that many public agencies are failing because of incompetence, dishonesty, and poor incentives and that these failures threaten the delivery of social services, the administration of justice, and the management of the economy, which in turn undermine free-market and democratic reforms.

[2] World Bank (1994, 8). The report doesn't make the reference explicit, but the source is apparently World Bank (1993, 174–80). Although this document stresses "incentive-based compensation," high pay for top officials, stiff penalties for malfeasance, and prizes for performance, it does not mention linking civil service pay to performance targets. The discussion in Wade (1990) of the economic bureaucracy in Taiwan and South Korea leaves it rather mysterious how the acknowledged high performance was achieved (for example, "we know rather little about the inner workings of East Asian bureaucracies generally," 337). He says salaries in government in Taiwan are 30–50 percent below those in the private sector (219).

African governments suffer from "recruitment based on subjective criteria; remuneration levels unlinked to productivity; and loyalty of employees to individuals rather than to the state" (10). But the report says nothing about how countries might learn from either East Asian or other examples of merit-based recruitment and promotion or from the linking of pay and careers to performance.

Why not? I wrote a colleague at the Bank and asked. She shared my question with others. Back came a memo from one of the authors of the report. He is suspicious of designing "pay schemes so that employees can be rewarded against the achievement of performance targets."

> This view has some support within the Bank's PSM [public service management] fraternity. Others [he lists himself and two others as examples] think it is dangerously naive, excepting in certain enclave situations and on a temporary basis . . . . First, you have to get base levels right . . . . Second, you have to get the rest of the budget right (no point in offering to reward performance if there are no materials for staff to work with). Third, you have to design a viable system of performance measurement. Fourth, you have to have a governance framework in place that is determined to reward performance and not patrimonial relationships. Call that a performance culture. Only now are the leading OECD reformers getting into performance pay, and gingerly (a badly designed performance pay scheme can just as easily demotivate staff). . . .
>
> In short, pay is important, incentives are central, but the answer does not lie in pay linked to performance measurement. Rather, we like to think about creating an "enabling environment" for the public sector. That's a much broader concept that embraces budgeting as well as the civil service. Performance measurement has a role in this, but to get a better handle on the outputs and outcomes associated with government interventions, with a view to learning how to improve performance. We see this as more important than using performance measurement as the basis for pay systems."

"We do think about incentives," the memo concludes, "but this doesn't lead automatically to performance pay linked to performance measurement." Incentives are recognized as a crucial problem but are downplayed as part of the solution. Why? This question is the focus of this chapter. Section 1 provides other examples of mixed feelings about incentives. Section 2 presents a simple economic framework for examining "incentive intensity." It enables us to identify the conditions under which "intense" incentives will and will not be desirable. And it suggests how these conditions might be altered to make incentives work better. Based on these considerations, section 3 tries to clarify the tension between an acknowledgment of the power of incentives and a deep suspicion of institutional reforms that place incentives at the center, and then suggests ways forward.

1   Mixed Feelings about Incentives

For six years I had the good fortune to work with Derek Bok when he was president of Harvard University, and so it was with eagerness that I acquired his recent book, *The Cost of Talent* (Bok 1993). Loaded with references and leavened with both caveats and wit, Bok argues that incentives in America have gone awry. Top managers and practitioners are paid from two to three times the amount necessary to attract able people and motivate them. (He justifies this statement using both cross-country and longitudinal data about pay levels. Understandably perhaps, he does not systematically justify the proposition through direct comparisons of productivity.) Moreover, civil servants, teachers, and social workers are paid too little, compared with those entering law or major businesses. In 1970, for example, a new graduate from a top professional or law school would earn a starting salary on Wall Street about equal to a starting salary in government and about two times the starting salary of a schoolteacher. By 1990, the multiples were Wall Street four, government two, schoolteacher one. At the top of U.S. businesses, big pay increases occurred in the 1920s and the 1980s, and the only explanation, he thinks, is zeitgeist and politics, not changes in markets and technologies and "economic factors."

The solution is, therefore, to change zeitgeist and politics, in part presumably via books like Bok's. But two questions arise. If skewed incentives are a problem, why aren't better incentives a solution? Wouldn't we move toward a solution by linking pay to performance?

Bok spends several pages on these questions. Merit pay, he says, has been tried for teachers, civil servants, lawyers, and chief executive officers, among others. "The striking fact about these attempts," Bok says, "is that they have all either failed completely or fallen far short of expectations" (243). Measuring performance proves difficult. Squabbling ensues, leading to unanticipated costs. Even when performance measures are implemented, employees undermine them by gaming, deceiving, even corrupting. He cites five other problems, including the fact that performance bonuses often remain puny compared to total pay, so no real incentive is provided.

In critiquing performance-based pay, Bok's tone seems to change. Earlier, when critical of relative pay levels, he is not critical of the ability of incentives to alter behavior. Indeed, his book is about the power of incentives. But when he turns to the possibility of systematically manipulating incentives within organizations, his skepticism surges.

As another example, consider Arturo Israel's 1987 book, *Institutional Development*. Its subtitle is intriguing: *Incentives to Performance*. The author, who was then the head of the World Bank's Public Sector Management and Private Sector Development Division, asserts that "the World Bank's experience suggests that distortions in wages and salaries are probably among the most costly obstacles to institutional development" (126)—in particular, paying highly productive people in the public sector too little. And yet his theoretical treatment plays down the reform of economic incentives. He emphasizes, instead, what he calls intrinsic incentives, having to do with the nature of the work and the availability of information about its results.

These are not isolated instances. Without having assessed the vast literatures on these subjects in personnel and in business administration, I think it is fair to say that the tension is chronic. On the one hand, analyses of highly successful firms often discover remarkable incentive systems based on performance. For example, a recent study of sixty major U.S. corporations examined compensation policies and the use of performance-based pay. Companies were classified into two categories, those using performance-based pay and those that did not. The former averaged almost 4 percent higher earnings per share over the previous three years, more than 5 percent higher profit margins, and almost 5 percent higher profits and cash flow per employee (Schuster and Zingheim 1992, 279). On the other hand, many personnel and management experts are reluctant to emphasize the *economics* of institutions.

In an early chapter of *In Search of Excellence*, Thomas Peters and Robert Waterman criticize the view that better incentives are the answer to institutional malaise.[3] Yet when reporting their results they acknowledge that the high-performing firms had more intense and variegated incentives than the others. "We found rich systems of monetary incentives; but we expected that. We also discovered an incredible array of nonmonetary incentives and an amazing variety of experimental or newly introduced programs" (Peters and Waterman 1982, 242).[4] The authors stress the noneconomic rewards, diminishing the economic ones as only to be expected.

As a final illustration, consider the most important empirical analysis of performance-based incentives, the Brookings volume *Paying for Productivity* (Blinder 1990). This compilation of both "anecdotal" and econometric evidence in the United States, Europe, and Japan shows that incentive-based pay leads to higher productivity.[5] Along the way, the Brookings book also provides evidence that employee "participation" does not work unless employees are paid more for participating effectively.[6]

However, the book's evidence is not decisive about the usefulness of employee participation in the design of incentive systems; in many cases, such participation was neither sufficient nor necessary for success. And yet,

---

[3]One of the eleven commonly held beliefs criticized by the authors is this: "Get incentives right and productivity will follow. If we give people big, straightforward monetary incentives to do right and work smart, the productivity problem will go away. Over-reward the top performers. Weed out the 30 to 40 percent dead wood who don't want to work" (Peters and Waterman 1982, 43).

[4]"As we did this research, we were struck by the wealth of non-monetary incentives used by the excellent companies. Nothing is more powerful than positive reinforcement. Everybody uses it. But top performers, almost alone, use it extensively" (269).

[5]Incidentally, Bok (1993) does not mention Blinder's book. Bok asserts: "At the most basic level, all pay-for-performance schemes proceed from a belief that the prospect of monetary rewards will motivate people to work harder and more efficiently. Although the premise seems obvious, there is surprisingly little empirical evidence to support it" (244). Precisely this sort of evidence is what Blinder's book overwhelmingly (in my judgment) provides.

[6]"The postulated link between participation and improved efficiency is one of information. . . . To an economist it should not be surprising to find that participatory arrangements, such as quality circles, that are designed to elicit better information without offering any stake in the returns to such information are usually short-lived." Daniel I. Levine and Laura D'Andrea Tyson in Blinder 1990 (186).

in the editor's introduction, after acknowledging the weakness of the statistical evidence about workers' participation, its importance is treated as one of the surprising conclusions of the book.[7] Calling for "participation" somehow tempers the call for "incentives"—perhaps a kind of sociological reassurance that no one is positing *homo oeconomicus*, even as economics is emphasized.

And here may be a clue to the tension about incentives. In part, at least, the causes are disciplinary, even temperamental. The economist approaching institutions tends to begin with the simplifying assumptions that employees are maximizing their incomes and that pay should be set equal to the value of the marginal product. In the limiting economic simplification of perfect markets and perfect information as in the Arrow-Debreu framework (or the Samuelson textbook), there is no role for managers. As Joan Robinson described it, the job of the manager of a firm is looking up in the book of blueprints the correct page corresponding to current (and future) factor markets (Stiglitz 1989, 3).

Understandably, this does not correspond to the reality appreciated by sociologists of organization, personnel experts, and professors of management. Many things matter besides money, they say.[8] And as James Q. Wilson says in his classic book, *Bureaucracy*, the economist's principal-agent model is far too simple a model for real organizations. On the other hand, it is worth noting this conclusion: "The principal challenge facing public managers is to understand the importance of carefully defining the core tasks of the organization and to find both pecuniary and nonpecuniary incentives that will induce operators to perform those tasks as defined" (Wilson 1989, 174).

Fortunately, recent work in economics provides an escape from the worst excesses (and nonsensical predictions) of reductionist economics. This work may help resolve the tension we have seen about incentives by showing that the importance of incentives linked with performance depends on various features of the specific situation. By analyzing a simple model and then introducing more complex considerations in a qualitative way, we

---

[7]For example: "It appears that changing the way workers are *treated* may boost productivity more than changing the way they are *paid*, although profit sharing or employee stock ownership combined with worker participation may be the best system of all" (13). I believe the book establishes no such conclusion.

[8]To which one wag has responded, "Pay isn't the most important thing. But it's way ahead of whatever is in third place."

can appreciate that, under the conditions faced in many developing countries, suspicions about the efficacy of incentive reforms are well founded. And yet, we also see the potential for better incentives and for more efficient bureaucracies as these conditions change (in part because of policy reforms).

2   The Optimal Intensity of Incentives

This section tries to convey the essence of an institutional economics approach to the incentive problem, using a variation of the principal-agent model. A central idea is that, since the agent's performance is only imperfectly measured, paying a wage based on what the principal can observe creates a risk for the agent. Because of risk aversion, the agent would prefer a fixed wage that does not depend on performance. But the principal dislikes fixed wages, because then the agent has no economic incentive for higher performance. The optimal wage agreement strikes a balance between risk sharing and incentives. Usually, this combines a fixed payment that does not depend on a measure of performance with a variable payment that does.

Suppose you are the principal, I am your agent. Your profits are a function of my efforts: Profit = $P(e)$. But my efforts are costly to me: Cost = $C(e)$. Ideally, you would pay me a wage equal to the value of my marginal product. But you don't know my effort e, at least not perfectly. You can observe an indicator of my effort, which is

$$z = e + x,$$

where x is a random variable representing the measurement error.

You can also observe a variable, y, that is not correlated to e but is correlated to x. For example, suppose z is sales of the product for this month. It is some function of my effort but also depends on industry demand, y. You might take y into account to enable a more precise estimate of my effort. The wage you pay me can be analyzed as having two parts, one fixed and one dependent on your assessment of my effort:

$$w = \alpha + \beta \, (e + x + \gamma y).$$

β is a measure of the incentive intensity of our wage contract. When it is zero, you pay me a fixed wage, α. The parameter, γ, measures how much weight you give to y in relation to z.

What contract would be socially optimal (for the two of us)? Assume that the expected values of x and y are normed to zero (for convenience), and assume no wealth effects. My certainty equivalent is equal to expected income minus the cost of effort minus a risk premium for the income risk I bear because $(x + \gamma y)$ is a random variable. That risk premium turns out to be approximated by $1/2r\ \beta^2\ \text{Var}\ (x + \gamma y)$, where r is a parameter of risk aversion. (Milgrom and Roberts 1992, 247). Your certainty equivalent as a risk-neutral employer is the expected profit minus the expected wage.

Both of our certainty equivalents depend on the four variables α, e, β, and γ. By the assumption of "no wealth effects," an efficient contract will maximize the sum of the certainty equivalents. But there is also an incentive constraint, which says that I as your agent will set my effort level such that the marginal benefit equals marginal cost. So an employment contract is efficient if and only if the choices α, e, β, and γ maximize the total certainty equivalent among all "incentive compatible" contracts where $\beta - C'(e) = 0$. The solution generally has some fixed pay and some variable pay that is a function of the two measures z and y.

From this model we can derive the incentive intensity principle. The strength of incentives should be an increasing function of the marginal returns to the task, the accuracy with which performance is measured, the responsiveness of the agent's effort to incentives, and the agent's risk tolerance.

$$\beta = P'(e)/\{1 + r\ [\text{Var}(x + \gamma y)]\ C''(e)\},$$

where $C''(e)$ is the slope of the marginal effort curve. This formula is computed by maximizing the total certainty equivalent of principal and agent with respect to e (Milgrom and Roberts 1992, 222–23). The incentive intensity principle suggests that under some conditions it is optimal to have "highly intense" incentives, but under other conditions a flat wage is the right choice. Below, I show some of the extreme conditions favoring or not favoring performance-based pay.

In many public bureaucracies, especially in developing countries, the conditions seem to resemble those in the right-hand column of Table 1. Of particular importance is the difficulty of measuring performance—in the model, reducing Var $(x + \gamma y)$. In part this is due to the nature of the goods being produced in the public sector.[9] In part it is due to the primitive technologies and insufficient funds available for evaluation in many poor countries.

The incentive intensity principle suggests a way to resolve the tension about incentives. Under some conditions, intense incentives will yield efficient bureaucracies. Under unfavorable conditions, trying to raise β will have meager and indeed perhaps unfavorable effects. But there is a third point. The four parameters of the incentive intensity principle are not immutable. In particular, when the measurement of performance improves, a wage package can be constructed that both enhances incentives and reduces risk. This is why better information is at the heart of institutional reform.

2.1   Poor measurement and low wages

We shall return to the point made above. But let us spend a moment more on what happens when performance measures are bad: it may be rational to have little or no incentive intensity. Using a different model of compensation, Timothy Besley and John McLaren (1993) show that very poor information and highly imperfect measurement can make it optimal to do what many developing countries actually do—pay tax collectors low

---

[9]Wilson (1989) distinguishes four types of public organizations, depending on the measurability of what might be called their efforts and their outputs. In production organizations, both efforts and outputs can be measured; here, the prospects for performance-based incentives are strong. At the other extreme, coping organizations, in which neither efforts nor outputs can be gauged, are weak candidates for incentive pay. Indeed, Wilson (175) says, "In coping organizations effective management is almost impossible." As prospects for performance pay, the two other corners of the table are in-between.

	Can measure effort	Cannot measure effort
Can measure outcomes	Production (e.g., internal revenue, social security, post office, FBI)	Craft (enforcement agencies, corps of engineers, forest rangers)
Cannot measure outcomes	Procedural (e.g., armed forces in peacetime)	Coping (foreign service, some schools, some police activities)

Source: Based on Wilson (1989, chap. 9). See also Clague (1994, 20–8).

wages with compressed salary scales. The alternatives—wages equal to those in the private sector and efficiency wages above private sector wages in order to deter corruption—will, under conditions of widespread dishonesty and very imperfect monitoring, yield less government revenue, even though low wages virtually guarantee that many officials engage in bribe taking. This result is similar to one of the points of Clague's (1993) analysis of compliance: unless enough people are induced to comply, a socially disastrous equilibrium can result.

Table 14.1

Conditions Favoring and Not Favoring Pay-Performance Links

Aspect of Incentive Intensity Principle	Favorable to Intense Incentives	Unfavorable to Intense Incentives
$P'(e)$ = marginal social benefits of more effort by agent	Additional efforts by public servants lead to big gains in effectiveness.	Because of other constraints, additional efforts by public servants yield no gains in effectiveness.
r = agent's risk aversion	Employees are almost risk-neutral, perhaps because plentiful opportunities exist and they are already well-off.	Employees are very risk averse, perhaps because poor.
Var $(x+\gamma y)$ = how accurately agent's effort can be measured	Effort and results are easy to measure.	Effort and results are almost impossible to measure.
$C'(e)$ = responsiveness of agent's effort to incentives	Effort is highly responsive to incentives (for example, high discretion).	Effort is not responsive to incentives (for example, fixed-pace activity).

But if monitoring effectiveness can somehow be improved—for example, if information is more widespread or more easily assessed—then the conclusion changes. Under many reasonable assumptions, with good monitoring and evaluation capabilities, the government's optimal wage strategy will be to pay efficiency wages.[10]

What about performance pay? Besley and McLaren's model rules it out in advance. Thus, in the model, wages cannot be varied according to performance—for example, according to revenues raised or frauds uncovered or quality of processing. Second, those who are caught offering or accepting bribes are not punished except that bribe takers lose their public sector jobs. Efficiency wages and steep hierarchies thus become the only way to reward officials for honest behavior (see Bulow and Summers 1986). But when these assumptions are relaxed and we allow the employer to use β, then if measurement is "good enough" a superior solution may be to reward tax officers as a function of their performance. But the point I wish to underscore in the Besley-McLaren result is the sensitivity of optimal pay schemes to the ability to measure. An employee's contribution to value added may be hard or impossible to gauge, and much of the resistance to incentive pay schemes in the literature is based on this undeniable difficulty.

2.2   Problems with incentive reforms

The following list summarizes some of the difficulties facing performance-based incentives. Beyond the categories suggested by the incentive intensity principle, it adds considerations of incentive dynamics, political economy, and layers of hierarchy.

> —How to afford incentive schemes (use nonmonetary incentives, samples, and partial fees-for-service; borrow measurement techniques; involve agents and clients in performance appraisal. Avoid bonuses that become standard.)
>
> —Extraneous factors determine $P'(e)$ (control for them statistically; use tournaments, contests, relative rankings, but these create side-effects)

---

[10]Besley and McLaren (1993) think Malawi may be a contemporary example. They also allude to the nineteenth-century case of Robert Hart taking over the corrupt Shanghai customs bureau, raising wages, increasing monitoring, using foreign inspectors, and dismissing officials guilty of improprieties. "The effect on tax revenues was resounding" (136). They cite Wright (1950) and, on Malawi, Medard (1986) and Lindauer, Meesook, and Subsaeng (1986).

—Teamwork (may need group incentives, but then free-rider problems; collusion)

—Dynamics and political economy (skewing agents toward the measurable to the detriment of the less measurable; "influence activities," including dissimulation, gaming, sabotage, and corruption; ratchet effect; creating disincentives for transfers, learning new skills, etc.: answers include a richer informational environment and processes that build transparency and credibility)

—Layers of bureaucracy (evaluators may not have correct incentives)

In particular, agents and principals may take dynamic steps that undermine incentives and information. Consider agents first:

—Agents distort activities toward those things easily measured at cost of those things not easily measured.

—Agents engage in influence activities: distorting information, influencing evaluators of information, not revealing useful private information.[11]

—If relative rankings of agents are used, agents may avoid useful teamwork or even sabotage others.

—Agents may avoid job transfers or the learning of new skills, for fear of losing bonuses attached to existing arrangements and competencies.

—Agents may act collectively to transmogrify performance bonuses into higher base pay.

Principals may also take steps that undermine the system:

—Ratchet effects: after learning more about the production function, principals move the goal posts, leaving agents worse off than before.

---

[11]Milgrom and Roberts (1988).

—Intermediate layers of the bureaucracy may simply lack incentives to undertake performance appraisal.[12] The appraisals are often limited to employee inputs, qualifications, or endowments, rather than to the much more difficult idea of contribution to value-added.

—In performance ratings, intermediate layers of the hierarchy collude with or extract rents from lower levels, undermining the system (and in extreme models leaving underlings no better off than before).

Such issues have been analyzed in the literature, and the complexities of reality soon overwhelm available economic models (see Holmstrom and Tirole 1989, 106–26). In particular, when dynamics are included, the incentive intensity principal no longer can be assured to hold.[13] Without a host of special assumptions, we cannot pretend to "compute" the optimal incentive intensity, even in theory. Nonetheless, the very categories suggested by theory as undermining performance incentives provide a framework for considering how in practice these problems might be mitigated. And building on the incentive intensity principle, the framework for policy analysis, below, suggests ways to make incentive reforms more likely to succeed.

---

[12]Although most organizations use formal appraisal systems—one estimate in the United States put the figure at 80 percent of manufacturing companies—in practice these systems are often said to be ineffective. For one thing, managers may lack incentives to report honestly on the performance of their subordinates. Unlike China of old, superiors are not themselves rewarded or punished on the basis of the subsequent performance of those they appraise. Around 1000 A.D. the Chinese possessed an elaborate system of recommendations. When you recommended someone, you were held partly responsible for the person recommended. If he did well, you could receive "requitement and commendation." If he did badly, you could be punished. For example, if he committed a crime punishable by death, you could be deported. If he was deported, you could be given forced labor. If he was sentenced to forced labor, you could be beaten with a heavy or a light rod. And so forth. (Kracke 1953, chap. 10.)

[13]Laffont and Tirole (1993, 663) note that optimal linear incentive schemes "were no longer so once dynamics, political economy, or multi-principal conditions were thrown in."

1. *Strengthen the link between employee effort and agency value-added.*

—Make sure everyone understands what the value-added is and how it is being sought. What are the "key tasks" of the organization? What does it take to perform them better?

—Incentive reforms require the participation of employees themselves in the specification of each agency's objectives, performance measures, and incentives. This helps educate everyone on the links between effort and value-added.

—Help employees improve the quality of their efforts (training, feedback on achievements).

—Sometimes P′(e) is close to zero for any individual but is large for groups of employees. In such cases team incentives are more feasible and desirable than individual incentives. (Free-rider problems may then emerge, which demand another iteration of solutions.)

2. *Reduce the risk aversion of employees.*

—Raise the level of the pay.

—Help remove employees' uncertainties about pay-for-performance by running transparent *experiments* in which employees (and clients) help to design quantitative and qualitative measures of performance, appropriate incentive schedules, and ways to evaluate the experiment's results in a relatively short time.

—Make credible commitments about the evolution of pay–performance formulas over time, to avoid the "ratchet effect." Again, a process is often important. For example, if employees, management, and clients help appraise progress and set new incentive schemes, along with a guarantee to return to *status quo ante* under agreed-upon conditions, this may engender the confidence to enable an experiment with incentive pay to begin.

—Avoid incentive master plans for all agencies and all time. Learn by doing. Make sure affected parties take part in the evaluation of the incentive experiments.

—Facilitate employee self-selection. Introducing performance-based pay can be expected to lead workers with lower risk aversion to prefer public sector jobs.

3. *Reduce the variance of measures of performance.*

—Include information from clients.

—Empower clients. Seek analogies to market power or joint management. Experiment with user charges and analogies to them such as in-kind contributions, sharing them with employees.

—Quantitative and qualitative outcome measures can be used. So can peer ratings, as long as ratings are forced to be "on a curve" (i.e., not everyone can be rated "excellent").

—Extraneous variables can be taken into account in the design of incentive schemes (the y in the incentive-intensity principle could try to measure such extraneous variables, which are given weight γ). Examples are controlling for students' social backgrounds in estimates of school contributions to learning, and in the Philippines Bureau of Internal Revenue controlling for the tax base of a local district in estimating the efficiency of the district office in raising revenues. Also, an incentive scheme may employ measures of relative performance, analogous to tournaments, which help "control for" the extraneous variables that affect everyone's performance up or down.

4. *Reduce the costs to employees of additional effort.*

—Begin with the easiest cases. In particular, try reforms in areas where performance is relatively easy to measure objectively and where the revenues raised or costs saved can make the experiment self-financing.

—Through training and better equipment, shift the cost-of-effort curve.

5. *Reduce the costs of providing incentives.*

—Incentives include money but also other things, which may be less expensive: promotions, training, travel, special assignments, transfers, awards, favorable recognition, and simple praise. Even information about how well one is doing turns out to function as an incentive.

—Remember the principle of the sample: incentives can be based on samples of performance. Especially in an experiment, there is no need for the comprehensive measurement of each and every outcome of each and every action.

—Cultivate political support, particularly from unions and foreign donors. The idea of an experiment reduces their worries and involves them in design and evaluation.

—Challenge technical assistance by foreigners. For example, learn by doing rather than attempting comprehensive studies that often end up being inconclusive or unsatisfactory. For example, use TA funds to finance experiments where local experts and even government officials carry out the required "studies" based on the participatory diagnosis of what is already known about problems and possible solutions.

—Privatize creatively. This can mean experimenting with hybrids of public and private sectors working together to provide services. Information about performance may incidentally be enhanced.

The problems raised by dynamics and by the political economy of incentive reforms do not yield ready solutions. Probably, however, part of the answer concerns the processes through which (1) performance measures are designed and (2) incentives are constructed and tested and reassessed.[14]

3   The Implications

It is widely asserted that "institutional development" has not worked as well as hoped. Increasingly, evaluations emphasize that incentives have often not been adequately taken into account.[15] Pay is too low to attract and

---

[14]Thus, Schuster and Zingheim (1992, 153) say that "the major thrust of new pay is in the area of introducing variable pay to employee groups where most organizations pay only base pay." But the process of doing this tends to involve important changes including formation of employee-organization partnerships, improved collaboration between organizations and employees, primary emphasis on customer interests, organizational success affecting all rewards, downplaying of tenure and entitlement, quality and customer value initiatives, and experimentation with new reward programs.

[15]On the failures of civil service reform, see Dia (1993). Even more broadly than civil service reform, institutional development efforts have foundered on pay levels too low to retain talented staff and incentives unconnected to

retain needed high-level talent in government, and performance does not drive reward schedules. On the negative side, for too long corruption has been neglected as an issue, and if it is raised, it is as a problem of law or ethics rather than of structures, incentives, and information.

On the positive side, when incentives are taken into account, good things can happen. Successful programs in developing countries have been built on appropriate bureaucratic incentives, which in turn depend on the generation of relevant performance measures. For example, in the mid-1980s, Indonesia reformed its rural credit program by creating performance-based incentives for local bank managers. First, information was developed about the savings generated from each village unit, the repayment rates, and who was getting the loans. Second, authority was decentralized to local bank managers so they could make decisions and respond to local conditions. Third, and crucially, local bank staff was paid depending on their results in getting loans to the poor, ensuring their repayment, and generating savings at local levels. Within three years, 82 percent of the village units were making money, and the rural banking system tripled its loan volume. By 1990 it was the second biggest rural credit program in the world.

Another success story is the Bolivian Social Emergency Fund. In 1986, after a year of stagnation, businessman Fernando Romero took over the SEF and introduced better systems of information and incentives. The SEF set up a process that asked the communities, working with the private sector constructors of schools, roads, sewers, and so forth, to submit proposals that were vetted centrally through a comparison process. In a second round, some technical assistance was given to communities that did less well in preparing projects.

Information and incentives again were crucial. The centralized information process included estimates of costs per unit of such things as rural roads and schools, so that when proposals came in with outrageous amounts officials had some way of knowing that. The process included

---

performance. In contrast, many successful projects and integrated rural development efforts paid close attention to these incentive problems (Rondinelli 1989; see also Israel 1987). In a related vein perhaps, a recent review of institutional development components of World Bank projects concludes: "Few ID projects or components have provided for monitoring progress against explicit performance criteria or dated targets. . . . As a result, ID issues repeatedly identified in successive projects often remain unresolved" (Operations Evaluation Department 1993, 2).

incentives for the people in the bureaucracy to monitor and evaluate operations in rural areas. Within two and a half years the SEF moved millions of dollars and created thousands of jobs. And it did so efficiently. Despite salaries considerably in excess of government norms and despite aggressive systems of promotions and incentives, the SEF's administrative cost per dollar moved to rural areas was less than 4 percent. This compared favorably with the amount USAID would pay the UNDP to administer a project in Bolivia, which was 7 percent (Klitgaard 1991, chaps. 7, 9).

There are many examples in the rich countries. The OECD countries, especially the United States, have experience with measuring and rewarding performance in the public sector.[16] In businesses, what has been called "gainsharing" and "the new pay" is growing in acceptance (Blinder 1990). Despite these successes, many people are skeptical about higher pay and performance-based incentives as solutions. The models in section 3 go some way toward resolving this tension. They show that the desirability and design of pay-for-performance schemes depend in predictable ways on aspects of the task environment. This has several implications. First, we should not expect the same incentive scheme to work equally well under all situations. Second, we should expect that incentive reforms will be differentially successful, depending on the variables we have identified. Third, these conditioning variables may themselves be subject to policy manipulation. Given the task environments found in many public bureaucracies in developing countries, performance pay will fail, and consequently low levels of performance and high levels of corruption will be chronic because, our models say, they are "rational" responses to a miserable organizational environment. For organizations to work better, this environment must change.

The last point opens new horizons for thinking about institutional development. From the perspective of a given manager or minister in a given system, reforming incentives may be impossible. Not only do civil service rules not permit it, but the manager may not have the authority or the resources to generate the measures of performance on which an effective incentive system depends. What is needed is analogous to structural adjustment: a change in the rules of the game, a new enabling environment.

---

[16]See, for example, the fourteen selections under the heading "Productivity Measures and Improvement in Government and Nonprofit Institutions," in Christopher and Thor (1993): see also Maguire and Wood (1992).

A key feature of the needed reform is better information about what government agencies do and what results they achieve.

"Efficient organizational design," writes Paul Milgrom, "seeks to do what the system of prices and property rights does in the neoclassical conception: to channel the self-interested behavior of individuals away from purely redistributive activities and into well-coordinated, socially productive ones" (Milgrom 1988, 58–59). There are interesting parallels between the free-market reforms that have swept the world in the past decade and incentive-based institutional reforms that I believe will sweep the world in the next two decades—not only in their advantages but also in their shortcomings, in the applicability of economic advice to conditions faced by developing countries, and in the surprising opposition to these reforms by some experts in development economics and "development administration."

There are important differences as well. Two stand out in my mind. First is the importance of *experimentation*. The idea of designing an incentive master plan is misguided. Performance measures are so problematic in the many senses we have uncovered that, especially in difficult cases, we are well advised to begin with incomplete experiments and learn from that experience. Second is the importance of *process* in institutional reform. It seems wise, especially in the challenging cases where performance is multidimensional and hard to measure, to involve employees and clients in the design of performance measures, the design of incentive schemes, and the evaluation of pay-for-performance experiments. What we have called the dynamics and political economy considerations of incentive reforms—such as the danger of manipulation and influence activities and the threat of ratchet effects later denying employees the benefits of their improved performance—can in many cases be mitigated only through a transparent process that builds trust, creates quasi-objective measures, and facilitates credible commitments. Thus, in comparison with free-market reforms, institutional reforms will be slower, will involve more participation by employees and clients, and will vary according to the conditions of different countries and ministries.

How can aid donors help? On the negative side, they can stop pushing the standard approach to civil service reform, which emphasizes more training, more foreign advisers, and more studies and which has the goal of horizontal equity and the "rationalization" of jobs. Table 14.2 contrasts this approach with a different one, building on information and incentives.

Donors can fund experimental projects that stimulate local people, including beleaguered and much abused public officials, to think more

Table 14.2

Two Approaches to Civil Service Reform

	Prevalent Approach	Proposed Approach
Ends of reform	Across-the-board pay increases; horizontal equity across jobs	Selective pay increases that eventually spread; incentives linked to performance targets
Means	Long-term studies leading to system-wide reform; foreign TA do the studies; learning by planning	Experiments with a few key elements of the civil service; public officials define measures of success; learning by doing
Constraints	Budgetary austerity; donor pressure to reduce wage bill	Begin with revenue-raising and cost-saving experiments that can pay for themselves; use aid to fund experiments
Facilitating conditions	Studies; technical assistance; political will to reduce the size of the public service	"Institutional adjustment," including better information, more client participation, competition.

creatively about what their institutions are trying to accomplish, how this might be measured, and how rewards might be linked to success. Donors can help create an enabling environment for such reforms. Most important are systemwide efforts to obtain better information on the performance of public institutions through a wide variety of mechanisms, including client surveys, partial fee payments, peer assessments, statistical data, ratings by immediate superiors, self-assessments, and critical incident studies. Better information promotes transparency. It also motivates bureaucracies—especially, of course, when it is linked with better incentives.

A lesson of this chapter is that, when incentives are poor, conditions may be such that performance-based incentives will not by themselves lead to improvement. But it is also true that, under the same conditions, bureaucracies exhibiting very low pay, weak links between career and performance, and corruption are unlikely to be improved by the usual approaches to civil service reform, institutional development, and public management. This suggests that the underlying conditions are what deserve systematic attention. It is time to experiment with new approaches. The chapter summarizes both the challenges facing incentive reforms and some possible ways to meet those challenges. I hope these serve as a framework for policy analysis of incentive reforms in developing countries. They show that although sometimes incentive reforms by themselves will work, more generally they should be one ingredient in a more wide-ranging effort of "institutional adjustment"—a strategic approach to public institutions that emphasizes the improvement of information, incentives, competition, and participation.

References

Blinder, Alan S., ed. 1990. *Paying for Productivity: A Look at the Evidence.* Washington, D.C.: Brookings.

Besley, Timothy, and John McLaren. 1993. "Taxes and Bribery: The Role of Wage Incentives." *Economic Journal* 103: 119–41.

Bok, Derek. 1993. *The Cost of Talent: How Executives and Professionals Are Paid and How It Affects America.* New York: Free Press.

Bulow, Jeremy, and Lawrence Summers. 1986. "A Theory of Dual Labor Markets with Application to Industrial Policy, Discrimination, and Keynesian Unemployment." *Journal of Labor Economics* 17: 376–414.

Christopher, William F., and Carl G. Thor. 1993. *Handbook for Productivity Measurement and Improvement.* Portland, Ore: Productivity Press.

Clague, Christopher. 1993. "Rule Obedience, Organizational Loyalty and Economic Development." *Journal of Institutional and Theoretical Economics* 149: 393–414.

———. 1994. "Bureaucracy and Economic Development." *Structural Change and Economic Dynamics* 5: 273–291. IRIS Reprint 57.

Dia, Mamadou. 1993. *A Governance Approach to Civil Service Reform in Sub-Saharan Africa.* Technical Paper 225. Washington, D.C.: World Bank.

Holmstrom, Bengt, and Jean Tirole. 1989. "The Theory of the Firm." In *Handbook of Industrial Organization.* Vol. 1, ed. R. Schmalensee and R. D. Willig. Amsterdam: Elsevier Science Publishers.

Israel, Arturo. 1987. *Institutional Development: Incentives to Performance.* Baltimore: Johns Hopkins University Press.

Klitgaard, Robert. 1991. *Adjusting to Reality: Beyond "State vs. Market" in Economic Development.* San Francisco: Institute for Contemporary Studies Press.

Kracke, E. A. 1953. *Civil Service in Early Sung China, 960–1067.* Cambridge: Harvard University Press.

Laffont, Jean-Jacques, and Jean Tirole. 1993. *A Theory of Incentives in Procurement and Regulation.* Cambridge: MIT Press.

Lindauer, D., O. Meesook, and P. Suebsaeng. 1988. "Government Wage Policy in Africa: Some Findings and Policy Issues." *World Bank Research Observer* 3: 1–25.

Maguire, Maria, and Robert Wood. 1992. "Private Pay for Public Work?" *OED Observer* 175: (April/May).

Medard, J. F. 1986. "Public Corruption in Africa: A Comparative Perspective." *Corruption and Reform* 1:2.

Milgrom, Paul. 1988. "Efficient Contracts, Influence Activities, and Efficient Organizational Design." *Journal of Political Economy.* 96: 42–60.

Milgrom, Paul, and John Roberts. 1988. "An Economic Approach to Influence Activities in Organizations." *American Journal of Sociology*, suppl. 94.

———. 1992. *Economics, Organization, and Management.* Englewood Cliffs, N.J.: Prentice-Hall.

Operations Evaluation Department. 1993. "Support for Institutional Development." *OED Précis* 57.

Peters, Thomas J., and Robert H. Waterman, Jr. 1982. *In Search of Excellence: Lessons from America's Best-Run Companies.* New York: Harper and Row.

Rondinelli, Dennis. 1989. *International Assistance for Institutional Development: Forty Years of Experience.* Research Triangle Park, N.C.: Research Triangle Institute.

Schuster, Jay R., and Patricia K. Zingheim. 1992. *The New Pay: Linking Employee and Organizational Performance.* New York: Lexington Books.

Stiglitz, Joseph E. 1989. "Incentives, Information, and Organizational Design." Working Paper 2979. National Bureau of Economic Research, Cambridge.

Wade, Robert. 1990. *Governing the Market: Economic Theory and the Role of Government in East Asian Industrialization.* Princeton: Princeton University Press.

Wilson, James Q. 1989. *Bureaucracy: What Government Agencies Do and Why They Do It.* New York: Basic Books.

World Bank. 1993. *The East Asian Miracle: Economic Growth and Public Policy.* New York: Oxford University Press.

———. 1994. *Governance: The World Bank's Experience.* Washington, D.C.: The World Bank.

Wright, S. 1950. *Hart and the Chinese Customs.* Belfast: Mullan and Son.

Rational Compliance with Rationalized Bureaucracy

Margaret Levi and Richard Sherman

Bureaucracy is known best for its failures. Criticisms of state intervention in the economy are more often than not attacks on large, faceless, and wasteful bureaucracies. The ideology of deregulation in the advanced capitalist countries and the dismantling of state-owned enterprises in developing countries and in the previously communist states are means to transfer functions from government to the private sector in the name of efficiency. However, government bureaucracy is not disappearing, nor should it disappear. Economic and political development requires a complex network of institutional arrangements, which includes a high-quality bureaucracy, as measured by adherence to meritocratic standards in promotion and recruitment and by effective means of detecting and deterring improper practices.

In this chapter, we examine the connection between the design of bureaucratic institutions and quasi-voluntary compliance by citizens and firms subject to bureaucratic regulation (Levi 1988, 52 and passim). Quasi-voluntary compliance involves a choice to obey even if the individual costs of compliance outweigh the individual benefits, but it is a choice within a situation of sanctions against those who break the rules. Given a positive evaluation of the collective good, the process by which decisions are made, or both, quasi-voluntary compliance requires confidence that other citizens and firms are also likely to comply and that government actors will keep their policy promises. Quasi-voluntary compliance lowers the costs of governance by reducing monitoring and enforcement. Moreover, the trust in government actors that facilitates quasi-voluntary compliance also facilitates citizen tolerance of experiments and occasional mistakes by government managers.

The policy implications of this approach are clear: the preconditions for development are manipulable by the state, and a well-designed bureau-

This chapter builds on an IRIS working paper written by the authors with Edgardo Campos. Additional funding for the research for this chapter came from the Royalty Research Fund, University of Washington. We especially wish to thank Christopher Clague, Barbara Geddes, and Elinor Ostrom for their helpful comments.

cracy can contribute to a well-functioning economy. Less evident but equally important is the probability that the kind of cooperation essential for democracy requires the existence of both relatively competent and relatively fair administration.

Weber (1968) observes the simple correlation between a modern economy and a bureaucracy characterized by a functional definition of duties, meritocratic appointment, full-time devotion to administrative tasks, and relative insulation from society. Bureaucracies, for Weber, depend on the existence of a monetary economy, but they are also an important tool in the construction of advanced capitalism.

There are at least three major objections to the Weberian view, with which our thesis shares some features. First, the relationship between bureaucracy and industrialization may be suspect. Silberman (1993, 37–38) even argues that there is no such relationship, citing evidence of variation in both the form of bureaucracy and the timing of industrialization in France, Japan, Britain, and the United States. Second, the traditional Weberian view overemphasizes bureaucratic insulation from politics. Evans (1992, 148) suggests that development requires a "developmental" state characterized by a bureaucracy with the corporate coherence of the Weberian ideal type, relative insulation from the cacophony of societal demands, and sufficient "embeddedness" in society so that the bureaucrats possess "accurate intelligence, inventiveness, active agency, and sophisticated responsiveness to a changing economic reality." However, as Evans notes, such embeddedness may initially increase but later hinder state capacity to promote economic growth. Third, the Weberian approach to development, even as modified by Evans, fails to identify, and occasionally misstates, the mechanisms by which a competent and relatively impartial bureaucracy promotes development. What work does the bureaucracy do in these cases? How, precisely, does that work improve the prospects of economic and political development? Is bureaucracy the only kind of institution that can perform those roles?

In this chapter, we discuss the institutional features and mechanisms that support a bureaucracy capable of producing credible commitments and credible threats that make compliance in the long-term self-interest of those being asked to comply. In our model, the institutional design of the bureaucracy and its agents' behavior signal to actors in the private economy the likelihood that current effort in the form of compliance will yield future rewards if not always immediate benefits. The signals are believed because of institutional arrangements that enable bureaucrats to provide high-quality service and to make credible commitments.

Weber focuses on modern bureaucracy's dependence on an advanced economy. We emphasize the dependence of an advanced economy, and perhaps even a democracy, on a rationalized bureaucracy that promotes rational compliance. Citizen compliance is more frequent where bureaucrats are competent, impartial, and nonpredatory. Where bureaucrats are incompetent or corrupt, compliance is seldom a maximizing strategy for agents in the private economy, since bribery and illegal activity will tend to yield higher rewards. Noncompliance leads to additional waste and economic misallocation, since both concealment of illegal practices and enforcement of the law are costly. Moreover, widespread noncompliance renders even well-designed and legally enacted development strategies unlikely to succeed.

Section 1 discusses the logic of rational compliance in response to a rationalized bureaucracy. The features of a bureaucracy necessary to promote compliance are related to institutional design. We suggest that effective monitoring is only a part of what makes a bureaucracy competent and honest. Equally important are incentives and other motivational structures that induce an identification with and commitment to the development project.

Briefly, the logic of the argument is as follows:

1. Quasi-voluntary compliance by citizens, firms, and bureaucrats is possible only where there is a rationalized bureaucracy. In the absence of the conditions that support such a bureaucracy, the prospects for both development and democracy are reduced.

2. Governments can increase compliance with government regulations by making it rational for individuals and firms to comply. This requires the "right" incentives (and sanctions), but at least as important are assurances of long-term benefits and enhancement of expectations of rewards from rule adherence and cooperation.

3. Rational and quasi-voluntary compliance by citizens and firms depends on the existence of a rationalized bureaucracy whose agents are both relatively competent and relatively impartial. Incentives and sanctions contribute to the construction of a rationalized bureaucracy but are not sufficient. Bureaucrats may also act upon nonrational or only partially rational motivations. The institutional design must provide not only rewards and credible commitments but also the basis for a corporate culture or corporate community that promotes trust, self-monitoring, and extra initiative.

Our primary focus is on bureaucracies that engage in regulation. We suggest but do not yet explore extensions of this argument to bureaucracies aimed at production, such as state-owned enterprises (see Waterbury 1993), delivery and transfer agencies, or those that are primarily responsible for policy making.[1] Our argument builds on available contemporary, historical, and comparative accounts of bureaucracy, especially in postwar Asia and in the period of industrialization in the United States and Europe. We do not test our arguments. Rather, we lay out what needs to be tested. Nonetheless, the logic of our argument suggests some important strategies for promoting economic and political development.

This research highlights the significance of institutional (in this case, bureaucratic) design in development. Research on the newly industrializing and would-be-industrializing economies has disproportionately focused attention on the way specific policies contribute to economic performance. Our research recognizes the importance of sound policy while demonstrating that sound policy is insufficient if problems of institutional design and implementation are neglected. We provide evidence to refute the naive view taken in some of the rent-seeking literature that the public sector is necessarily debilitating to the economy. Instead, we demonstrate that the state can play a central role in facilitating the successful organization of markets without supplanting those markets in favor of a system of centralized control.

1   Rational Compliance

A rationalized system of public administration is part of the transition between a traditional society with ascriptive authority relations and a modern society based on depersonalized rules. Rationalizing an administrative system entails eliminating or minimizing the wasteful rent seeking of corruption. Beyond this well-known effect, however, a rationalized admin-

---

[1]See Dunleavy (1991, 181–91) for a description and analysis of different kinds of agencies. He tends to distinguish among several kinds that we group as regulatory agencies, but nonetheless his taxonomy is useful. Wilson (1989, 158–71) also offers a typology of agencies: production, procedural, craft, and coping. His distinctions, however, bear little relation to either common language or common categories.

istrative system has additional economic and political benefits.[2] A bureaucracy that is known to be competent and impartial fosters quasi-voluntary compliance (Levi 1988). The compliance, although obligated by law, is voluntary because citizens and firms prefer to comply and may do so even in situations where narrow—or at least shortsighted—self-interest counsels noncompliance. Quasi-voluntary compliance is an effect (perhaps intended, perhaps a by-product) of a bureaucracy's capacity to make credible commitments regarding the division of gains from cooperation and compliance and to confer on compliant firms and individuals a valuable reputational asset. In addition, rationalizing the bureaucracy can transform the relationship between citizens and the state. More citizens become potential "winners" in a competitive environment, and those citizens generally have a greater incentive to participate in regulatory decision making.

1.1   Bureaucracy and rational compliance

Among the conditions that foster economic and political development are institutional arrangements and property rights that promote productive uses of resources and that minimize social waste (North 1981, 1990; Levi 1988; North and Weingast 1989; Weingast 1993). Crucial are efficient government regulations that reduce rent seeking and provide incentives for growth. Given efficient government regulations, of equal importance is compliance with those regulations. The state's ability to specify and enforce property rights is always imperfect, and some specification of rights is always left in the private domain. This private ordering can be noncompliant, as in the informal sector, or it can be compliant. Noncompliant ordering entails inefficiencies (since resources are spent avoiding detection or punishment and since the threat of detection influences firms' choices of technology), and noncompliance weakens the power of the state to implement policies that foster development. Development requires not only an appropriate property-rights regime but also compliance and cooperation in implementing that regime.

An impartial and competent bureaucracy increases the attractiveness of quasi-voluntary compliance by creating the basis for long-term gains from cooperation. To the extent that firms and individuals have confidence that

---

[2]Although there is some disagreement about whether corruption is always wasteful (see, e.g., Leff 1964), the most recent and important work suggests that corruption is more distortionary than taxation (Shleifer and Vishny 1993) and negatively correlated with investment (Mauro 1995).

government agents will be consistent in their application of the rules and will be effective in delivering promised services, including enforcement of the rules on others, they are more likely to take risks. Such risks may take the form of investments, a willingness to engage in implicit contracts, or a willingness to trust strangers as trading partners.

For example, one effect of regulation is to make rules regarding the division of gains from exchange, but regulation is effective in facilitating exchange only to the extent the bureaucracy is impartial and honest. Let us take the case of product quality regulations. Product quality is often imperfectly observable in advance of purchase. In the absence of regulations on product quality, producers might produce low-quality products and misrepresent them as high-quality goods. As a result, the gains from exchange may accrue largely or entirely to producers, and purchasers can suffer absolute losses as a result of the exchange. Knowing this, purchasers will be unwilling to pay a premium for high-quality goods, and some potentially valuable market transactions will not take place.

In an unregulated market, this problem can be overcome if producers invest in their reputations (Klein and Leffler 1981).[3] Investment in nonsalvageable assets—that is, assets that lose their value if the firm that owns them goes out of business—serves as a commitment mechanism in markets characterized by imperfect information. A firm with investments in nonsalvageable assets is vulnerable to the actions of consumers. If the firm cheats on its implicit contract with consumers by producing low-quality goods, consumers can punish the firm by refusing to buy its products in the future. Since the value of the firm's nonsalvageable assets is forfeited in this scenario, the nonsalvageable investment serves as an investment in the firm's reputation, signaling the firm's commitment to produce high-quality goods.

A corrupt bureaucracy can impede the construction of signaling and commitment mechanisms that facilitate exchange.[4] Since a corrupt bureaucracy can act arbitrarily—for example, by choosing to shut down a firm, perhaps by revoking its license to operate—investment in reputation is risky.

---

[3]Technically, in the Klein-Leffler model firms receive "quasi rents" from purchasers; the rents are dissipated in the form of nonsalvageable assets.

[4]Signaling in this context is distinct from signaling of the Spence (1973) variety, which intends to provide information about immutable characteristics of the signaler. Here, signals provide information about the signaler's course of future behavior.

The value of reputation is determined not solely by the firm's relationship with purchasers but also by the firm's relationship with the bureaucracy. The market solution to the problem of product quality works precisely because producers who cheat purchasers by producing low-quality goods have something to lose, namely the value of their investments in reputation. For the same reason, firms with investments in reputation are more vulnerable to the actions of a corrupt bureaucracy. Their willingness to pay bribes grows along with the value of their reputations, since the costs of a revoked license or forced bankruptcy increase with investment in reputation. Knowing this, firms may choose not to make such investments. Curbs on corruption reduce impediments to signaling and commitment mechanisms. An impartial bureaucracy can commit credibly to enforcing regulations faithfully, and regulations thus have the (intended) effect of setting rules for the distribution of gains from exchange.

At the same time, compliance with regulations itself becomes available as a market-signaling mechanism. Under an impartial regulatory system, noncompliant firms may be punished, and in general their violation of regulations becomes public knowledge. Therefore, a firm's partners in exchange have information about the firm's history of compliance. This is significant because compliance with regulations is itself a nonsalvageable asset (see Yarbrough and Yarbrough 1986; Ayres and Braithwaite 1992, 22). If a compliant firm loses a share of its future income stream as a result of cheating its trading partners, investments made by the firm in regulatory compliance cannot be recouped. Therefore, compliance is among the nonsalvageable investments that a firm can make in order to gain a valuable reputation, as in the Klein-Leffler (1981) model. Compliance, in other words, acquires a market value under an impartial regulatory system.

Commitment, participation, and regulation-induced scarcity

The emergence of quasi-voluntary compliance is facilitated by public institutions that not only make demands of citizens but also provide them with something of value in return. The reputational effects of compliance discussed above can increase the incentives of citizens to comply with laws and regulations. The value of a reputation for compliance, however, depends in part on the quality of bureaucracy, especially its freedom from corruption. As bureaucracies become less corrupt, the value of compliance increases, and citizens find it more in their interest to participate in the construction of an effective regulatory regime.

Among the many functions of a bureaucracy is the management of regulation-induced scarcity, by which we mean the allocation of property rights or government services through regulation. Regulation-induced scarcity plays a well-known role in generating opportunities for corruption, with the allocation of licenses through bribery (Krueger 1974; Manion 1994) serving as the canonical example. The effects of regulation-induced scarcity are not, of course, entirely pernicious, since they have the legitimate function of managing externalities (e.g., environmental regulation) and prohibiting socially undesirable behavior (e.g., child labor restrictions). The discussion in the previous section indicates that regulation-induced scarcity, aside from its other effects, can play a role in the construction of signaling and commitment mechanisms that facilitate exchange. This section elaborates this idea and discusses problems related to the participation of firms and citizens in devising regulatory regimes.

For purposes of discussion, we employ the example of the bureaucratic regulation of business licenses, with revocation of the license serving as the deterrent to noncompliance. A licensing regime may play one or both of two principal functions: allocation of licenses and monitoring of regulated firms. A thoroughly corrupt licensing regime is one in which both allocation and revocation of licenses is determined by payment (or nonpayment) of bribes to bureaucrats. This system resembles a protection racket in which firms protect themselves against closure by providing a stream of bribe payments to the bureaucrats empowered to revoke business licenses. It is under such a system that signaling and commitment mechanisms are most problematic. Investment in reputation renders the firm hostage to a predatory bureaucracy, and such investment is thus likely to be small.

A less dramatic abuse of bureaucratic power is the allocation of licenses through bribery coupled with an impartial system of monitoring, in which only firms that violate laws face revocation of their licenses. In this case, it is not difficult to construct an argument that bribery can serve as a second-best allocation system (second to allocation based on faithful application of laws or, in some cases, second to no allocation system at all, as in the complete absence of regulation-induced scarcity). Just as investment in compliance with regulations can serve as a nonsalvageable asset, so can a bribe paid to a bureaucrat; if the firm cheats customers and as a result is forced out of business, the value of the bribe cannot be recouped. By this logic, the bribe may itself signal an investment in reputation.

However, this type of argument is suspect. Since bribery is everywhere officially prohibited, taking bribes is a risky strategy for bureaucrats. Therefore, bribery takes place in secret and on an individualized basis. Consumers can only guess at the bribe cost of a business license, and the signal that the license sends to consumers is murky at best. Such a system, however, is a substantial improvement over the bureaucratic protection racket. When continued operation of a business does not require a continuing stream of bribe payments, firms are not deterred from making private investments in reputation. The implication is that a first priority for bureaucratic reform is to clean up the bureaucracy's role in monitoring compliance. Tackling corruption at the level of license allocation, while important, is of a lower order of urgency.

Mirroring these two types of corrupt licensing regimes are two "clean" systems of regulation-induced scarcity. The first is the allocation of licenses by rule of law, absent credible monitoring and enforcement roles for the bureaucracy. Although this system is a better signaling device than allocation of licenses by bribes, it also offers existing businesses an avenue to restrict competition by pressing for more stringent licensing requirements for new applicants. "Cleaner" still is a system of impartiality and rule governance in both the allocation of licenses and the method of monitoring. This system maximizes the signaling value of a license, since it represents not only an up-front investment in reputation but also continuing investment in regulatory compliance.

The crucial feature of such a system is the linkage of the signaling value of compliance with the quality of the regulatory system. Such a system generates incentives for regulated firms to participate in rationalizing the regulatory system and in constructing an appropriate regulatory regime. Regulations that filter out firms unwilling to invest in long-term commitments confer reputational benefits on firms that comply. The rationalization of a regulatory system involves the creation of a system of rule enforcement that correctly identifies violators so that the reputational signal of compliance can be trusted by consumers. A regulatory system governed by impartiality in license allocation and monitoring is thus a valuable institutional arrangement from the perspective of the compliant firm.

The danger inherent in participation is, of course, regulatory capture. Firms subject to regulations can use their access to bureaucrats both to restrict competition and to eliminate or hobble restrictions that are socially desirable. Eliminating channels of private sector input into the rule-making process, however, may also eliminate the bureaucracy's ability to develop the type of relationship with firms that facilitates low-cost compliance. Developing a sustainable regulatory system of impartial administration and industry participation is thus likely to require a political system that is responsive to the needs of those outside of bureaucratic clienteles and capable of placing a check on regulatory capture.

A typology of compliance problems

Bureaucratic rationalization does not have the same effect on rates of compliance in all areas of regulation. The Weberian ideal of a hierarchical and centralized bureaucracy can actually create opportunities for certain types of corruption by the regulators as well as the regulated (see Rose-Ackerman 1978, 173–79). To understand better how the existence of bureaucracy might support the sort of compliance that promotes economic development, it is necessary to distinguish which features of the bureaucratic structure influence which types of compliance. To do this requires, first, a typology of compliance.

Compliance problems can be classified into four basic types, each with distinct implications for the state's ability to induce compliance. First, the behavior that the state seeks to regulate can be either visible and, hence, easy to monitor or imperfectly visible and costly to monitor. Second, the benefits of cooperation can be either purely nonexcludable or partially excludable. That is, a single individual's decision to cooperate can result in benefits that are purely social—as when a person contributes to an orderly community by refraining from theft and violence—or in benefits that accrue in part to society and in part to the cooperating individual. Combining these two variables yields four distinct ideal-typical compliance problems, as depicted in table 15.1.

In general, compliance is less problematic when some of the benefits of cooperation are excludable (Olson 1965), as in the lower cells of table 15.1 (cells III and IV). As the size of the excludable benefit to a cooperator increases, compliance problems are transformed from prisoner's dilemma situations into assurance or coordination problems. When the private, excludable benefit is very large, compliance or cooperation becomes trivial, since cooperative behavior emerges strictly as a result of the private payoff to cooperation (or the private punishment for noncooperation). The latter case corresponds to simple coercion and presumes the existence of a centralized enforcer capable of manipulating costs and benefits.

The upper cells of table 15.1 (cells I and II) represent the standard problem of collective goods provision.[5] What distinguishes them is ease of monitoring (by the state, in the case of centralized monitoring, or by

---

[5]We are assuming, for the moment, that citizens value the result of mutual cooperation such that the total benefits outweigh the total costs of cooperation for any individual. For those who do not, this is not a collective goods problem but a straightforward instance of punishment for breaking rules established by others.

Typology of Compliance Problems

Benefits	Compliance Difficult to Monitor	Compliance Easy to Monitor
Not excludable	Coercion with costly monitoring, I	Coercion; conditional cooperation, II
Partly excludable	Assurance with self-enforcing contracts, III	Assurance with conditional cooperation, IV

individuals, in the case of decentralized monitoring). Where individual compliance is difficult to monitor (cell I), achievement of the collective good generally requires coercion. Taxation is a case in point—the state monitors compliance at a cost (and punishes noncooperators), but the state achieves economies of scale through centralized monitoring. Absent this centralized monitoring capacity, cooperation is unlikely since each individual must spend excessive resources monitoring each other's behavior. Even so, there is more compliance, at least in advanced industrial democracies, than an account based only on narrow self-interest can explain. Appeals to ethical standards and norms of fairness may account for a large part of the difference (Levi 1988; Pinney and Scholz 1992).

In cell II, where benefits are purely nonexcludable but low-cost decentralized monitoring is possible, compliance may be achieved by conditional cooperation. Citizens can condition their choices on the observed past behavior of others. For well-known reasons (Taylor 1987), conditional cooperation becomes more problematic as the size of the group becomes larger. When this is the case and when the polity cannot be federated into sufficiently small groups, coercion is the predominant solution.

The organization of informal sector markets, in which the state cannot generally be called upon to enforce property rights, provides an example of the compliance problems represented by cell II of table 15.1. Peddlers who occupy public property, perhaps illegally, have the incentive to locate in favorable locations and to monopolize the use of these sites. However, if many individuals seek to occupy the same site, resources are wasted in the competition, and property rights may be insecure. De Soto (1989) provides an account of the ways in which peddlers solve this problem through decentralized assignment of property rights.

A credible and competent bureaucracy is able to transform some compliance problems from prisoner's dilemma situations into coordination

A credible and competent bureaucracy is able to transform some compliance problems from prisoner's dilemma situations into coordination situations, and it is able in some cases to facilitate cooperation by providing centralized monitoring. First, the bureaucracy can confer reputational benefits on those who comply with regulations. These benefits are an excludable good available only to cooperators. Second, the bureaucracy has superior powers of monitoring. Through inspections, the imposition of fines, and issuance or suspension of business licenses, it provides public information about the behavior of firms and individuals in the economy. Even if the state does not have the coercive power to eliminate noncompliance, it can facilitate decentralized monitoring through these reputational effects if the bureaucracy is credible and competent.

A reputation for compliance, along with licenses that assist in decentralized monitoring, is of value only if gained through interaction with a reputable bureaucracy. If the bureaucracy is corrupt, a disreputable firm can gain licenses and operate free of government interference through bribery. This type of "compliance"—in which official approval results from rent seeking rather than from the honest application of rules—confers no reputational benefits on successful rent seekers. In addition, the monitoring function of the bureaucracy is ineffective, since it is public knowledge that possession of a license or a clean record of compliance is meaningless and may have been bought rather than earned.

1.2   The bureaucracy, the citizen, and the state

In this section we address three types of transformation in the relationship between citizen and state that a rationalized administrative system fosters. One involves the citizen as an economic agent and the citizen's expected income under corrupt versus rationalized administration. The second is a political-economic transformation that occurs as more citizens become potential gainers under a rationalized system. The third is mainly a political one involving the citizen's incentive to seek to influence the rule-making process as the administrative system becomes rationalized. Through each of these transformations the emergence of quasi-voluntary compliance becomes more likely, as citizens find the administrative system to be capable of providing a stream of benefits to those who comply.

Citizens as economic agents

Every bureaucracy takes actions that create winners and losers. Rationalized bureaucracies, however, do this in a fundamentally different way than corrupt ones. A corrupt bureaucracy allocates benefits on the basis of bribes and personal relationships, selecting specific individuals as winners and losers. A rationalized bureaucracy takes actions that influence individuals' incomes indirectly by implementing policies that influence the value of specific assets. Under a rationalized system, the citizen's identity loses some of its significance in the citizen-state relationship, and the citizen's economic behavior gains significance.

An implication of this difference between corrupt and rationalized bureaucracy is that the object of citizens' competitive behavior changes when bureaucracy is rationalized. Under a corrupt bureaucracy, citizens compete for favoritism. Under a rationalized system, citizens compete for assets that become relatively valuable due to the legislative and administrative actions. If favoritism is interpreted to mean that the assets of successful bribe payers acquire extraordinary value, then it is obvious that only a minority of citizens can receive favorable treatment. Under a rationalized system, the competition for valuable assets does not have the zero-sum character of the competition for favoritism under a corrupt system. For this, reason, we expect that rationalizing the bureaucracy creates more winners than losers in the competition for valued assets.

Citizens as potential winners under a rationalized system

Because corrupt bureaucracies directly influence the value of individuals' incomes, citizens are either losers or gainers under a corrupt system: a single dimension (their identity or their success in bribing regulators) is an important determinant of their income. However, individuals are differentiated along a number of dimensions not taken account of by the corrupt system, among them the content of their assets. Since the actions of a rationalized administrative system affect the relative value of assets, citizens are potential gainers (and, of course, potential losers) with respect to actions taken by or legislation implemented by the bureaucracy.

A system in which many (preferably most or all) individuals are potential winners is more stable than a system in which some or most are permanent losers. Przeworski (1991) clarifies this logic in regard to participation in government. One of the reasons that democratic systems of government survive is that current losers still face the possibility of gaining influence in government in the future. If a group is denied the possibility of influence, it has no interest in maintaining the system of government. This logic extends to the administrative system as well; a system that creates a permanent class of losers creates a group that has no interest in the maintenance of the current administrative (and perhaps political) system. The possibility of future gain under an administrative system gives the citizen a stake in the maintenance of that system, even if not all the actions of the bureaucracy benefit the citizen.

Rationalized bureaucracy and citizen participation

Under a corrupt administrative system, any influence a citizen might choose to exert over the policy-making process is wasted; a purely corrupt bureaucracy does not implement policies so much as it finds profit in permitting noncompliance with them. Policy initiatives will have little impact if the implementers of the policy fail to comply.

Under a rationalized system, policy initiative and citizen participation are valuable. The results of such efforts stand a chance of becoming not only statutory law but also real practice. A rationalized bureaucracy is therefore part of a transformation in the political relationship between citizen and state. Political participation becomes more valuable to the citizen as the bureaucracy becomes rationalized.

1.3   Quasi-voluntary compliance

Rationalized bureaucracy may also activate other and only partially rational incentives for compliance and cooperation. By increasing commitment to the goals of bureaucratic regulation and by increasing confidence in the relative honesty and competence of the bureaucrats, rationalized bureaucracy engenders a propensity to cooperate. The end result will be quasi-voluntary compliance (Levi 1988); individuals will comply both because they prefer to and because of sanctions and incentives that appeal to narrow self-interest.

Bureaucracy promotes quasi-voluntary compliance through several mechanisms. First, an impartial bureaucracy is relatively likely to promote and adhere to norms of fairness. Norms of fairness arise in circumstances that bring "an individual face to face with the same individual over a whole sequence of interactions" (Coleman 1990b, 254) but only if there is a horizontal relationship of relative equality (Putnam 1993, chap. 6) or a legal commitment to relatively equitable treatment. The existence of such norms signals the likely responses of those who have to interact.

Second, the regularity of interactions between bureaucrats and the citizens and firms they regulate produces a network of social relations in which a trustworthy reputation carries benefits. For the bureaucrat, this translates into superior access to information from private citizens or firms, an increased likelihood of successful implementation, and the willingness of the regulated to tolerate occasional experiments and mistakes. For the regulated, it translates into a higher probability of receiving licenses, contracts, and other government-provided goods for which a good reputation matters (and which themselves contribute to the reputation of firms). This line of argument is analogous to that of Putnam (1993) and others (see Yamagishi and Yamagishi 1994, 137–40; Coleman, 1990a, 300–24; Granovetter 1985) who argue that a dense network of social relations is a source of social capital in the form of trust and norms of reciprocity.[6]

2   Institutional Design

Recognizing the benefits of quasi-voluntary compliance for economic and political development and revealing the relationship between rational compliance and rationalized bureaucracy is only the beginning. The next step involves actually designing a public bureaucracy so as to ensure its competence, relative impartiality, and restraint and to promote what Clague (1993) labels "effort, initiative, and responsibility." A recent World Bank report (1993; see also Campos and Root, forthcoming), discussing the experience of the East Asian newly industrializing countries, searches for the aspects of bureaucracy that correlate with economic growth. What emerges are proper incentives, monitoring and sanctions, asset specificity, and reputation. Relevant institutional arrangements include (1) selecting a qualified pool of civil servants by filtering out those without the requisite skills, (2) linking promotion to performance while in office, (3) creating a well-defined and appropriately valued career path for bureaucrats, and (4) sanctioning bureaucrats found to be engaging in improper practices. The first two items on this list promote competence and the last two promote relative honesty. Linking hiring to qualifications and promotion to performance fosters the development of technical skills and expertise and signals the consequent commitment of bureaucrats to effective implementation of policy. The establishment of a well-defined career path for bureaucrats and of rewards for long years of service enhances investment in the job.

---

[6]Yamagishi and Yamagishi (1994) make a distinction between trust and assurance. The latter follows from regular and repeat interactions within institutional arrangements that sanction defectors and noncooperators. Trust, on the other hand, carries risks. A reputation for trustworthiness reduces the risks to a potential trading partner and is particularly important in conditions of social uncertainty. It is also a "booster" for moving out of commitment relationships and into a larger and more impersonal marketplace. They offer survey evidence to indicate that the Japanese have more assurance and the Americans more trust.

Bureaucrats are unlikely to jeopardize that valuable asset by engaging in improper practices, especially if they face sanctions for doing so. The well-defined career path, coupled with competition for posts, confers a scarcity rent upon a civil service career that bureaucrats will act to protect. Although corrupt civil servants also have investments in their posts,[7] the means to maximizing their ends is quite different where the incentives are for corruption rather than for relative honesty. Together, these factors also insulate bureaucrats from the demands of both very powerful governmental officials and powerful societal actors. Such insulation, or at least some form of bureaucratic autonomy, may be essential for the evolution of the kind of bureaucratic state capacity on which successful economic development policies rest.[8]

Incentives organized around reputation are powerful in public bureaucracies. Whatever assumption we make about the utility that bureaucrats maximize—personal income, budgets, or bureau shaping (Dunleavy 1991)—an institutional design that promises rewards to a reputation for honesty and competence will lead bureaucrats to improved performance. Large investments in maintaining and promoting civil service careers are comparable to purchases of visible, nonsalvageable assets. If high-quality civil servants receive adequate rewards for their efforts, then outsiders can expect a bureaucrat's nonsalvageable investment in a civil service career to signal credibility and trustworthiness. High-quality civil servants may be more costly to recruit and retain than those without equivalent merit, but they are more likely to provide good services.

These features in and of themselves only rehearse the Weberian ideal, modified slightly by the recognition of the importance of reputation and asset specificity. The addition of certain findings from transaction cost analysis may clarify why Weberian principles are important and effective, but they do not provide a satisfying recipe for institutional design. The imposition of the traditional Weberian bureaucracy, whose predominant features are hierarchical authority and selection and promotion by merit is not enough to promote the kind of behavior among bureaucrats that will lead

---

[7]Hilton Root pointed this out to us.

[8]There is an increasingly large literature that makes some form of this argument. See, for example, Campos and Root (forthcoming); Bates and Krueger (1993); Evans (1992); Geddes (1994); Grindle (1977); Haggard and Kaufman (1992, 3–37); and Wade (1990).

to either high-quality service or citizen compliance.[9] The design of bureaucratic institutions so they suit their regulatory purposes and so they can respond to their current and changing political economic environments is also critical. "Getting the incentives right" is only the beginning. A highly effective bureaucracy is one that evokes not only competence and honesty among its employees but also sustained extra effort and initiative. Its design includes a structure of costs, benefits, and monitoring that appeal to immediate and narrow self-interest and, concurrently, create an investment in the long-term success of the agency.

2.1   Corporate culture and corporate community

The new organizational and institutional economics stresses the importance of self-enforcing contracts and credible commitments. In public bureaucracies, the creation and maintenance of self-enforcing contracts and credible commitments depend upon the establishment of either a "corporate culture" or a "corporate community" within the bureaucracy. The principal-agent approach demonstrates that proper incentives are important, as are sanctions and monitoring. The literature offers important guidance as to which incentives and sanctions work in what situations, but the focus has been almost exclusively on constraining or using short-term and narrow self-interest to enhance the ends of the firm.

Two recent arguments take the literature on the firm in a new direction by focusing on long-term interests and on commitments to the interests of the organization as well as individual self-interest. Using the insights from iterated game theory, Kreps (1990, 90–143) and Miller (1992) reach two related, although distinct, conclusions about mechanisms by which to improve the performance of employees in firms. Kreps identifies two central problems that organizational leadership confronts: (1) assuring potential trading partners and hierarchical inferiors that their trust and cooperation will be repaid—and not abused, and (2) dealing with unforeseen contingencies not covered by contractual terms. The process by which corporate management signals and maintains this reputation and deals with uncertainties is through establishment of a "corporate culture," a set of consistent and simple principles that guide its behavior.

---

[9]Wilson (1989) demonstrates in case after case that organization and tactics are at least as important as the attributes, training, and professional commitments of bureaucrats. He discusses only the United States, but his observations are probably generalizable.

Miller also uses iterated game theory, but he relies as well on experimental evidence. He concludes that no set of incentives will motivate employees adequately and no institutional design can solve all the problems of monitoring. He stresses the importance of trustworthy leadership and of a multiplicity of goals. Unlike Kreps, he models organizational behavior and strategies that rely on motivations other than narrowly defined self-interest. In fact, what he argues for (although he does not label it as such) is a corporate community. These are individuals whose fates and sense of self are bound up in each other and in the service of some corporate end.

2.2 Creating a corporate culture and community within the bureaucracy

Both of these approaches offer means to promote an identification of employees with their firms and managers. Recent work on public bureaucracy recognizes the importance of this identification and of the consequent esprit de corps (Dunleavy 1991; Clague 1993, 1994; Taylor 1994; Waterbury 1993). Firms and public bureaucracies are not exactly the same, however. First, public bureaucrats usually depend on nonmaterial as well as material incentives. Second, public bureaucracies are more likely to suffer from problems created by the existence of multiple principals. Third, public bureaucracies require a link between agents and those they regulate that has a different character than that between employees of firms and their clients. Together, these problems suggest the need for alternatives to traditional hierarchy as means of both encouraging and monitoring agents and the need for reconceptualizing both bureaucratic autonomy and regulatory capture.

The employees of both firms and public bureaucracies respond to the incentives of salaries and promotions and to the sanctions of layoffs and demotions. However, there is considerable evidence that senior public officials in highly industrialized democracies, once they are assured of a certain level of income, care more about maximizing the quality of their work life than their incomes. They are likely to seek a collegial atmosphere close to the center of power (Dunleavy 1991, 200–2). At the lower ends of the bureaucratic employment ladder, relative job security and service orientation may be important motivators.

Equally important, for most public bureaucracies neither the standard for measuring output nor the principal-agent relationships are clear.[10] This makes rewarding performance extremely problematic. A

---

[10]This is one of Waterbury's (1993) central points.

public bureaucracy has a plethora of principals, including but not limited to taxpayers, legislatures, government executives, and ministers. Each of these sets of actors has a different mission. Even in the case of state-owned enterprises with measurable products, the ends include political goals that make it hard to assess bureaucratic effectiveness. Rarely do any of the principals have an incentive sufficient to overcome the free-rider problem; they have difficulty in coordinating to establish either a measure of performance or an effective means of monitoring. The end result is weak penalties for managerial performance (Waterbury 1993, 109–11). Where a means to measure the performance of the agency and to tie rewards of high-ranking bureaucratic managers to agency performance is missing, bureaucrats engage in protective or political strategies to move them up the corporate ladder.[11]

One promising approach to creating a work environment conducive to good performance stresses embedding bureaucrats in the local communities they are supposed to be regulating. This is Wade's (1994) explanation of why the Korean irrigation bureaucracy is so much more successful than the Indian one. Ostrom (1990, and this volume), Esman and Uphoff (1984), and others make similar claims for other localities. A related argument concerning regulatory bureaucracies in the advanced capitalist democracies is the institutionalization of a formal role for the groups being regulated and for those who have an interest in the success of the regulation (Ayres and Braithwaite 1992). Braithwaite (1995) goes one step further. She finds that regulatees who have strong social bonds with the regulators are more likely to be compliant than those who reject the goals of the regulating bureaucracy and feel no personal ties with the regulators. Institutional designs that emphasize building a relationship between the regulators and the regulated may not enhance impartiality and may promote capture, but they do seem to enhance competence and performance, at least for certain kinds of problems.

Another and related argument is the reduction of hierarchy and the establishment of a more level work environment (Miller and Cook 1994; also see Taylor 1994). Miller and Cook offer a fairly compelling case that, at least for certain kinds of tasks, the devolution of increased responsibility

---

[11]This is a problem, generally, of public bureaucracy. For example, one of the current complaints about university administrators is that they engage in popular, attention-getting programs that are vita-enhancing but that do little to build morale or quality at the university—which they are using as a stepping-stone to the next appointment.

to agents is more efficient in terms of both the quality and the quantity of the work done. Wilson (1989, 172) makes no such case, but he does argue that "managing any organization means not only finding incentives of high value and distributing them so as to reward the proper behavior but also providing access to them in ways that comport with the members' sense of equity."

Both Wilson (1989), in discussing American bureaucracy, and Geddes (1994), in discussing developmental bureaucracy, emphasize the importance of agency autonomy—as, of course, does Weber. However, after a detailed case study of reform efforts in Brazil, Geddes (81–82) concludes that, "The kind of autonomy that actually contributes to better economic performance is not autonomy from interest groups but instead autonomy from politically motivated pressures to distribute the resources needed for effective policymaking and implementation." She seems to share with Evans (1992, 46–49; also see Haggard and Kaufman 1992) a recognition of the importance of insulation in the earlier stages of development and some later embeddedness of bureaucrats within the society they are regulating, but her rationales are somewhat different. She argues for autonomy from political exchanges that undermine the selection and promotion of bureaucrats by merit and that use up crucial resources. She also argues for the positive democratic effects of popular demands for particular policies.

All of these approaches are in marked contrast to the Weberian, which is both hierarchical in structure and insulated from the pressures and politics of the public it is serving. They suggest important new directions for research on bureaucratic design.

2.3   Caveats

Discussions of bureaucracy are cyclical in their emphasis, first, on tightly supervised, hierarchical organization and, then, on the development of an attractive and equitable work environment. The advantages of the first approach are, following Weber, its insulation both from clients and, in its most advanced forms, from politicians. Furthermore, the Weberian bureaucracy is characterized by impartial treatment of clients and by promotion by merit. Thus, in principle, it enhances equity, honesty, and competence. In practice, however, this model of bureaucracy may evoke resistance. Such bureaucracies antagonize the regulated where tasks are not clearly specified (Wilson 1989; Ayres and Braithwaite 1992), where the resources to meet the tasks are not adequate (Lipsky 1980), or where the regulators treat the regulated as enemies (Lipsky 1980; Scholz 1984a, 1984b; Braithwaite 1995).

A response has been to emphasize creating a pleasant and cooperative work environment for bureaucrats and promoting a stronger bond
between bureaucrats and those being regulated. Compliance may go up, but
the price may be a cozy relationship between an agency and its clients that
makes access difficult for new entrants, encourages inequitable treatment of
those outside the core group, and facilitates capture of the regulators.

3   Conclusion

Bureaucracy is a subject of long-standing scholarly interest. Yet, as
this chapter demonstrates (also see Clague 1994), we are only beginning to
acquire an adequate understanding of its effects, its best designs, and the
political structures most compatible with an effective bureaucracy.
Nonetheless, we have made some progress in understanding bureaucracy as
an institution capable of promoting economic development. We have
considerable confidence that a strong empirical connection exists between
rationalized administrative systems and economic performance. Few
economies have developed successfully in the absence of a rationalized
bureaucracy, and countries with highly corrupt bureaucracies tend to exhibit
low levels of economic performance. The argument here isolates some of
the mechanisms through which rationalized bureaucracy contributes to
citizen compliance and explores the central issues involved in the establishment of a rationalized bureaucracy.

We also know that a rationalized administrative system is politically
demanding. It requires the insulation of regulators from direct political
manipulation, since political manipulation substitutes political partiality for
bureaucratic corruption. It requires policies effective in promoting economic
growth; otherwise, bureaucrats will be unable to sustain or implement the
policies. These requirements might explain why many states with successful
economic and administrative systems have given bureaucrats substantial
authority to formulate policy in addition to simple regulatory authority.

Although politically demanding, a rationalized bureaucracy is also
politically effective. A rationalized bureaucracy not only insures against the
willful subversion of state policies, it also contributes to a willingness on the
part of citizens and firms to comply with state policies. While some
political-economic systems can survive widespread noncompliance, none
thrives on it. Through its influence on the creation of quasi-voluntary
compliance, the institutional design of the bureaucracy provides a crucial
connection between development strategies and development itself.

References

Ayres, Ian, and John Braithwaite. 1992. *Responsive Regulation*. Oxford: Oxford University Press.

Bates, Robert H., and Anne O. Krueger, eds. 1993. *Political and Economic Interactions in Economic Policy Reform*. Oxford: Blackwell.

Braithwaite, Valerie. 1995. "Games of Engagement: Postures within the Regulatory Community." Working Paper. Administration, Compliance and Governability Program, Australian National University.

Campos, Edgardo, and Hilton Root. Forthcoming. *Rethinking the Asian Miracle: Institutions, Leadership, and the Principle of Shared Growth*. New York: Oxford University Press.

Clague, Christopher. 1993. "Rule Obedience, Organizational Loyalty, and Economic Development." *Journal of Institutional Theoretical Economics* 149: 393–414.

———. 1994. "Bureaucracy and Economic Development." *Structural Change and Economic Dynamics* 5: 273–91. IRIS Reprint 57.

Coleman, James. 1990a. *Foundations of Social Theory*. Cambridge: Harvard University Press.

———. 1990b. "Norm-Generating Structures." In *The Limits of Rationality,* ed. Karen Cook and Margaret Levi. Chicago: University of Chicago Press.

de Soto, Hernando. 1989. *The Other Path*. New York: Harper and Row.

Dunleavy, Patrick. 1991. *Democracy, Bureaucracy and Public Choice*. New York: Prentice-Hall.

Esman, Milton, and Norman Uphoff. 1984. *Local Organizations: Intermediaries in Rural Development*. Ithaca: Cornell University Press.

Evans, Peter. 1992. "The State as Problem and Solution: Predation, Embedded Autonomy, and Structural Change." In *The Politics of Economic Adjustment,* ed. Stephan Haggard and Robert R. Kaufman. Princeton: Princeton University Press.

Geddes, Barbara. 1994. *The Politicians' Dilemma*. Berkeley: University of California Press.

Granovetter, Mark. 1985. "Economic Action, Social Structure, and Embeddedness." *American Journal of Sociology* 91: 481–510.

Grindle, Merilee Serrill. 1977. *Bureaucrats, Politicians, and Peasants in Mexico*. Berkeley: University of California Press.

Haggard, Stephan, and Robert R. Kaufman, eds. 1992. *The Politics of Economic Adjustment International Constraints, Distributive Conflicts, and the State.* Princeton: Princeton University Press, 3–37.

Klein, Benjamin and Keith B. Leffler. 1981. "The Role of Market Forces in Assuring Contractual Performance." *Journal of Political Economy* 89: 615–41.

Kreps, David M. 1990. *Perspectives on Positive Political Economy.* New York: Cambridge University Press.

Krueger, Anne O. 1974. "The Political Economy of the Rent-Seeking Society." *American Economic Review* 64: 291–303.

Leff, Nathaniel. 1964. "Economic Development through Bureaucratic Corruption." *American Behavioral Scientist* 8: 8–14.

Levi, Margaret. 1988. *Of Rule and Revenue.* Berkeley: University of California Press.

Lipsky, Michael. 1980. *Street-Level Bureaucracy.* New York: Russell Sage.

Manion, Melanie. 1994. "Corruption by Design: Bribery in Chinese Enterprise Licensing." Paper prepared for the American Political Science Association Meetings, New York.

Mauro, Paulo. 1995. "Corruption, Country Risk, and Growth." *Quarterly Journal of Economics* 110: 681–742.

Miller, Gary. 1992. *Managerial Dilemmas.* New York: Cambridge University Press.

Miller, Gary, and Kathleen Cook. 1994. "Leveling and Leadership in States and Firms." Paper prepared for conference "What Is Institutionalism Now?" University of Maryland, October 14–15.

North, Douglass C. 1981. *Structure and Change in Economic History.* New York: Norton.

———. 1990. *Institutions, Institutional Change and Economic Performance.* Cambridge: Cambridge University Press.

North, Douglass C., and Barry R. Weingast. 1989. "Constitutions and Commitment: The Evolution of Institutions Governing Public Choice in Seventeenth-Century England." *Journal of Economic History* 49: 809–32.

Olson, Mancur. 1965. *The Logic of Collective Action.* Cambridge: Harvard University Press.

Ostrom, Elinor. 1990. *Governing the Commons: The Evolution of Institutions for Collective Action.* Cambridge: Cambridge University Press.

Pinney, Neil, and John Scholz. 1992. "Can Cognitive Consistency Cure Collective Dilemmas? Self-Interest versus Duty to Pay Taxes." Working Paper 28. Russell Sage Foundation, New York.

Przeworski, Adam. 1991. *Democracy and the Market.* New York: Cambridge University Press.

Putnam, Robert. 1993. *Making Democracy Work: Civic Traditions in Modern Italy.* Princeton: Princeton University Press.

Rose-Ackerman, Susan. 1978. *Corruption.* New York: Academic Press.

Scholz, John. 1984a. "Deterrence, Cooperation, and the Ecology of Regulatory Enforcement." *Law and Society Review* 18: 179–224.

————. 1984b. "Voluntary Compliance and Regulatory Policy." *Law and Policy* 6: 385–404.

Shleifer, Andrei, and Robert W. Vishny. 1993. "Corruption." *Quarterly Journal of Economics* 108: 599–617.

Silberman, Bernard S. 1993. *The Cages of Reason.* Chicago: University of Chicago Press.

Spence, A. Michael. 1973. "Job Market Signaling." *Quarterly Journal of Economics* 87: 355-74.

Taylor, Michael. 1987. *The Possibility of Cooperation.* Cambridge: Cambridge University Press.

————. 1994. "Good Government: On Hierarchy, Social Capital, and the Limitations of Rational Choice Theory." Paper prepared for Wesquassett Workshop, July 8–9.

Wade, Robert. 1990. *Governing the Market.* Princeton: Princeton University Press.

————. 1994. "Organizational Determinants of a 'High-Quality Civil Service': Bureaucratic and Technological Incentives in Canal Irrigation in India and Korea." Background Paper. World Bank, Washington, D.C.

Waterbury, John. 1993. *Exposed to Innumerable Delusions: Public Enterprise and State Power in Egypt, India, Mexico, and Turkey.* New York: Cambridge University Press.

Weber, Max. 1968 (1922). "Bureaucracy." In *Economy and Society,* ed. Guenther Roth and Claus Wittich. New York: Bedminister.

Weingast, Barry R. 1993. "The Political Foundations of Democracy and the Rule of Law." IRIS, College Park, Md.

Wilson, James Q. 1989. *Bureaucracy: What Government Agencies Do and Why They Do It.* New York: Basic Books.

World Bank. 1993. *The East Asian Miracle: Economic Growth and Public Policy.* New York: Oxford University Press.

Yamagishi, Toshio, and Midori Yamagishi. 1994. "Trust and Commitment in the United States and Japan." *Motivation and Emotion*, 18: 129–66.

Yarbrough, Beth V., and Robert M. Yarbrough. 1986. "Reciprocity, Bilateralism, and Economic 'Hostages': Self-Enforcing Agreements in International Trade." *International Studies Quarterly* 30: 7–21.

VI   IMPLICATIONS FOR DEVELOPMENT PRACTICE

16   Putting Institutional Economics to Work: From Participation to Governance

Robert Picciotto

The new agenda for sustainable development calls for a mix of market-friendly, people-friendly, and environment-friendly policies. It is equidistant from the failed interventionist doctrines of the left and the "state minimalist" precepts of the right (Streeten 1993). Given complex and highly differentiated development problems, policy makers need relevant support from the academy in their search for pragmatic, tailor-made solutions. In particular, the design of responsive and accountable institutions has become a central preoccupation of practitioners. Therefore, institutional economics has been put to work to enhance the impact of development programs and projects. In this context, section 1 describes the privileged role of projects in development assistance; section 2 proposes a systematic approach to their organizational design; section 3 deals with the governance dimension of development assistance; and section 4 attempts a global synthesis.

1   The Institutional Economics of Development Projects: The Project as an Institution

Development is a long-term, incremental process. A key instrument of development is the investment project.[1] Projects aim at finite, specific, monitorable objectives. They incorporate resources commensurate to the task and aim to overcome market failures. They are the building blocks of development programs, and their selection for external assistance implies that they have priority for concentrated attention.

Thus, according to Hirschman (1967), projects are "privileged particles of development." They are meant to address problems that are especially relevant to the achievement of priority development objectives. They are expected to produce benefits well in excess of their costs, including the opportunity cost of the capital invested in them.[2] Often, they bring in

---

[1]It is consecrated as the major vehicle of World Bank assistance by the Bank's Articles of Agreement.

[2]The basic project evaluation methodology used by the World Bank is summarized in World Bank (1994, 57–58).

new technologies and skills or help to capitalize on forward and backward linkages. Their indirect and external benefits are as important as their direct benefits. Conversely, they frequently involve unintended social and environmental costs. The project achieved initial prominence as a development instrument because it reflected the experience of wartime planning. The presumption of a direct and unambiguous relationship between public expenditure inputs and development results made it easy to "retail" development programs for external support and was consistent with the blueprint approach to development then in vogue. Thus, development projects were originally conceived as "one-shot" efforts geared to physical investment carried out over a limited period of time. Such a straightforward approach appeared well adapted to public sector activity.

As development experience accumulated, it became evident that policies and institutions matter more than public investment. In turn, the requirements of a new development agenda emphasizing social, environmental and institutional concerns led to gradual changes in the very conception of what constitutes a project. Increasingly, projects came to be viewed as policy experiments and as instruments of institutional reform. Precisely because the project proved a flexible tool, adaptable to changing priorities, it has survived as an effective and influential development institution.

1.1   Project modalities

The institutional architecture of projects reflects the principles of economic organization elaborated by business economists (Milgrom and Roberts 1992). Fundamentally, a project is a set of contracts linking principals and agents, such as owners, employees, contractors, consultants, and beneficiaries. An overarching contract also links the country and the external development agency in the form of a negotiated project agreement that incorporates rewards and penalties. Standard clauses define rules for the procurement of goods, the disbursement of funds, the auditing of accounts, the evaluation of impact, and so on. Tailor-made clauses raise the costs of noncompliance with respect to project-specific performance objectives.

Incentives for effective performance are embedded in project agreements. Reporting requirements provide for the monitoring of contract compliance. Disbursements may be suspended or project loans canceled if misprocurement takes place or if fundamental provisions embedded in the agreements are violated. Conversely, effective project performance produces positive spillover effects, for example with respect to the use of project savings, the provision of implementation support, or the financing of "repeater" projects.

1.2   Project dilemmas

Moral hazard is a central preoccupation of development lenders. For reasons of efficiency and reciprocity, the cooperative handling of unexpected problems is the norm. Yet, opportunistic behavior must be discouraged. While relatively minor infractions are not penalized, egregious free riding is inhibited by incentives and penalties. These considerations translate into transaction costs. Some are borne by the borrower, others by the development agency. The benefits of development learning arising out of individual projects are shared throughout the membership. At their best, projects act as pathfinders for the overall development enterprise.

The familiar trade-offs explored by business economists—with respect to the depth of monitoring versus the capacity constraints affecting information processing, the degree of contractual completeness versus the resort to performance incentives, and the demandingness of performance standards versus the risks of adverse selection—are routinely faced in development assistance operations.

1.3   An evolving development instrument

Projects tend to reflect the development conceptions of their time. As long as planning dominated development practice, projects were perceived as slices of a public investment program. Their design was geared to the achievement of physical goals and government expenditure targets. Optimization was sought through systems analysis. Project preparation focused on issues of size, physical characteristics, and technical parameters. Economic analysis concentrated on shadow pricing to compensate for market distortions. In short, projects reflected the then prevalent production function metaphor of development.

Once the neoclassical resurgence set in, projects no longer took economic distortions for granted and, instead, began to address the policies that created them. New lending instruments were forged to provide quick-disbursing assistance explicitly targeted at policy adjustment. Thus, projects have become more demanding, complex, and process oriented to respond to the remarkable enrichment of a development agenda that now encompasses social and environmental concerns and also aims at greater participation. Projects increasingly incorporate policy and institution-building features. This is producing more ambitious operations, involving higher benefits but also higher transaction costs and risks (World Bank 1995). In response, improved internal management programs have been introduced to manage portfolio risks, to enhance the development impact of projects, and to streamline lending procedures (World Bank 1993). The very cycle through which projects are conceived and implemented is being reconsidered (Picciotto and Weaving 1994).

These shifts are consistent with the precepts of institutional economics. The problem of imperfect commitment to project objectives having been identified as a major cause of unsatisfactory development outcomes, more effective routines of project preparation and approval directed at building borrower "ownership" emerged (Johnson and Wasty 1993). Information asymmetries having been found to affect the development impact of projects, more rigorous inspection and evaluation arrangements have been put in place (World Bank 1993b). The streamlining of internal information flows, shifts of administrative resources toward client relations, strengthening of management accountability for results, and tighter budget policies have come to dominate development agency reforms. These measures aim to enhance the incentives for successful development performance and to lower transaction costs.

2   The Fundamentals of Institutional Design

However astute the contractual arrangements, however tight the monitoring, and however relevant the objectives of development assistance, projects are highly vulnerable to implementation dysfunctions and poor organizational designs. Institutional economists have yet to focus directly on such issues. The balance of this chapter suggests a possible approach to this challenge.

2.1   Choosing among institutional alternatives

Just as reorienting the role ascribed to the state in economic management is a recurring feature of macroeconomic adjustment, the judicious assignment of responsibilities to the public, private, and voluntary sectors is critical to the design of institutional arrangements at the project level. Traditionally, the institutional design of projects was dominated by an a priori public sector orientation. As government capacity and fiscal constraints came to light, there was greater emphasis on mobilizing private resources for development. At the same time, in response to pressing social and environmental problems, voluntary organizations multiplied and attracted substantial development funding. The same societal shifts made the involvement of beneficiaries in achieving project objectives (participation) an article of faith for the entire development community (Organization for Economic Cooperation and Development 1991).

Thus, as disillusionment with the capacity of states to control the "commanding heights" of developing economies set in, the role of the private and voluntary sectors increased and the assumptions governing the design of project organizations had to be reconsidered.

2.2   Enter institutional economics

Missing so far has been a systematic approach to the choice among hierarchy, markets, and participation so as to enhance development performance. Yet, the elements for a concerted approach to organizational design are available: the potentials and the limits of government, markets, and organizations have been extensively analyzed by institutional economists. In particular, the literature has brought to light the difficulties of aligning individual incentives to the common good in large and heterogeneous groups (see Olson 1965, a pioneering work on the dilemmas of collective action).

By now, the powerful incentives to "free ride" that are inherent to large groups are well understood. Similarly, the transaction-cost literature has illuminated the contractual enforcement difficulties associated with excessive reliance on hierarchy and control. Whereas, under the traditional public investment planning approach, there was a presumption in favor of command and control organizations, institutional theory has established that the desirable point of departure for reviewing project design options is the market. Specifically, where markets can be used efficiently they should be, since—compared to the alternatives—they save on scarce administrative capacities, avoid the public choice obstacles associated with large organizations, and tend to be responsive to consumer needs. This said, not all development problems are amenable to market solutions.

In particular, private transactions are effective only for goods that are consumed by one person at a time (subtractability) and in circumstances in which individual consumers can be excluded without incurring substantial costs (excludability). It is the combination of these characteristics that, along with competition, provides the conditions of free entry and exit that result in market efficiency. The implications for institutional design are fundamental (Kessides 1993). Four major classes of goods can be distinguished, even though the boundaries between them are not always clear cut (see table 16.1). Thus, the production of private goods is overwhelmingly determined by market considerations. But nonmarket factors prevail within the firm, and intermediate goods often require the production of other goods, for example, common pool goods where natural resource use is involved.

Table 16.1

Nature of Project Goods

Excludability	Subtractability	
	Low	High
Low	Public goods	Common-pool goods
High	Toll goods	Private goods

2.3   Common-pool projects

The management of common-pool goods (common pastures, irrigation water, etc.) is especially challenging because such goods lack excludability while possessing subtractability. This hinders market operation. With subtractability high, competition for access to the good is heightened by its finite supply. In most instances, hierarchy is not an effective deterrent to free-riding, because effective rationing requires an elaborate monitoring infrastructure, which may not be available, or an administrative apparatus so vast that it is easily subverted.

The failure of market mechanisms combined with the impracticability of controls explains why common-pool goods are best managed through persuasion and cooperation. Uninhibited market incentives or technocratic management modes unaccompanied by appropriate participatory arrangements are frequent causes of project failures for common-pool projects. In particular, projects that depend on the management of finite natural resources tend to fail when they disrupt traditional arrangements for resource preservation and equitable distribution of benefits. In such cases, new resource management alternatives must be designed to avoid social tensions and resource depletion. Thus, the allocation of water at the watercourse level, access to community pastures and natural forests, or the use of scarce fisheries resources can turn into tragedies of the commons unless effective participatory institutions are in place. In such situations, individual incentives left to themselves can clash with the common good, and regulatory institutions imposed from the top down are frequently undermined by corruption or collusion.

The privileged role of participation in the management of community projects is illustrated by the Matruh natural resource management project in Egypt, supported by the World Bank and undertaken in collaboration with Bedouin communities; in the national irrigation administration program carried out in the Philippines to improve water management; and in the Pakistani Oragi pilot project, which aims to develop affordable sewerage for Karachi's squatter settlements.[3] In all these instances, community involvement and local contributions are combined with technical improvements and reduction of corrupt practices through peer group pressures.

Thus, cooperative scenarios with happy endings do exist (that is, natural resources can be managed for sustainability) if institutional design takes due account of the prerequisites—selective incentives, relatively small groups, and strong leadership—identified by Olson (1965) with respect to the solution of collective action dilemmas.

2.4 Exit and voice

Where consumption by one beneficiary does not reduce availability of the good to others (that is, when subtractability is missing), powerful incentives to free ride exist as well, but control requirements are less demanding, and hierarchy is a more effective antidote to institutional decline. However, hierarchy is not enough. It needs to be complemented by market mechanisms (exit) where control of access is feasible (toll goods) and by voice mechanisms where it is not (pure public goods). Table 16.2 illustrates the exit and voice characteristics associated with the four types of project goods pictured in table 16.1. And, just as gaps in the periodic table have guided scientists toward the discovery of missing elements, table 16.2 suggests the existence of two other types of project goods—government goods in the northwest quadrant and civil goods in the southeast quadrant.

Government goods share the low subtractability characteristics associated with public and toll goods. Some goods supplied by government (for example, national defense, justice, and police) imply low excludability and, from this perspective, are akin to public goods: law and order is supplied, at least in principle, to all citizens, and the enjoyment of public tranquility by one citizen does not detract from the benefits derived by other citizens. On the other hand, the government also produces equity goods

---

[3]The World Bank Learning Group on Participatory Development was launched in December 1990. In August 1994, it produced recommendations to increase participation in Bank work. The recommendations were endorsed by the Bank's management and its board of directors. Many of the illustrations provided in this chapter are drawn from the work of the Learning Group.

through such redistributive measures as taxation and subsidies, whose high excludability evinces an affinity with toll goods. What distinguishes pure government goods from public and toll goods is their limited reliance on exit (on which toll goods are highly dependent) and voice (which public goods creation requires). It is government's monopoly of legitimate coercion that underlies the low-exit/low-voice characteristics of government goods.

Table 16.2

Exit and Voice Mechanisms

	Voice	
Exit	Low	High
Low	Government goods	Public and common-pool goods
High	Private and toll goods	Civil goods

Similarly, civil goods have much in common with private goods and common-pool goods; they are characterized by high subtractability. On the other hand, they may or may not evince excludability. A professional association delivers services only to its members, while a traveler's aid agency delivers services to any wayward passenger in need of assistance. Civil goods are products of charitable organizations, professional associations, public advocacy groups, clubs, and sundry voluntary organizations. They are shaped by threshold protocols associated with membership and access to benefits. They differ from private and common-pool goods in terms of their heavy reliance on voice (which private goods do not normally require) and exit (an option of which common-pool goods are usually deprived).

2.5 Hierarchy

A World Bank-financed railways project in Nigeria pointed Hirschman (1970) to the discovery of what is arguably the most influential trilogy of institutional economics: exit, voice, and loyalty. Because of the ease with which the railways corporation could tap into the national treasury, Hirschman noted that exit of important customers weakened the very voice option that might have triggered recuperative mechanisms within the public agency. Thus, Hirschman concluded that loyalist (that is, exit-postponing) behavior is a key factor of organizational resilience. Loyalty is activated by leadership and relies on hierarchy. Table 16.3 contrasts the differential roles that loyalty-inducing hierarchy and the market play with respect to the six types of goods defined above. Hierarchy counts for a great deal with respect to government and public goods, since their production requires the exercise of legitimate authority. On the other hand, the market matters most where the production of private and civil goods is concerned. Toll goods, by contrast, require both hierarchy and the bracing effects of market competition, while common-pool goods require neither, highly dependent as they are on cooperation and participation.

Table 16.3

The Role of Hierarchy

	Hierarchy	
Market	Low	High
Low	Common-pool goods	Public and government goods
High	Private and civil goods	Toll goods

Organizational design can now be defined as the selection of appropriate exit, voice, and hierarchy mechanisms. When the market represents the most appropriate mode of project operation, exit mechanisms should be given pride of place. When participation is the answer, it makes sense to nurture voice mechanisms. Loyalty and its ally, hierarchy, intervene when exit needs restraint to give full scope to the recuperative benefits of voice. Thus, for pure public goods (for example, a more rigorous tax policy or a traffic-signaling scheme), full benefits occur when loyalty is encouraged by effective policing (hierarchy) or when users are involved and motivated (participation).

2.6   Public goods projects

World Bank experience with rural roads and water supply projects confirms the importance of loyalty-building mechanisms and the need for a mix of hierarchy and participation for public goods projects. In the Gurage roads organization in Ethiopia, local maintenance has been handled effectively since 1962 through community involvement, training, and adequate compensation of service operators. Under a pilot program in Côte d'Ivoire, villages were explicitly required to maintain hand pumps at their own expense and were provided with training. The program resulted in more reliable water service.

In the Côte d'Ivoire case, collective action dilemmas arose when the authorities attempted to organize competing interests into water management committees. The problem was especially serious in the larger villages, and in a revealing manifestation of hierarchy, the village chief simply took over the selection of committee members. Similarly, in the Zambia social recovery fund project, boreholes were dug to relieve severe water shortages without local contribution and, given the perceived urgency of the scheme, with minimal consultations. When pumps failed, the beneficiaries refused to contribute to the needed repairs.

The corroding impact of vested interests illustrates the need to align individual incentives with the common good lest the public venture become a hostage of minority vested interests, as predicted by public choice theory (Gerson 1993). Thus, the authoritative role of hierarchy is vital when a small part of the beneficiary population involved in a project exercises undue influence. In the Central Visayas regional development project (Philippines), community organizations were allowed to organize forest residents in reaping traditional benefits from protected forest areas. This arrangement had to be revoked when the leaders of these organizations colluded with timber merchants to harvest live trees.

2.7 Toll goods projects

Toll goods projects (such as for piped water) can be managed effectively only through organizational options that combine market and hierarchy. The choice of options (ranging from regulated private water companies, concessions, and autonomous public corporations to contracting) depends on a variety of project characteristics (such as network features and whether costs are sunk), the administrative resources available, the feasibility of regulation, and initial conditions. The sequencing of reform requires judicious assessments of institutional potentials and constraints.

The regulation of utilities illustrates how systematic institutional design can encourage private investment while maintaining competition and efficient pricing. Institutional economics can help shape regulatory arrangements that ensure compatibility with domestic legislative, executive, and judicial institutions (Levy and Spiller 1993).

Credible commitments that regulatory discretion will be restrained within fair bounds, that basic changes in the enabling environment will not take place, and that effective and independent recourse will be available in case of conflict are basic determinants of private utility investment and operation. This is why policy options regarding regulatory reform must take account of the initial conditions characteristic of the country's institutional environment. In the design of appropriate institutional solutions for toll goods projects, the existence of a respected and independent judiciary has been shown to be fundamental. In its absence, reliable external conflict resolution mechanisms must be specified. Safeguards can be provided through legislation (as in Chile) or embedded in the operating license (as in Jamaica). Where existing institutions are incapable of effective and flexible enforcement of broad regulations, complex rules are needed, which presumes, of course, that strong administrative capacity is available. In certain situations, as a transitional measure, international mechanisms may be able to offset domestic administrative weaknesses. For example, World Bank guarantees against noncommercial risk have been used to encourage investment while core institutions are strengthened and a constituency for domestic capacity building and reform is nurtured.

2.8   Government and civil goods projects

Where both subtractability and excludability obtain—as they do for most agricultural and industrial products—efficient resource allocation and consumer satisfaction prevail, provided the market is allowed to operate freely and market participants are intent on maximizing their incomes (as producers) or their satisfaction (as consumers). This implies, of course, that a suitable policy framework is in place. The dilemma is that the enabling environment itself is a public good. A market cannot operate effectively without the likelihood of contractual enforcement, that is, without the production of such government goods necessary for effective market operation as regulatory functions and compliance mechanisms. Policy formulation involves a mix of hierarchy and participation, while policy implementation relies largely on hierarchy. Thus, policy is a public good, but different kinds of policies require different admixtures of hierarchy and participation, ranging from a highly hierarchical mix for monetary policy to a highly participatory mode for school district management.

The administration of commercial law, the management of safety nets, and the implementation of environmental regulations are examples of government goods. Such goods are the fruits of the executive and judiciary branches. They differ from the regulations and laws themselves, the production of which typically involves both the executive and the legislative branches of government in a mix of hierarchy and participation. Government goods are important because, without enforcement and the deterrence it produces, opportunism prevails. Government has a monopoly for legitimate coercion, and therefore, the market needs the state just as the state needs the market. But this cohabitation is not trouble free, since overzealous reliance on one automatically undermines the other, for example through bureaucratic constraints associated with the state or the rent-seeking behavior associated with private parties.

That is why civil goods are also needed for effective market operation. Delivered by private voluntary organizations of bewildering diversity, civil goods have grown rapidly precisely in those countries where the market and the state are poised in relative balance. In totalitarian regimes, the civil society is weak precisely because hierarchy brooks no dissent. Equally, in countries where the state is failing and government functions are moribund, voluntary action is stunted. By exhorting, motivating, and restraining the state and by calling attention to the excesses of free and unrestrained markets, civil society plays a vital supporting role by filling gaps in private and government activities. Civil organizations are breeding grounds for participation and cooperation. They operate with minimal reference to hierarchy. Indeed, they often define themselves in opposition to the state—as the nongovernmental sector. They thrive on debate and make use of advocacy to achieve their objectives. Their ascent parallels the growing dissatisfaction with the failings of both state and market.

To be sure, there is no guarantee that all components of the civil society are benign or genuinely concerned with the fate of the downtrodden. Indeed, theory suggests that the smaller and more motivated the group, the more vocal and effective it is in maintaining cohesion and achieving results. This means that the extremes often rule. Thus, some private voluntary organizations are created specifically to advance the interests of narrow and privileged constituencies. Therefore, failing effective self-policing, the civil society must be restrained to work for the common good both by the workings of the market and by the enabling environment of the state. Figure 16.1, which draws on Keidel's (1995) approach to "seeing organizational patterns," shows the array of project categories described above and their relationship to the three major development institutions: the state, the market, and the voluntary sector. Obviously, the dividing lines between the six categories of goods are not sharp, and there is considerable synergy among them. The market depends on the parallel provision of infrastructure (common-pool, toll, and public goods). The state requires a mix of

Figure 16.1

Institutional Design Parameters

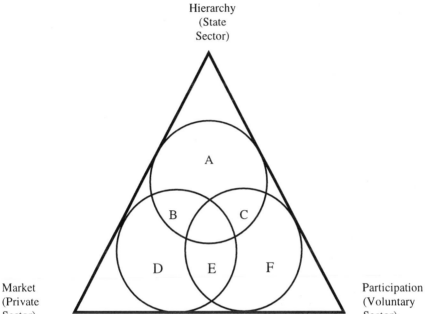

Hierarchy
(State
Sector)

Market
(Private
Sector)

Participation
(Voluntary
Sector)

	Nature of Project Goods	Dominant Parameters	Institutions	Example
A	Government	H	State agencies	Justice, police
B	Toll	M, H	Public or regulated private corporations	Public utilities
C	Public	P, H	Hybrid organizations	Policy, rural roads
D	Market	M	Private corporations, farmers, and entre-preneurs	Farming, industry, services
E	Civil	P, M	NGOs, PVOs	Public advocacy
F	Common pool	P	Local organizations, cooperatives	Natural resource management

Parameters: Hierarchy = H; Participation = P; Market = M

government goods (for enforcement) and of public goods (for representation of various interests) so as to yield legitimacy and social responsiveness. The framework can be used to initiate organizational design at the micro (project) level. It can also facilitate institutional design at the macro (country) level, as section 3, below, shows.

2.9   A delicate balance

Development requires government and civil goods in addition to a judicious mix of private, public, common-pool, and toll goods. Projects are mechanisms through which such goods are supplied. The art of governance consists of achieving an appropriate balance between the products of various institutional goods so as to achieve a positive interplay between the state, the market, and the voluntary sector. There is a natural tension among these actors, given their contrasting mandates and their different constituencies. An appropriate balance is struck when excessive power by any one sector is counteracted by one or both of the others. If one sector is patently weak, judiciously selected capacity-building projects can help redress the imbalance. Thus, effective governance involves cross-cutting and shifting alliances as well as deliberate capacity-building efforts aimed at mutually supportive operation of the state, the market, and the civil society.

The actual mix is highly dependent on initial conditions. In low-trust societies, improved public sector management enjoys greater priority than in high-trust societies, given the greater role that the state must assume. Through judicious project selection, the institutional endowment of society can be gradually modified. External advice may be needed to design arrangements combining well-engineered exit, voice, and loyalty mechanisms. Moving from one institutional equilibrium to the next without losing ground can be an acrobatic maneuver, the success of which may be facilitated by an outside party.

3   The Governance Dimension of Development Assistance

Section 1 describes projects as public goods designed to overcome failures in development markets. Section 2 proposes an analytical framework for the design of project institutions within a macroinstitutional structure taken as given. In this section, the institutional resource endowment of the country is the focus. Institutional capital is a primary determinant of economic and social performance, and its quality is characterized by judicious admixtures of state, market, and voluntary institutions. From this perspective, depending on their relevance to the country's institutional development needs, projects deplete available institutional capital or contribute to its accumulation. Inappropriate organization design leads to the excessive use of institutional capital. On the other hand, well-designed projects can help generate institutional capital by reinforcing participatory processes, improving the workings of government, or facilitating market operations. Thus, beyond their proximate role as producers of goods and services, development projects can contribute to the reduction of transaction costs throughout society.

3.1   Taking account of initial conditions

Development suffers as a consequence of corrupt, misdirected, or weak government, because only government can create an enabling environment for the development of efficient markets and, together with civil organizations, can sponsor programs to protect the poor and the environment. Institutional endowment varies across countries. In some, traditions, rules, and organizations render development efforts effective. In others, characterized by poor governance, economic performance is hindered by a tendency to divert public resources for private gain; arbitrary, unpredictable government behavior; excessive rules and regulations; or unresponsive, opaque decision making. Poor development performance (typically induced by external shocks and misguided policies) also contributes to poor governance. Stagnant economies induce weak public finances, dissatisfaction among citizens, and pervasive distrust of government. Just as good governance facilitates the introduction of effective economic policy, good economic management facilitates the reform of governance arrangements.

3.2   Reorienting government

The recognition of the crucial importance of an appropriate role for the state explains why, in addition to providing developing member countries with funding and policy advice, development assistance now addresses governance issues in their own right (World Bank 1992). With the introduction of policy-based lending, the focus has shifted toward the enhancement of countrywide institutions. One important way of improving governance has been to help ensure that scarce public resources are concentrated on functions that only the government can provide while encouraging a greater role for the private sector and the civil society.

Therefore, taking account of country conditions and objectives, the principles illustrated in figure 16.1 for the micro level apply equally well at the macro level. For example, public capacity-building activities are best geared to the discharge of functions for which the state is well suited, while policy advice is best directed to establishing positive enabling environments for private enterprise and voluntary activities to fill whatever gaps are left. Figure 16.2 illustrates a sequential approach to policy reform, focusing first on reorienting the role of the state and next on encouraging the voluntary sector to assist in the adjustment process.

3.3   Financial sector development

Changes in financial systems illustrate how the redefinition of the role of the state has induced pervasive changes in the institutional fabric of developing countries.

In the 1950s and 1960s, almost all developing country governments took control of private financial systems and set up specialized banks for agriculture and industry under public ownership and control. The state directed financial institutions to lend to selected industries on subsidized terms. The limitations of this approach were not apparent as long as there was easy access to foreign funding.

After the onset of the debt crisis, high interest rates, low commodity prices, and devaluations increased the domestic burden of borrowing firms' foreign debts, and governments had to borrow domestically for their needs, exacerbating inflationary pressures. Given the artificially low lending rates in force, as well as the poor quality of the loans made, the banking system became unviable in many countries, and financial sector reform became a top priority. In some countries, reforms of company, banking, securities, and bankruptcy laws were required. In others, fiscal policy, banking supervision, and regulation had to be directed away from credit allocation and interest rate controls toward the maintenance of a healthy and efficient financial system. In Eastern Europe and the former Soviet Union, wholesale restructuring had to take place in parallel with reform in the regulatory framework and the stabilization of the economy.

More recently, the emergence of substantial private flows has put the emphasis on securities-based systems and the development of capital markets. Partly as a result of policy reform, private capital flows to developing countries have risen. They represent portfolio investment (through bonds and equities) as well as foreign direct investment fueled by privatization. They are concentrated in countries that have achieved effective economic stabilization, policy reform, and institutional development in their financial sectors and capital markets. Just as governments set the rules for markets, markets are now setting constraints on the role of governments.

Figure 16.2

Governance Reform

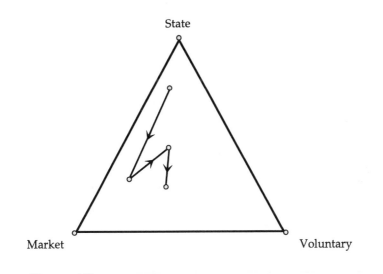

State

Market   Voluntary

3.4   Public sector management

In sum, given the fundamental dilemmas of collective action highlighted by theory, the concentration of public sector activities on appropriate functions has emerged as a necessary condition of effective governance. Hence, the focus of the new development agenda on civil service reform; the increased competitiveness of the business environment; the improved effectiveness and efficiency of public agencies; the restructuring, liquidation, and privatization of public enterprises; and the decentralization of government administration. Experience shows that the success of such programs depends not only on the effective transfer of skills and practices but also on the broadly based "ownership" of reform objectives and the construction of workable coalitions (Johnson and Wasty 1993).

The focus on government commitment to reform is relatively new. Public choice theory has shaped practice by highlighting the gap that often exists between public policy pronouncements and actual implementation and by identifying strategies aimed at aligning individual incentives and social goals.

3.5   Accountability

Accountability requires mediation among three distinct groups: recipients of public services, political leaders who oversee service providers, and the service providers themselves. The goals and interests of each group differ from those of the other two, and a useful role for development assistance agencies is to help prevent capture of the public good by one of the groups to the detriment of the others—and of the public interest. Where such capture is prevented, loyalty is enhanced.

It is not practical to expect sustainable reform toward accountability through actions limited to the micro (project) level, since the role of the modern state involves myriad interrelated functions, and projects have a limited focus and a finite life. Macro-level accountability, on the other hand, calls for sustained shifts in public attitudes and government practices, and "path dependence" is a powerful drag on wholesale reform. Given these obstacles, a judicious mix of micro and macro interventions is needed, and the mobilization of scattered energies in support of reform is often feasible only in periods of crisis. This explains the links between financial crises, governance reform, and policy adjustment. Beyond the management of public finances and the design of investment projects, policy dialogue, public education, nurturing of consensus, and carefully sequenced strategies of reform have become central to the development enterprise. Ideas matter.

Among government goods that are underproduced for public choice reasons are those that enhance accountability for financial and economic performance. Financial accountability at the project level faces obstacles linked to generic weaknesses in countrywide public accounting, expenditure control, and cash management. To address this issue, technical assistance can be devoted to build up domestic institutional capacity. Similarly, accountability for economic performance may be addressed through budget policy reforms, improved public expenditure management, the removal of white elephants from investment programs, the decentralization of public administration, the elimination of ghost workers from public employment rolls, the closure and privatization of public enterprises, the commercialization of public entities, and the building of evaluation capacity. Thus, the World Bank has provided assistance to Poland and Romania for decentralization, to Indonesia for financial accountancy development, to China for evaluation capacity building, and to Ghana and Madagascar for public financial management. To improve accountability for environmental programs, the Bank has required the preparation of environmental impact assessments for the projects it finances and has assisted its member countries in the design of countrywide environmental action plans. Research into appropriate indicators for environmentally sound management of natural resources is under way.

3.6 The rule of law

Still another dimension of building governance capacity is the establishment of a sound and predictable legal framework for development. Five elements are involved: (1) rules that are known in advance, (2) the enforcement of rules, (3) monitoring, (4) conflict resolution, and (5) the timely amendment of rules. Together, they facilitate the production of what was earlier defined as government goods essential to the reduction of transaction costs. To this end, the World Bank has assisted Mauritania and Guinea in disseminating information about the law through official gazettes. In Laos, the Bank has helped to fund legal training and the promulgation of business legislation. In Romania and in the Czech Republic, contradictions and inconsistencies in legislation have been identified and removed. In Sri Lanka, financial sector adjustment lending has helped to reform the laws allowing financial institutions to foreclose on collateral.

Under the Philippines financial sector adjustment loan, the bankruptcy law has been revised to make it less punitive to debtors and more rehabilitative in the interest of both debtors and creditors. In Bangladesh, a financial sector adjustment credit has helped establish courts, appoint judges, and dispose of cases to implement a law designed to reduce the time needed to settle suits brought by financial institutions against defaulting borrowers.

3.7 Transparency and participation

Voice mechanisms are the lifeblood of participatory modes of governance. Since these mechanisms depend heavily on information dissemination, suitable rules of the game concerning disclosure and dissemination of public information are part and parcel of improved governance. Considerable experimentation has taken place in building solidarity and incentives for participation at the project level and in strengthening voice mechanisms used by beneficiaries vis-à-vis public agencies. To take hold, these mechanisms often require the provision of special incentives and the involvement of an outside party.

In a pilot project in Bangladesh, for example, where tradition normally excludes destitute women and widows from gainful employment, nongovernmental agencies organized landless contracting societies to involve these women in construction to preserve flood-prone embankments. In Pakistan, during implementation of the integrated hill-farming project, it became clear that communities organized to undertake reforestation were not disposed to maintain and protect the saplings during their five-year maturation period since the returns were too distant to motivate collective action. Accordingly, undergrowth plants were added to the plantations, to be harvested on a rotating basis.

The emergence of a strong voluntary sector depends on a host of cultural and historical factors. In some countries (Bangladesh, Chile, Colombia, India, Kenya, Mexico, and Zimbabwe), voluntary agencies have mushroomed. In others, they have not and remain dependent on official sponsorship and support. Pressures to co-opt nongovernmental organizations are ever present and must be resisted. Yet, there is great scope for complementary action as NGOs, despite frequent administrative weaknesses, can be cost effective in reaching low-income groups. Today, NGOs act as effective partners of the state (and of development agencies) in a wide range of development operations.

3.8   Country institutional development strategies

Institution building is a time-consuming, complex process. It requires long-term vision, sustained efforts, and well-sequenced operations. The paradox of institutional development is that it is most needed in the very countries where it is most difficult to achieve. Where commitment from the political leadership is not available, it needs to be nurtured without major resource outlays. Where, on the other hand, ownership is assured, nimble and responsive external assistance can yield high returns. A judicious choice of instruments and a partnership among development agencies is central to cost effectiveness and selectivity.

4   The Global Dimension of Institutional Development

It should be clear by now why, in the words of Williamson (1994), "institutional economics has been invited to join the arena" of development economics. A pragmatic reaction against the orthodoxies of planning and neoclassicism, institutional economics aims to bridge, encompass, and transcend these orthodoxies so as to provide more reliable guides to development decision making. In the neoclassical world, a "hidden hand" manages resource allocation. In nonmarket environments, a providential or dictatorial "hiding hand" seeks to maximize social utility. Both conceptions are unrealistic; they ignore transaction costs and take little account of the incentives and interests that underlie policy.

By contrast, institutionalists are concerned with the costs and benefits of transactions and suspicious of the "immaculate conception" school of economic decision making. They seek to understand the motivation of economic agents in order to build effective strategies for reform. Thus, the ascent of institutional economics is partly related to supply factors—the production of realistic and relevant concepts by the new institutionalists. But it also reflects demand factors, such as the urgent need for new ideas to assist principled and practical decision making in the rapidly evolving development business of an increasingly interdependent world.

4.1   Global factors

Underlying this demand are vast changes in the global economy. The urgent need to reform economic institutions arises from three main factors: (1) the growing interdependence of the international economy and the physical environment, (2) the explosive impact of demography and technology, and (3) the tight fiscal constraints on governments and development agencies. These factors are interrelated. The world economy has become global not only as a result of trade liberalization but also because of innovations in telecommunications and information technologies. These technologies have made governance failures more visible. The fiscal constraints that plague the public sector are themselves the indirect result of unstable monetary and fiscal policies triggered by global shifts in exchange rates, interest rates, and capital flows.

Conversely, fresh opportunities have arisen as a result of the new agility, responsiveness, and location-independence of multinational production (Lindbaek and Rischard 1994). Improved economic policies and new financial instruments are unlocking the enormous potential of private capital markets to meet the pent-up needs for infrastructure investment in developing countries. At the same time, major ecological threats requiring collective action are looming. Global warming, water scarcity, acid rain, deforestation, public health crises, and large-scale migrations transcend national borders. The need for multilateral action is especially dominant with respect to failed and failing states. The centrifugal forces unleashed by the end of the Cold War are fueling regional conflicts, famines, and refugee movements precisely in areas where population growth is galloping, environmental stress is high, and development has lagged.

It is no accident that, where development has failed, basic governance and institutions have usually been weak. Enhancement of domestic capacities simply cannot be handled within reasonable time frames without sustained international cooperation and development assistance. In a sense, government goods and civil goods have become internationally traded services. Shifting boundaries for market solutions, the rise of the voluntary sector, and rising returns to investment in ideas confirm the continuing need for responsive international development cooperation.

4.2   Shifting boundaries for market solutions

Specifically, technological developments have reduced the natural-monopoly characteristics of major infrastructure services. Containerization has introduced competition in port services. The wireless revolution is inducing small telecommunications operators to compete with large wire-based networks. Independent power producers can construct and operate relatively small power plants in competition with large public generation plants (Bond and Carter 1994).

Innovative financing techniques offer institutional investors and venture capitalists opportunities to diversify their portfolios in emerging markets. Learning from the experience of developed and reforming developing countries has also played a role in igniting institutional reform, not only with respect to the encouragement of foreign direct investment, privatization, and financial sector reform but also in the social and environmental areas.

4.3   Rise of the global voluntary sector

According to Salamon (1994, 4), "We are in the midst of a global associational revolution that may prove to be as significant to the latter twentieth century as the rise of the nation-state was to the latter nineteenth." The growth of self-governing private organizations is tapping into the enormous benefits that small groups are known to enjoy. Voluntary agencies are able to mobilize grassroots energies through small-scale, flexible interventions. At the same time, the new communications technologies and the rise of global mass media have allowed them to network and influence public opinion on an unprecedented scale.

In the developing world, 4,600 international voluntary organizations are now active and support approximately 20,000 indigenous nongovernmental organizations. A growing share of concessional development assistance is being channeled through them. Similar developments are evident in Eastern Europe and the former Soviet Union. The economic and political significance of this trend (at a time when the institutions of the state have been rolled back) are considerable and are especially relevant with respect to the global environmental challenge.

4.4 Growing returns to investment in ideas

Fiscal constraints have also played a role in shifting institutional boundaries. According to Larry Summers, "With money scarce, we need ideas." Rates of return on the generation of good policies and their dissemination are enormous. As noted earlier, policies are public goods. Their production and delivery calls for a combination of hierarchy and participation. But policies are useless without an institutional machinery capable of implementation. The travails of the economies in transition as well as those of sub-Saharan Africa illustrate this simple proposition. Self-help and internal determination are the keys to success, but external support has been shown to be instrumental in overcoming public choice obstacles and in laying the foundations for sustainable growth. New institutional capital created by the voluntary sector has also come into play in the search for effective institutional development strategies.

A remarkable global consensus about development strategies has emerged over the past decade, due in significant part to the research and evaluation outputs of multilateral institutions. A great deal of experimentation has taken place to find the right balance between markets, the state, and the voluntary sector in the design of development institutions. Demographic stress on environmental resources, advances in technology, and greater insights about the role of markets and property rights derived from recent advances in institutional economics have shifted the institutional equilibrium throughout the developing world. These trends underlie the growing relevance of institutional economics to the development business and the new role of projects as agents of institutional change.

4.5 The case for multilateralism

In this evolving global framework, the rationale for official multilateral intermediation arises from imperfections in information markets, global development challenges, and the risk-bearing advantages related to the special contract enforcement abilities within an international setting of multilateral organizations.

The high transaction costs involved in cross-border capital flows aimed at developing countries are caused not only by information asymmetries but also by the difficulties of international contract enforcement. The cooperative characteristics of multilateral development agencies give them privileged access to development information. Disclosure of development information and dissemination of analytical work help overcome the information asymmetries that plague international capital markets and concessional aid flows. Since the obligations of multilateral institutions are backed by all their members, and since they have built up a superior global monitoring capability, they have been entrusted with concessional resources targeted at poor countries and at the delivery of financial intermediation services to developing countries on terms and conditions that no private agency can replicate.

Economies of scale in information gathering, interpretation, and monitoring as well as in raising long-term funds in capital markets and in sharing portfolio risk also come into play. This combination of money and ideas is synergistic. At early stages of a country's development or market transition, external support can be critical in triggering private or concessional flows. Similarly, by reducing the transaction costs of participants, multilateral institutions can help coordinate international funding.

The end result is an improved allocation of development information and global capital and the attenuation of market failures, especially from the perspective of the poorest and least credit-worthy member countries. Thus, the economic rationale for development assistance lies in its public goods character—its contribution to redressing market imperfections with respect to information and risk bearing and to the design of cooperative solutions to the looming problems of the global commons.

References

Bond, Gary, and Laurence Carter. 1994. *Financing Private Infrastructure Projects*. Discussion Paper 23. Washington, D.C.: International Finance Corporation.

Gerson, Philip R. 1993. "Popular Participation in Economic Theory and Practice." HRO Working Paper 18. World Bank, Washington, D.C.

Hirschman, Albert O. 1967. *Development Projects Observed*. Washington, D.C.: Brookings Institution.

———. 1970. *Exit, Voice, and Loyalty: Responses to Decline in Firms, Organizations, and States*. Cambridge: Harvard University Press.

Johnson, John, and Sulaiman Wasty. 1993. *Borrower Ownership of Adjustment Programs and the Political Economy of Reform*. Discussion Paper 199. Washington, D.C.: World Bank.

Keidel, Robert. 1995. *Seeing Organizational Patterns: A New Theory and Language or Organizational Design*. San Francisco: Berret-Koehler.

Kessides, Christine. 1992. *Institutional Options for the Provision of Infrastructure*. Discussion Paper 212. Washington, D.C.: World Bank.

Levy, Brian, and Pablo Spiller. 1993. *Utility Regulation: Getting the Fit Right*. Policy Views from the Policy Research Department, Outreach 14. Washington, D.C.: World Bank.

Lindbaek, Jannick, and Jean-Francois Rischard. 1994. "Agility in the New World Economy." *Finance and Development* 31: 34–35.

Milgrom, Paul, and John Roberts. 1992. *Economics, Organization, and Management*. Englewood Cliffs, N.J.: Prentice-Hall.

Olson, Mancur. 1965. *The Logic of Collective Action*. Cambridge: Harvard University Press.

Organization for Economic Cooperation and Development. 1991. *Development Cooperation*. Paris: OECD.

Picciotto, Robert, and Rachel Weaving. 1994. "A New Project Cycle for the World Bank?" *Finance and Development* 31: 42–44.

Salamon, Lester M. 1994. "The Rise of the Nonprofit Sector." *Foreign Affairs* 73: 109–22.

Streeten, Paul. 1993. "Markets and States: Against Minimalism." *World Development* 21: 1281–98.

Williamson, Oliver. 1994. *Institutions and Economic Organization: The Governance Perspective*. Washington, D.C.: World Bank.

World Bank. 1992. *Governance and Development*. Washington, D.C.: World Bank.

———. 1993. *Getting Results: The World Bank's Agenda for Improving Development Effectiveness*. Washington, D.C.: World Bank.

———. 1994. *1992 Evaluation Results*. Operations Evaluation Department. Washington, D.C.: World Bank.

———. 1995. *1993 Evaluation Results*. Operations Evaluation Department. Washington D.C.: World Bank.

17 The New Institutional Economics and Institutional Reform

Christopher Clague

The research program of the New Institutional Economics (NIE) in the field of economic development is the assessment of the determinants and the consequences of different institutional structures. These structures include the constitutional order (the fundamental rules), the institutional arrangements (the operational rules devised within the constitutional order), and the cultural endowments (the behavioral norms and mental models shared by society; see Feeny 1993). Greater progress has been made in understanding the role of institutional arrangements than in understanding the roles of the other two, mainly because institutional arrangements exhibit more variety and change more frequently than constitutional orders and cultures.[1] With regard to institutional arrangements, it is probably fair to say that the study of their consequences has proved more amenable to intellectual progress than the study of their determinants. That is, by theoretical and empirical methods scholars have identified some institutional arrangements that are highly conducive to economic progress and other arrangements that are not. But how these institutional arrangements come into being is less well understood. This chapter elaborates on what we think we know about the consequences and determinants of institutions and draws out the implications for the design of external assistance.

With respect to the consequences of economic institutions, there is a broad consensus among economists that a certain set of economic arrangements is conducive to economic progress. The superior economic performance of countries with competitive markets, secure property and contract rights, stable macroeconomic conditions, and efficient government provision of public goods is supported by numerous studies. A similar broad consensus exists in society at large that democratic political institutions are the ones most conducive to human welfare. There are disagreements and debates about particular features of these arrangements, such as the choice of fixed or flexible exchange rates, the nature of antimonopoly policy, the

---

[1] In the terminology of Olson (1990), constitutional orders and cultures are *scant* sets. While institutional arrangements are not exactly *multitudinous* sets, they do contain many more members than the other two and, hence, offer more opportunities for the study of cause and effect relationships.

desirability of universal banking, the advantages of presidential versus parliamentary systems, and the responsibilities of local versus national government, and different arrangements seem to work reasonably well in different countries. But these variations and disagreements do not obscure the point that the institutions of competitive markets and democratic politics, which are by and large the arrangements that exist in the rich countries of the world, are not found or do not function well in most of the less-developed and formerly socialist world. Those poor countries with the appropriate economic arrangements in place are generally growing rapidly.

Thus, the ultimate goal of institutional reform in poor countries is fairly clear. That goal can be described as a market-friendly environment, with supportive government services provided by a democratic polity. But agreement on this ultimate goal does not resolve the crucial issue of how to get there. One way to frame this question is in terms of sequencing. In a country with a poor set of policies and institutions, which steps should be taken first? In other words, what is the optimal order of changes in economic and political arrangements? In framing the question this way, I do not suggest that we have enough knowledge to lay out a precise blueprint of a sequence of changes—far from it—or that the sequence should be the same in all countries; differences in constitutional orders, cultural endowments, and inherited institutional arrangements imply that reforms must be path-dependent. But in thinking about the order of reforms in terms of the participants' incentives, we can see that certain sequences offer higher probabilities of success than others.

There is a great temptation for external donors to ignore the sequencing issue. Observers from highly successful and rich countries go to poor countries and find economic arrangements to be very different. What happens next was well put by Kindleberger (1952, 391–92) some time ago: "These are essays [World Bank country reports] in comparative statics. The missions bring to the underdeveloped country a notion of what a developed country is like. They observe the underdeveloped country. They subtract the former from the latter. The difference is a program." One hears the same criticism of aid programs today. To do better than that, donors need to understand the determinants of institutional arrangements and how they can be changed.

The NIE approach to the determinants of institutional change may be contrasted with two other approaches that are prominent in the minds of development professionals. These are "institution-free" standard economics and "incentive-free" social engineering. With regard to the first, standard economics of a couple of decades ago analyzed market failures and proposed government remedies for them, with little attention to the determinants of the economic institutions of capitalism (see chap 2). Although the emphasis was on getting the economic policies right and on the implications of these policies for private sector incentives, problems of policy implementation by the government bureaucracy were generally not addressed, and there was little analysis of why policy makers behaved as they did. Much of this literature expressed the view, either explicitly or implicitly, that there were good policy makers and bad ones and that reform depended on the emergence of "political will."

By incentive-free social engineering, I mean any approach to social change that neglects the incentives facing individual actors or that relies for its success on moral exhortations to people to do things that are quite contrary to their self-interest as they perceive it. Such thinking pervades the development assistance literature. For example, in dealing with the miserable performance of the government bureaucracy in Bangladesh, one author (Blair 1994) recommends a strategy based on accountability, that is, making the political leaders and government bureaucrats accountable to the public for their performance, but there is no consideration of why the individual citizen would find it in his interest to become well enough informed for this strategy to be effective. Similarly, governments are urged to respect human rights and to channel resources toward the provision of basic human needs of the entire population, without consideration of why government leaders would want to do these things.

An approach to external assistance based on the NIE attempts to suggest strategies for reform that are incentive-compatible. That does not mean that people are assumed to be narrowly selfish all the time. There is abundant evidence that people do form groups and internalize norms that constrain their opportunism—without such behavior, the arrangements in the successful countries would not function—but by and large this behavior emerges in environments in which the payoffs to antisocial actions are not too large. What is required are reform strategies based on a careful understanding of the incentives facing actors in the current situation and on an examination of avenues for changing the institutional equilibrium.

An important distinction between different types of reform has been well expressed by Naim (1985), who refers to the launching of economic liberalization as stage I and to its consolidation as stage II. (A similar distinction is made in Klitgaard 1991; and in Haggard, chap. 6 of this volume.) Stage I includes cutting the government budget, stopping inflation, liberalizing prices, opening the economy to trade and investment, and deregulating the private sector. These steps can be implemented by the national government, relying on a team of technocrats insulated from normal political pressures. If the program is credible, the private sector is likely to respond productively. Stage II, or the consolidation phase, includes improving tax administration, public service delivery, civil service, environmental and antitrust regulations, labor-management relations, and judicial institutions; it also includes decentralization of tax collection and public functions. Stage II reforms require broad participation, and the outcomes are much less visible than those of stage I reforms.

Let us look at the issues raised by these two types of reform. There are occasions in which a technocratic team of reformers is given wide latitude to devise and launch a stage I program. When conditions are right and the program is well designed and executed, there are gains to many parties, including the technocrats and their political mentors. Thus the incentive problem is not so severe for this type of reform. But when the issue is stage II reform, designing an incentive-compatible package is much more difficult.

Naim's schema represents one view of the appropriate sequencing of reforms. It incorporates the idea that a number of macroeconomic and structural reforms can be packaged together and implemented quickly and that, if they are successful, they will be sustained. Experience supports this strategy, and political economy models have been developed to explain the phenomenon (see, for example, Bates and Krueger 1993; Williamson 1993; for a nice review of the theoretical models, see Tommasi and Velasco 1996). Several ideas appear in these models. The packaging of reforms, each of which adversely affects a particular interest group, can enable a coalition to emerge in which all members benefit. This packaging may be possible only during a crisis, in which the normal rules of politics are suspended. In addition, people's mental models of how the world works can be abruptly altered by dramatic events. The "information" aspect of reform strategy is illustrated by the "Nixon in China" syndrome: several of the successful reforms have been carried out by formerly left-wing or populist politicians (Cukierman and Tommasi 1994).

There are alternative views on the sequencing of reforms, and of course circumstances differ among countries. Some observers emphasize strengthening government administration or civil society as a first step in the process or, at least, as tasks that should be undertaken without delay; we return to this issue below. Apart from the sequencing issue, the reforms listed under stage II are institution-intensive. They involve reforming bureaucracies, overcoming the resistance of well-organized interest groups (during normal rather than extraordinary politics), and changing people's attitudes and expectations about the role of government in society. What does the NIE have to offer with regard to this type of reform? Below we consider lessons from various types of investigation.

1   Lessons

1.1   Irrigation associations and rural development projects

The work of Ostrom (chap. 7) and others shows that irrigation and rural development organizations function well when rules are consistent with behavior. The collection and transmission of information are central to the operation of such organizations. Successful organizations constrain opportunism, usually by a combination of gentle norm-enforcing sanctions backed up by stronger sanctions where necessary. From Narayan (chap. 9) and others, we learn that participation in rule making is positively related to efficiency in water use, a finding fully consistent with Ostrom's conceptual scheme.

An appealing form of intervention for outsiders (national governments or external donors) is to offer resources to support the creation of a community organization to accomplish a particular purpose. The hope is that, once the collective action problem is resolved for accomplishing one purpose, the organization will be able to tackle successfully other group goals, including the goal of raising its own resources so that it becomes self-sustaining. This is not a new idea in development assistance, however, as Ruttan points out in chapter 10, and enthusiasm for it has waxed and waned over time. Outsiders need to ask themselves why the community organization they have in mind has not already been created. Sometimes what the donors offer is protection from local or national government authorities. Potential donors need to understand what they might be contributing to existing arrangements before suggesting strategies for improvement.

1.2   Government bureaucracy and corruption

There seem to be multiple equilibria in the operation of government agencies. Even within the same country, some agencies function well while others are inefficient and corrupt. An institutional analysis of the incentives facing employees helps to explain this phenomenon; in the good equilibrium, information flows within the organization in such a way that slackers are noticed and sanctioned, while in the bad equilibrium there is no reward for conscientious behavior. The patterns of behavior are reinforced by the evolution of attitudes of the members toward the organization (Clague 1993; Levi and Sherman, chap. 15, this volume). If multiple equilibria exist, then efforts to reform inefficient or corrupt organizations must make nonmarginal changes in the way they operate. Similar considerations apply to the relations between government bureaucracies and the private sector; there is often an existing equilibrium resistant to small changes, but it may yield to large changes in top leadership or the external environment. The role of leadership in tax administration reform is illustrated by Tanzi and Pellechio (chap. 13), whose essay also contains many useful suggestions for reform strategies. In bureaucracies, as well as in local organizations, the flow of information is critical, as Klitgaard illustrates (chap. 14). In developed countries, governments are making major efforts to measure the performance of government agencies and to link rewards to these measures; such efforts may be productive in poor countries, as well.

The extent of corruption in government is affected by the types of task that government undertakes. When government is protecting property rights and enforcing contracts, it can normally rely on help from at least one of the parties to the dispute. The victim of theft or of contract nonfulfillment is usually willing to provide information to government authorities in their efforts to enforce the laws. When government attempts to prohibit trans-actions between willing partners, as when it tries to set prices or limit imports, both parties to the illegal transaction have incentives to conceal their activity from the government, and they are often willing to offer substantial bribes to government officials to look the other way in the event their transaction is detected (Olson 1995). This is one reason it makes sense to follow Naim's sequencing of reforms—in this case, to get the government out of the price regulation business before attempting to clean up corruption.

1.3   Civil society

Political scientists often emphasize the profound effects of the institutions of civil society on the performance of both the government and the economy. Both markets and government work better in societies with institutions that support horizontal ties (Putnam 1993) or the relationships based on reciprocity (Oakerson 1993). These ideas resonate with the results on the beneficial effects of participation in irrigation associations.

These results do not, however, resolve the issue of how to devise a reform strategy. The horizontal ties and reciprocal relationships that function in the United States and parts of Italy are not necessarily feasible in societies with long traditions of unequal social relationships (see Chantorn-vong 1993 for an interesting comparison of the United States, as described by de Tocqueville, with Asian societies). An institutional analysis may help explain these unequal social relationships. In poor rural communities there often exists the threat of starvation, and arrangements have evolved to provide insurance and transfers to ensure survival. According to a game theory analysis (Fafchamps 1992), people join solidarity networks to pool the risk of crop failure, illness, or other disasters. People who are part of the network contribute to take care of others, so that they themselves will have the right to draw on the assistance of others in the event of need. The solidarity network will benefit if richer individuals remain members, for this increases the resources available in the event of disaster. However, richer members might have an incentive to drop out of the network, since they could self-insure via their own savings. One way to keep them in the network is to permit patron-client relationships, in which poor clients perform services for the rich other than insurance. For example, poor clients may provide labor, gifts, and social support to their rich patron. When external donors visit such a community, they may find that poorer members defer to a small number of wealthy patrons. Attempts by outsiders to displace the patrons may fail if the function of these relationships is not recognized.[2]

1.4   Autocracy versus democracy

The results reported in chapter 5 indicate that durable democracies at a given income level tend to provide more secure contract and property rights than autocracies. However, the shift from autocracy to democracy does not tend to improve the state of these rights. Long-lasting autocracies tend to provide more secure property and contract rights than short-lived ones. This result is consistent with theoretical expectations based on the incentives facing autocratic rulers. There is also considerable evidence that economic development increases the probability that democracy will emerge and endure.

The major task of development, according to the arguments developed here, is the reform of policies and institutions. The New Institutional Economics offers a way of thinking about how to meet this

---

[2]Wade (1992) suggests, based on his study of Indian villages, that it would be counterproductive to prescribe majority rule rather than elite decisions for the selection of members of the council of an irrigation association, in part because the enforcement of the rules of the association depend on traditional sources of authority and, in part, because the large landowners form a privileged group in Olson's sense, in that they are a small group that gets a large share of the benefits of the association.

above illustrate, the NIE deals with questions that are not addressed by institution-free standard economics, and it offers ideas for the reform of institutions that are quite different from the moral exhortations of incentive-free social engineering. What we think we know about institutions suggests that they are not easy to change, but careful thought about information flows, incentives, and sanctions will surely enhance the effectiveness of reformers' efforts. While institutional reform requires local ownership of reform programs, poor countries can learn from the experiences of more successful societies. Just as agricultural development has been enhanced by building an indigenous "capacity for transfer" (Evenson and Kislev 1975; Hayami and Ruttan 1985), institutional reform can be facilitated by building an indigenous capacity for institutional design.

2   Conclusion

Probably the main uses of the NIE in development work will be in the hands of local practitioners. But its intellectual framework does have implications for the activities of external donor agencies such as the World Bank and bilateral aid-giving agencies. The remainder of this chapter offers some personal observations about strategies appropriate for external assistance in development.

With the collapse of communism in the Second World and the failure of government planning and inward-oriented development programs in the Third World, there has emerged a greater receptiveness among elites in these countries to market-friendly policies and institutions. There is of course a yearning on the part of the population for the standard of living enjoyed by the developed democracies. But there is in many quarters a lack of understanding of how a market economy, with its supportive governmental institutions, is supposed to function. One of the ways in which institutions change is that people change their mental models of how the world works. That is, ideas matter in institutional change. An important, and not particularly expensive, task for donors is to contribute to the education of elites and broader populations about incentive-compatible mechanisms for cooperation (see Murrell, chap. 11; Cadwell, chap. 12). In many cases, the relevant examples are not the institutions in the rich countries but the successful patterns of cooperation in similarly situated countries.

A great deal of current bilateral foreign assistance takes the form of delivery of goods and services directly to poor people. Without changing patterns of behavior in the recipient country, this activity cannot make a dent in world poverty. In Olson's analogy (chap. 3), this is fishing with hooks rather than with nets. This direct assistance is a natural response of human compassion to the misery observed, and it is encouraged by the lobbying of the nongovernmental organizations that administer funds provided by governments. However, assistance programs targeted on poor people could be administered in such a way as to encourage institutional change. An example is the microenterprise lending programs of the U.S. Agency for International Development, which not only have provided funds to individual recipients but have encouraged institutional innovation in lending institutions (Rhyne 1994). Given the complexities of human behavior, it is to be expected that efforts to stimulate institutional change will often fail. In this respect, institutional change is like technological change; there may be many false starts before success is achieved, but the return to investment can still be high. Part of the strategy of using assistance funds productively is that donors should be willing to pull the plug on projects that are not working. Donors need to conduct impartial evaluations of ongoing projects, to counter the natural tendency of both the donor staff involved in the project and the host country to exaggerate their accomplishments.

One of the themes of the NIE is that the collection and dissemination of information is important to the functioning of institutions. In the international arena, data on income levels, distribution, growth, and nonmonetary measures of human welfare have highlighted the differences that good policies can make. There is now a need for more data on institutions: on the delivery of government services, on measures of the output of government agencies, on the state of property and contract rights in the private sector. The World Bank data base on institutions in the housing sector (Mayo and Angell 1992) is an excellent example of the kind of information that is needed.

An analysis of the incentives facing autocrats suggests that donor pressure for sharing power is unlikely to succeed. The resources that an autocrat can extract from his domain are likely to exceed by far the resources that he can obtain from the proffered aid. In addition, the autocrat may fear for his safety if he loosens his grip on power. Moreover, even if donor pressure or other events lead to the holding of an honest election, that step does not imply that a stable democracy will emerge. The incentives of potential political entrepreneurs depend on their positions and expectations regarding rivals' behavior. While it is true that stable democracy has emerged in very poor countries (virtually always following British tutelage), the conditions do not seem ripe in many poor countries. As Olson points out in chapter 3, the creation of democratic institutions in an unpromising environment is not a short-term task. Donors should be wary of biting off half the cherry.

There is perhaps a prima facie case for donors to emphasize Naim's stage I reforms in countries that are not following these basic policy guidelines. Successful stage I reforms provide more resources for the society and they probably tend to increase the degree of legitimacy of government institutions, both of which are conducive to carrying out stage II reforms. In fact, it is hard to see how stage II reforms can be implemented in an environment of macroeconomic chaos, extensive government intervention, and declining national income. Stage I reforms mainly involve getting the government out of the economy, while stage II reforms involve the more difficult task of improving the quality of government services. By withholding major assistance until countries make serious attempts at basic policy reforms, donors may change the incentives facing political leaders and thus increase the benefits of launching economic reforms.[3] In most cases, external assistance will not make reformers out of traditional politicians; the benefits of conditional assistance may lie in increasing the probability that a reform program will restore growth.

Some of the ways in which the international community could help the populations of poor countries involve infringements on what their leaders claim to be their "sovereignty." Foreign observers of elections, or international arbitration courts, do constrain the freedom of action of political leaders, and naturally they resent it. We should distinguish the interests of poor people from those of the people who claim to represent them.

References

Bates, Robert H., and Anne O. Krueger, eds. 1993. *Political and Economic Interactions in Economic Policy Reform.* Oxford: Blackwell.

Blair, Harry W. 1994. "Analyzing and Closing the Performance Gap in Bangladesh: Three Approaches." In *Puzzles in Productivity in Public Organizations,* ed. Norman Uphoff. San Francisco: Institute for Contemporary Studies Press.

Chantornvong, Sombat. 1993. "Tocqueville's Democracy in America and in the Third World." In *Rethinking Institutional Analysis and*

---

[3]Countries in which the political conditions are not ripe for serious reform may still be good candidates for educational efforts.

Development: Some Issues, Choices, and Alternatives, ed. Vincent Ostrom, David Feeny, and Hartmut Picht. San Francisco: Institute for Contemporary Studies Press.

Clague, Christopher. 1993. "Rule Obedience, Organizational Loyalty and Economic Development." *Journal of Institutional and Theoretical Economics* 149: 393–414.

Cukierman, Alex, and Mariano Tommasi. 1994. "Why Does It Take a Nixon to Go to China?" Department of Economics, Harvard University.

Evenson. Robert E., and Yoav Kislev. 1975. *Agricultural Research and Productivity.* New Haven: Yale University Press.

Fafchamps, Marcel. 1992. "Solidarity Networks in Preindustrial Societies: Rational Peasants with a Moral Economy." *Economic Development and Cultural Change* 41: 147–74.

Feeny, David. 1993. "The Demand for and Supply of Institutional Arrangements." In *Rethinking Institutional Analysis and Development,* ed. Vincent Ostrom, David Feeny, and Hartmut Picht. San Francisco: Institute for Contemporary Studies Press.

Haggard, Yujiro, and Vernon W. Ruttan. 1985. *Agricultural Development.* Baltimore: Johns Hopkins University Press.

Kindleberger, Charles. 1952. "Review of 'The Economy of Turkey; The Economic Development of Guatemala; Report on Cuba'." *Review of Economics and Statistics* 34: 391–92.

Klitgaard, Robert. 1991. *Adjusting to Reality: Beyond " State vs. Market" in Economic Development.* San Francisco: Institute for Contemporary Studies Press.

Mayo, Stephen, and Shlomo Angel. 1992. "Housing: Enabling Markets to Work." Policy Paper. World Bank, Washington, D.C.

Naim, Moses. 1985. *Latin America's Journey to the Market: From Macroeconomic Shocks to Institutional Therapy.* Occasional Paper 62. San Francisco: Institute for Contemporary Studies.

Oakerson, Ronald J. 1993. "Reciprocity: A Bottom-Up View of Economic Development." In *Rethinking Institutional Analysis and Development,* ed. Vincent Ostrom, David Feeny, and Hartmut Picht. San Francisco: Institute for Contemporary Studies Press.

Olson, Mancur. 1995. "The Devolution of Power in Post-Communist Societies." Paper prepared for conference Russian Reform: Established Interests and Practical Alternatives, Moscow, April 13–15.

Putnam, Robert. 1993. *Making Democracy Work: Civic Traditions in Modern Italy.* Princeton: Princeton University Press.

Rhyne, Elizabeth. 1994. "Microenterprise Finance as Institution-Building." Paper prepared for conference, Economic and Political Institutions for Sustainable Development: Implications for Assistance, Washington, D.C., October 24–25.

Ruttan, Vernon. 1992. "The Sociology of Development and Underdevelopment: Are There any Lessons for Economics?" *International Journal of Sociology of Agriculture and Food* 2: 17–38.

Tommasi, Mariano, and Andres Velasco. 1996. "Where Are We in the Political Economy of Reform?" Paper prepared for conference, Economic Reform in Developing and Transitional Economies, New York, May 12.

Wade, Robert. 1992. "Common-Property Resource Management in South Indian Villages." In *Making the Commons Work,* ed. Daniel W. Bromley. San Francisco: Institute for Contemporary Studies Press.

Williamson, John, ed. 1993. *The Political Economy of Policy Reform.* Washington, D.C.: Institute for International Economics.

Contributors

CHARLES CADWELL: Director, Center on Institutional Reform and the Informal Sector at the University of Maryland at College Park.

CHRISTOPHER CLAGUE: Professor of Economics, University of Maryland at College Park; Research Director, IRIS Center.

STEPHAN HAGGARD: Professor, Graduate School of International Relations and Pacific Studies, University of California at San Diego.

PHILIP KEEFER: Economist, Finance and Private Sector Division, Policy Research Department, World Bank.

ROBERT KLITGAARD: Professor of Economics, University of Natal, Durban, South Africa.

STEPHEN KNACK: Assistant Professor, School of Public Affairs, American University; Faculty Research Assistant, IRIS Center.

MARGARET LEVI: Professor of Political Science, University of Washington.

PETER MURRELL: Professor of Economics, University of Maryland at College Park.

DEEPA NARAYAN: Social Scientist, Social Policy and Resettlement Division, the World Bank.

MANCUR OLSON: Distinguished Professor of Economics, University of Maryland; Principal Investigator and Chair, IRIS Center.

ELINOR OSTROM: Arthur F. Bentley Professor of Political Science, Indiana University; Co-Director, Workshop in Political Theory and Policy Analysis.

ANTHONY PELLECHIO: Economist, Tax Administration Division, International Monetary Fund.

ROBERT PICCIOTTO: Director-General, Operations Evaluation, World Bank.

VERNON RUTTAN: Regents' Professor of Applied Economics and adjunct professor in the Hubert H. Humphrey Institute of Public Affairs, the University of Minnesota.

RICHARD SHERMAN: University of Washington.

MELINDA SMALE: Research Economist, International Maize and Wheat Improvement Center (Mexico).

VITO TANZI: Director, Fiscal Affairs Department, the International Monetary Fund.

Index

Library of Congress Cataloging-in-Publication Data

Institutions and economic development : growth and governance in less-
developed and post-socialist contries / edited by Christopher Clague.
      p.   cm. — (The Johns Hopkins studied in development)
Includes index.
ISBN 0-8018-5492-X (hc : alk. paper). — ISBN 0-8018-5493-8 (pbk. : alk.paper)
1. Developing countries — Economic policy — Citizen participation —
Case studies. 2. Developing countries — Politics and government — Case studies.
3, Post-communism — Case studies. 4. Institutional economics — Case studies.
I. Clague, Christopher K.   II. Series.
HC59.7.I543   1997
338.9'009172'4 — dc21   97-5135